COLD WAR RECKONINGS

Cold War Reckonings

AUTHORITARIANISM AND THE GENRES OF DECOLONIZATION

Jini Kim Watson

FORDHAM UNIVERSITY PRESS   NEW YORK 2021

This book is freely available in an open access edition thanks to TOME
(Toward an Open Monograph Ecosystem)—a collaboration of the
Association of American Universities, the Association of University Presses,
and the Association of Research Libraries—and the generous support
of New York University. Learn more at the TOME website, which can be
found at the following web address: openmonographs.org.

Fordham University Press has no responsibility for the persistence or
accuracy of URLs for external or third-party Internet websites referred to
in this publication and does not guarantee that any content on such websites
is, or will remain, accurate or appropriate.

Fordham University Press also publishes its books in a variety of electronic
formats. Some content that appears in print may not be available in
electronic books.

Visit us online at www.fordhampress.com.

Library of Congress Cataloging-in-Publication Data available online at
https://catalog.loc.gov.

Printed in the United States of America
23 22 21   5 4 3 2 1
First edition

for Bryce and Mateo

Contents

Note on Romanizations

In general, I use the McCune-Reischauer system for romanizing Korean texts and names, except where other romanizations are more widely known (for example, Park Chung Hee, not Pak Chŏng-hŭi). For proper names from translated texts, I use the romanization employed by the translator and the McCune-Reischauer system for clarifications.

Chinese texts, names, and terms are romanized in pinyin, except for Taiwanese and other names that have been commonly transliterated using other systems. I use standard contemporary Indonesian and Malaysian spelling and clarify where names have variants (for example, Sukarno and Soekarno).

COLD WAR RECKONINGS

Introduction

Ruling Like a Foreigner: Theorizing "Free World"
Authoritarianism in the Asia-Pacific Cold War

Hitler's Moustache

I'm surely in good company
with Mao's pate,
Pinochet's smirk,
Mussolini's jaw,
Hitler's moustache,
Franco's height,
Kim's jowl,
Gaddafi's nose,
Mugabe's philtrum . . .
all the very best of them.[1]

Singaporean poet Cyril Wong published his sly rendition of the dictatorial personality, *The Dictator's Eyebrow*, in 2013. In this extended fifty-page poem, the dictator's own eyebrow becomes the narrating subject of history, finding itself "in good company" with other trademark authoritarian facial features from Hitler's moustache to Mao's hairline to Mugabe's upper lip. The eyebrow-narrator goes on to describe a series of humdrum duties as the typical "work" of the dictator:

Another witchhunt; another day.
A leader's work is never done.
How many colleagues, journalists, teachers,
opposition-members, artists and students

1

have you brought to their knees
with the threat of imprisonment[?][2]

Wong's satiric poem plays on one of the great political tropes of the twentieth
century: the larger-than-life, over-the-top dictator, whose personal excesses
and unchecked power have long been recognizable traits ripe for parody. As a
whole, the fifty-one-stanza poem functions as an identikit image of the
twentieth-century tyrant. As Gwee Li Sui writes in the introduction, the eyebrow expresses "the inevitable fusion in time of power and personality, power
and idiosyncrasy."[3] Wong's poem is indicative of the way we often view the
problem of dictatorship, and its cognate authoritarianism, as a single and unified phenomenon or substance focalized through the larger-than-life personality of a tyrant. At the same time, the poem seems to suggest an implicit
geographical and temporal transfer, whereby mid-century European fascist
leaders (Hitler, Mussolini, Franco) appear alongside past, recent, and even
current Third World autocrats (Mao, Pinochet, Gaddafi, Mugabe, Kim).
Wong's satire, I suggest, pokes fun at the tyrant's recognizable and interchangeable traits, while raising questions about the way authoritarianism
"travels" from Europe and becomes naturalized as part of a larger, generaliz-
able deficit of the Global South.

In a collection of essays from 1999, postcolonial critic and anthropologist
David Scott also tackles the problem of illiberal political forms in the postcolonial world. He takes stock of the independent nationalist project some
forty years after the heyday of decolonization, a period often referred to as the
"Bandung Era" after the historic 1955 Conference of African and Asian nations
in Bandung, Indonesia. For Scott, several things signal the decisive end of the
"Bandung project": the end of the "bipolar global order," until which time
"the Soviet Union . . . maintained at least a strategic interest in blocking U.S.
hegemony in the Third World"; the "lost years" of structural adjustment
during the 1980s; and the rise of the U.S. as "unipolar hegemon."[4] In contrast
to the possibilities that arose out of Bandung, the post-1991, post–Cold War
period confirms liberal capitalist democracy as the only viable political model,
reinforcing the binary of modern West and backward Global South. Worse,
accounts of liberal democracy have "set the standard for the assessment of all
political institutions and political discourses"[5] such that illiberalism has all but
come to function as a signifier of the political defects of the non-West:

> Postcolonial formations must fare badly inasmuch as their moderni-
> ties can only be questionable (questionably adequate, questionably
> secure) ones. Their nonmodern, nonliberal, and nondemocratic
> forms of political community can only appear as, at best, a safely *past*

past, and they can only be urged to enter more conscientiously—that is, less ideologically—upon the project of perfecting their modernities, where it is assumed of course that this task can *only* take place within the concepts and institutions through which their social lives have been reshaped by the intrusion of Western power.[6]

For Scott, with the end of the Soviet and non-aligned blocs and the potential moral authority of socialism gone, the ideology of neoliberal capitalism appears more and more hegemonic as the "end of history" famously posited by Francis Fukuyama.[7] The fraught democracies and struggling economies of postcolonial societies—with their seemingly interchangeable autocratic leaders—are cast as backward, belated, and politically empty vessels waiting to be filled up with adequate amounts of tutelary "liberalism" and "modernity."

But if we shift our locus of analysis from the Caribbean to the Asia-Pacific region, things look somewhat different.[8] From this vantage point, we might rather say that it is less the unrelenting political and moral dominance of the West that has triumphed over alternative socialist national projects, and more that certain illiberal Asian states—with a different relationship to the Cold War—have emerged as credible models for Global South capitalist modernity.[9] Focusing on East and Southeast Asia, this book tells a new story about authoritarianism, the Cold War, and the global shift from colonialism to independent nation-states. In it, I examine cultural production on and of a number of authoritarian, non-communist states variously aligned with the United States—those paradoxically unfree spaces within the "free world"—for what they reveal about the supposed divisions between First World and Third World, liberalism and illiberalism, and capitalist "free world" democracy and socialist tyranny. As Scott suggests, it is obvious that we cannot think of Third World or Global South illiberalisms in terms of an inherently stagnant, Orientalist, and non-modern deficit. And yet neither can we think of them only as the failure of Bandung national projects to materialize in the face of a monolithic "Western power." *Cold War Reckonings: Authoritarianism and the Genres of Decolonization* argues that the question of authoritarian capitalist states demands an accounting of the specific conditions and modalities of Cold War decolonization as they unfolded in the region. Consequently, its focus is certain modernizing, autocratic capitalist states that were birthed by this Cold War–decolonizing matrix. Put otherwise—and contra Scott—it is not the *end* of the Cold War, but its *congealed presence* in forms of East and Southeast Asian developmental state-formations that needs to be accounted for. The book is structured as the working-through of five clusters of theoretical-aesthetic tropes (one cluster per chapter) in which I bring together cultural production, the Cold War, and postcolonial illiberalism in new ways. These clusters are freedom, decolonization, and alignment; writerly freedom and the state; separation and futurity; exile and anachronism; and atrocity, justice, and the post–Cold War. While these tropes in themselves are not exclusive to these regimes, they become pronounced flash points of tensions that structure Cold War decolonization. I focus on cultural texts that reveal the way the Cold War violently meets decolonization in the context of the following Asia-Pacific regimes: the South Korean military dictatorship (1961–87); the Marcos period in the Philippines (1965–86); illiberal Singapore under Lee Kuan Yew (1959–90); and Indonesia's Suharto regime (1965–98). Taiwan under the Kuomintang is also addressed in certain sections.[10] The book begins by examining regional writers' conferences of the 1960s to the early 1980s before moving to poetry, essays, and fiction of the early Cold War period. I then turn to the recent proliferation of novels and films that retrospectively look back to these decades. Writers and artists include F. Sionil José, Kim Chi-Ha, Pramoedya Ananta Toer, Ninotchka Rosca—writing during the high Cold War years—and Mohamed Latiff Mohamed, Sonny Liew, Jeremy Tiang, Hwang Sŏk-yŏng, Tan Pin Pin, Han Kang, Joshua Oppenheimer, and Yoon Je-kyoon—whose retrospective gazes look back from the late 1990s or after.[11] To be clear, I do not mean to celebrate these regimes as some victory of a non-Western "alternative" modernity or as the heroic defeat of Enlightenment rationality by something deemed "Asian" and therefore resistant. Rather, my goal is to historicize and better understand their constitution and contestations—especially the role played by internal leftist struggles that seem to push back from the "wrong side of history." This book's cultural archive constitutes an attempt to grasp the political and cultural genres pertaining to non- and anti-communist, illiberal formations both as they were emerging and as retrospective objects. Part of its goal, therefore, is to denaturalize the occurrence of authoritarianism in the Global South, where "Kim's jowl" and "Mugabe's philtrum" too easily become synecdoches of a far more complex historical, political, and cultural conjuncture.

Cold War/Postcolonial

The methodological approach of Cold War Reckonings aims to move us beyond both typical postcolonial conceptions of power and a "three-worlds ideology." Articulated by Sharad Chari and Katherine Verdery, the latter concept refers to the academic partitioning of the world into separate objects of study: mainstream social science and history for the First World, socialist or post-socialist studies for the Second World, and postcolonial studies for the

Third.[12] In moving beyond "three worlds" thinking, we can recognize the ways in which what Odd Arne Westad has called the *global* Cold War produced specific responses to problems of decolonization:[13] "US and Soviet interventionisms to a very large extent shaped both the international and the domestic framework within which political, social, and cultural changes in Third World countries took place."[14] And yet in Cold War studies, the cultural and literary histories of the worlds that grew under the war's shadow are just being written. Conversely, as Monica Popescu notes, the shaping influence of the Cold War on Global South cultural production has been little recognized by postcolonial studies or world literature.[15] In fact, as Chen Kuan-hsing has argued, to think about the Cold War's epistemological legacy is an intellectual project on par with that of postcolonial studies:

> Just as the formal end of colonialism did not lead overnight to a dissolution of its cultural effects, so the subjectivities formed during the cold war remain within us. Our worldview, political and institutional forms, and systems of popular knowledge have been deeply shaped by the cold-war structure.[16]

If Chen calls for scholars to "de-cold war" alongside the critical project of decolonizing knowledge and institutions, Bhakti Shringarpure argues that "a renewed postcolonial Cold War historiography is urgently needed."[17] Such critical projects require that certain assumptions of postcolonial studies be revised. Writing of the influential theories that have emerged to "provincialize" Europe and pluralize modernity, Heonik Kwon notes that in these critiques "there are no traces of a modern Europe as we know it; that is, the Europe that, after experiencing a catastrophic war, was divided into mutually hostile forces in an undeclared ideological war."[18] Such a perspective thus misapprehends the object of critique—Western imperialist power—by "relegat[ing] bipolar history to an analytic void."[19] This is especially relevant for East and Southeast Asia, a region in which the "bipolar Manichean rivalry between the United States and the Soviet Union was triangulated,"[20] and the Cold War unfolded not merely as a "historical epoch or event, but as itself a knowledge project or epistemology."[21] And just as the "Cold" War is a misnomer for violent conflicts in Asia and other parts of the Third World, the marker of 1989 or 1991 as the "end" of the conflict "pertains only to the Western Hemisphere's temporality."[22] In that sense, this book is also about the production of our broader post-socialist present, even though it does not engage directly with territories that were formerly socialist.

To interrogate the oxymoronic formation of "free world" authoritarianisms in East and Southeast Asia is therefore to consider "how Cold War representations have shaped and continue to shape theory and politics."[23] Caroline Hau reminds us that by being enmeshed in the U.S.'s hegemonic web that replaced European and Japanese colonial power, states in "free Asia" experienced a freedom from communism rather than a substantial postcolonial democracy.[24] Moreover, the logic of a temporary militarization of society was acceptable in areas of the world where "Communists or left-wingers had already staged attempts at gaining political power." Here, the "combination of [military] training and technology would enable the soldiers to hold the ground while the political and economic forces of modernization took hold of society, removing it from the danger of a Communist take-over."[25] The U.S. Cold War imaginary tried to resolve these ideological con-tradictions by distinguishing those tolerable Third World right-wing regimes from the "true" enemy of communist totalitarianism via the notion of *transi-tion*. Speaking of Latin America during the Cold War, historian Greg Gran-din writes, "Washington found that it greatly preferred anti-Communist dictatorships to the possibility that democratic openness might allow the Soviets to gain a foothold on the continent."[26] U.S. foreign policy partly jus-tified itself through the belief that political liberalization "was more likely" to occur under right-wing dictatorships, making an implicit distinction between these merely transitional autocratic forms and the more perma-nent, essential totalitarianism of communist regimes.[27] With a focus on the way conceptions of human rights became narrowed to U.S.-style individual liberal freedoms, Crystal Parikh has noted that mid-century U.S. adminis-trations "saw radical or socialist politics as vehicles of dangerous unrest, and they limited support for nationalist movements to those that championed *stable* states, free of the taint of communism."[28] Like these scholars, I emphatically refute the notion of "free world" autocracy as a tutelary, tran-sitional stage on its way to liberal democracy. Rather, I consider such regimes to be the concrete and specific result of the way decolonization unfolded *through and as* the Cold War. Whereas Western Cold War ideology has insisted on the spurious distinction between (il)liberal capitalism and com-munist tyranny, in a reverse tendency certain strands of postcolonial think-ing continue to lament democratic failures primarily in terms of the enduring half-life of European colonial rule; its symptoms are most visible in the failure to industrialize and the extravagance of dictatorial, clientist states. In my telling, however, authoritarian rule is not only compatible with (sometimes stupendous) economic growth, but emerges as the political form *necessary* for a certain kind of postcolonial economic development. Within the Cold War matrix, such regimes paradoxically aim to advance decoloni-zation by reproducing elements of the colonial state.

Put otherwise, this book aims to make visible a certain genealogy of authoritarianism that troubles analytic frameworks produced both by Cold War and
postcolonial epistemes. The most dominant (and enduring) of the former is
the theory of totalitarianism that emerged at mid-century; William Pietz has
noted that totalitarianism was "the theoretical anchor of cold war discourse."[29]
It posited a historically new kind of regime that, emerging in Nazism and
finding full realization in Stalinism, wields utter and total ideological control
over the individual through the modern technologies of surveillance, prisons,
and police terror.[30] Articulated in the influential mid-century writings of
George Orwell, Hannah Arendt, Aleksandr Solzhenitsyn, Arthur Koestler,
and others, it became a keystone of Western anti-communist discourse and
policy and was the foil to Western liberal democracy.[31] Although totalitarianism found its "ultimate ground of meaning and authority" in the "literary
works of certain writers,"[32] Hannah Arendt's major work *The Origins of Totalitarianism* (1951) perhaps advanced its most influential definition by conjoining Nazism and Stalinism into a single phenomenon: "Up to now we know
only two authentic forms of totalitarian domination: the dictatorship of
National Socialism after 1938, and the dictatorship of Bolshevism since 1930."[33]
For Arendt, this form of domination is historically novel and exceeds simple
dictatorship, tyranny, or one-party rule because of the "onion-like structure of
the movement [Nazism or Bolshevism]," which aims to penetrate every level
of the bureaucracy and state machine. Such "organizational omnipotence"
famously results in "the fictitious quality of everyday reality" where lying and
subterfuge reign.[34] Totalitarianism's other distinctive trait, memorably fictionalized in Orwell's *1984*, is thus the destruction of the private sphere. A totalitarian government not only "isolat[es] men, their political capacities," but
"destroys private life as well.[35] Yet Arendt provides a far richer account than
simply an account of "the ingenious devices of totalitarian rule."[36] In her wide-
ranging study, there are two crucial historical roots to totalitarianism: anti-
Semitism and imperialism, which together constitute a genealogy of modern
state violence. While Arendt was certainly no postcolonial theorist, her
approach importantly invokes the operations of colonial rule as what set the
stage for totalitarianism in Europe: "Lying under anybody's nose were many
of the elements which gathered together could create a totalitarian government on the basis of racism."[37] The striking formula Arendt arrives at is that
the totalitarian ruler or dictator is simply *ruling like a foreigner* "in the same
sense as a foreign conqueror may occupy a country which he governs not for
its own sake but for the benefit of something or somebody else."[38] In short,
"The totalitarian dictator is like a foreign conqueror who comes from nowhere,
and his looting is likely to benefit nobody."[39] Paradoxically, despite the fact that

Arendt's "totalitarianism" is partially theorized in historical reference to colonial domination, her focus on European political formations—and her study's uptake in Western Cold War discourse—means it has been less useful in diagnosing the specificity of modes of unfreedom that actually emerge *in* the formerly colonized world. Equally, the outsized influence of the mid-century notion of totalitarianism has meant that today's resurgence of ethno-nationalist autocrats is often understood as a "return" of something that had long been in abeyance. As I shall address in the Epilogue, such narratives miss the constitutive role of Global South decolonization struggles in producing our own authoritarian moment.

Meanwhile, from works that would form the canon of postcolonial studies, the most prescient early account of Third World dictatorship is surely Frantz Fanon's *The Wretched of the Earth* (*Les Damnés de la Terre,* 1961). The book is at once the extraordinarily powerful "handbook" of Third World liberation and a cautionary tale of betrayal by the national bourgeoisie. The latter, notoriously, "discovers its historical mission as intermediary" at independence and seamlessly steps in where the colonizers left off to exploit and rob the nation.[40] Fanon is also under no illusion that the Soviet-U.S. standoff is anything but another ruse of Third World domination: "Today the peaceful coexistence between the two blocs maintains and aggravates the violence in colonial countries."[41] And while the global Cold War escalates every local conflict into a bipolar power contest, the colonized people respond with greater awareness of the internationalist dimensions of struggle: "They no longer limit their horizons to one particular region since they are swept along in this atmosphere of universal convulsion."[42] Nevertheless, Fanon's main objection to the bipolar conflict is the impossibility of the Third World's development and neutrality.[43] Although the latter "allows underdeveloped countries to receive economic aid from both sides,"[44] the Cold War

> does not permit either of these two sides to come to the aid of underdeveloped regions in the way they should. Those literally astronomical sums invested in arms research, these engineers transformed into technicians of nuclear war could raise the living standards of the underdeveloped countries by 60 percent in fifteen years. It is therefore obvious that the underdeveloped countries have no real interest in either prolonging or intensifying this cold war.[45]

While Fanon's trenchant critique of the neocolonialist elite and Cold War pressures would prove devastatingly accurate in many sites, he did not live to see the full extent of the shaping role of the Cold War on postcolonial societies. That Third World nations should "refuse to get involved in such rivalry"[46] also misses the fact that for some new nations such refusal was an impossibility.

Put more strongly: In some sites, the Cold War constituted the very form that decolonization took. Kwon writes, "The bipolar political conflicts in the Asia-Pacific region *advanced as part of* decolonization," which was not the case in all other parts of the world.[47] Fast-forwarding to contemporary postcolonial thinking, the figure (along with Scott) who has most influentially grappled with repressive state forms of the Global South is Achille Mbembe, whose notion of *commandement* elegantly describes the reactivations of colonial dictatorship in the post-independence period.[48] For Mbembe, focusing on sub-Saharan postcolonial states, *commandement* does not function by the coercion, violence, or exploitation of colonial rule, but is legitimated by a symbolic regime defined by the grotesque, lascivious, and extravagant personal rule of its leaders. The pressures of the Cold War, however, do not play a part in his analysis. Moreover, by way of the Orwellian notion of "double speak," postcolonial tyranny tends to slide into depictions of communist totalitarianism: "This is why the rhetorical devices of officialese in the postcolony can be compared to those of communist regimes—to the extent, that is, that both are actual regimes given to the production of lies and double-speak."[49] Here, postcolonial authoritarianism is readily accessed through the tropes of mid-century fascism. While such a brief and partial summary of each of these rich thinkers ignores many nuances, I want to suggest that from both Cold War discourse and postcolonial studies, we have few analytic models through which to think autocracy simultaneously in its bipolar *and* decolonizing dimensions.

Cold War Reckonings seeks to critically synthesize and reconnect a number of historical processes and cultural discourses usually addressed in separate disciplines: cultural accounts of decolonization and postcolonialism; Cold War ideological contests and alignments; and the concrete problems of repressive states in the postcolonial world. In resituating the "postcolonial" with regard to "post–Cold War,"[50] my goal is to think about postcolonial authoritarianism less as a monolithic essence that besets the Third World via the dictator's "fusion of power and personality" or "symbolic regime,"[51] and more as the process by which decolonization is crosshatched by the structure of global bipolarism.[52] Indeed, the cultural texts I assemble in this study reveal how the experiences of decolonization in the Asia-Pacific region are theoretically and experientially inseparable from the Cold War. For these reasons, I look especially to texts that open up other worlds, political imaginaries, and temporalities from the supposed certainties about this period. However, this book does not argue for literature's unmediated access to political reality—in which we would read a fictional narrative as directly illustrative of history, culture, or identity.[53] Nor does it recover a politicized textual agency that depends on stylistic subversion and innovation for its impact, whereby formal devices are "said to serve as signs of 'resistance' and opposition to the dictator."[54] Finally,

I am not importing the significant study of the "dictator novel"—largely a Latin American and African genre—to the Asia-Pacific region.[55] I am interested, rather, in the way a variety of cultural genres transpose and organize the raw materials of social and historical worlds in ways that map certain rationalities of power while helping us reimagine the sedimented narratives that inhere in Cold War and postcolonial discourses. In particular, I argue that the struggles and imagined futures of leftists, radical nationalists, and others who occupy the "wrong side" of neoliberal history are necessary for a more nuanced understanding of autocratic rule in the region.

Throughout, my book intentionally crosses boundaries of area studies and postcolonial studies by comparing cultural production from East Asia alongside that from Southeast Asia, thereby examining the postcolonial aftermaths of British, Dutch, American, and Japanese colonial empires. I bring further comparative axes to the project by incorporating insights from scholars of temporality and postcolonial time (Reinhardt Koselleck, David Scott, Gary Wilder); the global politics of anti-communism and human rights (Greg Grandin, Crystal Parikh, Vijay Prashad, Joseph Slaughter); state-formation in other Global South contexts (Akhil Gupta, Naomi Schiller); and post-dictatorship transitions (Lisa Yoneyama and scholars of South Africa's Truth and Reconciliation Commission). This book argues for the ability of imaginative texts to dislodge a number of conceptual certainties: of authoritarianism "there" and freedom "here"; of the assumed temporal boundaries of colonial/postcolonial and Cold War/post–Cold War; and notions of repressive state control versus economic liberalism—assumptions we have inherited from both postcolonial and Cold War epistemes. In short, *Cold War Reckonings* seeks to bring Chen's call to "de-cold war" critical thought together with postcolonial studies' attention to decolonizing Euro-American knowledge forms and institutions. In it, I seek to develop a critical idiom that brings together two hermeneutics—the postcolonial analytic of "Europe and its other" and the critical Cold War lens of bipolar global restructuring—in ways that challenge and enrich each other. In seeing these struggles as connected and entangled in new ways, we better understand the ways these histories are embedded in our present—helping, perhaps, to explain the residues and reactivations of autocracy today.

Revolutionary Promotion:
The Authorities of Cold War Development

In East and Southeast Asia, perhaps the most obvious legacy of the Cold War is simply war: the Chinese civil war, the Korean War, the Vietnam War, and its "sideshows" the Cambodian and Laos conflicts.[56] Intimately related but less discussed than those conflicts are the instances of "free world" state violence carried out in the name of suppressing domestic communism and other political opponents. A chronology here might include the 2.28 massacre of 1947 and subsequent White Terror period in Taiwan; South Korea's Cheju Island Uprising and massacres of 1948–49; the 1950s counterinsurgency military actions that crushed the Huk Uprising in the Philippines; Singapore's 1963 purge of leftists in Operation Cold Store; the 1965–66 massacre of leftists in Indonesia; and the violent crackdown of the 1980 uprising in Gwangju. As we already noted, for U.S. foreign policy such violence was often understood as the unfortunate cost of keeping the even larger evil of communist totalitarianism at bay. As Richard Nixon notoriously commented in 1971 of Latin American dictators, "It is an orderly way which at least works relatively well. They have been able to run the damn place."[57] It was hoped, of course, that after economic development and more tutelage in liberal democracy, such violence would recede.

Usually disconnected from such accounts of state violence is the other major legacy of Cold War decolonization in this region, the "developmental state," which has been credited with creating the Asian economic "miracles" and consolidating capitalism in the region.[58] First modeled on the Japanese economic engine of the 1950s and '60s, the developmental state is typically characterized by authoritarian rule, strong state-business relations, tight control over labor, and the overriding imperative to create economic growth. It was able, moreover, to harness "very real fears of war and instability toward a remarkable developmental energy,"[59] not forgetting, of course, that "American and other imperial ambitions helped create the disorder in the first place."[60] Confounding the usual terms of political analysis, the developmental state is at once "strong" in terms of the "struggle to industrialize" but "weak" in terms of the "enmeshment" in the web of U.S. power; in short, they are "semisovereign."[61] By the 1990s the "Asian miracle" economies were widely lauded and had inspired hundreds of studies from the perspective of U.S.-based modernization studies.[62] Later sections of Wong's poem succinctly illustrate its characteristics, indicating that *The Dictator's Eyebrow* may be less about a transhistorical, generic dictator, and more about a form of political rationality particular to the Asia-Pacific:

Let's call oppositional forces
anarchists. Let's call us "we".
Let's term "them" anything we like.
Let's insist that they threaten

everything we stood for and built.
I bristle with indignance at the podium,
enthralling newfound allies,
enemies cowering in dingy basements.
I fall on all the right words like
"stability", "progress" and "nation".
. . .

Stick on "democracy" like a price-tag
then pick it slowly off the dulled back
of society caught up in its pragmatisms
and material pursuits. Every part of the plan
is in place, oiled and ready. You can only
move on up from here. Gather intel
to ensnare rebels on bogus charges;
terrorism is so in this year. Let me do my job
on the news, suffusing your face with regretful
authority. The future's now ready for capture.[63]

Although tropes of "gather[ing] intel" to ensure "stability" and "progress" may
speak to any authoritarian government, references to "a society caught up in
its pragmatisms" where "You can only/move on up from here" explicitly evoke
the U.S.-aligned Cold War developmentalist state in the region. Such catch-
phrases (and the author's country of origin) make it hard not to identify the
implied subject of the poem: Lee Kuan Yew, Singapore's "founding father,"
who began his career as an anti-colonial lawyer and would remain prime minister for three decades. Lee ruled through the People's Action Party, or PAP,
the only governing party independent Singapore has known. Between the
1960s and 1990s, the PAP delivered astonishing material progress and security
to its citizens while crafting a flexible economic and financial system highly
responsive to global fluctuations,[64] making it a touchstone of successful Third
World development and globalization. Yet Singapore reinvented itself, paradoxically, by "borrow[ing] many of the elements of self-fashioning from the
colonial state,"[65] that is, by limiting liberal freedoms, disciplining labor, and
quashing political opponents. To borrow Arendt's phrase, it succeeded in part
by "ruling like a foreigner."

Further, as Chua Beng Huat observes, Singapore accepted and leveraged
its "frontline" status in "resisting the spread of communism" in return for a
lucrative alliance with the U.S.-led free world.[66] Citing the priority of
national survivalism whenever challenged, the PAP found that "fighting
communism was not only financially lucrative but also a convenient excuse

for domestic political repression by any politician with a tenuous hold on power."[67] The relationship of the stupendous export-oriented growth of Singapore, along with that of South Korea, Hong Kong, and Taiwan, to Cold War U.S. military backing, loans, and infrastructure—not to mention the massive regional economic boost from both the Korean and Vietnamese conflicts—has been well documented.[68] Notwithstanding significant differences in economic and political formations, the second tier of "Newly Industrializing Countries" in the Asia-Pacific, including Indonesia, Malaysia, the Philippines, and Thailand, charted similar developmental course. Paul Hutchcroft notes, for example, that due to the importance of military bases in the Philippines for the U.S.'s Vietnam War effort, "the United States rewarded [Marcos's] martial law with large increases in grants and loans."[69] During Suharto's New Order period, the Indonesian economy similarly benefited from "the political victory of counter-revolutionary social forces" as well as the "generous levels of foreign aid, privileged access to lucrative Western export markets, and access to important new technology" afforded by Cold War exigencies.[70] As the Cold War–era dissident writers analyzed in Chapter 2 reveal, capitalist developmental states paradoxically emerged not merely alongside but *in response to* the early successes of People's Republic of China, the unified Vietnamese state, and the Democratic People's Republic of Korea.

We must further recognize that—especially after the Sino-Soviet split by the early 1960s—China was the more relevant Communist power in the region. Robert Young writes of the significance of the 1949 revolution: "For the first time, a non-white, formerly semi-colonized country achieved an independent communist government through a military campaign: national liberation and socialist revolution had been brought together."[71] While communist revolution was made newly tangible for the region's anti-colonialist nationalists, a side effect was that communism would become partly coded through Chineseness, both supplanting and reproducing colonial epistemologies of race, with particular consequences for the multiracial postcolonies of Southeast Asia. We will see later in this book how both departing colonizers and non-communist national elites would view Chinese communities with sometimes lethal suspicion. The larger point to be made, however, is that in many respects these authoritarian regimes might be viewed as the less revolutionary mirror images that sought to compete with both the revolutionary appeal and modernizing capabilities of their communist siblings.[72] In the most material sense, Cold War binarism and its triangulation through decolonizing Asia created the conditions for programs of transpacific capitalist accumulation and authoritarian repression in these states.

How might we further probe the imbrications of decolonization and the Cold War via the developmental state? Having already noted the mixed inheritances of Arendt's major work on totalitarianism, I turn here to her lesser-known theoretical work on the problem of authoritarianism. We might note here that the term "totalitarianism"—which for Arendt connoted power that colonized even the most private aspects of the individual—is rarely in political parlance today (except as hyperbole). "Authoritarianism" and its slightly stronger cognate "dictatorship," on the other hand, seem resurgent.[73] In Arendt's 1954 essay "What Is Authority?" she usefully makes the distinction between authority and violent coercion:

> The authoritarian relation between the one who commands and the one who obeys rests neither on common reason nor on the power of the one who commands; *what they have in common is the hierarchy itself,* whose rightness and legitimacy both recognize and where both have their predetermined stable place.[74]

Arendt describes a situation—unlike the case of tyranny or outright dictatorship, in which brute power issues from the person of the dictator—where the source of authority defers to a force outside itself. Arendt recalls Plato's appeal in *The Republic* to the "rightness" of the authority of the doctor over his patient and of the ship's captain over the sailors. In this account, external authority is a source that "transcends the political realm, [and] from which the authorities derive their 'authority.'"[75]

While Arendt goes on to examine the appeal to external authority in Greek and Roman thought (through Plato's notion of "the good" and the role of ancestors and founders of Rome, respectively), I wish to bring her thinking to bear on the way decolonization can be understood as a nation's forced entry *into* a "a global political scenario."[76] To do so allows us to consider how this historic moment of restructuring—the simultaneous dis-embedding from colonial rule and re-embedding into a bipolar matrix—enabled novel kinds of appeals to outside authorities. Despite vehemently rejecting the West's racialized logic of colonial tutelage, nearly every decolonizing nation aspired to modern industrial development to "catch up" with the West, as many speeches from the 1955 Bandung Conference make clear; such desires would be echoed in the Asian Writers' Conferences that I examine in Chapter 1.[77] As long as one essential task of the new nation-state was to overcome the lack of material development understood as colonialism's legacy, the desire for development could be construed as an indisputable *external authority* that legitimized the *internal hierarchy* of the authoritarian state, whether of communist or capitalist inclination. This is not to say, of course, that such authority did not also work by outright violence as well, as we have mentioned.

Popescu, building on the work of Susan Buck-Morss, has written of the profound desire for Soviet-style modernization on the part of certain Third World intellectuals. In her analysis of the Soviet travelogue, *A Soviet Journey* (1978) by South African political exile Alex La Guma, Popescu notes the way in which it appears to La Guma that "Soviet people can speed up time."[78] Thanks to Lenin's revision of Marxist historical progress, the USSR "aimed to fast-forward the Soviet nations through stages deemed inevitable in the development of a society."[79] In an opposing but complementary mode, Park Chung Hee envisioned the righteous restoration of Korean sovereignty through a rapidly accelerated and rabidly anti-communist modernization, measured above all by export earnings. The national export target even took physical form in the Seoul export tower (Fig. 1), which kept a running annual tally of the country's exports in U.S. dollars.

Figure 1. Seoul's Export Tower, December 1970, listing US$1 billion as the achieved target export earnings.

The point is that, although we typically think of the Cold War as a spatial-ized confrontation between blocs, spheres of influence, and curtains—whether iron, bamboo, or color[80]—Third World *futurity and temporality* is of crucial importance to understanding Cold War decolonization.[81] The logic of prog-ress promised by the export tower may best be described as revolutionary pro-motion. Theodore Hughes has described how "President Park offered the *promise of promotion* through the world system, from periphery to core power, as the one-way road to achieving autonomy and reunification."[82] Anti-communist, developmentalist "promotion" would thus actively resolve the problems left over from decolonization, namely, the divided peninsula, pov-erty, and U.S. military occupation. In a similar logic, Lee Kuan Yew saw his nation's progress as one of revolutionary advancement from poverty-ridden Third World nation to First, attested to in the very title of one of his best-selling memoirs, *From Third World to First: The Singapore Story 1965–2000* (2000). In this formulation, of course, "Third World" is stripped of its earlier meanings of solidarity and self-determination among once-colonized nations. Instead, the logic of promotion offered through capitalist modernization—widely disseminated through W. W. Rostow's 1960 theory of stagist economic development—was interpreted as the promised leap into the future and escape *from* Third World backwardness, and could explicitly compete with the fast-forwarding of time modeled by the communist world.

The Cold War could intersect with and bolster right-wing authoritarian appeals to development with special intensity because of the perceived "time lag" of colonial underdevelopment. Particularly in the "free world," the authority of the bipolar contest structured the very nature of nationalist prog-ress. As we will see in texts such as Jeremy Tiang's *State of Emergency* (Chap-ter 3), Han Kang's *Human Acts*, and Joshua Oppenheimer's *The Act of Killing* (Chapter 5), the figure of the communist threatened national development and could send the country on the road to unholy collectivist ruin. Such threats, in turn, were manipulated to control political opposition and disci-pline labor, subduing workers for the sake of building export-oriented indus-tries and attracting foreign investment. Although the Philippines is not usually included in the Asian Tigers honor role, Marcos's "transnational accumula-tion strategy" was explicitly modeled on the authoritarian successes of South Korea and Taiwan and, accordingly, required the militarized enforcement of "political stability."[83] Caroline Hau duly notes that we ought to view the Mar-cos state and the more lauded "Asian miracles" as "occupying the same con-tinuum."[84] Relatedly, in writing of the mass killings in Indonesia in 1965–66, Hilmar Farid points out that state violence is too often understood solely through the lens of human rights: "State violence in this case played a crucial role in creating a cheap and submissive labour force and Indonesia's selling point for attracting foreign capital during the New Order period."[85] We might, then, better understand the intersection of the Cold War and decolonization as not merely producing the unfortunate side effect of violence and authoritarian governance, but as inaugurating and *authorizing* the frantic competition to fast-forward the time of national development. In "free world" Asia, this intersection made illiberalism the necessary counterpart to a translocal formation of postcolonial capitalism.

To return to Arendt again, if Plato was "looking for a relationship in which the compelling element lies in the relationship itself and is *prior to* the actual issuance of commands,"[86] for authoritarian postcolonial leaders, the a priori element sustaining their authority could always be evoked through the gap between actual and desired development, between the impoverished and shameful now and the materially secure future. Versions of this basic formula are, of course, all too common on the left and the right of the political spectrum: Soviet and Chinese Five-Year Plans were echoed in Park Chung Hee's own Five-Year Plans, part of his "Yusin" or "revitalizing" reforms, while similar visions for the future are implied in Suharto's "New Order" regime, Marcos's "New Society," and Lee Kuan Yew's vision of Singapore as a "first world oasis." Important differences between these regimes will be explored in the following chapters, but, returning once more to Wong's poem, we might term this general style of authoritarian rule "regretful authority."[87] Neither lagging outside Western modernity nor explained by the racialist concepts of Asian model minorities or "Confucian Capitalism,"[88] "regretful authority" corresponds to a mode of autocratic postcolonial rule in which decolonization is pursued through, not despite, bipolarity. By conflating economic growth with national time, and by replacing political revolution with revolutionary development, the conceit of such regimes is the long-anticipated restoration of a national community.[89] Sovereignty is reclaimed via a necessarily painful—but perhaps only temporary—process of modernization that suspends or brackets discussion about the political processes of modernization itself. As Wong's indignant eyebrow reassures us, "The future's now ready for capture."[90]

I have been arguing that it is not enough to understand Asian capitalist, developmental states as merely the result of fortuitous structures left by colonialism and redeployed by a canny, complicit postcolonial elite. They are, I suggest, characterized by a novel political-economic grammar—or, to use Ann Laura Stoler's phrase, "genre of rule"—that emerged in the Cold War–decolonizing matrix.[91] Nor is the Asian developmental state a retreat to the specificity of a regional anomaly or historical outlier. Hughes describes how under the military dictatorship of Park Chung Hee, South Korea "became in the early 1970s—and remains as of this writing [in 2012]—a favored site for the display of successful development; it followed Japan's postwar lead as a model-minority case in the world system."[92] From our supposedly post–Cold War moment, the constitutive authoritarianism of these capitalist success stories has been all but occluded, and they are heralded retrospectively as being on the "winning" side of (neoliberal) history, whether or not their transitions to democracy are complete. Wong's poem—to which I turn one last time—satirizes such a one-sided view:

> . . . And let's
> inventory the tangible successes: a flourishing
> banking sector, industries and bottomless
> reserves; laws hammered into place
> so with each election there can be
> no contest; a resentful minority shrinking
> out of sight as we speak.[93]

But the influence of the Asian developmental state has not gone unrecognized by the left. In Vijay Prashad's 2007 elegy for the Non-Aligned Movement (or NAM), *The Darker Nations*, he observes that that the "tangible successes" of the East Asian Tigers of South Korea, Taiwan, Singapore, and Hong Kong were not just outliers of postcolonial development but actively "dampened the enthusiasm for the Third World's exertions to transform the world order."[94] Their enviable economic success by the 1970s and '80s "enabled the Tigers to exert themselves in the NAM forums against the line proposed by Castro and the Left."[95] These Asian states not only bucked the trend of Third World developmentalism—in which developmentalist programs in Latin America and Africa stalled for a variety of reasons[96]—but contributed to the pushing back of socialist and leftist political possibilities more generally. In particular, the economic rise of Singapore was to have several lasting effects, of which perhaps the most far-reaching was to "uncouple the linkage between economic and political reform of the world order."[97] Prashad explains:

> By the 1980s, NAM [the Non-Aligned Movement] was infected with the belief that economic development is a technical problem that should not be bothered with the question of power. The Tigers' example and leadership drove the Third World abandonment of the political critique of the economic order. The debt crisis shook the Third World agenda at about the same time as the Tigers experienced their economic takeoff. Whereas the Tigers continued to attend the Third World forums, they now did so to promote their path as well as combat the ideas of import substitution and anti-imperialist cooperation.[98]

What Prashad's otherwise astute account occludes,[99] I argue, are the *internal* contestations around the "abandonment of the political critique of the economic order." The now-globalized logic of "pragmatic survivalism" that places a firewall between the political and the economic cannot, I contend, be properly understood *without* returning to the vicissitudes of Cold War–decolonization struggles in Singapore, Malaysia, Indonesia, the Philippines and the Korean peninsula. Anti-communist development is not only what routs a leftist Third Worldist orientation à la Prashad, but comprises a set of fought-over reorderings that struggled to overcome certain contradictions of colonial society in the name of regaining sovereignty. Thus, one final claim of this book is that the triumphalism of the West in "winning" the Cold War—confirmed by Fukuyama's "end of history" thesis—has disavowed the role of communists and leftists not only in the Soviet-aligned Third World, but also *within* those U.S.-aligned postcolonies where nationalist historiographies also tend to hold fast to a Cold War lens.[100] A more nuanced understanding of the global Cold War emphasizes "the unequal relations of power among the political communities that pursued or were driven to pursue a specific path of progress within the binary structure of the global order."[101] Such a perspective, in turn, demands a "more complex, multidimensional matrix of 'us' and 'them'"[102] beyond the assumed civilizational power binary between metropole and periphery, and East and West. It is precisely to see these formations as *simultaneously* postcolonial and a result of bipolar complications that is at stake for this study. I read the retrospective cultural productions of the second half of the book as a kind of historical auditing of, or reckoning with, the developmental states forged by Cold War decolonization, revealing how their internal struggles have been passed down to the present. These texts revisit this era not in order to provide a neutral balance sheet of its pros and cons—economic growth here, human rights violations there—but to specify, as Paik Nak-chung has put it, "the precise weight to be given to each, and determine the actual relationship between the two aspects."[103] What did those struggles and desires look like, and how do cultural texts map, take stock of, and reimagine them? What are the ethical and political stakes of remembering them?

Genres of Cold War Decolonization

In the final section of the Introduction, I outline the stakes of the book in terms of my cultural archive and reading practices. The first thing to note is that the complex internal and external underpinnings of authoritarian governance are much less legible than those of colonialism proper. Because the problem of "free world" native dictatorships scrambles both the foreign oppressor/native resister paradigm, *and* the totalitarian East/liberal West dyad, *Cold*

War Reckonings traces a set of new motifs, tensions, debates, and the literary and filmic forms they take. As I have already suggested, I am interested not only in the "exit narrative" of European or Japanese colonialism, but the way that decolonization was "an entry, with considerable baggage, into a new world order with its own delimiting determinations for civil and political practices."[104] Such dilemmas suggest that strategies for representing and critiquing postcolonial regimes will necessarily depart from those that animated various anti-colonial writings.

In his well-known 1986 essay on Third World literature, Fredric Jameson discusses the literary responses by canonical postcolonial writers such as Senegal's Ousmane Sembene and Kenya's Ngũgĩ wa Thiong'o to their countries' neocolonial realities. Such writers, he notes,

> find themselves back in the dilemma of [Chinese nationalist writer] Lu Xun, bearing a passion for change and social regeneration which has not yet found its agents. I hope it is clear that this is also very much *an aesthetic dilemma, a crisis of representation*: it was not difficult to identify an adversary who spoke another language and wore the visible trappings of colonial occupation. When those are replaced by your own people, the connections to external controlling forces are much more difficult to represent. The new leaders may of course throw off their masks and reveal the person of the Dictator, whether in its older individual or new military form: but this moment also determines problems of representation.[105]

Jameson's important point here, overshadowed by the controversy around his essay,[106] concerns finding adequate expressive form for the specificity of *post-colonial*—rather than colonial—unfreedoms. For writers and cultural producers, questions of visualizing "connections to external controlling forces"—or indeed the domestic power of the "Dictator"—constitute a distinct problem that emerges in the latter part of the twentieth century. In 1976, Ngũgĩ wa Thiong'o himself had theorized the "crisis of unclarity" in "Black run neo-colonial states."[107] He observed that "the native comprador bourgeoisie are the most dangerous because they confuse the people. The real powers behind the neo-colonial throne are invisible. The visible rulers have the same colour of skin and hair as the rest of the population."[108] Where Ngũgĩ goes on to call for the strengthening of democratic cultures,[109] Jameson's essay discusses the special role of allegorical and satirical genres, speculating that "under the circumstances, traditional realism is less effective."[110] For both, representations of postcolonial authoritarianism demand new critical and aesthetic tools.

Correspondingly, certain accepted wisdoms of postcolonial literary analysis and its dominant genres may need revisiting. We can recall that much classic anticolonial writing—from José Rizal's *Noli Me Tangere* (1887), Gandhi's *Hind Swaraj* (1909), C. L. R. James's *The Black Jacobins* (1938), to Frantz Fanon's *The Wretched of the Earth* (1961)—was, despite the diversity of its genres, often characterized by the careful *analysis, refusal, and opposition* to the imperial state's racial, economic, and cultural organization in the service of anticipating national sovereignty and self-determination. In the tradition of anticolonial "combat literature" à la Fanon, the raison d'être of such literature is to call "upon a whole people to join in the struggle for the existence of the nation."[111] As Jameson intuits, such a politico-aesthetic strategy is inadequate for what he calls (somewhat sweepingly) "the poisoned gift of independence."[112] Or, as Duncan Yoon has more recently noted in an essay on the Afro-Asian literary organizations that followed Bandung, "however critical 'revolutionary literature' was of colonialism, it would take another aesthetic to address the antagonism of the independent nation. That is, as important as 'combat literature' was to the birth of the postcolonial, it was not able to address the various entanglements of the postcolony."[113] These observations square with the problem Christopher J. Lee has aptly called the "tensions of postcoloniality." Lee elaborates how the contradictions at hand are no longer the "tensions of empire," but the "inherited colonial legacies and possible postcolonial futures that African and Asian countries had to negotiate."[114] Put otherwise, if earlier genres often privileged the *colonial state* as an unambiguous object of critique, what representational logic is demanded by authoritarian postcolonial regimes?[115]

We may note that the autocratic turn in the Global South has been rendered visible through a variety of genres, including prison literature (for example, Ngũgĩ wa Thiong'o's 1981 *Detained* and Pramoedya's Buru Quartet, examined in Chapter 2), the *testimonio* (most famously *I, Rigoberto Menchú* from 1983), magical realism, especially in the portrayal of Latin American potentates (such as Miguel Angel Asturias's 1946 *El Señor Presidente* and Gabriel García Márquez's 1973 *Autumn of the Patriarch*), and what may be called "failed state fiction."[116] In this book, I am interested in cultural forms that mediate the emergent "genre of rule"[117] of postcolonial authoritarianism within the Cold War–decolonizing matrix. I contend that imaginative works that reckon with "tensions of postcoloniality" in non-communist Asia do so most profoundly through an impure mix of genres that historicize and theorize these fundamental shifts in political terrain, doing so in order to grasp "the crisis of unclarity." One consequence is that this book dwells less on those genres and thematics mentioned above, as well as those most established within postcolonial studies. In terms of privileged genres in the field, "the novel under decolonization was clearly a medium for the expressiveness of national consciousness" and has garnered the lion's share of scholarly attention.[118] This project, by contrast, takes a more promiscuous approach to genre, reading across novels, poetry, reportage, conference proceedings, the *Bildungsroman*, the graphic novel, documentary and fiction film. More than defining a "new" privileged genre to replace the novel or the *testimonio*, I am interested in the way these adulterated forms raise questions about the very relationship between decolonization as both political and cultural genre. In Peter Hitchcock's useful discussion of the "genre of postcoloniality," he warns us that "the gauntlet of genre definition is a sign of hubris—the manner in which the literary critic asks to be shot." Better, he suggests, to define genre "in more open, relational terms. Rather than fixing a point of origin the genre is defined by a particular combination of characteristics that may surface and subside at different moments in history."[119] In a similar tack, my use of genres is less about taxonomies, classifications, or the "being of genre," and more about "the intricate workings of the process of genre."[120] For example, I am interested in the way writing against the state might take on—and trouble—the genre of historical fiction, while narratives of leftist exile surface in conjunction with the trope of anachronism. Such intermixings, I suggest, are strategies to map the double transformation *from* colonialism *into* postcolonial developmentalism, a process that might be described by Antonio Gramsci (in different circumstances) as "restoration-revolution."[121] These forms parse the postcolonial as both reproduction and possibility through a range of genre mixings, borrowings, and recombinations.

This approach takes me in two directions, explored in Parts I and II of the book respectively. In the first, via an admittedly more familiar mobilization of genre, I examine certain cultural modes and conventions that Cold War decolonization precipitated, namely, the regional writers' conference and the genre of "persecuted" or dissident literature, exemplified by three "Asian Solzhenitsyns." We see there how geopolitical contests produced distinct debates around freedom of expression, "engaged" versus "pure" literature, and individual versus collective liberty. Both genres draw on longer traditions that enshrined the free passage of literary exchange, and yet here are indelibly marked by the bipolar historical conditions—and contortions—of possibility. In the second half of the book, I grapple more directly with local mediations of a newly global political genre: anti-communism. As we will see, anti-communism is not only the ideological entry fee for alignment with the "free world," but it is a versatile political-aesthetic concept that can articulate with a number of other authorities, such as colonial race thinking (which begets "red" bloodlines), boundary definitions of the "other" of the postcolonial nation, and an all-purpose justification for frenzied capitalist development. Importantly, the texts in this section critically incorporate the tropes of anti-communism by adapting a range of literary-political modes such as the

Bildungsroman of the new nation, the tale of historical anachronism, and the legal form of the truth commission. One further motif drawing together the heterogeneous archive of these three chapters is that of temporality. If the external authority of anti-communist development short-circuits the richness of possible decolonizing futures—internationalist, democratic-socialist, or other—many of the book's texts locate coercion and violence in the state's infrastructures of temporality. They take us from tyrannies of colonial domination to dictates of developmentalism through narrative genres that experiment with and reflect upon foreclosed futures of the past and sedimented histories of our "post–Cold War" present. Together, I consider these texts genres of Cold War reckoning. My title is an attempt to capture both the tensions at a specific geopolitical conjuncture and the gesture of "settling accounts" with the past.

Chapter Outlines

Finally, let me briefly outline the structure of the book and the terrain of each chapter. Part I, "Authorities of Alignment, 1955–1988," examines the pressures that reshape notions of literary and political freedom under bipolar recruitment. Chapter 1, "Writing Freedom from Bandung to PEN International," lays the historical groundwork for regional debates over decolonization, "free world" incorporation, and development. Scrutinizing the proceedings of a number of PEN Asian Writers' Conferences held in different Asian cities from the early 1960s to 1980s, I trace the dilemmas of literary and cultural producers as they attempt to theorize a collective future beyond both colonialism and superpower subordination. Reading the conference form itself as a distinctly Cold War genre, we see how notions of freedom and cultural autonomy prove to be anything but stable: They range from the PEN-endorsed defense of "free words" and exchange across the "free world" to radical calls for political solidarity and "cultural import substitution."

Next, for several high-profile writers whose works have been typically categorized as "dissident writing," I consider the way their aesthetic retooling of prominent oppositional literary genres exposes the fault lines around postcolonial sovereignty and the Cold War reproduction of colonial rule. In this chapter, "In the Shadow of Solzhenitsyn: Pramoedya Ananta Toer, Kim Chi-ha, Ninotchka Rosca, and Cold War Critique," I compare writings of and on three literary figures who ran afoul of the South Korean, Indonesian, and Philippine governments, respectively. Although the works of Pramoedya, Kim, and Rosca continue longer traditions of allegorical and satirical writings that critique state power, their imaginative renderings theorize authoritarianism specifically as the withholding of national sovereignty for the reproductive imperatives of a transpacific capitalism. I argue that, despite differences in literary form, languages, and postcolonial contexts, these figures challenge liberal, human-rights notions of the dissident Third World writer via their emphasis on global political economies, regional histories, and Cold War restructuring.

In Part II, "Genres of Cold War Reckoning, 1997–2017," I shift my attention to post-1990 texts that look back to the Cold War decades. This part examines how retrospective accounts of decolonization scrutinize anew the relationships between state violence, anti-communism, and developmentalism. Chapter 3, "Separate Futures: Other Times of Southeast Asian Decolonization," turns to narrative inscriptions of the tumultuous independence, merger, and separation of Singapore and Malay(si)a. The chapter looks closely at Mohamed Latiff Mohamed's *Confrontation (Batas Langit)* (1997), Jeremy Tiang's *State of Emergency* (2017), and Sonny Liew's *The Art of Charlie Chan Hock Chye* (2015) for the ways they work through separation, unification, and division as processes of decolonization that foreclose radical nationalist and leftist energies. Employing the literary forms of fictionalized memoir, a multi-perspectival family drama, and a graphic novel, these loose *Bildungsromane* provide a window onto those other "futures past" (Koselleck) that were available at decolonization.

In the final two chapters of the book, I endeavor to trace the repressed aftermaths of the Cold War in the present. There I argue for a textual and filmic poetics of untimeliness that challenges the linearity of both postcolonial historiography and the triumphalism of (post–)Cold War epistemes. First, in pondering the problem of the "meritorious dictator" in Singapore and South Korea—that is, acknowledging the period of remarkable economic growth as simultaneously one of political repression—Chapter 4, "The Wrong Side of History: Anachronism and Authoritarianism," argues for the poetics of anachronism as a defining (post–)Cold War genre. Hwang Sŏk-yŏng's fictionalization of the failed 1980 Gwangju Uprising in *The Old Garden (Oraedoen Chŏngwŏn)* (2000) and Tan Pin Pin's banned documentary on political exiles *To Singapore with Love* (2014) narrate former leftist and anti-imperial struggles of liberation from the perspective of defeated political dissidents, communists, and student leaders. The figure of anachronism, I contend, indexes the fraught continuities between an apparently "past" era of Cold War anti-communism and our triumphant neoliberal present.

Then, the fifth chapter, "Killing Communists: Transitional Justice and the Making of the Post–Cold War," examines Joshua Oppenheimer's controversial documentary *The Act of Killing* (2012) and Han Kang's *Human Acts*

([*Sonyŏni onda*] (2014) for their intimate reckoning with past state atrocities. Framing my analysis in terms of the temporal logic of transitional justice, I consider Han's exquisite portrayal of pain and Oppenheimer's striking aestheticization of killing to ask whether the genres of truth commissions—individual truth-telling, commemoration, reconciliation, and official mourning—are able to proffer notions of justice and ethical reckoning within today's authoritative temporality of the "post–Cold War." Together, the retrospective reckonings of Part II question the historical turning point of 1991 and disclose how forms of anti-communist, capitalist orthodoxy continue to haunt and shape our "post–Cold War" present.

Finally, the book's Epilogue, "Authoritarian Lessons for Neoliberal Times," considers the apparent resurgence of authoritarian and populist regimes in our political present. While rightly highlighting the role of neoliberalism in creating today's authoritarianisms, recent works of political theory on the subject are still largely limited to a North Atlantic perspective. I turn to accounts of neoliberalism that, in contrast, underscore the way Cold War decolonization helped create the very conditions for the neoliberal victory of capitalism. I return to questions of "success and failure" and the historical balance sheet via a reading of Yoon Je-kyoon's blockbuster 2014 film *Ode to My Father (Kukje sijang)*, a film that spurred controversy for representing the Park Chung Hee regime for its developmentalist triumphs while downplaying its human rights violations. I argue, instead, for the unavoidable *ambivalence* of the capitalist developmental state, which renders the choice between economic triumphalism *or* authoritarian human rights abuses a false one. The rise of today's neoliberal authoritarianism, in sum, can be understood only by a proper reckoning with the entangled processes of decolonization and the Cold War.

PART I

Authorities of Alignment, 1955–1988

1
Writing Freedom from Bandung to PEN International

Relatively speaking, all of us gathered here today are neighbours. Almost all of us have ties of common experience—the experience of colonialism. Many of us have a common religion, common cultural roots, and the so-called "underdeveloped" nations have more or less similar economic problems . . . and yet, we know so little about each other.

—PRESIDENT SUKARNO, SPEECH AT THE OPENING
OF THE ASIAN-AFRICAN CONFERENCE IN BANDUNG, APRIL 1955

"We have to recognize our being part of Asia, our being Asian."
"But Asia means backwardness" . . .
"And even if we had a revolution and won in the end, what would we do? We would still have to produce and sell—sell to, yes, America."

—F. SIONIL JOSÉ, MASS, 1978

In the years spanning 1962 to 1981, five Asian Writers' Conferences were held in different Asian cities under the auspices of PEN, the international literary organization founded in London in the 1920s. Following the inaugural meeting in Manila in 1962, the next four conferences would be held in Bangkok in 1964, Taipei in 1970, Taipei again in 1976, and finally, Manila in 1981.[1] These meetings brought together writers, critics, university academics, and the occasional politician or diplomat to exchange ideas and debate trends in literature and culture in an ostensibly pan-Asian forum. Attended by delegates from a number of countries in the region, including the Philippines, the Republic of China (that is, Kuomintang-governed Taiwan), South Korea,

South Vietnam, Hong Kong, Japan, India, Thailand, Malaysia, and Indonesia, these conferences brought together writers from societies that had recently emerged from colonial rule and now largely found themselves—with some important exceptions such as India—in the U.S.-aligned camp of the Cold War. At the 1964 conference held at Thammasat University, Bangkok, the formal luncheons, plenaries, and a royal reception with the king and queen of Thailand at the Grand Palace were followed by a panel titled "The Contribution of Asian Writers to World Understanding." In his paper, Vu Hoang-Chong, delegate from Vietnam, opined that,

> culture constitutes the most lasting and efficient means of arriving at mutual understanding between peoples of different languages and civilizations. The emphasis has been the more significant after the Second World War when colonialism, the once-dominant factor in East-West relationships, has been virtually eliminated in free Asia. In our "crisis of growth," we, the newly independent countries, are but too willing to make our voices heard throughout the world, and the heritage of culture bequeathed us over the centuries is but too willing to display itself on its way to gaining more friends and better understanding.[2]

Vu's quote underscores some significant aspects of these early PEN-sponsored conferences. Most obvious is the optimism that infuses this literary gathering, where colonialism has been "virtually eliminated in free Asia" and gives rise to "the newly independent countries." With colonialism gone, a central motivation of the conference is to promote "mutual understanding" and friendship between peoples who had been arbitrarily kept apart by colonial borders, giving voice to their rich but hitherto obscured "heritage of culture." Yet these are countries also grappling with the "crisis of growth" that pertains to newly won independent nationhood:[3] the conditions giving rise to this inter-Asian conference are therefore not simply those of emancipation and the opportunity to gain "more friends." The key expression, I wager, is "free Asia," which demands to be read for its double meaning: both "free" from colonialism, and "free" as in the U.S.-led and non-communist, capitalist "free world."[4] This chapter argues that the PEN regional meetings are a unique lens through which to see how tensions between newly won postcolonial freedoms and Cold War pressures of alignment are worked through on the terrain of literary exchange and cultural cooperation. Moreover, the conferences themselves may be read as a distinct genre of Cold War decolonization, in which debates over freedom, self-determination, and futurity are especially intense.

We can immediately note that the form of the writers' conference incites multiple modes of reading. On one level, we can read these meetings for the content of their preambles, speeches, papers, keynotes, and resolutions; some conference proceedings even include detailed transcripts of discussions that followed formal papers, providing access to their ephemeral dimensions. The proceedings also gesture toward the extra-literary aspects of the meetings: the welcome speeches, luncheons, sight-seeing excursions, receptions with local dignitaries, and even—in the case of the 1981 Manila Conference—the full budget and financing details (24,000 pesos were provided by the Ford Foundation, 3,027 pesos of which went toward "Beer and Snacks").[5] The conferences, therefore, are more than neutral intellectual exchanges. They are performances of inter-Asian hospitality; opportunities for cultural diplomacy and Cold War political propaganda; and material events that require substantial funding, labor, and international coordination. They exemplify one definition of Cold War literature provided by Andrew Hammond: "an intertwined, multi-generic set of socio-political concerns and textual practices produced by, and productive of, the historical conditions of the times."[6] I read these debates and performances as part of a much larger literary history of the global Cold War.[7]

As such, this chapter, unlike the ones that follow, does not focus on close readings of individual literary works. It serves as a condensed cultural history of a particular institution, PEN Asian Writers' Conferences, whose participants self-consciously struggled to theorize a decolonized Asian sphere of letters—a realm of cultural exchange beyond the fetters of colonial subordination—but within rapidly hardening Cold War boundaries. If, as Joseph Keith has observed in U.S. Cold War discourses, "the principle of freedom became increasingly mobilized to define the struggle against the Soviet Union,"[8] what kinds of "principles of freedom" were invoked and theorized in the domain of postcolonial, non-communist Asia? How does the notion of writing as a privileged *object* of freedom—as stressed by PEN's founding values and charter—rub up against ideas of culture's larger role in national and regional anti-imperialist liberation? How are fears of communist takeover negotiated alongside the realities of new U.S.-backed authoritarian regimes led by such figures as Marcos, Chiang Kai-shek, or Suharto? And finally, how might reading the conferences as a *simultaneously* postcolonial and Cold War genre enable us to think in new ways about the intersections of literary freedom, cultural imperialism, and Cold War authorities? The "principle of freedom" at stake, as we will see, is threatened by at least two major contaminants: on the one hand, communist takeover, and on the other, the betrayal by authoritarian comprador regimes. In asking these questions, this chapter aims to present a broader landscape of the literary-political networks, debates, and tropes through and against which the book's later case studies and textual examples can be read.

In what follows I first give a brief history of the PEN organization, paying special attention to its Cold War expansion in Asia. I then move to an analysis of how different permutations of freedom—literary, individual, national, anti-communist, and anti-imperial—are deployed and contested in this Cold War matrix. In particular, I'm interested in what happens to the revolutionary energies of anti-colonialist nationalism when the very notion of revolution appears to be ceded, under Cold War bipolarity, to the socialist-aligned block. In the final section of the chapter, I address questions of translation and the problem of neocolonial authoritarian rule as it manifests in PEN resolutions supporting imprisoned writers around the world. The Asian Writers' Conferences, in sum, raise the fraught question of freedom *after* independence,[9] as read through a little-studied genre of Cold War decolonization.

PEN at the Cold War

Arguably, one of the most dominant conceptions of international cultural exchange and freedom of expression has been advanced by the organization PEN International. Deriving its name from the acronym for Poets, Essayists, and Novelists, PEN was founded in Britain in 1921 by Catharine Amy Dawson-Scott and John Galsworthy and is now a sprawling international federation that boasts 145 centers in over 100 countries.[10] PEN's official stance has always been a liberal one of freedom of expression and political neutrality. Its charter states that literature and art "should be left untouched by national or political passion" and remain the "patrimony of humanity at large"; it exhorts its members to "pledge themselves to oppose any form of suppression of freedom of expression in the country and community to which they belong."[11] Following its founding, the organization soon established overseas chapters in Iraq, Egypt, and Argentina in the 1920s and in India (where Rabindranath Tagore was its first president), China, and Japan by the 1930s.[12] Originally conceived as a literary social club in London whose liberal founders promoted "international friendliness for writers," the organization's vocation was profoundly shaped during the interwar period and the rise of fascism.[13] Following the book burnings in Nazi Germany and the expulsion of German Jewish writers, PEN—then under the leadership of H. G. Wells—came to see "literary texts, now tied to the fate of authors, [as what] required international protection from state suppression."[14] In the 1930s it defended the writers Federico García Lorca (unsuccessfully) and Hungary's Arthur Koestler (successfully) against Spain's Franco. In sum, "Humanitarian [or human rights] ideas of speech beyond national boundaries, gender equality, international cooperation and education"[15] were predicated on the idea of literary expression as a special moral and aesthetic object that above all demanded protection.

By 1949 it had consultative status at the UN and by the mid-1960s, as Frances Stoner Saunders relates, "International PEN had seventy-six centres in fifty-five countries, and was officially recognized by UNESCO as the organization most representative of all the writers of the world."[16] The global spread of PEN Centers during the Cold War, in turn, made it a target of the CIA-backed Congress for Cultural Freedom. Established in 1950, the CCF was a front organization whose mission was to "nudge the intelligentsia of western Europe away from its lingering fascination with Marxism and Communism towards a view more accommodating of 'the American way.'"[17] As Peter McDonald writes of the CCF, "It set out to create an elite worldwide liberal alliance that would promote Western ideas of culture and act as a bulwark against communism and the broader threat of totalitarianism."[18] Saunders provides a pithy history of the extensive maneuvering within the American PEN Center, concluding that by the mid-1960s "the CIA had achieved excellent penetration of PEN."[19] Indeed, *Comment: The Filipino Journal of Ideas, Discussion and the Arts*, which published the proceedings of the 1962 conference in Manila, was published jointly by PEN and the CCF. Thus, although PEN's original mission may have been shaped by European debates on fascism, art, and humanism, it found a particular calling in the postwar geopolitical conjuncture, where Third World decolonization was subtended by the Cold War. Paralleling the trajectory of postwar human rights generally, PEN's prominent cases tended to highlight dissident writers of the Soviet bloc (the Soviets would not affiliate with PEN until 1988) and Third World authoritarian states. Doing work in the literary realm analogous to that of Amnesty International and other human rights NGOs, it is today the preeminent international NGO promoting literary freedom of expression and continues to actively oppose the state persecution of writers.

In many ways the work of PEN and the CCF dovetailed to promote similar liberal notions of culture as "free" from political contamination, privileging the individual autonomy of the writer/creator. Yet studies such as McDonald's have explored the conflicted role that PEN centers and conferences played in postcolonial national contexts such as in South Africa and India.[20] At one level, PEN's emphasis on freedom of speech, "unhampered transmission of thought," literature as "common currency between nations," and the dispelling of "race, class and national hatreds"[21] fits well with the aspirations of writers and intellectuals emerging from the restrictions of colonial borders and institutions. On the other, PEN's commitments were profoundly complicated by decolonizing contexts, where vastly different conditions would challenge its anti-political notions of freedom of expression. Furthermore, even if Saunders reminds us that the PEN executive was well "penetrated" by the CIA's cultural front—ensuring that "free speech" remained the gift of the U.S.-led "free world"—we cannot assume that the writers, critics, and scholars that attended its international meetings were simply supporters of U.S. efforts in the Cold War. Despite being primarily funded by the Ford Foundation, for example, the 1981 Manila Conference gave airtime to Marxist literary critic Domingo Castro de Guzman, who vehemently indicted "trivial, superficial and smallminded" American poets for being "intoxicated by their nation's imperial successes and benefit[ing] directly therefrom."[22] F. Sionil José's long-time participation in PEN is perhaps a more substantial rejoinder. A prolific writer whose novels on colonialism and class struggle troubled the Marcos government (as did writings by many journalists and writers, many of whom were imprisoned),[23] he founded both the Philippines PEN Center and the bookshop and publishing house Solidaridad. He was a key participant at four of the five PEN Asia Writers' Conferences; Singaporean critic Dudley de Souza would give an entire presentation on his novels, subtitled "An Extended Study in Social Injustice," at the 1981 Manila conference. José also edited the *Asian PEN Anthology*, published by his Solidaridad Press in 1968 and reprinted by Taplinger Press in New York the same year. I use brief excerpts from José's 1978 anti-Marcos novel *Mass* throughout this chapter to give literary grounding to some of the lively debates at the conferences.

Instead of collapsing PEN with the ruses of the CCF, I suggest that the PEN-sponsored writers' conferences participate in a set of political-cultural concerns not unrelated to those articulated at the historic 1955 Asian-African Conference in Bandung, in which representatives from twenty-nine newly decolonized and decolonizing nations came together to assert their independence from both colonial rulers and the new Cold War superpowers. Vu's comments on the shared "heritage of culture" and desire for friendship I quoted above, for example, might well remind us of the welcome speech made by Indonesian President Sukarno at Bandung: "Many of us have a common religion, common cultural roots and the so-called 'underdeveloped' nations have more or less similar economic problems . . . and yet, we know so little about each other."[24] "Bandung" has since come (sometimes nostalgically) to signify the birth of the Afro-Asian solidarity movement and the subsequent Non-Aligned Movement established in Belgrade in 1961; the more radical anti-imperialist movement of the Tricontinental would follow with the 1966 Havana conference, "expand[ing] the Bandung alliance to the Americas."[25] By extension, as I discussed in the Introduction, for scholars such as David Scott, Samir Amin, and Partha Chatterjee, the Bandung Era signals an entire modality of Third World nation-formation, those "experiments with anti-imperialist self-determination, with political and economic nonalignment."[26]

It is more helpful, however, to view Bandung less as an origin point, and more as a container of diverse and sometimes competing sentiments. I follow Christopher J. Lee in his assessment of the complexity of Bandung, a conference so often considered "a foundational moment of the early postcolonial moment." He notes that "it equally"

> contained the existential predicaments of a newfound sovereignty
> and the internal and external political claims and responsibilities that
> would soon challenge it, particularly those generated by the cold war.
> . . . Bandung contained both the residual romance of revolution, as
> well as the *realpolitik* of a new world order in the making.[27]

In other words, Bandung was never only about the romance of revolution, or what Scott has elegantly delineated as the overcoming of colonial alienation via a "narrative of liberation" (a point I return to at the end of this chapter). It was also a moment inexorably struck through by Cold War tensions and alignments. If Lee returns to Bandung as a way to chart "the possibilities and predicaments of the early postcolonial period" in relation to our political present,[28] I suggest that the PEN Asian Writers' Conferences provide a window onto a particular subset of those early postcolonial predicaments, whose contradictions have persisted until, and continue to inform, our present. In one of the regions of the world most polarized by the conflicts of the Cold War, we see how "the residual romance of revolution" was refashioned by "the *realpolitik* of a new world order." Whether debating translation goals, realist versus abstract literary styles, or issuing resolutions of solidarity with detained writers, the particular form of the conferences indexes the multiple desires as well as pressures reshaping the region.

By historical coincidence, the inaugural PEN Asian Writers' Conference 1962 was held in the same year as the second Afro-Asian Writers' Conference in Cairo. The latter followed on the successes of the first Afro-Asia Writers' Conference convened in 1958 at Tashkent, Uzbekistan, under the umbrella of the Afro-Asian Peoples' Solidarity Organization established in 1957, which itself drew direct inspiration from the anti-imperialist Bandung spirit. (The Afro-Asia Writers' meetings were subsequently formalized into the permanent Afro-Asian Writers' Bureau, or the AAWB.) To be sure, the PEN Asian Writers' meetings were not governed by the Third Worldist anti-imperialist aesthetics of the literary journal *Lotus* or Afro-Asian Writers' Bureau, as recently discussed by Hala Halim, Rossen Djagalov, and Duncan Yoon.[29] One clear parallel with the AAWB, however, was PEN's interest in literary translation, which I discuss in the final section of the chapter. And there were overlaps in themes as well as some common participants at Bandung, the Afro-Asian Writers' Conferences, and the PEN Conferences. Diplomat, author, and president of the UN General Assembly from 1949 to 1950, Carlos P. Romulo, represented the Philippines at Bandung with one of the opening speeches and would give the keynote "José Rizal" lecture at the 1962 PEN meeting. At the 1981 PEN Writers' Conference, literary scholar C. F. Bautista alludes to the 1975 Afro-Asian Writers' Symposium as an important thematic precursor to the recent 1977 Philippines PEN Conference, where the latter meeting "functioned as a follow-up to the proposals drawn up in that symposium."[30]

My point is that the literary energies of this period cannot be neatly assigned into categories of aligned and unaligned. The particular forum of PEN Asian Writers' Conferences ought, rather, to be understood as part of the larger post-war political and cultural milieu that developed out of the 1950s and '60s, a period when competing articulations of freedom, self-determination and national futures were in global circulation. Functioning primarily as a venue for cultural and intellectual exchange by writers and critics in non-communist Asia, the conferences also received the imprimatur of politicians, diplomats, and university leaders, and in that sense, they may be read at the intersection of cultural and diplomatic history. Most interesting, the conferences attest to a historical moment in which decolonization gives rise to new forms, genres, and experiments in regional and interregional organizations, demanding attention to the "interpersonal, sociopolitical practices that constituted such efforts."[31] These efforts, in turn, allow us to map distinct transformations and fissures around the Cold War–decolonizing conjuncture. In Romulo's Rizal speech he credits the great nineteenth-century Filipino writer for showing us "what things were, and how it was then thought the future would be."[32] We might approach the Asian Writers' Conferences from the 1960s to the early 1980s in the same way.

Anti-Communist Friends

How might we parse the complex positionality of these participants from non-communist or "free world" Asian nations? Admittedly, we must note that, if the Afro-Asian Writers' Bureau sought "a definition of culture that took anti-colonial struggle as its starting point,"[33] early PEN Asia writers sometimes took *anti-communism* as its cultural starting point. The strongest articulations, unsurprisingly, come from writers in Taiwan, (South) Korea, and (South) Vietnam. One extreme articulation is presented at the 1962 Manila Conference by M. K. Li from the Republic of China, who provides a brief history of Chinese literature on Taiwan thus: "In a short period of thirteen years our writers have created worthy literature in Free China. And I would frankly call it Anti-communist literature."[34] South Korean delegate Mun Chon No, meanwhile, describes his nation's "thirst for liberty" as the result of Asia being the "foremost battlefield where democracy and communism face each other,"[35] handily deploying the standard Western ideological shorthand for the Cold War contest. Addressing questions of literary style and form, Hsiao I Hung from Hong Kong warns against the collapsing of literature with propaganda, which would dangerously "subordinate [the writer's] creation to a certain practical authority,"[36] synonymous with the communist agenda. At the 1970 Third Asian Writers' Conference in Taipei, delegate participant Arved Viirlaid from Estonia, identified as "Writer in Exile" in the proceedings, could express delight and camaraderie with his Asian colleagues precisely because of their shared Cold War context:

> But here, I feel you understand me better than the people in Canada, the United States, or the Western world. You understand what Communism is. You know what tyranny means to a writer. . . . [If only] we can send our free words, our free thinking to Red China or the Soviet Union we would find so many friendly writers over there who would help us to tear down any kind of Iron or Bamboo curtain.[37]

For Viirlaid, Asian writers understand his plight so much better than Westerners because they are living among the actual conflicts of the Cold War rather than its abstract ideologies. In his formulation, it is nothing other than the free flow of literature—"our free words"—that would demolish Cold War barriers. We cannot help but notice the way Viirlaid echoes the Eisenhower administration's stress on transnational flows as the perceived counter to communism. As Christina Klein has documented, Eisenhower and Dulles deployed the "intertwined concepts of flow and exchange . . . as central ideas during the Cold War." They defined "the 'free world' as a place where people, commodities, resources, and the products of intellectual activity could move easily across national boundaries, and distinguished it from the Soviet 'bloc' where all of these things were trapped behind iron and bamboo curtains."[38] An editorial in Taipei's daily newspaper *Lianhe bao* (*United Daily News*) confirms this view. In a write-up of the opening of the 1970 Writers' Conference, the editorial lays blame on the "the Iron Curtain of the West" (*xifang de tiemu*) and "the Bamboo Curtain of the East" (*dongfang de zhumu*) for hindering free communication and common prosperity.[39] Similarly, for Viirlaid, PEN's defense of free cultural exchange and the "unhampered transmission of thought" model the very "principle of freedom" which alone is needed to combat the tyranny of communism. PEN's liberal defense of freedom of expression, in which literature moves freely from external constraint, is therefore a useful analogy of the "free flows" whereby capitalist liberalism is defined against the inherent blockages of the Soviet system.[40]

Nevertheless, the actual form of the conferences indicated their own ideological blockages. Not surprisingly, no writers from the communist Mainland or North Korea appear to have attended any of the conferences. Moreover, a Vietnamese delegate at the 1970 Taipei meeting, Nghiem Xuan Viet, complained about the absence of discussion of his country's war at the conference, arguing that the first value of any cultural politics must be liberty: "Without liberty and without surrounding protection of that liberty, we can not live, therefore, we can not write."[41] Evoking "the common struggle for liberty in Asia, liberty for mankind," Nghiem urged other writers to work against "the denying of basic spiritual values"[42] that the encroaching threat of communism represents. We may surmise that the final Saturday evening's reception given by "His Excellency President of the Republic of China Chiang Kai-shek and Madame Chiang" at Chung Shan Hall would have repeated such themes (Figure 2).[43] Further, occurring in the midst of the PRC's Cultural Revolution (1966–76), delegate tours to Taipei's magnificent Palace Museum, the Chinese Opera, and the National Museum of History would have performed a visceral contrast between the Nationalist (Kuomintang [KMT]) Party's protection of cultural treasures and the Chinese Communist Party's subordination of art to political exigency. Such extraliterary activities remind us of the way the conference as a whole may function as a performative genre of cultural diplomacy. Put otherwise, efforts staged by the 1970 Taipei conference map the region's concrete experience of Cold War conflicts—especially the competition between the KMT and the Chinese Communist Party—into a cultural ideology that posits both writerly freedom and freedom in general at odds with the depredations of communism. If PEN centers helped consolidate a universal language around the protection of literary freedom as a basic human right, in decolonizing Asia it did so via the simultaneous construction of Cold War boundaries between nations that valued "liberty" and those that didn't. By extension, a similar boundary operated between literature that was aesthetically autonomous and that which descended to propaganda.

Paradoxically, the "free flows" and unhampered transmission of thought are even less evident at the 1976 conference in Taipei, where the trend of increased international representation by delegates is sharply reversed. Compared to 1970, this meeting counted participants from only four countries beyond the Republic of China: Japan, Hong Kong, (South) Korea, and Saudi Arabia.[44] Such a decrease reflects the fallout following Henry Kissinger's and

Figure 2. President Chiang Kai-shek and Madame Chiang (Soong Mei-ling) entering a reception hall at the 1970 Asian Writers' Conference held in Taipei.

U.S. President Richard Nixon's visits to Beijing, in 1971 and 1972 respectively, after which the United States changed its diplomatic affiliation from the Republic of China (ROC) to the People's Republic of China (PRC). The UN seat and powerful Security Council membership also switched from the Taipei-based Nationalist government to Beijing's Communist Party;[45] Chiang Kai-shek had died just the previous year. The isolation of Taiwan is further evidenced by the fact that the 1981 Manila meeting calls *itself* the Fourth PEN Asian Writers' Conference, apparently ignoring the 1976 Taiwan meeting altogether.[46] At the latter, the geopolitical standoff across the Taiwan Strait (which continues today) results in a more explicitly anti-communist sentiment than at earlier meetings, while the "principle of freedom" is ever more narrowly defined.

The 1976 opening remarks by Y. C. Chen, president of the Taipei PEN Center, seek to underscore the different experience of the Cold War in Asia from that in Europe. Chen points to the irony of holding the 40th International PEN Congress in Vienna the previous year (1975) under the theme "European Writers in Three Decades of Peace"; the latter is obviously the negative inspiration for the Taipei meeting's theme "Thirty Years of Turmoil in Asia." Chen elaborates: "In the 30 years from the end of World War II, Europe has had cold war but in general no large-scale hot war. But what about this Asia of ours?"[47] He concludes the conference by again emphasizing Asia's ongoing instability: "In those countries that have been afflicted by new wars and disturbances, countless people have lost their lives. . . . Unrest weighs heavily upon our whole region."[48] In one sense, Chen's comments anticipate recent scholarly interventions such as those from Odd Arne Westad, Jodi Kim, Andrew Hammond, and Heonik Kwon, whose work has stressed not the "long peace" experienced in the North Atlantic, but an "epoch of 'unbridled reality' characterized by vicious civil wars and other exceptional forms of political violence."[49] Yet although Kwon and other scholars of the global Cold War have helped widen scholarly attention to the "multitude of these locally specific historical realities and variant human experiences,"[50] delegates at the 1976 conference remain locked in a defensive geopolitical reality. At its most reductive, the very notion of "freedom" of literature and culture is reduced to nothing *but* the battle against communism, as Wang Chi-tsung attests in a brief paper titled "Literature in Agitated Time":

> Judging from the thirty years of Asian literature created in turmoil, we can say that the worst enemy of free literature are the Communist theories, both in literature and in general. The anti-communist theme is the most important one in Asian literature, I believe. In the progress of time, it is likely that there will be great writers like Pasternack [*sic*] and Solzhenitsyn, who will show to the world the essence of Asian culture and will be a part of great world literature.[51]

In this strained formulation, Asian literature will ascend to the status of "great" world literature precisely by virtue of its anti-communism. Note here the assumed correlations between "free literature," the "essence of Asian culture," and world literature, even as the reduced conference attendance makes clear the shrinking world of allies for the KMT's republican stronghold on Taiwan.[52] Obviously, no mention is made of the KMT's own increasing repression around publishing and literary freedom, which would culminate in the accusation of leftist, "nativist" (*hsiang-t'u*) writers at the 1977 KMT-convened Symposium of Writers for promoting Taiwanese separatism.[53]

Finally, we can observe the strangeness of a debate on social realism that follows a paper by Yen Yuan-shu of National Taiwan University. In a discussion on the avowedly anti-communist fiction of Chen Jo-hsi, the author's choice to write in a social realist mode is not critiqued for the reason we might assume—its perceived ideological alignment with the Soviet world. As Hammond reminds us, Soviet ideologue Andrei Zhdanov's anti-formalist prescriptions for Soviet art were frequently contrasted to the U.S.'s sponsorship of modernism's experimental aesthetics.[54] Instead, the Taiwanese conference participants fault social realism for portraying the Mainland as anything other than a horrific, intolerable state of misery. That such portrayals can be published in Taiwan gives rise to puzzlement at the "freedom of speech of our island that allows stories like that . . . to be printed at all."[55] Rather than see these debates as irredeemably ideological, however, I suggest we read them as attempts to make sense of the shifting "principle of freedom" as it is navigates both bipolar geopolitical standoffs and the liberal insistence on free communication and exchange. Refracting such tensions into the domain of the literary conference, PEN's commitment to "freedom of expression"—which in Taiwan in 1976 can officially refer only to "anti-communism"—grates against liberty as defensively defined in Cold War Asia. In envisioning a world of letters created negatively through the artistic principle of freedom from (communist) constraint, other possibilities for world-making, solidarity, and futures forged *against* bipolarism itself are foreclosed in the 1976 KMT-sponsored PEN Conference.

By the 1981 Manila Conference (technically the fifth Asian Writers' Conference), with the theme "Literature and Social Justice," the European PEN executive itself seems to have recognized the way "freedom of expression" had become an "aligned" concept in the cultural Cold War. International PEN secretary, former soldier, and novelist Peter Elstob opens the conference with a general disclaimer as to PEN's ideological allegiances:

A principle which has emerged very clearly in recent years is that a P.E.N. Centre never speaks for its government and its delegates can never be called to account for the actions of their government. . . .

I mentioned that we considered the cases of writers imprisoned in more than thirty countries and that member will immediately tell you that no one political ideology is responsible for oppressing and suppressing writers.

Perhaps the two worst countries for an independent-minded writer to live in today are Argentina and Cuba, and their politics could hardly be further apart; two others almost as bad are Czechoslovakia and Chile.[56]

Elstob strategically calls out pairs of repressive governments, one communist and one capitalist, with the assurance that neither right-wing nor left-wing governments have a monopoly on repression. But his comments also suggest a certain symmetry of authoritarianism during the Cold War, acknowledging that the "free world" may not be as liberal as advertised.

Between Revolution and Development

If anti-communism looms large as a primary contaminant to freedom, a different but parallel articulation of unfreedom also comes into focus at the early conferences. The latter stresses common colonial histories, poverty, and persistent underdevelopment as the problems Asian nations face during and after decolonization. As we saw earlier in the quote from Sukarno, economic "backwardness" as a shared Asian and African characteristic was a trope repeatedly used at the 1955 Bandung conference. Romulo's speech there well evokes the shared sense of urgency around this issue:

> Lastly, I have said that all of us here are concerned with peaceful economic growth. This brings us closest of all to the hub, the center, the heart of our common preoccupations, because the political forms and methods we seek and choose, the social ideas and ideals we embrace, are all wrapped up in the way in which we strive for *growth*. Economic growth, economic change, transformation of our backward and inadequate economies—these we all seek. These we *must* seek, else we stagnate and die.[57]

In his speech at the closing session, Prime Minister of India Jawaharlal Nehru confirms the urgent need for development: "We have been backward; we are backward. We have been left behind in the race, in the world race, and now we have got a chance again to make good."[58] It is not difficult to agree with Dipesh Chakrabarty's assessment that the discourse of Bandung "often displayed an uncritical emphasis on modernization" to the extent that "the figure of the engineer was one of the most eroticized figures of the postcolonial developmentalist imagination."[59] We might, in fact, perceive here a central tension of postcoloniality as that between cultural modernity and modernization, expressed in the jostle between the figure of the writer and the engineer.[60] The preoccupations with modernization at Bandung would permeate the PEN conferences, as we see in the opening statement at the 1962 Manila Conference by Philippines Vice President Emmanuel Pelaez. Like the young protagonist in F. Sionil José's novel *Mass* who claims "Asia means backwardness" (in the scene I quoted as the epigraph), Pelaez describes poverty as Asia's "only common factor."[61] Yet it is precisely the shared experience of colonialism across almost all of Asia that simultaneously gestures toward a resurgent pan-Asian identity: as a region of proud civilizations no longer subordinated to the West or to Japan, it is poised now for an era of national rebirth, sovereignty, and prosperity.

A central problem that PEN Asian writers grapple with, then, is defining the role of culture and letters—embodied in the figure of the writer—in the "striving for growth" that Romulo and Pelaez give voice to. At the 1970 Taipei conference, a panel featuring F. Sionil José, longtime PEN member from India Sophia Wadia, and Iranian delegate Dr. Z. Rahnema, for example, debate issues of tradition and modernity; multilingual, vernacular, and regional language politics; the influence from the West of "realism, romanticism, symbolism, surrealism and so on";[62] and the technological problems of printing presses and literary dissemination. Catalogued under the problems of culture and modernization, these questions of reforms, mass education, and the pressing task of developing their nations are discussed again and again by delegates. In this sense, the threat to freedom comes not from communists on the other side of the Iron or Bamboo Curtains, but from the internal struggle to transform those "backward and inadequate" economies (Romulo). At the 1962 Manila conference, N. V. M. Gonzalez, one of the Philippines' most esteemed twentieth-century authors, describes the task of the writer as seeking a form adequate to the complex temporality of the postcolonial Asian nation, that is, of "a society living simultaneously, as it were, several hundred years in time."[63] For Gonzalez, the literary artist "can be the most deceptively effective in *cutting away the drag of centuries* with which like a sea-anchor Asian societies float about in the storms of the present."[64] Indonesian delegate S. Takdir Alisjahbana,[65] meanwhile, looks forward to a "new worldwide literature" and corresponding humanism made possible by "the accomplishments of science, technology, and economics which characterize modern culture."[66] There is a sense among these speakers that the fundamental struggle of the postcolonial nation is that of *temporality*: The present is compelled to vanquish the "drag of centuries" in order to build, as Vice President Pelaez has it, "a whole new structure of society."[67] For the writers, this is not viewed merely as technological progress but one that must produce a new culture, a new humanism and society. One of the more intractable conceptual and political problems that emerges is how to articulate collective desires for "a whole new structure of society" in a world where revolution was now unavoidably associated with communism.

In other words, PEN Asian writers find themselves in the peculiar dilemma of vehemently *desiring* the social revolution that should follow formal political emancipation, but lacking the vocabulary to describe it because of Cold War proscriptions. We may recall here Reinhart Koselleck's fertile discussion of the temporal implications of revolution in his study of historical time, *Futures Past*. Since the French Revolution, he argues, revolution involves not just the overthrowing of a political regime, but promises "the social emancipation of all men, *transforming* the social structure."[68] In one of his few comments on the non-European world, Koselleck notes that, "while the political emancipation of former colonies may be nearly complete, political freedom becomes a reality only if emancipation is construed as a *social process*."[69] If, in non-communist Asia, national "growth" and "development" are precisely the social processes thought to effect such a transformation, these require a different set of social and cultural energies than those that helped to overthrow colonialism. At the 1962 conference, liberal Indonesian critic Alisjahbana—a staunch defender of universal, nonpolitical literary values—describes the apparent delay between political emancipation and social change as due to the necessary collective "cooling off period" after national awakening.[70] S. M. Kismadi, also of Indonesia, similarly credits anti-colonial nationalism with the achievement of Asia's recent independence, but identifies revolutionary energies as what must now be reined in. If the role of the Asian writer has hitherto been to help "set in motion the Asian revolution," what, he ponders, is the writer's present role?[71] Lamenting the double-edged sword of "collective passions"—so essential to national revolutions but which risk submerging "individual passions"—Kismadi suggests that the writer's role is the "defense of individual rights against the new order."[72] (Although we can assume he is speaking against the communists, the phrase "the new order" unwittingly and proleptically names the Suharto regime that would follow on the heels of the anti-leftist massacres of 1965–66.) Perhaps Filipino delegate Raul S. Manglapus puts the dilemma most succinctly in his speech "Progress and the Writers of Asia": "The leadership of almost one half of the world today believes also in revolution, in the struggle of class against class. In our half of the world—what revolution is there to believe in?"[73] An instructive scene from José's novel *Mass* raises a parallel quandary. The young protagonist Pepe discusses the possibilities for revolutionary action with his mentor, legendary peasant leader Ka Lucion. In response to Pepe's enthusiasm for action, the older man cautions, "This is not the time. . . . The Americans are here. . . . They will interfere. The oligarchy will convince them that your revolution is communist, *even if it is not*."[74] Radical change, in this historical-geographical conjuncture, can only be interpreted as communist.

José's warning is diagnostic of the specific entanglements of decolonizing Asian countries and the demands of bipolar alignments. If, as Leo Ching has suggested, we see here a *trans-imperial* shift from formal Japanese, European, and U.S. colonial occupations to a configuration of nation-states inserted within a new U.S.-led transpacific bloc,[75] conference participants express deep anxieties over both uncontainable revolutions on the left *and* a hovering suspicion about the ability of this new international order to deliver the goods of modernity and social emancipation, a disappointment that would be forcefully articulated in 1965 by Kwame Nkrumah as neocolonialism.[76] They thus recall an earlier moment of Romulo's speech at Bandung, in which he warns—à la Fanon—against the mere replacement of a foreign ruler with a local oligarchy. Even Romulo, the U.S.-allied liberal diplomatic, recognizes that the situation of ruling *like* a foreigner reproduces "autocratic rule, control of the press, and the police state [which were] exactly the worst features of some colonialist systems against which we have fought." Thus, "it is perilously easy in this world for national independence to be more fiction than fact."[77]

What emerges in these discussions is twofold: on the one hand, a vehement desire to conquer postcolonial temporality and modernize society as the means to self-determination and autonomy; on the other, a haunting suspicion about whether modernization under alignment will resist—or reproduce—imperialist, authoritarian forms of rule. The epithet "free Asia"—used enthusiastically by some conference participants—again reveals the ambivalence of "free": free from colonialism, but forced into anti-communist military alliances and dependent trade and development with the so-called "free" world. Underwriting what Gilbert Rist has called "the development age" of the postwar period is the accepted tenet that underdevelopment was a "lack" that impelled all societies to replace tradition with modernization.[78] And yet the desire to vanquish those "backward and inadequate economies" (Romulo) to achieve national autonomy places the political *present* in a state of abeyance. As I examine more fully in the following chapters, the future-making ambitions of these regimes—such as Suharto's "New Order" and Park Chung Hee's "Revitalization reforms"—tap into decolonizing desires to claim an accelerated path to national prosperity,[79] while restricting the route toward that modernity to one of "technical measures outside the realm of political debate."[80] These technical measures, in turn, were often used precisely to deflect bipolar political tensions, such as when the KMT "responded to [its] political crisis [by] accelerating the modernization process, determined to strengthen Taiwan's global position by building it into an economic powerhouse."[81] In this formulation, authoritarian development and anti-communist repression are mutually reinforcing.

Let us pause here to reflect on the previous two sections. First, I have noted that PEN's foundational defense of freedom of expression, international "friendliness," and cosmopolitan cultural exchange is recoded through anti-communist friendships as a defense of Asian territories *from* the tyranny of collectivism. The older literary trope of writerly freedom against the state is thus mobilized as a geopolitical bulwark against possible communist take-overs and, at its extreme, anti-communist literature is conflated with ("free"-) world literature, confirming a notion of literature as "anti-political, individualist, moral and aesthetic."[82] Second, parallel discussions of postcolonial development, reform, and tradition versus modernity reveal an emerging anxiety around unfreedoms precipitated by developmental imperatives and U.S. hegemony. To return to *Mass*, José's character Pepe voices the double bind of non-communist Asia's development: "Even if we had a revolution and won in the end, what would we do? We would still have to produce and sell—sell to, yes, America."[83] The larger point is that PEN's supposedly universal concepts of "freedom of expression" and literary exchange as baseline goods for organizing post-imperial cultural flows come under pressure from Cold War exigencies. Indeed, they prove inadequate for—and indeed mask—the complex transformations occurring at this conjuncture. Let us move forward to the 1981 Asian Writers' Conference to see a different "principle of freedom" elaborated.

New Authorities

The 1981 Manila Conference—and the last regional conference I examine—may be readily contrasted with the 1976 Taipei Conference, in which we saw increasingly contorted literary theories to preserve the fiction of freedom "here" and authoritarianism "there." In fact, the two conferences offer seemingly divergent views on liberation's contaminants: an overwhelming, monolithic sense of communist tyranny, on the one hand, and the increasing disappointments and new authorities of the "free world" postcolony, on the other, the latter made unavoidably visible by the Marcos regime. We should bear in mind, however, that we cannot read the conference materials as representative of all cultural energies of the period; too much remains unknown about who was invited, who wasn't, who refused to attend, and why. Furthermore, if we attend to the distinct political-cultural landscapes in Taiwan in 1976 and the Philippines in 1981, we can avoid reading the differences between the two conferences as a simple evolution of political consciousness. The Republic of China, recall, had already been under martial law for going on thirty years (and would be for another ten); ongoing tensions across the Taiwan Strait would keep a lid on organized resistance and the KMT would remain exclusively in power for another two decades. The Philippines, by contrast, saw a more uneven postwar political development with five different presidents of the Republic preceding Marcos's presidency in 1965. The rapid growth of protest movements and the rise of radical nationalism in the late 1960s and '70s was due to a multitude of causes, including "the Vietnam War and opposition to it, the French student revolt, the Chinese cultural revolution, [and] the rigged election of 1969 [when Marcos was reelected]."[84] Marcos's martial law of 1972 itself was justified to prevent government overthrow by two forces: the Moro Liberation Front of Muslim separatists and the newly resurrected Communist Party of the Philippines (CPP), largely inspired by the Chinese and Vietnamese struggles.[85] Even as Marcos's switch in policy to export-oriented industries and agricultural and land reforms saw some success by the mid-1970s, by the early '80s his regime was in crisis both financially and politically, while his repressive tactics were actually drawing more people into communist and other opposition movements.[86] Until his ouster following the EDSA Revolution of 1986, it would be a regime largely dominated by the military and technocrats "who shared his idea of national development," that is, massive foreign debt, U.S. military aid, and extravagant public spending, while most economic benefits went to the Marcoses' patronage networks.[87]

The shadow of eleven years of martial rule under President Marcos—only lifted earlier in the same year as the 1981 conference—and the increasingly strident resistance to the regime obviously influenced the conference's tone and theme of "Literature and Social Justice."[88] In a paper titled "The Filipino Writer and Social Justice," Mauro R. Avena speaks of Marcos's duplicity in no uncertain terms:

> We were a nation stunned when Marcos, his legitimate term as President about to terminate for good the following year, imposed martial law in 1972. He had—if anyone outside the First Lady, his cabinet, the military, and the would-be civilian community guards believed then—the noblest of motives: ". . . to save the Republic, and to reform society."[89]

If Marcos's turn to martial law was rationalized as "saving the Republic" from the MLF and the CPP,[90] it bears a family resemblance to Park Chung Hee's own Emergency Declaration in South Korea just three weeks earlier. Indeed, by the end of the 1970s the consolidation of right-wing authoritarianisms in East and Southeast Asia forces a new complexity to the "principle of freedom." In turn, we see that theorizations of literature, culture, and freedom at the Manila conference respond more directly to a set of emerging contradictions in the region. One symptom is that the terms "Third World" and "developing society" replace "free world" used in the earlier conferences, indexing a stronger sense of shared Global South dilemmas.

The final keynote lecture included in the 1981 proceedings begins with a sense of the now-generalizable predicament of Third World authoritarianism, and does so through the critical lens of human rights—a lens that, like PEN's defense of freedom of expression in the Third World, comes of age in the postwar decades.[91] The speaker is Salvador P. Lopez, liberal journalist, professor, president of the Philippines PEN Center, former Secretary of Foreign Affairs, and Philippine ambassador to the UN.[92] In "Some Reflections on Human Rights," he extols the innate rights that all humans are born with and reminds his audience that the Philippines was represented at Eleanor Roosevelt's 1947 UN Commission on Human Rights in Geneva (by none other than Carlos Romulo, speaker at both Bandung and the inaugural PEN Asian Writers' Conference in 1962). Speaking of the shared disappointment in the state of the Third World, he poignantly asks "What has gone wrong?"[93] In articulating an answer, he lays firm blame on approaches to the problem of underdevelopment. For Third World societies, "the presumed advantages" of authoritarian rule "can become irresistible" since "the democratic process is often slow and time-consuming and tends to act as a brake on the engine of national development."[94] Although ignoring the larger, more persistent global inequalities that might play a role in reproducing underdevelopment, Lopez exhorts his audience to think of individual political rights and social-economic rights as two sets of freedoms that cannot be separated: "The development of the human being requires an integrated process that addresses itself to body, mind and spirit."[95] I wish to read Lopez's speech as symptomatic of a moment when the authoritarianism of the *non*-communist Third World—personified by Marcos—has become perceivable in a new way, and is thereby opened up to theorization and critique.

Indeed, the conference theme of "Literature and Social Justice" allows for not just an assessment of Marcos-style repression—which perhaps was unwise at this forum—but the diagnosis of the multiple, wider problems besetting postcolonial societies, from economic underdevelopment, class and gender oppression, the problem of minorities, and environmental destruction. Throughout the various papers, we see a multilayered indictment of the betrayal of the national liberationist project—or what was earlier discussed as the Bandung Era—but from the specific location of a region still squarely caught in the bipolar contest. South Korean delegate Duk-yong Kong, for example, could speak of Choi In-hun's 1960 novella of the Korean War, *Forum* (*Kwangjang*, more commonly translated into English as *The Square*), in which the protagonist falls into nihilistic despair after experiencing the disappointments of repressive systems in both the North and the South.[96] Although there are a wide range of analytical frameworks—from Lopez's liberal human rights approach to literary histories, surveys, and polemical position papers—such indictments fall most readily into two prominent, although related, strains: Marxist and cultural nationalist.

Although writers and critics from North Korea, Vietnam, and the PRC are still absent, the presence of Marxist and pro-socialist understandings of literature at this conference is striking. Cecil Rajendra, lawyer, poet, and critic from Malaysia, for example, excoriates the Cold War liberal assumptions that view social commitment and literary autonomy as incompatible, a standpoint which is unwittingly complicit with authoritarian rule:

> It is pertinent also here to observe how authoritarian regimes and the literary establishment, often poles apart on questions of censorship, security and individual freedom, join hands and seem almost to echo each other in their vociferous denunciation of the creative writer who, directly or tangentially, intercedes for social justice.[97]

Rajendra refutes exactly the sentiments of earlier PEN participants from South Korea, Hong Kong, Taiwan, and Indonesia who worried about the dangers of literature succumbing to the "practical authority" of communism and insisted on the containment of anti-colonial energies. Bangladeshi participant and novelist Selina Hossain goes even further:

> The capitalist or the so-called Western democratic way of life includes literature and art in its system of manipulation. The goal of this system is to limit the development of individuals, to make it conform to the requirements of modern capitalist production. On the other hand, the literature of socialist orientation selects and assimilates the best achievements of humanity and is deeply-rooted in the consciousness of the class struggle of the toiling masses. This socialist orientation views the writer not as an indifferent observer but as an investigator of life. He analyses real phenomena and passes judgement on them according to his *aesthetics*.[98]

Hossain submits that Western literature and art function as nothing less than ideological alibis for capitalism and, flipping the usual connotations, condemns Western art for promoting conformism. In contrast, "reflecting social relationships, which are primarily production relationships" is the remit of a presumably socialist realist Third World literature.[99] And if the role of literature and art in the developing world is qualitatively different, this is because it is where "chaos reigns, tyranny rules and agents of imperialists sow havoc."[100] Domingo Castro de Guzman's piece "Notes on Art, Freedom and Society" concurs by proclaiming that "it is impossible to be a true or great artist in the present anywhere in the world without being anti-capitalist."[101] Radically departing from both anti-communist fears and concerns over rapid modern-ization, such a conception of tyranny is predicated on the explicit awareness of the profound *difficulty* in transforming the material relationships of the former colony in relation to both new and old imperial powers (noting, of course, the unique position of the Philippines in having the same colonial ruler as new Cold War hegemon). Literary prescriptions that cordon off art from social struggle therefore have no place in the Third World. Conse-quently, unfreedom refers not to the menace of Soviets or Maoists as at earlier PEN meetings, but emerges as a corollary of the *effort* to contain the commu-nist challenge through expanded capitalist production. Thus, in something of an echo of Fanon's famous description of the colonized word, the Third World as a whole "is a tragic land, tyrannized in the name of democracy, religion and civilization."[102]

Alongside the Marxist critiques, a related strand of analysis emerges that we might label cultural nationalist. Replacing those discussions from the 1964 Bangkok Conference—that seem naive just a decade and a half later—on the way Asian "contributions" to world literature will revive the conti-nent's proud cultural heritage in a post-imperial world, speakers now describe embattled cultures struggling to contend with the continued cultural impe-rialism of the West. Four different papers use the analogy of "excess foreign consumption" to diagnose the problem of subordinated national cultures. Michio Ochi, in a brief overview of modern Japanese literature, claims the "imported modernization" of Western literary genres "caused a peculiar dis-tortion in Japanese literature,"[103] a problem that writers are still struggling to overcome. In a paper on the state of publishing in the Philippines, the direc-tor of New Day Publishers in Quezon City, Gloria F. Rodriguez, decries the literal problem of import/export imbalance: "Take a typical National or Ale-mar Bookstore, the two largest multi-branch bookstores in the country; a comparative study of the non-textbook titles carried would, I am sure, show that at least 85% of them are from abroad."[104] Rodriguez laments that "the Filipino people are mainly English-speaking and reading" and compares the situation with more fortunate Indonesia, where "publishers don't have as much competition from abroad since the majority of their readers are literate only in Bahasa Indonesia."[105] But it is poet and critic Virgilio S. Almario who makes the analogy between economic trade balances and literature most explicit.[106] He blames Filipino writers' "consumerism" of Western modernist literature as what diverted their attention away from social issues and "towards intensely subjective and personal experimentation."[107] In terms of a solution, he offers the following:

Experiences of developing countries in the economic and political
fields can be a guide in the formulation of a sounder educational and
cultural policy. Selective and conditional importations with more and
more incentives for local industries characterize the developing countries' program for economic self-sufficiency. An analogous procedure is
undergone to attain political independence. Without totally ignoring
the value of cultural interdependence, similar restrictions on the
importation of ideas must be imposed in literature and culture.[108]

In short, Almario proposes an import-substitution model for nurturing
national cultural production in the Third World. His thoughts productively
anticipate those of Marxist literary critic Fredric Jameson, whose 1992–93 article, "On Literary and Cultural Import-Substitution in the Third World," takes
seriously the notion of import-substitution as a way to theorize literary and
cultural influence beyond simple cultural imperialism.[109] Jameson explains its
appeal: If consuming American cars or films may be "politically disgraceful
for a Third World nation . . . to set up your own automobile factory or your
own film studio is surely not."[110] Jameson's larger point is to show how "cultural
import-substitution" produces innovative forms and genres that are not merely
derivative of the Western original. In a provocative analysis of the Latin American *testimonio* narrative form, he traces a shift from the centered, bourgeois
subject of Western autobiographical narrative to "a new conception of collec-
tivity and collective life . . . specific to the culture and experience of the Third
World itself."[111] Similarly, for Almario, it is the specificity of the social and the
collective that is lacking in Filipino literature too imitative of the "intensely
subjective and personal" style of Western modernist literature.

Striking here is the departure from cosmopolitan writerly exchange and
freedom of expression as the master cultural values appropriate for a world of
formally equal, independent nation-states. In formulations like Almario's, it is
the *unevenness* of Third World economic and cultural development that
demands a new theorization of literature's relation to freedom. Replacing the
self-evident value of "free words" and their power to break down barriers, a
deliberate "restriction" on foreign cultural consumption may be required in
order to nurture the development of an aesthetic form adequate to local conditions. We can place this discussion in the larger global context of uneven
media and publishing power, a topic brought to light by Sarah Brouillette's
study of UNESCO and the developing world. In reconstructing this little-
known history, Brouillette describes the struggles that took place under the
banner of UNESCO during the 1960s and '70s to correct the dominance of
Western media and publishing power in the Third World. Tallying with

perspectives at the 1981 Manila Conference, Brouillette describes UNESCO's
(ultimately stymied) efforts to even the playing field as

> sometimes about unearthing the total interdependence of economic
> and intellectual systems and recognizing that the book had become
> a specific kind of tool: a tool controlled by a small part of the world's
> population, but needed for participation in a global conversation
> about what kind of global order would unfold in the wake of
> colonialism.[112]

We can think of the Asian Writers' Conferences as a forum in which the supposedly universal, liberal defense of cultural exchange is challenged in the
face of a growing awareness of the "interdependence of economic and intellectual systems" and the betrayal by neocolonial, authoritarian regimes. We
can therefore chart a certain shift in the tenor of debates, from individual
freedom as the basic (anti-communist) condition for writing liberty, to concerns with the material and intellectual authorities left in place by colonialism
and reactivated by the "free world's" capitalist integration. In the final section
of this chapter, I briefly take up two final features of these meetings as a lens
through which to access this complex landscape: the conference resolution
and translation projects.

Resolutions and Translations

The conference resolution is a distinct subgenre that carries within it many of
the contradictions of the period's debates that we have already discussed. The
resolution itself, after all, is a curious formal addendum to the conference
genre. Usually placed at the end of the proceedings, it appears as a de facto
conclusion to all that has preceded it, as if the many papers and discussions
were all just preamble to its declarations. Unlike the individual papers, which
may well contest and contradict each other, the resolution indicates a collective will and implies that a democratic process has already occurred in its
production. Like the form of the "communiqué" (the "final communiqué" of
Bandung being one well-known example), it is consensual, democratic, and
outward facing, while its performativity also makes it a relative of the genre of
the manifesto. For these reasons, I suggest that the conference resolution
functions as a peculiarly concentrated literary-political genre that invokes sovereignty, agency, and international solidarity even as it subscribes to a fundamentally liberal form of protest.[113] In their own way, the resolutions from 1962
to 1981—ranging from modest translation projects to calls for the release of
detained writers—make visible the larger regional complexities that ultimately

frustrate both ideals of liberal postcolonial cultural dialogue and attempts to recognize larger, structural problems of decolonization.

At the Bangkok PEN Writers' Conference of 1964, only two resolutions—or "recommendations" as they are called there—were passed: one dedicated to founding an ongoing translation project for inter-Asian publications and one for the compiling of an Asian Writers' Bibliography. As I have suggested above, the concerns of PEN Asian Writers around the nature and conditions of post-colonial freedom were not wholly unrelated to those of avowedly anti-imperialist writers in the Afro-Asian Writers' Bureau. As with the latter, PEN translation projects emerged out of the conviction that the boundaries of the colonial world had artificially kept Asians ignorant about each other's societies and histories, and that no sense of solidarity could proceed without familiarity with each other's cultures. Norman Cousins, the liberal American journalist and longtime editor of the *Saturday Review*, wrote the introduction to the 1968 *Asian PEN Anthology* (edited by F. Sionil José), in which he announced that "the primary purpose of this volume . . . was to introduce Asian writers to Asians" (xv).[114] We must note the heavy irony, of course, that it required an American writing in English to make this pronouncement. By the same token, there seems to have been little discussion over non-European languages as the target language for the translations, at least in its initial stage. The Bangkok proceedings allude to three different motions which would translate works into (1) English, (2) English and/or French, and (3) English or French or any other major language,[115] with the last motion declared passed with only the Philippine delegate dissenting; they had voted for the second option. There is no recorded discussion about what "any other major language" would include. A proposed second stage would use English as "the common language from which further translations to other Asian languages could proceed."[116]

PEN's language politics can be here contrasted with those of the Afro-Asian Writers' Bureau. Hala Halim's work underscores the importance of Arabic for the association's publication *Lotus*, which was published trilingually along with French and English from the late 1960s to the early 1990s. Arabic, Halim argues, "contests the hegemony of imperialism's linguistic legacy,"[117] and advances the "impetus to reorient intercultural dialogue, as no longer primarily between metropole and colony but between former colonies" along a "south-south" axis.[118] One challenge for PEN writers is that no obvious equivalent to Arabic exists in Asia. Of two possible contenders for a regional East Asian language, Chinese and Japanese, the latter was tainted by being the language of the enthusiastically "pan-Asianist" Japanese empire, and, although widely spoken in Korea, Taiwan, and beyond at mid-century, it was not even raised in the proceedings. Chinese, we can surmise, was difficult both because of its association with communism (we can think of a non-communist postcolony like Singapore and its vexed relationship to Chinese language education) as well as its own complex imperial history in Asia. Either Malay or Indonesian might have been a possibility for Southeast Asia, but again are not mentioned. Revealingly, the Japanese PEN Center was tasked with the Asian Writers' Bibliography project precisely because of a shortage of *English* language skills in the Thai PEN Center. At the 1976 Taipei conference, mention is again made of a possible translation center to be established so "that all the countries in Asia could participate,"[119] a somewhat ambitious goal given the limited attendance at this conference. It is then lamented that "even among the nations of Asia we do not have a common language that we can understand each other. We still have to resort to English. It's a great pity but it's a fact."[120]

Japan's curious status in the translation debate discloses larger paradoxes concerning that former imperial power, whose delegates were present at all PEN conferences discussed in this chapter, as well as at Bandung (think, for example, of the outrage if the French or British had appeared at the latter). The country's odd positioning can be best analyzed through the vector of decolonization's intersection with the Cold War, noting that the massive swath of the Pacific under Japanese control by 1945 (including its longtime colonies in Korea, Taiwan, and Manchuria) scrambles the binary of transcending Western colonial rule in order to enter independent sovereignty. While the leaders of communist China, North Korea, and North Vietnam could make great political use of their anti-Japanese credentials, this was more difficult in "free Asia." Leo Ching, following Yoshimi Shun-ya, describes how "the United States has replaced, displaced, and subsumed the Japanese empire in the region." In its decision to promptly occupy, demilitarize and repurpose Japan as the region's capitalist motor, the U.S.'s anti-communist bloc "created a division of labor among the Asian nations" with other countries serving as American military installations.[121] As a result, Japan's strategic and economic roles effectively blocked attempts to reckon with its past status as colonial aggressor.[122] Kuan-Hsing Chen elaborates:

> Historical issues of Japanese colonialism in Taiwan and Korea could not be tackled because the Japanese, South Korean, and Taiwanese states were locked into the pro-American side; to address such historical issues would have entailed confronting internal contradictions within the capitalist bloc.[123]

Partly as a result of these "internal contradictions" that could not be addressed—especially clear regarding the role of Japan—the Writers'

Conferences had difficulty affirming a horizontal, "south-south" language politics. Moreover, that Japan becomes the site of English translation resources triangulates and obscures the actual regional hegemon, the United States.[124] The translation resolutions, therefore, speak both to the desires for a post-imperial cultural sphere, and the limits to its possible realization.

If, at the earlier conferences, the resolutions are limited to inter-Asian translations and the bibliography, by the 1981 Manila conference, three of six resolutions aim squarely at the plight of writers detained by repressive governments.[125] These are Poland (Resolution 1), the Philippines (Resolution 2), and South Africa (Resolution 3). Extracts from each are as follows:

[Resolution 1] The Asian Writers Conference meeting in Manila, hosted by the Philippine Center of International P.E.N., expresses deep concern over the situation of P.E.N. members and writers in Poland. We ask you urgently to inform us about your present condition. We extend to you our fraternal greetings.[126]

[Resolution 2] The Conference expresses concern over the continued detention, including solitary confinement, of some writers in prison; the continuing threat to rearrest writers who have been provisionally released; and the reports that at least one poet-journalist has disappeared under mysterious circumstances.

The Asian Writers Conference therefore appeals to his Excellency the President of the Philippines, to release writers in prison against whom no charges have been filed . . . .[127]

[Resolution 3] The Asian Writers Conference . . . notes with great concern the continuing flagrant repression of the basic human rights of the black African people in South Africa, and the freedom of black African writers, artists and intellectuals.

The Conference expresses its strong sense of solidarity with the black African people . . . and appeals to all writers, artists and intellectuals in the world to help and support their struggle in South Africa.[128]

Note that in terms of speech acts, each resolution has a slightly different structure, addressee, and appeal. Resolution 1 is the most intimately worded. It "expresses concern" for Polish writers and "ask[s] you urgently to inform us about your present condition." Contrast this with Resolution 2's expression of similar concern followed by direct personal appeal to Marcos, "his Excellency the President of the Philippines," to release writers in prison. Finally, Resolution 3 moves beyond the concern for specific writers. It invokes the larger political situation of the "flagrant repression of the basic human rights of the

black African people in South Africa" before expressing the conference's solidarity with them. These resolutions are bold articulations of solidarity, especially the Philippines one, given the many local writers implicated in the
direct appeal to President Marcos. They exemplify PEN's founding principles
of "humanitarian ideas of speech beyond national boundaries" and international cooperation,[129] returning us to the liberal notion of literary texts primarily as *objects* whose aesthetic autonomy is to be protected from the overreach
of authoritarian states. When read more closely, however, we see that the resolutions again index a number of "internal contradictions" (Chen) that the
Cold War's intersection with decolonization has produced, even if the resolutions cannot name them per se. In a sense, what draws the Third World—and
some countries of the Second World—together now is less the optimism of a
new era of post-imperial cultural exchange, but a shared experience of
repressive governments. In fact, we can read the three appeals as corresponding to three possible authoritarian permutations of the global Cold
War: the Soviet repression of intellectuals and writers on the Eastern European front of the Cold War; the U.S.-support of an anti-communist dictator in
the Third World; and the South African apartheid state, where an anti-
colonial liberation struggle was prolonged and intensified by the support of
NATO countries for the white-minority government and Soviet backing for
the ANC's armed wing, Umkhonto we Sizwe.

The genre of the conference resolution, nevertheless, hews to a postwar
vision of a world composed of formally equal and sovereign nation-states.
McDonald has noted the way the original PEN charter "echoed the ideals of
the League of Nations,"[130] and as we have seen, each of the conferences identifies individual "delegates" by his or her nationality, with the conference
room setups themselves sometimes bearing not a little similarity to the UN
General Assembly meetings. In such a bureaucratic arrangement of formal
national equality, it is difficult to imagine other kinds of indictment being
expressed, for example, against the U.S.'s backing of Marcos (or Park Chung
Hee or, more quietly, of Suharto). Tightly codified by PEN's liberal-
bureaucratic principles, the very form of the conference resolution itself deter-
mines what kind of statements can and cannot be made. While individual
national governments may be named accurately enough as repressive regimes
and dissident writers as their antagonists, the genre has difficulty addressing
larger economic or structural problems of decolonization. Perhaps more prob-
lematically, literature as a possible mode of *theorizing* freedom, solidarity, or
oppression is displaced, as are the "interdependenc[ies] of economic and intellectual systems" (Brouillette) discussed earlier. The effect, though unin-
tended, is the casting of an equivalency across the three different national

situations of unfreedom. The resolutions thus reinscribe and naturalize a notion of discrete state power as what violates the rights of individual writers. Elided is the complex and uneven role of blocs, alignments, and reconstituted imperial hegemonies, as well as the military and strategic aid and loans that drove the frantic "bipolar pursuit of modernization"[131] typical of many authoritarian regimes. The naming of repressive regimes by the resolutions—as performatively significant as it is—can only go so far in diagnosing those Third World disappointments emerging by the 1970s.

To conclude, let me return to David Scott's rich thinking on the temporalities and predicaments of postcoloniality that I raised in the Introduction. In discussing the once viable "Bandung Project" of non-aligned, cooperative Third World self-determination, Scott describes how that project's guidebook and manifesto, Frantz Fanon's 1961 *The Wretched of the Earth*, provided the clearest "narrative of liberation." The latter offered "a structured story that progressively links . . . a past and a present of Domination to an anticipated future of Freedom," in part by "constructing a subject who moves from alienated dehumanization to self-realization."[132] It is difficult, Scott admits, not to remain seduced by Fanon's lucid moral-political account of decolonization. Yet in a post-bipolar, and post-Bandung world, he suggests that such nostalgia is misplaced: The political present calls forth a new "problem space" for postcolonial politics to be worked in and through.

I am entirely sympathetic with Scott's analysis, which remains relevant some twenty years after its publication. My point in this chapter has obviously not been to use a Fanonian model of liberation to assess the PEN Asian Writers' Conferences. What I've sketched out is not a recuperative account of a literary internationalism and its resistance aesthetics, and we will only be disappointed if we approach the meetings with this goal. Rather, my brief account intends to bring further complexity to those narratives of decolonization's vicissitudes already produced by Scott, Vijay Prashad, and others.[133] The latter have usefully mapped out the "exhaustion" of non-aligned and Bandung projects whose death knells sounded in the 1980s and burials could be confirmed by the 1990s. Yet in the experiences of certain non-communist Asian postcolonies—those predominantly represented at the PEN conferences—we see another "problem space" and experience of decolonization being worked through. The PEN conferences tell a different story of the career of the "national-modern" (Scott) project inaugurated by Bandung, one in which Cold War conflicts and pressures contaminate and co-produce notions of freedom, autonomy, authority, and futurity. In particular, we see how the core liberal principle of "freedom of expression" becomes recoded, challenged,

and retheorized within the changing landscapes wrought by the Cold War–
decolonizing conjuncture. Investigating the specific figure of the dissident
writer is the task of the next chapter. In turn, later chapters demonstrate how
narratives of radical nationalists, leftists, and communists who attempted to
redefine freedom at this conjuncture are all the more relevant to the struggles
of our neoliberal moment.

In sum, the PEN Asian Writers' Conferences, their form, debates, and resolutions can be viewed simultaneously as conflicted artifacts of a newly independent Asia forged against its former colonial identities, and of a region
grappling with the new political-economic restructuring of Cold War world-
making. They index the often-compromised politics of literary friendships and
alignment; the blurring of hospitality and propaganda; the paradoxes of staging "free" intellectual interchange while excluding one half of Asia; and the
fraught attempts to parse economic, political, and cultural "freedoms." It is for
these reasons that I read them as a distinctly Cold War–postcolonial genre that
attends to both power formations. And perhaps it is by the very failures of this
Third World without third*ness*—the failure to distinguish "free words" from
the "free world"; to articulate a postcolonial revolution beyond development;
to find an inter-Asian language—that we appreciate the contestations over
such world-making.

2

In the Shadow of Solzhenitsyn

*Pramoedya Ananta Toer, Kim Chi-ha, Ninotchka Rosca,
and Cold War Critique*

On the 15th August 1945, and then on the 17th August 1945, first
Vietnam, then Indonesia declared independence. . . . These two
countries began a struggle for freedom which spread through Asia and
Africa. After this, in reaction against these anticolonial independence
movements, the Northern countries began the Cold War.
                                   —PRAMOEDYA ANANTA TOER, 1995

By all accounts, the 1960s and 1970s saw an efflorescence of Third World
and socialist authoritarianism. Russian writer Aleksandr Solzhenitsyn published his best-known work, *One Day in the Life of Ivan Denisovich*, in 1962,
a novel composed while he was imprisoned in Stalin's labor camp system and
which quickly became a touchstone of Cold War dissident writing.[1] Founded
in 1961, Amnesty International would become crucial to publicizing such dissident work and, by the late 1960s, began naming a number of political prisoners for its annual "Prisoner of Conscience Week."[2] In 1972 these included
Indonesia's best-known writer, Pramoedya Ananta Toer, alongside "an anti-
Castro doctor in Cuba, a Taiwanese satirist and two Roman Catholic priests,
one in South Africa and the other in Hungary."[3] In a *New York Times* article
of November 1972, Ivan Morris, professor of Japanese at Columbia University
and spokesperson for Amnesty International USA, spoke of the organization's
appeal to UN Secretary-General Kurt Waldheim to assist in freeing the twelve.
"More and more countries are turning to police methods," Morris notes, "sus-
pending human rights, making arrests without charges and torturing prisoners."[4] Reported in similar articles across major Western newspapers, the plight
of each of the twelve prisoners was briefly noted, constituting a snapshot of the

unfreedoms raging in the non-West. Pramoedya, who was imprisoned for fourteen years from 1965 until 1979 by the Suharto government, is referred to in a number of articles as the "Indonesian Solzhenitsyn."

Other international campaigns included "The Committee to save Kim Chi-ha," a group formed by Japanese academic Tsurumi Shunsuke. The committee sought international publicity for Kim, the South Korean poet who was jailed—and later sentenced to death—after publishing his withering satire of the Park Chung Hee regime, "Five Bandits," in 1970. In 1973 Tsurumi traveled to Seoul with a petition signed by notable figures including Jean-Paul Sartre, Simon de Beauvoir, Alex La Guma, Oe Kenzaburo, and Herbert Marcuse.[5] In the international press Kim is referred to as the "Korean Solzhenitsyn."[6] Finally, although lesser known than the other two writers, Filipina journalist and writer Ninotchka Rosca was detained, along with hundreds of others, by the Marcos government during its sweeping 1972 crackdown on journalists and writers. Since her release, she has lived in exile in the United States; she published her novel on the Marcos regime, State of War, in 1988. A number of its plots and character sketches, however, appeared in her 1983 short story collection, The Monsoon Collection, which was conceived during her imprisonment in the notorious Camp Crame. In a 2012 magazine article, Lourdes Gordolan interviews a number of writers who had been detained by the regime, and wonders about the paucity of Philippine literature documenting this period: "Why is there no One Day in the Life of Ivan Denisovich for the Philippine experience?"[7]

All three cases help confirm that the figure of the imprisoned dissident writer, epitomized by Solzhenitsyn, is one of the most recognizable tropes of Cold War authoritarianism.[8] But why exactly does the fate of "prisoners of conscience"—and the genre of dissident literature in general—become such a flash point for diagnosing unfreedom during the Cold War? Given the appellations of "Indonesian" or "Korean Solzhenitsyn," what is occluded when the Second and Third Worlds are collapsed in an assumed shared condition of tyranny, despite obvious variations in the political orientations of those regimes (communist, socialist, capitalist, pro-West, non-aligned, and so on)? Put otherwise, how has a Cold War lens shaped the way we view typical genres of dissident literature, such as historical allegory, political satire, and the novel of resistance? Conversely, as I discussed in the Introduction, in the field of postcolonial studies, the privileging of colonial power forms and epistemologies has tended to occlude the way global bipolar restructurings shaped new states. Despite the plethora of literary texts concerned with the unfreedoms of the postcolonial state, Neil Lazarus observes that "scholars in the field have evidently not known how—other than through [a] wholesale repudiation—to

account for the setbacks and defeats of the post-independence years."[9] Moreover, while "nearly all of the discussion has centred on the 'Janus face' of
nationalism in general . . . very little of it has addressed the *specific agency of
the postcolonial state*, captured by the political class at independence, and
actively deployed by it—for better and, mostly, worse—thereafter."[10] Pramoedya
Ananta Toer, Kim Chi-ha, and Ninotchka Rosca are writers whose works force
us to grapple with an interpretative quandary: No longer part of the exemplary
anti-colonial struggles "that emerged significantly as part of the organized
national liberation struggles and resistance moments,"[11] neither do they fit the
model of anti-Stalinist dissident literature. My goal is, again, to trace the
uneven fault lines between the decolonizing world, the "free world," and the
"unfree" Soviet bloc by asking how the shorthand liberal notion of "dissident
writer" has continued to shape our conceptions of twentieth-century dictatorships and authoritarianism. In the preceding chapter we saw how PEN Asian
Writers debated the values of literary freedom in an era defined simultaneously by new regional writerly networks and the hardening of Cold War
boundaries and nationalist projects. Here, I consider three specific instances
of clashes between writers and governments for what they reveal about the
subject of postcolonial freedom at this particular conjuncture.

In three sections, this chapter works through Pramoedya's final novel in his
Buru tetralogy, *House of Glass* (*Rumah Kaca*, published 1988, read in transla-
tion); Kim's poetry of the early 1970s, especially his "talk poems," "Five
Bandits" and "Groundless Rumors" ("Ojŏk" and "Pi'ŏ," 1970 and 1972); and
Rosca's novel of resistance, *State of War* (1988). While these writers exemplify
the figure of the dissident writer as defined by organizations such as PEN and
Amnesty International (Pramoedya would win PEN's Freedom to Write
Award in 1988), my goal is to investigate the dissident *theorizations* of postcolonial freedom and autocracy that we find in their works, which have often
been overlooked in the emphasis on their arrests and trials. Despite differences in literary form, languages, and national contexts, I suggest that these
figures both challenge assumptions of an indistinguishable Third World/Sec-
ond World tyranny and nuance colonial legacies by accounting for the specific violence of Cold War capitalist modernization. While I appreciate the
profound, often life-saving work of human rights campaigns such as Amnesty's, I mean to think through the tensions inherent in the categories "freedom
of speech," "dissident writer," and "prisoner of conscience" as they operate
within the matrix of Cold War decolonization in the Asia-Pacific.

Before moving on to the texts, I want to briefly dwell on the construction of
the dissident writer in international human rights discourse. Joseph Slaughter
has discussed the original *Amnesty Campaign* of 1961, led by Peter Benenson

and other lawyers, in which "prisoner of conscience" is defined as "Any person who is physically restrained (by imprisonment or otherwise) from expressing (in any form of words or symbols) any opinion which he honestly holds and which does not advocate or condone personal violence."[12] The definition itself draws from the 1948 Universal Declaration of Human Rights, especially articles 18 and 19, which recognize freedom of thought, conscience, religion, and opinion,[13] and from a longer tradition of the committed writer in whom "artistic autonomy is opposed to institutionalized politics."[14] These ideas, however, took on newly charged significance in the Cold War discourse on totalitarianism, in which individual autonomy was thought to be the very target of state power. Extreme ideology combined with police terror would enable "the will of the political state to dominate the very process of thought and subjectivity."[15] What was novel about the Amnesty campaign was its strategy of "publicising the personal stories of a number of prisoners" over "publicising [their] political views."[16] Prisoners of conscience were thus valued less for the content of their political critiques, and more for the degree to which their personal stories dramatized the ruthless domination of the state's ideology over individual will. Moreover, Amnesty's letter-writing campaign and publicity strategies stressed the "centrality of literary expression" to its efforts[17] because the literary capacity—corresponding to the realm of internal, private thoughts and beliefs—was precisely what totalitarianism most threatened. As a result, "the modern Amnesty campaign emerged, at least in part, as a defence of literature, or literary values, forms, and figures of free expression."[18] Such a defense is advanced in a *Guardian* article on the 1972 "Prisoner of Conscience Week," which describes the collective plight of the twelve as stemming from their *"refusal to adapt* their writings, teaching, religious or political beliefs to political requirements."[19] Similar notions motivate the journal *Index on Censorship*, founded by Czech exile George Theiner in 1972, which specifically sought to defend dissident writers "who'd challenged the might of an authoritarian state."[20] A 1988 *LA Times* article on the death of Theiner names the "great figures of persecuted literature" who appeared in the *Index*: "Solzhenitsyn, Miloran Djilas, Vaclav Havel, Ngũgĩ wa Thiong'o, Wole Soyinka and Ariel Dorfman," while mentioning Pramoedya and Kim Chi-ha as two other prominent figures. In this formulation, the genre of dissident literature expresses the unyielding of an individual's artistic expression to Third World or Soviet state pressure. Literature itself becomes "persecuted."[21]

As we saw in the preceding chapter's history of PEN International, such a clear-cut conceptional opposition—artistic will versus the state machine of terror—has the effect of endowing literature with its special status as artifact of liberty to be protected. An article on the "Korean Solzhenitsyn" summarizes this terror in decidedly Cold War imagery, where the all-powerful dictator is "sustained by an army. . . , a ubiquitous secret police, and unknown number of informers and wire-tappers, and the terror of life where no one dare trust his neighbour."[22] Such stark renderings of power tend to present censorship and repression, as Peter McDonald puts it in his study of Apartheid South Africa, as "an abstract drama played out between 'literature' and the 'modern state,'"[23] and risk flattening out and de-historicizing contestations over the *meanings* of freedom or oppression, that is, the very contestations that the "persecuted" texts themselves might articulate. By contrast, I argue that the writings by Pramoedya, Kim, and Rosca disclose a form of authoritarianism conceived less as the violation of an individual's expression or subjectivity by the state, and more as the historical complication of national sovereignty in the entry to transpacific capitalism. If Amnesty-type campaigns sought "to introduce a third character (world opinion) into the two-person drama of political imprisonment, to interpose public opinion between the state and the individual,"[24] the three writers I focus on recast this drama entirely. They arrogate literature to the more ambitious, and perhaps riskier, role of theorizing the complex historical and material entanglements of the colonial, neocolonial, and bipolar.

I explore these claims by comparatively attending to two facets that the very different texts of Pramoedya, Kim, and Rosca evidence: first is their interest in documenting the recursiveness of colonial authoritarianism. Their works necessarily go beyond the positivist tropes of Cold War arbitrary violence and secret police in their effort to depict the nonlinear, or sedimented nature, of postcolonial historical time. At first glance, all three authors employ genres that are traditionally well associated with the critique of state power: allegory, satire, and the resistance novel. Yet all three perform distinct genre-mixing to capture the ongoing pastness in the present, whether it be via historical fiction that dwells on newness (Pramoedya); a ribald poetic reinscription of folk opera (Kim); or a novel of resistance-turned-family saga that foregrounds resistance *and* reproduction (Rosca). In depicting the unfinished business of decolonization[25] through formal attempts to link and question temporalities of past and present, each writer challenges the historical marker of "independence" as the dividing line between eras. Second, I explore how each writer forwards critiques of developmentalist authoritarianism that emphatically challenge the liberal notion of individual freedom *from* politics. In particular, we will see how each text—via very different literary strategies—figures postcolonial liberation as the ability to imagine political alternatives to the capitalist logic of promotion within the "free world" system, short-circuiting the will to colonial reproduction. In other words, the problem of authoritarianism and the

writer is not to be found in the neat, ahistorical "two-person drama" of a ter-
rorizing police state encroaching on individual creative expression. It is rather
to be grasped through layered and meandering stories of historical returns,
entangled sovereignties, and (non)capitalist futures.

Looking Back toward the New: Pramoedya's *House of Glass*

From Pramoedya's large oeuvre, I choose to focus on the fourth and final
novel of his acclaimed "Buru Quartet," a tetralogy so named because it was
famously composed while he was incarcerated on remote Buru Island during
the 1970s.[26] The first three novels in the tetralogy are *This Earth of Mankind*
(*Bumi Manusia*, 1980), *Child of All Nations* (*Anak Semua Bangsa*, 1981), and
Footsteps (*Jejak Langkah*, 1985), all of which were suppressed by the Indonesian government for their supposed promotion of Marxist-Leninist ideologies.
House of Glass (*Rumah Kaca*), like the others in the series, was promptly
banned by the Suharto government after its publication in 1988.[27] The biography of Javanese-born Pramoedya (1925–2006) reflects his country's troubled
passage from Dutch colonial territory to independent nation. During the Japanese occupation he worked for the Japanese newspaper *Domei*; after independence he taught and attempted to run his own literary agency, at a loss.[28]
He has had the dubious distinction of being incarcerated by not one, but three
regimes: by the returning Dutch colonists; by the Sukarno state (for one
month) for his "overzealous support of the Chinese in Indonesia"; and, finally,
by Suharto's long-lived New Order regime.[29]

   The literary milieu in Indonesia preceding the 1965–66 anti-communist
massacres and Suharto's rise to power is worth briefly recalling.[30] Following
the conclusion of the four-year revolutionary struggle (1945–49) against the
Dutch,[31] a number of national literary debates emerged that echoed those
discussed in the preceding chapter. Non- and anti-communist cultural critics
such as S. Takdir Alisjahbana (present at the first Manila PEN Asia conference
and quoted in Chapter 1) advocated a universalist, non-ideological conception
of literature. He and his allies argued that Indonesia "should embrace Western
culture and continue to seek access to it by cementing close, postcolonial cultural relations with the Netherlands."[32] This approach assumed that free cultural exchange—including that with the former Dutch colonizers—was an
unmitigated good. In contrast, Ki Hadjar Dewantara, Indonesia's minister for
education, and others looked to recently decolonized neighbors such as India
for cultural inspiration. In his exhaustive study, Keith Foulcher relates: "In
their search for a modern culture," Hadjar and his allies worried that the
"Roundtable Conference [on Indonesia sovereignty], the Marshall Plan and

the United Nations [were] all driving Indonesia towards capitalism and American influence."[33] It is in this context that in 1954 the Lembaga Kerbudayaan Rakyat, or Institute of People's Culture, LEKRA, was founded, an organization that was closely linked to the Partai Komunis Indonesia (PKI).[34] Pramoedya would work closely with LEKRA until his arrest in 1965.

As early as 1955, LEKRA had established "twenty-one branches throughout the archipelago" along with "media channels in Jakarta, Surabaya and Medan" while supporting cultural works and activism in literature, visual arts, music, drama, film, philosophy, and sports.[35] Two aspects of LEKRA are especially salient here. First is that its overall goal was to promote culture that should be "both nationalist and anti-imperialist"; culture was explicitly conceived as actively helping shape an authentic, modern Indonesian nation through the selective adoption of Third World and socialist influences to counter an encroaching Western neo-imperialism.[36] National culture was thus conceived as part of a revolutionary new international culture. Not surprisingly, LEKRA emphasized Afro-Asian links, and Pramoedya himself attended the 1958 Afro-Asian Conference in Tashkent and visited China in 1956.[37] As Foulcher summarizes:

> It is through [Chinese and Soviet] sources such as these that LEKRA theorists obtained their sense of internationalism, seeing the ideals of the Indonesian revolution and indigenous-oriented cultural national-ism as belonging to a world-wide movement towards the progressive development of the cultural potential of humanity.[38]

Pramoedya himself was profoundly influenced by a wide array of Western, socialist, and Chinese works, and he published translations of Steinbeck, Tolstoy, and Gorky.[39] The second aspect to note—and in explicit contrast to the PEN and Amnesty-endorsed literary value of "freedom of expression" pit-ted against an overreaching state—LEKRA conceived of art as deeply embed-ded in nationalist development under the Sukarno government. Indonesian artists, it followed, should be supported by the government for their important role in building the nation. Foulcher gives the example of a PKI electoral slogan in 1955: "For artists, voting PKI means freedom to create and an improvement in working conditions."[40] Like the argument about cultural import substitution in the preceding chapter, this position was logically con-sistent with the rejection and even censorship of imperialist (American) cul-tural products, such that LEKRA would lead boycott campaigns of certain Hollywood films.[41]

The cultural vibrancy—with all its contradictions—of LEKRA came to a resounding halt in the 1965–66 bloody purges of the PKI and its supporters as

General Suharto came into power and deposed the PKI's close ally Sukarno.[42] Pramoedya, as we know, was arrested along with an estimated 500,000–750,000 others and classified as a "B-class" prisoner, which "consists of persons suspected of having played roles similar to the ones of those in Category A [those clearly and directly involved in the 1965 attempted coup] but for whose suspected guilt there is insufficient evidence."[43] The leftist-oriented concept of socially engaged literature, and its *kerakyatan* or popular aesthetics, was all but buried in official Indonesian literary circles as part of the "anti-communist norms of post-1965 cultural hegemony in Indonesia."[44] Even after the global publicity around the banning of *This Earth of Mankind* and *Child of All Nations*—which precipitated two national seminars on literature and society in 1982—the mainstream orthodoxy that understood socialist art "as a challenge to 'free' art" remained largely unchallenged in Indonesia for years to come.[45] It is in this context that we can place Pramoedya's tetralogy, noting the historical irony that it is the very liberal conception of "persecuted literature" that catapults Pramoedya to worldwide recognition.[46]

Set in the early twentieth century, the historical realist novels of the tetralogy center on the character of Minke, a young aristocratic Native who attains a European education, comes gradually to reject the superiority of European civilization, and is instrumental in the awakening of the Dutch East Indies toward a nationalist consciousness. The character of Minke is closely based on the journalist Tirto Adi Suryo (1880–1918), evidence of Pramoedya's efforts to "restore to historical memory" this pioneering nationalist.[47] Through Minke, Pramoedya's detailed descriptions of the new journals, newspapers, trains, and common language (the use of the lingua franca Malay, today's Bahasa Indonesia) bring together the hitherto fragmented spaces of the Indonesian archipelago into a profoundly new sense of world-historical modernity.[48] By *House of Glass*, however, the first-person narrative of Minke, our exemplary witness to history, gives way to that of Jacques Pangemanann. Pangemanann—"with two n's," as he repeatedly reminds the reader—is a Native police commissioner who rises to become a valued "expert" on Native affairs employed at the Dutch Algemeene Secretariat (General Secretariat). Minke, meanwhile, is exiled to Ambon early in the novel and effectively remains off-stage for the five-year duration of the novel.[49] Like Minke, the historical Tirto was exiled to Ambon in the remote Moluccas (Maluku islands), not far from Buru. With Minke removed from the narrative, we instead follow our antihero, Pangemanann, and his rise (and fall) as he is tasked with monitoring and suppressing the emerging local organizations, especially the Sareket Islam (the Islamic Association or Union) founded by Minke.

For a series of novels that was composed while Pramoedya was imprisoned by the Suharto regime, the choice to conclude with what is effectively the state's narration rather than Minke's has been puzzling to critics. Peter Hitchcock describes *House of Glass* as "the most difficult of the *Buru Quartet* for it challenges the inevitabilities of national awakening."[50] Indeed, the troubling allegorical dimensions of the novel are hard to ignore: The repressive Dutch state that exiles and censors Minke's work obviously evokes the New Order regime's arrest of Pramoedya (and hundreds of thousands of others) in the name of anti-communist "national security." Hitchcock rightly identifies "a double time"[51] of the novel which layers the 1910s with the 1960s–80s. Where the previous novels seemed to chart the inexorable rise of anti-colonialist, nationalist consciousness, the final novel constitutes a decisive rolling back of such a movement toward liberation. As such, *House of Glass* seems to confirm the very "two-person" drama of repressive state and dissenting individual discussed above. Benedict Anderson, commenting on the novel's unusual narrator, describes Pangemannan as "the file-keeper and file-contaminator of *The Glass House* who is also the ultimate narrator . . . [and] a dystopic prolepsis,"[52] foreshadowing the unfreedoms to come under the Suharto regime. Read as an allegory for the later regime, the novel pointedly asks its readers, "Who are the new tyrants?"[53]

Yet Pramoedya's final novel is much more than a proleptic augur of the New Order's unfreedoms. If, as Chris GoGwilt suggests, the tetralogy is a complex reconsideration of "the significance of a nationalist historiography in light of the events of 1965,"[54] *House of Glass* explicitly asks the question of political and social *reproduction*. What political structures have been revived or reconstituted in the gap between the Dutch and the New Order regimes, and how? Conversely, what was lost and must be recovered from the early decades of nationalist awakening? On closer examination we find that the problem of ruling like a foreigner is not one of simply "too much state" and its unchecked repressive apparatuses (the police, jails, surveillance networks). Nor is it a straightforward lag or "holdover" from the colonial period, expressed in neat allegorical parallels between the Dutch and the Suharto regimes. We could say, rather, the novel is an aesthetic investigation into the dialectical structures of repetition and newness.

The novel is, nevertheless, focalized through a servant of the repressive colonial state. Like Minke, Pangemannan is something of a singular figure in the Dutch Indies: Menadonese and Christian by birth, he was raised in Lyons by a French apothecary, and attended the Sorbonne. His wife is French; two of their children are studying in the Netherlands and they live a culturally

European life.[55] It is precisely due to Pangemanann's hybridity that he is tapped by the government to study the Native organizations springing up, a task that generates much ambivalence.

> And so it was that the police had become both my life and my prison. I was a policeman and, at the same time, the prisoner of the police . . . .
>   I had read many books in Europe and I had gained much knowledge about the liberation of men from oppression—spiritual and physical, economic and political. So I fully understood that colonial rule over any part of the world was evil.[56]

At one level, Pangemanann personifies the native collaborator of colonialism. Constantly slighted by his white superiors and experiencing firsthand the system's embedded inequalities, he is hypocritically content to reap its benefits. His conflicted allegiances, however, are often addressed to the absent but admired Minke—"my teacher"—in the second person, making Pangemanann's narrative voice simultaneously a vehicle for colonialist discourse and the nascent anti-colonial movement. This tension is played out in Pangemanann's relationship to Minke's manuscripts, which are stolen from Ambon and delivered to him.

> There were 123 notebooks. They were all full of Minke's terrible scribble and there were many words and phrases scratched out and replaced. The notebooks were tied together in separate bundles. They were all written in Dutch. The first bundle contained a story that had already been published in Malay, entitled *Nyai Permana*. I put that bundle aside. The second bundle was entitled *This Earth of Mankind*, the third *Child of All Nations*, the fourth *Footsteps*.[57]

In a deft narrative conceit, it is now revealed that the three previous novels of Pramoedya's Buru Quartet are in fact nothing but Minke's own writings (although the latter are in Dutch not Bahasa Indonesia)—drawing even clearer parallels between Minke's incarceration and exile and Pramoedya's. Hitchcock observes: "We read Pangemanann reading Minke as if the New Order . . . were trying to read Pramoedya."[58] Through almost obsessive study of the manuscripts, Pangemanann becomes both the state's exemplary spy—the manuscripts are used to understand the organizations he must repress—and Minke's most devoted student and co-conspirator. Minke's stolen notebooks thus allow for a meta-fictional critique of the repressive function of the Suharto state. Given these canny narrative constructions, it is tempting to assume that Pramoedya's abiding concern is writerly freedom during both the Dutch and the Suharto period. Authoritarianism, whether Dutch or postcolonial, is nothing other than the breach of an imagined boundary that should separate the state from the sovereign interiority of the individual; Minke's stolen manuscripts are the external correlative of a violated inner consciousness.

I want to argue, however, that Minke's singular, dissenting consciousness is not the sole, nor even the main, focus of *House of Glass*. If Pangemanann is a character who presages the political failures of Bandung under Suharto's Cold War repression, he is also the perfect narrative device to survey and methodically record the exuberant proliferation of organizations, reform movements, unions, women's groups, and other associations blossoming in the Indies during the early twentieth century. In the process of studying archives, journals, newspapers, stolen letters, and notebooks "so that the government might forever perpetuate its rule,"[59] Pangemanann unwittingly records the very diversity and irrepressible growth of these emergent organizations. Moreover, if the "action" of the novel is "focus[ed] on reading and interpretation,"[60] this labor is anything but passive. Early in the novel, Pangemanann spends many months at the state archives researching Native organizations and movements in order to "make some conclusions about their caliber, the direction of their thinking, and their attitude toward the government of the Netherlands Indies."[61] The intelligence report takes him almost one year to complete.[62] Although the government subsequently bans the movements and exiles its leaders, Pangemanann's workload only increases throughout the remainder of the novel: We follow him rushing to meetings with concerned Dutch officials, traveling between towns, arranging more exiles, and desperately following another new movement's leader. In the process, the state reveals itself to be in a permanently reactive position vis-à-vis the constant innovations of Native society. By the end of the novel, Pangemanann is completely overwhelmed: "The political situation had changed. I couldn't keep up with it. There were new developments each day flowing on from earlier developments which had already left me behind."[63]

Pangemanann's Sisyphean labor is thus at once evidence of the long arm of state surveillance and repression—his "house of glass"—and an indication of its inadequacy. Under the guise of surveillance work, the reader is paradoxically offered a rich ethnography of the Indies' emergent political society rendered in its transnational historical context. We thus learn of the "Indische Partij, or the Indies Party, the first political party in the Indies . . . formed just one year after the Kuomintang was formed in China,"[64] which we may compare with Boedi Oetomo, the moderate reform movement promoting Native education.[65] Another party with former members of the Indische Partij subsequently emerges, while the Indies Social Democratic Association is established by political exiles from the Netherlands.[66] In one memorable scene,

Pangemanann's own nephew urges him to join the new Sarekat Menado,[67] one of the many regional ethnic organizations sprouting up, to Pangemanann's extreme discomfort. Meanwhile, Minke's Sarekat Islam—the prime target of the government—is described by Pangemanann as a veritable force of nature: "a great wave formed by the ocean of life, which had been whipped into a storm by new modern ideas and ways."[68]

Even as Pangemanann works to eliminate the Sarekat by exiling its leader Minke, the organization continues to incubate new leaders. But each leader is not to be read allegorically as the possible postcolonial liberator from Suharto's rule. Rather, each new leader opens the narrative to yet more social and historical layers of authority. In one chapter, for example, Pangemanann must study the writings of one of the Sarekat's emergent leaders, Marco Kartodikromo, which have been seized from a newspaper office. Another autobiographical narrative thus enters Pangemanann's house of glass, but also the *House of Glass* we are reading.[69] The investigation into Marco provides the occasion for a detour into the hardships suffered by peasants under the Dutch agrarian policy of Cultuurstelsel (culture system), introduced in 1830, a forced-labor system for plantations that grew export crops. Importantly, not only is Dutch colonial rule indicted for its racialized labor exploitation, Marco's diary delineates a state within the state, or the way the economic structure of imperialism is embedded within the functions we usually consider "the state's." In this case, the Dutch state colludes with foreign, often British, oil companies that effectively controlled labor and land distribution in the rural areas. As Marco puts it, "In the government, there was also an Oil Government, and the people of our village had to obey both of them."[70] As a result, "From being free farmers they had been turned into the coolies of their former guests."[71] Marco's embedded autobiography demonstrates Pramoedya's skillful use of framed narratives and historical fiction to simultaneously look back from the novel's present to the Cultuurstelsl period, while also looking forward to firmly indict the 1970s and 1980s of the New Order. It forces us to ask: What structures of imperial power—economic, political, social—have been reactivated in the Cold War conjuncture?

This repetition with a difference allows us to recall the way Suharto's regime was crucially supported by American, British, and Japanese foreign investment and access to global markets, especially during its oil boom of the 1970s.[72] More precisely, the New Order's "victory of counterrevolutionary violence" meant it could act "in a manner conducive to the interests of capital in general" and recruit back colonial-era economic players after Sukarno's efforts to nationalize the economy.[73] Historians have noted that, "to a large extent, it was US-trained economists at the Army Staff and Command College who

indoctrinated the anti-Sukarno officers with the developmentalist ideology."[74]
Pramoedya's narrative diversion demonstrates the way the state works not just
by its typically recognized apparatuses of bureaucracy, police, and prisons, but
as anthropologist Naomi Schiller notes, through "the workings of the economy and society"[75] more generally. By concealing itself as a monolithic entity,
the state "hides the social-economic structures of inequality" that lie behind
its false coherence.[76] Marco's autobiography reveals how such structures were
often established in the *longue durée* of imperial rule and are actively reconstituted by the bipolar restructuring underwritten in the Asia-Pacific by the
United States. *House of Glass* thus functions as both a piercing indictment of
the longevity of colonial-capitalist state structures in the postcolony, but also
of the way such structures are actively revived by Cold War economic and
geopolitical imperatives. Freedom, in this rendering, is not simply freedom of
consciousness *from* the state, but the freedom to refigure historical material in
a way that engenders new ways to think the state in its wider political and social
entanglements.

One of the more humorous ways Pramoedya intervenes in dominant Cold
War notions of liberal freedom is via the character of Pangemanann's America-
loving Dutch boss, Meneer L—. Determined to speak only in English, Meneer
L— reveres Thomas Edison and talks incessantly of the "new continent or the
continent of freedom, as he called it."[77] While Pangemanann quietly recalls
to himself "the American Indians who had been systematically annihilated"
and the "big plantation fields of America and the Negro nation who slaved in
those fields,"[78] his boss sees only a country "where every man can live freely
and lives to be free!" Unaware of his own absurdity, Meneer L— explains,
"There is so much freedom there that there is none left for outside America."[79]
He then compares the freedom of the Indies with that of America:

> I feel free here in the Indies—free to oppress the Natives. But this is a
> different kind of freedom than the freedom to truly make something
> of yourself, to become a millionaire who knows no limits to his power
> and influence, whose influence will be felt in every corner of the
> earth. That can only happen in America—a country of freedom with a
> freedom that is unrivalled anywhere.[80]

In the boss's enthusiasm, Pramoedya satirizes the Cold War ideal of America
as quantitatively *more* free than anywhere else. This exalted freedom of individuality—"Where every man can live freely and lives to be free!"—not only
disavows the country's own historical conditions of settler colonialism and
slavery but also that it is underwritten by its global military power: "Only
America, with its unrivalled technical abilities, can defeat Germany,"[81] points

out Meneer L—. "Freedom" in America, it turns out, is not very "different" from that in the colonial Indies after all. As theorized by Meneer L—, it is still the freedom to oppress natives and accumulate wealth, but cloaked in the rhetoric of entrepreneurialism, to "make something of yourself." Pramoedya again reveals how freedom cannot be sufficiently theorized in terms of minimalist conceptions of individual civil and political rights, but must refer to historical and structural conditions that produce freedom for some and not others. After trying to discuss the dangers of an arms buildup with his boss, Pangemanann is forced to give up: "There was nothing more I could say to this fan of America."[82]

For the most part, however, Pramoedya forges an alternative sense of freedom less through debates between characters, and more through the narrative recovery of the dizzying plurality of the many different organizations—elite, Indo (that is, Eurasian), Native, worker-based, ethnic-based, women's, regional—viewed through the policeman's eyes. Their sheer number and variety present opportunities for micro-histories of dispossession and economic injustice—as we have seen—as well as micro-narratives of agency, bravery, solidarity, and occasional failure and disappointment. The brilliant young feminist writer, the aristocratic Seondari, is an example of the latter. A former acquaintance of Minke, she renounces her titles of nobility and appears briefly in the narrative as a new leader of exceptional promise. However, no sooner has she emerged as a character than she is tracked down by police (with the help of Pangemanann's surveillance) and given the choice of either marrying and disappearing from public life, or causing her father to lose his official position and title.[83] As we see also in the quartet's other installments, Pramoedya is highly attentive to the gendered effects of the intersections of colonial rule and local patriarchy.[84] The result: "It was as if Seondari had vanished into thin air."[85] The effect is an oddly centripetal, or distracted narrative style such that the further the narrative proceeds, the more minor characters appear and the more diluted the plot feels.

If the "*over*-significance of minor characters"[86] has been analyzed for ways it can "restructure the narrative worlds of the novel,"[87] I suggest that in *House of Glass* the serial appearance and disappearance of new, minor characters has a specific literary-political function. Despite Pangemanann's dogged efforts at cataloguing all these new leaders, the narrative refuses to sustain focus on any one of Minke's successors as the reader might expect. Pangemanann himself complains, "The situation was not getting any simpler at all. New figures emerged and then disappeared. But there were also names that did not go away—Soerjopranoto, Djojopranoto, Sostrokardono, Sostrokartono, Goenawan, Gunadi, Soekandar, Seokendar. I could hardly tell one from the other

. . . no less than ninety names!"[88] Pangemanann's distress is echoed by the reader who, similarly, has trouble keeping track of the multiple minor characters and narrative threads which refuse to coalesce. Indeed, the novel strains to contain the stories of all "ninety" or so budding leaders, registering the groundswell of different movements at the level of literary form. These multiple leaders suggest that the true protagonist of *House of Glass* is neither Minke nor his antagonist Pangemanann, but the forging of the new space of political activity itself. Indeed, our surveiller-narrator instructs the reader:

> The role of the individual, be he named Raden Mas Minke or Si Ana or Siti Ainu, was not important at all. The times guaranteed the birth, growth, and development of organizations as the vehicle for different ideas and for the ideas themselves. Of course, the individual left behind deep marks, . . . but what was more important was the role of the organizations on the modern history of the Indies, in the way they changed the Indies and its people, in accordance with the ideals that had been formulated, struggled for, and developed as the essence of these organizations' activities.
>
> And the role of the former police commissioner called Pangemanann was not important either.[89]

By the time the new, liberal Governor General Van Limburg Stirum arrives, Pangemanann observes: "Java was beginning to move. There was wave after wave of strikes. . . . The government faced more and more problems as these actions resulted in a decline in the national income."[90] What the novel narrates then, is not the exemplary but thwarted leadership of Minke as an allegorical figure of the dissident writer, but rather, the importance of the multiple spheres of action that he and others were able to bring into being. If Pangemanann concedes that "writing in public with your name right up front . . . certainly originated with Raden Mas Minke,"[91] its potential is only actualized when the political action it inaugurates becomes anonymized and collectivized: "Java was beginning to move."

In the final two chapters of *House of Glass*, Minke returns from his exile in Ambon. Stripped of his family, his resources, his house (into which Pangemanann has moved), friends, and networks, he wanders Java disconsolately under Pangemanann's ever-vigilant eye. After falling ill and being denied proper medical care, he dies penniless and unrecognized, with only Pangemanann his paradoxical admirer, jailer, and censor, as witness: "Here upon my desk I had created magic threads that connected me with him. I could feel every move of his fingers, I could hear his heartbeat. So I also knew that he did not leave a single word when he died."[92] On the very last page of the novel,

Pangemanann partially redeems himself by giving Minke's manuscripts and notebooks to Nyai Ontosoroh, aka Sanikem, the inspiring, strong-willed Native businesswoman and mother of Minke's first wife Annelies.[93] Although this leaves the manuscripts with a potential future life, we are still left with the final novel's emphatic sidelining of Minke. In a sense, the first three novels appear to have been something of a "false lead" all along.

Such a narrative trajectory is, I suggest, precisely the point. *House of Glass* is not a dramatization of the "mindless force of state power . . . against creative, critical subjects"[94] that the genre of Cold War dissident literature typically invokes; it instead serves as a literary vehicle that contains the proliferating organizations, strikes, riots, and youth groups that emerge, each with meandering narrative detours and often short-lived leaders. Counterintuitively, the final installment of the quartet is above all a novel of unfinished *beginnings*; it is about the capacity to begin and create something new. In one of the only instances of direct speech from Minke after his return from exile, he discusses the future of the Indies with his one remaining friend, Goenawan, who tries to urge moderation and acceptance of the status quo. Minke retorts: "We all have to accept reality, yes, that's true. But just to accept reality and do nothing else, that is the attitude of human beings who have lost the ability to develop and grow, . . . to create new realities."[95] When Pangemanann visits Minke's grave he notes, in his characteristic doubled voice, "It was I who did that [visit the grave], alone, as a mark of respect for a man *who had set new things in motion in the Indies.*"[96] We come to understand that Minke isn't the privileged subject of Indonesian nationalist historiography after all; rather, the minor characters whose lives fall in and out of Pangemanann's panoptical gaze may be considered the proper subject of *House of Glass*. If the Buru Quartet as a whole clears, as Hitchcock suggests, a "space for politics," it is precisely Pramoedya's backward glance that makes this perceivable.

In both her major work *On Revolution* and her essay "What Is Freedom?" Arendt identifies a fundamentally diminished notion of "freedom" in the modern era that especially takes shape during the postwar reckoning with totalitarianism's legacy.

> We are inclined to believe that freedom begins where politics ends, because we have seen that freedom has disappeared when so-called political considerations overruled everything else. Was not the liberal credo, "The less politics the more freedom," right after all? Is it not true that the smaller the space occupied by the political, the larger the domain left to freedom? Indeed, do we not rightly measure the extent

of freedom in any given community by the free scope it grants to apparently nonpolitical activities, free economic enterprise or freedom of teaching, of religion, of cultural and intellectual activities? Is it not true, as we all somehow believe, that politics is compatible with freedom only because and insofar as it guarantees a possible freedom *from* politics?[97]

Arendt's characterization of freedom here as "free economic enterprise, or freedom of teaching, of religion, of cultural and intellectual activities" resonates with the conceptions advocated by Amnesty and the *Index on Censorship* discussed above. In the tendency to view freedom as the freedom *from* politics, the space of politics is conceived as a narrow and subtractive one. In contrast, and in a typical Arendtian return to the ancients, freedom is better conceived as the faculty to *act* in a politically constituted space. In the classical world, "freedom needed, in addition to mere liberation the company of other men [*sic*] who were in the same state, and it needed a common public space to meet them—a politically organized world, in other words, into which each of the free men could insert himself by word and deed."[98] Arendt's understanding of freedom as the ability to "call something into being which did not exist before,"[99] or "the sheer capacity to begin,"[100] helps us understand Pramoedya's decision to conclude the Buru Quartet with Pangemanann's narrative. Above all, the policeman's tale emphasizes the ability to "set new things in motion."

Further, the novel's implicit diagnosis of tyranny and freedom necessarily complicates the figure of Pramoedya as the "Indonesian Solzhenitsyn." If this moniker discursively merges the Third World with the Second via the privileged Cold War tropes of secret police, censorship, and arbitrary imprisonment, *House of Glass* theorizes freedom and unfreedom through repetition and difference, the dialectics of the individual and the masses, and the national and transnational determinations of state and economic power. Mindful of his roots in the LEKRA movement, Pramoedya's writing is not primarily an expression of individual artistic consciousness that must remain untouched by state power, but is the attempt to reimagine the very condition of moving toward liberation through collective political action. In a 1995 interview, three years before the fall of the Suharto regime, Pramoedya observed that "the further we get away from the moment of independence in 1945, the further away Indonesia is from independence."[101] *House of Glass* gives us a way to imagine postcolonial futures beyond colonial reproduction and toward radical newness.

Kim Chi-ha and Disfiguring Development

In the Cold War Western press, the "Korean Solzhenitsyn" Kim Chi-ha was lauded as another dissident hero speaking truth to an oppressive regime. Author of the scandalously satirical narrative poem "Five Bandits" ("Ojŏk"), published in 1970 in the journal *Sasanggye*, which was subsequently shut down, South Korea's "representative poet"[102] famously earned the wrath of the Park Chung Hee military dictatorship. Born in 1941, the poet—whose nom de plume "Chi-ha" literally means "underground"[103]—was in and out of prison for most of the late 1960s and '70s and sentenced to death in 1974 for speaking out about the regime's use of torture; his sentence was commuted to life imprisonment in 1975. He would be pardoned after Park's assassination and the regime change in 1979. Charged with violating the state's anti-communist laws as well as President Park's Emergency Decree Number 9 prohibiting anti-government criticism, Kim's arrest and very public 1976 trial spurred an international outcry, alluded to above.[104]

In a 1978 profile article on Kim in the *Index on Censorship*, Shelly Killen draws on Albert Camus's influential 1957 lecture "Create Dangerously" to elaborate on the artist's predicament.[105] Camus's essay, Killen points out, reflects on "the role of the artist in a society whose existence was threatened daily by barbarism and the rising power of the totalitarian state."[106] In Camus's words, the artist's battle with the oppressive state is nothing less than a confrontation between "the martyr and the lion" in "History's amphitheatre."[107] In his call for artistic freedom in "Create Dangerously," Camus charts a course between the effete "art for art's sake" movement and the dangers of social realism, which "sacrifices art for a purpose that is alien to art."[108] Camus goes on to champion the transcendent powers of art, which triumph over "modern tyrannies, whether they are right-wing or left-wing".[109] "Tyrants know that great works embody a force for emancipation. . . . And even thousands of concentration camps and prison cells cannot obliterate this moving testimony of dignity."[110] We again recognize the key Cold War imaginary of totalitarianism's prison camps and arbitrary tyranny, against which the genre of dissident literature stands uncorrupted. Disregarding the actual political characteristics of the Park regime, Killen firmly inserts the Korean poet at "the centre of this blood-drenched arena," praising Kim's "incandescent poetry . . . [that] has the power to rekindle faith in our intrinsic capacity to transcend our present savagery."[111] She goes on to defend his impeccable Catholicism and mock the Park regime for casting him as a communist. Without mentioning the grotesque, lewd, and often funny nature of his satirical poetry, Kim is lauded as the paradigmatic defender of freedom against a savage and totalitarian state: The "martyr" faces off against the "lion" of the Park regime.

As with Pramoedya, I argue that Kim muddles such clear-cut renderings of liberal freedom versus totalitarianism, writer versus tyrant, artistic autonomy versus ideological state. As we saw in the preceding chapter, it was precisely the apolitical notion of "pure literature" that many right-wing regimes used to legitimate anti-communist artistic repression. Youngju Ryu's study of Park's "Winter Republic" sheds light on this literary milieu. The state's cultural policies were advocated partly through the government's Korean Culture and Arts Foundation, whose head, Mun Tŏk-su, happened to be the president of the PEN-International Korean Center,[112] attesting again to the curious alignment of principles of "freedom of speech" with right-wing regimes. Emerging in the early 1970s in opposition to this alignment was the Association of Writers for Freedom and Praxis (chayu silch'ŏn mumin hyŏhŭihoe), also known as Chasil.[113] By focusing on both aesthetic autonomy *and* praxis, it sought to resist the false dichotomy of the Park regime's cultural program, in which "pure literature" was contrasted with that infected by proletarian ideology.[114]

A more uncomfortable alignment was the U.S.'s prominent role in South Korea. By the early 1970s, the beacon of the free world had been forced to recognize its own complicity with the increasingly repressive regime that had imprisoned and tortured Kim. The U.S. was, after all, financing the anti-communist fight on the Korean peninsula to the tune of $1.5 billion, which aimed to "modernize [South Korea's] armed forces"[115] and help protect U.S. security interests there. For U.S. liberals, Kim's show trial was one of the great scandals of the Cold War Pacific alliances and highlighted a "central paradox" about South Korea during the Cold War:[116] The "show trials" and "blatant violation of liberal democratic ideas" were "taking place not in the communist North Korea, as one might expect, but in the anti-communist South Korea."[117] Ryu observes with irony: "Solzhenitsyn would have found his great writer in Kim Chi-ha."[118] But how might we read the work of this exemplary "dissident poet" in terms other than as a "paradox" of the Cold War? This chapter has been arguing that the dominant epistemic lens of the Cold War dissident writer—seen so well in the press on both Pramoedya and Kim—cannot account for the compatibility between the free world's liberal capitalism and a transpacific authoritarianism. It has therefore prevented us from seeing *other* possible approaches to oppositional literature. In what follows, I read Kim's "Five Bandits" and "Groundless Rumors" from the 1970s for the way their aesthetics bring to life not just the "paradoxically" repressive nature of the

U.S.-backed Park regime, but the more scandalous compatibility between capitalist development and "present savagery."[119] Kim's satire must be read, I suggest, for its literary innovations in depicting the new contours of a transnational political economy that articulates with, rather than contradicts, the authoritarianism of the South Korean state.

In the second part of this section, I then look briefly to Kim's reception in *Lotus*, the journal of the Afro-Asian Writers' Bureau I touched on in the preceding chapter. The year after the English-language collection *Cry of the People and Other Poems* was published in 1974 by Japan's Autumn Press, Kim was awarded the Lotus Prize alongside a number of prominent Third World writers. A very different Kim emerges in these pages, one that expresses the shared struggle against neocolonialism across the Third World. Such a reading usefully challenges liberal notions of individual artistic dissidence versus a monolithic totalitarianism (the "martyr" and the "lion") to emphasize issues of national sovereignty and ongoing anti-imperialist struggles. My readings of Kim's poems show how the poet forges a specific aesthetic that attends to both imperialism's recursivity and Cold War complications.

If Pramoedya's fictional narratives relied on a firm, historically realist return to the 1910s in order to pose questions of post-1965 Indonesia, Kim Chiha's "Five Bandits," presents us with a less than clear approach to time. Early in the poem, the speaker ironically invokes a premodern, precolonial era of plenitude when the nation "enjoyed perfect peace, the most prosperous peaceful peace" (*t'aep'ŏng t'aep'ŏng t'aep'ŏng sŏngdaera*).[120] The poem's initial use of archaic Korean literary forms ("Whoever writes poetry . . . Write straight, like this"; "*sirŭl ssŭdoe . . . irŏhk'e ssŭryatda*")[121] seems to confirm an ancient setting. Throughout the poem are references to an array of premodern Korean and Chinese historical figures and battles, including Dongzhuo, a general of the first century Han dynasty; Wu Cheng'en's famous sixteenth-century novel, *Journey to the West*; and General Wan Li of the Choson dynasty. The genre of both "Five Bandits" and "Groundless Rumors" is, however, decidedly modern. Ko Won describes Kim's narrative poems as "marked by comedy, colloquialisms and unrestrained vulgarisms."[122] In them, Kim draws from *p'ansori* elements—a traditional form of folk opera—as well as shaman rituals and vernacular slang in a free verse arrangement the poet called "talk poem" or *damsi*. Chan J. Wu has defined *damsi* as "an open genre in which narrative and poetry, drama and song, lyric and epic, drama and epic can mix and interact freely,"[123] while Ryu reminds us that *p'ansori* itself was a "hybrid genre that mixed erudite learning and classical allusions with lewd, ribald, and often scatological humor."[124] Kim's "revived form of *p'ansori*"[125] is thus ideal for representing the larger than life figures of the Park regime, while drawing on traditional Korean genres of song and verse.

Although the regime seems to exist in an unspecified historical time, the title of the poem makes clear Kim's allegorical gesture. In Korean, the phrase "five thieves or bandits" (*ojŏk*) was "used to characterize the five government ministers who in 1910 signed over Korean sovereignty to the Japanese to start Japan's colonial occupation of Korea."[126] In Kim's poem, the five titular subjects are thus neocolonial agents of the Park regime. They are the conglomerate businessman (*chaebŏl*) or, "ConglomerApe" in the excellent translation by Brother Anthony of Taizé, the National Assembly member (*kukhoi ŭi wŏn*) or "AssemblyMutt," the high-ranking government official (*kogŭp kongmuwŏn*) or "TopCivilSerpant," the military general (*changsŏng*) or "General-in-Chimp," and the government minister (*changch'aguan*) or "HighMinisCur."[127] Ostensibly, the occasion for the poem is the gathering of the five thieves as they meet to celebrate ten years in "the thievery business"[128] with a golf match. The gathering is the opportunity for an extended, grotesque, and satirical description of these five branches of the authoritarian state and their various "talents." First under scrutiny is the *chaebŏl*, or business magnate, synonymous with those enormously powerful conglomerates like Samsung, Hyundai, and Lucky-Goldstar (LG), which took off during the Park Chung Hee period. Draped with gold accessories from his tiepin to his shoes, the *chaebŏl* tycoon and his talents are described in culinary terms:

> He grills ministers yellow, he boils vice-ministers red,
>
> adds vinegar, soy sauce, mustard, pepper paste, loads of monosodium glutamate, garnishes all that with shredded peppers, leeks, garlic, then gobbles, *yum-yum*,
>
> gulps down bank money replenished by tax funds, money borrowed from overseas, plus every kind of privileged concession, in a flash,
>
> seduces pretty girls to be his whores, keeps pounding on them day and night, breeding kids with all his might.[129]

As has been well documented, the *chaebŏl*-state alliance was a developmental model that took advantage of the unusual degree of industrialization and centralization implemented by the Japanese, and was explicitly modeled on the Japanese *zaibatsu* conglomerate system.[130] It rode the economic boom driven by the demand for material and supplies for the U.S.-led war effort in Vietnam (as Japan had done during the Korean War), helping many *chaebŏls* in their takeoff. After bringing the economic elite firmly under control by arresting "illicit profiteers," the Park regime gave preferential loans and contracts to selected businesses,[131] effectively creating a class of powerful *chaebŏl* who benefited from lucrative Cold War military and development loans.[132] Kim's rendering of the *chaebŏl* ecology gives aesthetic form to this novel alignment of business, state, and transnational capital: The *chaebŏl* enjoys "tax money, foreign loans" (*segŭmpadŭn ŭnhaengdon, woegugsŏ pitnaen don*) from Japan and the U.S., enthusiastically consumed with traditional Korean seasonings such as "vinegar, mustard, pepper paste," and so on.

The remaining four thieves are described in similarly withering terms. The Assembly member shouts out nonsensical slogans to "stupid citizens" such as, "Revolution! New wrongs for old!" (*hyŏngmŏngidat, ku'akŭn sinakŭro*), and "Modernization! . . . Priority to farming! Make poor farmers quit farming!" (*kŭndaehwadat, . . . chungnonidat, pinnong'ŭn inong'ŭro*).[133] Meanwhile, Top-CivilSerpant specializes in taking bribes; the military general steals his soldiers' rice and "fills the sacks . . . with sand";[134] and the minister demands ever higher export productivity as he embezzles money on government contracts. Pramoedya's attention to the gendered effects of colonial rule are paralleled in Kim's depiction of the HighMinisCur, who emerges

> glaring eyes veiled by disgusting mucus, his left hand conducts the national defense with a golf club.
>
> His right hand fumblingly scrawls *production, export, construction* [*chŭngsan such'ul kŏnsŏl*] on a girl's breast: *Ha ha*, hey, that tickles, Sir!
>
> You ignorant bitch! [*irŏn musikhannyŏn*] How dare you say that affairs of the state tickle?
>
> Export even though people starve. Produce though nothing sells. Use the bones of those who've died of hunger to build a bridge to Japan: let's go over and greet their gods! [*kamisama bae'alhajat!*]][135]

In images such as the misogynist minister, Kim mobilizes the *damsi* form to succinctly encode the material logic undergirding the "miracle" of Korean industrialization: the reliance on foreign loans, the unrelenting pursuit of export dollars, fierce anti-communism, labor repression, and low domestic consumption levels in part enabled by the use of young, female factory labor.[136] One telling poetic result is the renewed aesthetic relevance of the commodity form. In "Five Bandits," modern consumer goods—the shoes, electronics, and textiles produced by Koreans for the world market, as well as the Western commodities that began to trickle in at this time often through

American military black markets—take on an aura and authority of their own. Indeed, the description of the bandits' space- and time-stretching mansion actually takes up more lines than the descriptions of the five thieves themselves. Although most critical attention has focused on the personal satires of the latter, the poem is as interested in the arrangement and description of grotesque *things* as in their owners, inspecting the regime's material economy in exhaustive poetic detail. In the setup to the following quote, the chief of police hears of the royal decree for the arrest of the thieves and naively goes to the mansion intent on capturing them and becoming a hero. As soon as he arrives, however, he is instantly seduced by its decadent architecture and amenities:

Then peeping in through the slightly open door, he sees:

nacre cabinets, matte-surfaced steel trunks, phoenix-adorned dragon chests, dragon-adorned phoenix chests, a chest with three thousand three hundred and thirty-three levels, flowered wardrobes ornamented with painted carnations, a jade salver the size of a playing field, candlesticks in gold, silver, and bronze, soaring high as buildings, electric clocks, electric rice bowls, electric kettles, electric chopsticks, electric vases, electric mirrors, electric books, electric briefcases. . . .

pewter earthenware, Tang vases, Japanese vases, American vases, French vases, Italian vases, a television sheathed in a tiger-skin rug, a Sony recorder in a marquetry chest, a Mitchell camera on a tortoise-shell table, an RCA projector beside a coral bookcase [*hwaryu mun'gapsoge ssoni nogŭmgi, taemo ch'aeksang wi'e mitch'el k'amera, sanho ch'aekjang kyŏt'e alssi'ei yŏngsagi*], a Parker fountain pen in an amber writing-brush holder, chandeliers with candles lit, castor-oil-burning standing lamps . . . [137]

The picture that emerges here (and in many pages that follow) is one of an unnaturally proliferating and decidedly hybrid commodity culture: Traditional luxury goods coveted by Chinese and Korean emperors or *yangban* (landed elite) merge with the latest modern gadgetry from Japan and the U.S., "Sony" and "Mitchell," to produce a monstrous transpacific commodity form. The objects function as material sediments of several kinds of authority at once: the absolutist rule by premodern kings, colonial rulers, and the specific Cold War character of South Korea's development. The accumulated loot of the ruling elite harbors the material traces of the peninsula's fraught decolonization process, resulting in a poetics of delirium. I suggest that Kim's disfiguring aesthetics thus mark the specific, material "juncture between two epochal political forms": the "colonial" and the "bipolar."[138]

"Five Bandits" must be read simultaneously as a damning satire of the corrupt personages of the Park regime and as a cutting political-economic critique of South Korea's incorporation into the capitalist "free world" bloc. Put otherwise, what is most scandalous about Kim's poem is the way bipolarized national development so closely resembles colonial exploitation, or rule by a foreigner.[139] Such repression is neither the generic fall into totalitarian "savagery" depicted by Killen or Camus, nor is it simply due to the lingering aftereffects of colonial dictatorships.[140] Rather, tyranny here is a reactivated and re-formed authority that emerges out of the growing material network of development schemes, investment apparatuses, anti-communist military loans, and the transnational political economy of imports and exports. When the chief of police mistakenly arrests Kkwesu, a poor farmer from rural Chollado, the latter defends himself by insisting he is merely a poor gum peddler.

> A gum seller? So much the better. Gum seller, Cigarette seller, Stockings seller, Sweets seller, Chocolate seller, all taken together,
>
> selling foreign goods, [they] make up the Five Bandits, right?[141]

Power here is precisely the ability to define crime as whatever might hinder the nation's development strategy, whether by selling gum or cigarettes. Kkwesu is subsequently arrested, tortured, booked for "calumny" (*mugojwe*),[142] and perishes in jail.

Indeed, the strident public opposition to the Park dictatorship was largely motivated by the neocolonial dimensions of South Korea's developmental push. Popular outrage erupted at the news of the normalization of Republic of Korea–Japan relations in 1964–65, prompting campus protests that continued for 532 consecutive days, to which President Park responded with both "martial law and a garrison decree."[143] Kim, a student at the time at Seoul National University, would go on to write a scathing poem on the "death" of Korean democracy,[144] helping consolidate his place in the anti-dictatorship cultural movement. But diplomatic normalization with Japan was not merely a matter of nationalist pride. Writing about the reestablishment of relations, Tadashi Kimiya has explained how South Korea's initial demands for massive legal reparations from its erstwhile colonizer were eventually placated, with the help of the U.S. as mediator. Instead of a legal resolution and payment, Japan provided a total of US$8 billion in "money, goods, and services as economic aid or gifts in order to clear away the South Korean claims against the Japanese."[145] This strategy alleviated both Japan and the U.S.'s major concern about maintaining South Korea as a stable capitalist economy in the face of North Korea and China's threat.[146] At the same time, as Lisa Yoneyama has argued, it testifies to the way postwar transpacific "victor's justice" "instat[es] the victorious as overseers and protectors of besieged sovereignties," and thereby "legitimiz[es] prolonged occupations after cease-fire."[147] The American military occupation coupled with the "gift" of Japanese economic aid precisely indexes South Korea's "besieged sovereignty."

Heonik Kwon, following Jacques Derrida, has written of the peculiar "geopolitics of forgiveness" that emerged in the decolonizing–Cold War matrix. Around the globe, bipolar imperatives required uncomfortable alliances, such as the pardoning of French Nazi collaborators in the face of Europe's rearmament for the Cold War,[148] and the backing of the South African state by the U.S., with the latter becoming "apartheid's reluctant uncle."[149] For newly decolonizing Third World states, "The amnesty concerned collaborators with the colonial regimes, and these acts of forgiveness, often conducted against the population's expectations and wishes, weakened the state's moral legitimacy and distorted subsequent political developments."[150] In South Korea, the demand for colonial accountability was "distorted" by the free world's counter-demand for anti-communist security and militarized industrial development. Kim's poem well demonstrates how, with the U.S. Cold War military machine on one side and the effort to "greet Japanese gods,"[151] on the other, any alternative, decolonized path to South Korean modernity was foreclosed. "Five Bandits" thus anatomizes and satirizes tyranny as the forced participation in a specifically Cold War developmental-security matrix.

The Western press was not the only keen outside observer of Kim's case. If the U.S. and British media were largely fixated on the Park regime's recalcitrant illiberalism and its "wave of political trials,"[152] a different reading of Kim emerges in Lotus, the journal sponsored by the Afro-Asian Writers' Bureau.[153] In 1975, as mentioned above, Kim was awarded the prestigious Lotus Prize alongside the prominent Third World writers Chinua Achebe of Nigeria, Faiz Ahmad Faiz of Pakistan, and M. Mahdi El Gawahri from Iraq.[154] A Lotus issue of 1976 included a special section on the four prize winners, with brief author profiles of each. Additionally, the issue carried a four-page review of The Cry of the People and Other Poems and reprinted three of its shorter poems. In the prizewinner's profile, Kim is described as fighting for "the sovereign rights of the Korean people" against the "dictatorship of foreign powers."[155] With obvious resonances of Fanonian "combat literature," and in contrast to the liberal understanding of literary freedom from politics, the Lotus editors remind the reader that "poetry and political action are inseparable."[156] For the journal's editors and readers, Kim's oeuvre is exemplary for its struggle for national self-determination in a broader field of global politics.

Maher Shafik's four-page review of *Cry of the People* expresses such an appreciation yet—like Keller's piece—is remarkable for how little it actually refers to Kim's poetry. After providing biographical information and describing Kim's arrest and imprisonment after the publication of "Five Bandits," the bulk of the review is concerned with explaining the many political and historical "topical references" behind the poems.[157] To do so, Shafik assembles direct (and unattributed) quotes from the volume's explanatory footnotes. Thus, he explains how "Groundless Rumors" refers to "the mysterious Daeyunkak Hotel fire of Christmas Eve, 1971," and summarizes President Park's emergency declaration and his repressive Yusin Constitution of 1972. The largest single unattributed quote reproduces a lengthy footnote from "Groundless Rumors" on the political economy of the regime:

> President Park dangled a cheap, skilled and docile work force before foreign investors. In addition to passing laws outlawing labor strikes in foreign enterprises; "tax-free" zones have been set up. . . . "Export zones" have also been established "to increase employment and improve technology," all goods produced therein being for export only. Profit transfer rights offered to foreign investors allow hundreds of millions of dollars of untaxed profits to flow out of Korea annually, profits which derive primarily from the low wages paid to Korean labour.[158]

The phrases in quotation marks are in the original Autumn Press publication, where they presumably refer to the state's discourse. For Shafik, such details are important because the "topicality" of the Korean situation "does not mean that Kim's poems do not have a universal appeal."[159] The review concludes with some brief sections of "Five Bandits" and "Groundless Rumors" and the reviewer's final assessment: "Certainly [Kim's poetry] is not as witty as Brecht's great political satires, but it has its own distinction, and is definitely a revolutionizing force that seeks to change the world."[160] What matters most to Shafik, in other words, is how much the conditions referred to in Kim's poems can be translated to other anti-imperialist Third World locations, and whether or not his works constitute a "revolutionary force."

The concerns of the *Lotus* editors and readers can be readily contrasted with those of the Western press. Rather than being read as the work of the exemplary prisoner of conscience wielding the torch of artistic freedom against a "savage" regime, Kim's poetry is read for the way it charts the South Korean experience of neocolonialism—a process perceived to be "universal" across the decolonizing world. The *Lotus* coverage effectively replaces concern with the sovereignty of the individual's conscience to a concern with the sovereignty of the Third World nation. Yet despite their interest in postcolonial sovereignty, the *Lotus* writers curiously make no mention of the fact of Korea's divided peninsula, the conflagration of the Korean War, the U.S. military occupation in the South, or the triangulation between Japanese economic hegemony and U.S. military power. While useful for considering South Korea in a shared, Third World framework, the writers do not recognize that certain postcolonies *cannot* be Third Worldist in the sense of being unaligned, for this is precisely the neocolonial situation they find themselves in.

Just one year later, one of Africa's most prominent writers (himself famously imprisoned by the Kenyan state), Ngũgĩ wa Thiong'o, would use Kim's "Five Bandits" as a representative text to discuss neocolonialism.[161] Indeed, Ngũgĩ noted the inspiration for his 1980 *Devil on the Cross* as his encounter with Kim's work on a trip to Japan in 1976.[162] In his essay "Africa and Asia: The History That Refuses to Be Silenced," he writes that the poem

> could be talking about many countries in Asia, South America and
> Africa. The Bandits, a combination of business tycoons, top bureau-
> crats, national assembly men, the top military brass and cabinet min-
> isters, all the elements that make up the comprador social stratum,
> are compared to the slavemasters of old who drove people to work
> harder and harder with the resulting wealth going into the lifestyle of
> the few and their foreign connections in the centres of world imperi-
> alism. These bandits are reproduced by imperialism in a neo-colonial
> system engulfing the peoples of Asia, Africa and South America. So
> when he talks about the alliance of the Five Bandits with Japanese
> and US imperialism as helping in the plunder and murder of our peo-
> ples, he is speaking all our histories.[163]

For the Kenyan writer, Kim's poem gives aesthetic form to the latest of three general stages of Western imperialism—the first two being slavery and "classical colonialism," and the third stage neocolonial comprador capitalism.[164] "That is why," Ngũgĩ reiterates, "the Korean people's struggle for democracy and unity is the struggle of all oppressed peoples."[165] Like the *Lotus* editors, in claiming Kim's universality Ngũgĩ suggests a South-South solidarity that provocatively links postcolonial East Asia with Africa. (Kim himself would cite Frantz Fanon in his 1976 trial in another linking of the two continents.)[166] Yet Ngũgĩ is more cognizant of the profound role of the Cold War in shaping decolonization, a process that had devastating effects on the African continent as well as in Asia. First, his mention of Japanese imperialism in the above is not insignificant given that *Lotus*—like the PEN conferences discussed in the preceding chapter—often included Japan and its cultural production as an unproblematic part of postcolonial Afro-Asia. For Ngũgĩ, "Japanese and U.S. imperialism" firmly signals the Cold War capitalist alliance between the two powers, necessarily complicating a smooth notion of Afro-Asian solidarity against the West.[167] Second is Ngũgĩ's insight on the specific use of anti-communism by the neocolonial native elite. Toward the conclusion of his essay he notes, "[the native comprador bourgeoisie] kill democracy and they kill national initiatives. They kill unity of the people under the pretext of fighting the demon they call communism."[168] I suggest, though, that in East and Southeast Asia, we must go further than merely naming the "pretext" of anti-communist violence as an opportunistic tool of repressive regimes. As I have been arguing, Kim's poetry reveals the *necessary* relationship between the expansion of Cold War capitalism and authoritarian rule. That is, Kim's critique is not simply that South Korea's regime is repressive, exploitative, and beholden to foreign powers. It is that these characteristics are *normal and necessary* in the pursuit of a decolonizing modernity that emerged as part of the peninsula's "division system." As influential literary and cultural critic Paik Nak-chung explains, the "division system" (*pundan ch'eje*) is not merely the bloc confrontation between "two opposing ideologies—capitalism (or liberal democracy) and socialism (communism),"[169] but a radically interdependent form, a "peninsula-wide structure" that itself forms a subset of the world-system as a whole.[170] That is, the workings of the rightest South Korean security state can only be understood in relation to the North Korean state which it opposed and competed against but, in many ways, mirrored.

Kim's 1972 *damsi* poem "Groundless Rumors" (*Pi'ŏ*), to which I now turn, demonstrates precisely the interlocking of Cold War capitalist and illiberal modes of authority. Divided into three sections, the poem's imagery manages to exceed even the monstrous couplings of "Five Bandits"; David McCann calls it "the best of the long satires."[171] The first section, "Origin of a Sound," follows the story of the impoverished An-do, who is charged with "the crime of standing on his own two feet and spreading groundless rumors [*yu'ŏn pi'ŏ*]."[172] Satirizing the Park regime's paranoid response to dissident writers, An-do is condemned at a sham trial, after which his body parts are cut off one by one. Only his un-dead torso remains to roll around his cell with an unsilenceable "Kung!"— a sound that "is heard even now, day and night."[173] Part 2, "Ko Kwan," or "high official," tells the story of the Daeyunkak Hotel fire of Christmas Eve 1971 mentioned above. In Kim's hands, the event is the opportunity to make fun of the sleazy politicians, business elites, Japanese cronies, and their respective illicit lovers, who flee as a fire engulfs the hotel. The final section, "Adoration of a Six-shooter," descends further into bodily vulgarity and obscene violence as a king—identified only as ruling "in the year of the pig"—becomes pregnant and is told by his shaman that he must eat 30 million human livers, preferably communist ones, in order to abort.

Let us briefly unpack the gruesome fate of An-do in the section "Origin of a Sound" ("*sori naeryŏk*"). The lingering "Kung!" emanating from his torso offers a clear, if macabre, rejoinder to the Park regime's attempt to silence all dissent. Yet the poem's show trial, I contend, satirizes more than just the regime's disproportionate violence. The prosecution against An-do presents a ludicrous litany of crimes, poetically rendered as an enormous single run-on line of mostly Sino-Korean characters, as opposed to the rest of the poem which predominantly uses *han'gŭl*, pure Korean letters. Unlike the bulk of the poem with its free verse lines, frequent exclamation points and onomatopoeic vocabulary, the legal charges comprise a torrent of formal, bureaucratic vocabulary, rhythmically united by the repetition of "crime of—" (*—choe*) in each phrase. The accusations include "crimes" that speak to the obvious illiberalism of the regime: speaking out against the government, disgracing the fatherland, and anti-government conspiracy. However, several charges explicitly challenge capitalist values and policies that, on their own, would not be considered particularly "authoritarian." These crimes include "the crime of insolently avoiding the national policies for more production, export, and construction without a moment's rest" (*ch'onbon muhyu chŭngsan such'ul kŏnsŏljŏk kukka chŏngch'aek kip'ijoe*)[174] and "Disturbing the environment for capital investment" (*t'uja hwan'gyŏng kyoranjoe*).[175] Syntactically and poetically, these violations operate at the same level of ridicule as the crimes in other stanzas, such as "the crime of possibly organizing an anti-government body through telepathic means."[176] Whether fomenting a supernatural anti-government conspiracy or avoiding export policies, An-do's charges receive the same satirical treatment of exaggeration, disproportion, and disfigurement. The *equivalence* of these outrages is partly what is at stake in Kim's poems.

We see a similar equivalence between illiberal and capitalist authorities in his more traditionally lyrical "The Cry of the People" ("*minjung ŭi woech'um*"), the title poem of the Autumn Press English translation. Here, lines decrying the betrayal of democracy by the Park regime are formally commensurate with the injustices of an export economy and foreign investment. Beginning with such outrages as "Dictatorship has been established" and "The people's leaders thrown in prison / For espousing democratic rights,"[177] the poem continues with:

> To improve the investment environment,
> Compradors appear;
>
> Tax exemptions, transfer rights,
> Offered like ancestral gifts;
>
> But rights of labor brutally suppressed,
> Special laws are written;
>
> Industrial zones, export centers,
> Create only regional gaps.[178]

Remarkable here is the attempt to craft a poetics of protest *through* the very language of growth-oriented economic policy: "Tax exemptions, transfer rights," and "special laws" for taming labor. In formally presenting such policies alongside the more obvious human rights violations of a dictatorship, we understand that labor disciplining is not an unfortunate by-product of a generic authoritarianism. Rather, it is the linchpin of the South's bipolarized ascension into the free world. Meanwhile, the question of reunification with the North—the unfinished nature of decolonization on the peninsula—must take second place to the industrial push: "Economic independence but a distant vision;/Unification a receding dream."[179]

For Kim, therefore, at stake is not merely the violation of the classic individual, political, and civil liberties that would, as Joseph Slaughter has argued, come to "hijack" more capacious, Third Worldist understandings of international human rights.[180] Nor is it simply the fact of neocolonial foreign control, as Shafik's review stressed, nor even the egregiously rushed nature of development that contributed to the Daeyunkak fire: As one victim of the latter wryly asks, "Is the lack of an emergency staircase modernization?"[181] Many of the national policies Kim indicts are precisely those that have now been standardized as part of the playbook of successful globalized development: export-oriented industrialization, courting foreign investment, rapid urbanization, anti-union and anti-labor laws, and the externalization of environmental costs.[182] Indeed, the shock of reading Kim's poetry from a twenty-first-century vantage point is the way these typical "growth" policies were so firmly entwined with a dictatorial, neocolonialist regime. We can now read the concern with the normalization of the 1965 Japan–Republic of Korea relations with a doubled lens: What Cold War modernization produces, above all, is the *normalization* of a certain mode of capitalist development that arises at the intersection of decolonization and the bipolarization of modernity. The Park regime scrambles both the time and goals of decolonization such that the "postponement (of democracy) becomes a condition for acceleration (of industrialization)."[183]

Kim's delirious, grotesque satires are therefore not only directed at the bloated cronies of the Park regime. They critique South Korea's subjection to militarized, anti-communist capitalist development, which is portrayed poetically at its frenzied and unnatural endpoint: grotesque couplings of commodities and the equally monstrous demands for the creation of capital-friendly environments. We must, finally, recognize the profound transformation of imperialism in the decolonizing Asia-Pacific. If bipolarized restructuring was coeval with decolonization,[184] what we see is less an unchanging, durable form of Euro-American imperialism and more the "novel imperial order of the Cold War era."[185] Anti-communist state tyranny is not a convenient "pretext" for repression; it is the enabling condition for the postwar incorporation of South Korea and other Asian postcolonies into the promise of Pax Americana.

Ninotchka Rosca's Blurred Boundaries of the State

In many ways, Ninotchka Rosca is another exemplary Third World dissident writer. Born in 1946, and roughly the same generation as Kim Chi-ha, she attended the University of the Philippines. As Marcos tightened his grip in the late 1960s and early '70s, his regime "launched one of the largest government media operations in Asia."[186] Immediately after Marcos declared martial law in 1972 (just weeks before Park Chung Hee would dissolve the South Korean legislature), the arrests of news and television journalists on the grounds of "communist infiltration" began en masse, with a number of media outlets closed for good and "4,500 employees of the print media and 3,500 of the broadcast media" losing their jobs.[187] To control the media, Marcos established his own National Media Trust "modelled after a similar body in Indonesia."[188] Rosca was imprisoned for her anti-government writings in 1973, and spent six months in Camp Crame, where torture was not uncommon. In the years following her detention, she lived in exile first in Hawai'i and then in New York. As mentioned above, she published her scathing novel of the Marcos dictatorship, *State of War*, in 1988, basing some of her characters on her 1983 short story collection, *The Monsoon Collection*, conceived during her imprisonment. Rosca would write another novel more directly indicting the dictator, *Twice Blessed*, in 1992, and remain committed to the cause of writerly free speech in her activist work. While based in New York, she has made a name as a respected literary and human rights activist, especially in her role as founder of the GABRIELA network, a Philippine–U.S. women's solidarity group, which works to stop the trafficking of women.[189] From 1991 to 1995 she served on the Board of Trustees of the New York–based PEN America Center, along with such literary luminaries as Allen Ginsberg, John Irving, E. L. Doctorow, and fellow Filipina Jessica Hagedorn, while Salman Rushdie served as honorary vice president. A *New York Times* article of January 24, 1996, even cites her objection to proposed changes to PEN America's membership rules that would have allowed non-writers (read donors) to join.[190] Her protest letter, ironically enough, appears to have been censored by the Center.

Unlike Pramoedya and Kim, who achieved international recognition because of their imprisonment, Rosca's case garnered no special media attention, perhaps because of the relatively brief period of incarceration and her subsequent exile. A 1984 *New York Times* review of the *Monsoon Collection*, nevertheless, opines that its nines stories "seem fringed by barbed wire,"[191] confirming the major motifs of the genre of "persecuted literature" discussed earlier. Rosca's Anglophone work, however, is recognized as "writing within the [Philippine] radical-nationalist tradition as a feminist activist,"[192] and she has also been canonized within U.S.-based Asian American studies as an exemplary exilic writer. Scholars of the latter field have noted that Philippine writing in the United States departs from the more established Asian American thematics of immigration, assimilation, and the U.S. nation precisely because of "the vagaries of the (neo)colonial U.S.–Philippines relationship,"[193] a topic well explored by Rosca. For these reasons, we can read her as part of "a literature of exile and emergence rather than a literature of immigration and settlement."[194] Moreover, in Rosca's work, "the return to the homeland is not the return to paradise, utopia, or precolonial purity,"[195] and her writings can be characterized as an ongoing feminist engagement with the violent legacies of colonialism and neocolonialism in Philippine politics, history, and identity. In placing Rosca alongside Pramoedya and Kim Chi-ha, I wish to read her work as part of a larger Asia-Pacific archive of literary critiques of Cold War authorities. In particular, I use her fiction to think about postcolonial state-formation and literary form in a way that again complicates tropes of pure artistic opposition against a generic Third World or Soviet authoritarianism. It is with these questions in mind that I read Rosca's *State of War*, with its action-packed account of the resistance movement opposing the Marcos state (though he is never named other than as "The Commander"). If the preceding sections sought to complicate historical allegory and political satire as two dominant genres for reading autocracy, how might we reread a novel usually understood within the category of resistance literature?

The novel's main story is set on an unnamed island during a religious festival and eventually culminates in an attempted armed uprising against the
regime. The festival—modeled on the Ati-Atihan festival held in the province
of Aklan—provides the background for a dizzying, carnivalesque three-day
intermingling of locals, visitors, tourists, transgender people, revolutionaries,
and soldiers, focalized through the relationship between three young protagonists: the serious revolutionary and widow, Anna Villaverde; the beautiful
and fickle Eliza Hansen; and Adrian Banyaga, the son and heir of a wealthy
Manila industrialist family. Drawing syncretically on native and Catholic elements, Rosca's festival has been read as an exemplary site of oppositional culture: Myra Mendible notes that the carnivalesque festival functions as both
"literary and political device," and "hints at the prospect of revolution."[196] In a
similar vein, Rocio G. Davis understands Rosca's work as reflecting a subversive "literary repossession of homeland and its history."[197] Yet the novel complicates the simple affirmation of resistance culture against the state by
providing a very different kind of narrative as well. It is, in fact, formally composed of three separate books: Books One and Three follow the festival's political and personal dramas, while Book Two is a self-contained 200-page historical
novel that simultaneously gives us the ancestral genealogies of the three protagonists and the prehistory of the Marcos regime itself.[198]

Titled "The Book of Numbers," Book Two's long historical narrative begins
in the waning years of the Spanish colonial era and carries us through the
short-lived Philippine revolution (1896–98), the subsequent invasion by and
war with the new Yanqui colonizers (1898–1903), the Japanese occupation of
World War II (1942–45), and the Huk Uprising and American-sponsored counterinsurgency campaigns of the early post-independence years. Throughout,
Rosca's controlling literary theme is that of conflict and survival; indeed, four
hundred years of Philippine history appear here as one extended, interminable
"state of war." While the first and third books—with their biblical-sounding
titles "The Book of Acts" and "The Book of Revelations"—are set over a mere
three-day period of the festival, the middle "Book of Numbers" covers about
one hundred years of history. I am thus interested in how we might read what
Pheng Cheah has called the novel's "heterotemporality"[199]—its disjunctive
narrative temporality—as a complex articulation of the formation of the postcolonial present. I suggest that the inextricability of historical and contemporary struggles is formally staged by the structure of the novel itself: It is a
bifurcated or hybrid novel that wants simultaneously to be a tale of revolutionary immediacy and a plodding family saga; a book of anti-dictatorship
political urgency and the historical *longue durée* of repressive rule. The very
melding of literary genres, with their alternately stretched and compressed

temporalities, is what I see as one of the main achievements of *State of War*: the formal attempt to explain the constitution of the present authoritarian state by reaching back into history to unveil its complex temporalities and entanglements. This demands we read the novel in ways other than for its well-discussed aesthetics of resistance.

As touched upon at the beginning of this chapter, such habits of reading for resistance are due partly, at least, to the formation of postcolonial studies and its foundational interest in exemplary anti-colonial struggles, nationalist constructions, and subversive hybrid identities. If the field does not subscribe to a notion of liberal freedoms along the lines of Amnesty or PEN, it has nevertheless been informed by the long tradition of reading artists in opposition to states. A deep interest in reading and writing against colonial dictatorships is exemplified in the large body of work on resistance and prison literatures. Starkly at odds with Amnesty International's avowedly liberal, cosmopolitan, and anti-communist approach, Barbara Harlow's scholarship on protest literatures has been particularly influential. Perhaps best known for her concept of "resistance literature" from her influential 1987 study, Harlow's oeuvre made visible activist writers from a number of Third World political contexts, including the Kenyan liberation struggle against the British, South Africa's anti-apartheid movement, the Palestinian fight for sovereignty, and Latin American dictatorships. In contrast to Amnesty or PEN's minimalist conception of the right to free expression, for Harlow, literature's purchase on the political is decidedly "maximal." Literature is nothing less than "an arena of *struggle*"[200] integral to the larger liberation movements, and possesses the power to indict, analyze, and combat colonial oppression while "reconstructing . . . the history of the relation of power between [what have] been variously designated as First and Third worlds."[201] Poetry and narratives produced within these movements evidence "their manifold role as historical documents, ideological analyses and visions of future possibilities produced out of the contemporary struggle against oppression."[202]

We must credit Harlow's pioneering work for renewed scholarly interest in what Lazarus calls "the centrality of the category of resistance in anti-colonial nationalist literature."[203] Nevertheless, despite the radical leanings of Harlow and the consequential body of work inspired by her, there is a curious alignment between Harlow's "resistance writer" and the liberal "prisoner of conscience." In both approaches, the primary adversary remains the undifferentiated state. In her readings of prison literature in *Barred: Women, Writing, and Political Detention* (1992), Harlow collates a number of influential works and genres that "translate protest against torture into a demand for a collective political accounting."[204] Analyzing the reports produced by

Amnesty International, Harlow describes torture as the "failure of governments to exercise their legal responsibilities to prevent it."[205] The task of "writing human rights," then, is to resist "tyranny and oppression" of those
"governments that once signed the [UDHR] declaration."[206] Although figuring literature as maximally endowed with political agency, Harlow's writing
resistance, akin to Amnesty's "two-person drama," presumes a clear moral and
political boundary between the "state machine of terror"[207] and the writing
subject of resistance.

As with my discussion of Amnesty and PEN, it is not my aim to deny the
"centrality of resistance" in the literary genres powerfully brought to light by
Harlow, or its important influence on much postcolonial scholarship. I aim to
point out, simply, that in postcolonial studies, literatures of freedom or resistance often turn on the figuring of an unproblematic state sovereignty as the
object against which they constitute themselves, with little theoretical distinction between colonial and postcolonial dictatorships.[208] How, I ask, might
such texts interrogate the uneven reproduction of oppressive rule itself and
depict *other* forms of authority—economic, bipolar, religious, gendered,
racial—that both align with and confound what we are typically quick to recognize as "the state machine of terror"? We can usefully enrich our discussion
of dissident writers and oppressive states through the substantial body of work
on non-Western state-formations from the field of anthropology. Resonating
with David Scott's work discussed earlier in the book, Akhil Gupta has identified the ways the so-called "backward" nature of postcolonial states is seen
to be eternally deficient.

> In many analyses of what was *lacking* in the postcolonial state . . . [at
> fault is] the failure to construct adequately the boundary between state
> and society: The state was permeated by society and failed to remain
> autonomous and sovereign; or society was dominated by the state and
> unable to constitute an environment for civil society to flourish. . . .
> By this yardstick, non-Western states would always be deficient.[209]

In this account, the correct "boundary between state and society" is an ahistorical gauge for reaffirming the transcendent liberal values of autonomy and
sovereignty, a version of which we see in the Western Cold War emphasis on
the noninterference of political ideology into the sphere of art.[210] In contrast,
Gupta provocatively theorizes the "blurred boundaries" that characterize
many of the world's states. Furthermore, he suggests that in order for states
to work they must be actively constructed through symbolic and discursive
representations as well as in everyday practices.[211] In that sense, they are akin
to Benedict Anderson's well-known "imagined communities" of the nation

(1983).[212] However, whereas for Anderson, print culture and notions of homogenous time help us to imagine a "we," the state most often is figured more ambiguously, as both us *and* not us. Following insights from Gupta and others, I suggest we read literature on postcolonial authoritarianism as not merely concerned with representing and critiquing those given immutable, discrete structures of state power. With its competing and contested stories of the state, *State of War* less depicts a dramatic "fall" into some recognizable state tyranny to be resisted, and more the uneven reworkings of colonial modes of extraction and accumulation, reconstituted to serve the new priorities of the Cold War postcolonial state. The Marcos state is therefore not only to be understood in vertical relation to its subjects of resistance. Rather, its decentralized and porous bureaucratic infrastructure, military and militias, landowning and political elite, and entanglements with foreign powers constitute a complex and shifting site of struggle as both idea and practical arena.[213] In short, if Rosca presents the violence of the Philippine state as repetition and entanglement, she does so by simultaneously entangling familial, social, state and interstate authorities. Crystal Parikh has argued that "the family saga is never simply about the heroics or fortunes of an individual protagonist, not even the paterfamilias; rather it concerns the reproduction and status of a family line," and is a genre that " intrinsically situates its characters in a social world."[214] I therefore read *State of War* less as novel of resistance or work of dissident literature—in which resistance and complicity are clearly demarcated—but as a literary interrogation into the *reproductive capacity* of certain state and non-state arrangements. The family saga is the narrative form for such an investigation.

Let me work through these claims more closely. At one level, *State of War* depicts the straightforward inheritance and longevity of repressive colonial state forms with an emphasis on military violence and gendered torture. Thus, we understand scenes of sexual abuse in the Marcos-era narrative "as a continuation of the sexual violence set in motion by the [Spanish] colonizers"[215] rather than an innovation of that dictatorship. *State of War* also vividly reveals that the brutal techniques of military counterinsurgency go back to the first Philippine–American war, famously described by Mark Twain as a conflict in which "thirty thousand killed a million."[216] Yet Book Two's drawn-out family saga complicates the notion of inheritance as merely the aftereffects of colonial governance. During the postwar anti-communist suppression of the PKP (Partido Komunista ng Pilipinas)-led Huk rebellion, U.S. "anticommunism dovetailed with elites' efforts to recover power and control over the countryside,"[217] laying the ground for Marcos's vehemently anti-leftist regime. Moreover, "U.S. aid and advisors helped establish the infrastructure for martial rule, and it is not unlikely that the CIA recruited and trained Filipino officers in torture techniques."[218] The results are graphically narrated in scenes of the torture of Anna Villaverde by the repulsive Colonel Amor. Such scenes alert us to the very limits of a liberal model of reading that would condemn the human rights abuses of the Marcos regime without understanding its conditions of possibility within both colonial and bipolar histories. The novel thus places the time of the autocratic postcolonial state within a larger historical and transnational frame, squarely acknowledging "the role of former empires in what a nation [and I would add, a *state*] can become."[219]

The plot of Book Two revolves around Maya, first introduced as "a dark, Malayan girl with an acacia tree's sturdiness,"[220] who becomes the mistress of a Capuchin friar and later matriarch of an industrialist family in Manila. In contrast to the explicit binaries of the Marcos-era narrative—state violence versus the festival's oppositional politics—the middle book's extended historical narrative offers a less clear-cut model of both political agency and the boundaries of the state. In the long chronicle of colonization, abuse, and repression that characterizes the archipelago, we are unable to name who is complicit and who represents resistance. Moreover, we see that sexual unions and unconventional kinship structures result in reconfigurations of state or state-like authority, which often blend official, religious, gendered and economic power. This is largely narrated through character and family lineage. Maya's elevation to the ambiguous position of "priest's whore," for example, effects such a shift. Being "both in the center of and yet outside the half-pagan, half-Catholic society,"[221] she attains a certain degree of independence and autonomy:

> Perched on the driver's seat of her caleche, her tiny hands with wrists of iron controlling the palpable power of her black horse, her small, hard body with its mahogany skin costumed in an extravagant embroidered blouse of woven pineapple fiber . . . her lips clasped about the lighted end of a brown cigarillo, she drew in her wake men, women, and children who stared at, ran after, and hailed her passing, calling her witch, whore, saint, patroness, insane. She would stop at intersections and accept rolled-up petitions from peasants, petitions which, for a coin or two, she promised to bring to the attention of the proper saint, prodding the statue with whip lashes every twilight until the request was granted.[222]

It is precisely Maya's uncertain status as "witch, whore, saint, patroness" that allows her to mediate between the peasants and the colonial authority of the Catholic Church. Her function is neither simply collaborative nor straightforwardly oppositional. While she clearly defies gendered and racialized norms, the narrative goes on to reveal that "the peasants somehow inverted her idea of coercing the holy powers and began flagellating themselves instead"—a practice that her descendant Anna Villaverde will later witness at a "festival confused by time and history."[223]

After the friar's death, Maya rises to middle-class respectability in early twentieth-century Manila by negotiating both Spanish legacies and the new American occupation. Her son Carlos Lucas, a successful gin distiller, ponders joining the American-installed political system with the rationale, "I'm rich. . . . That's the only requirement."[224] We eventually follow the next generation of the family now focalized through a renewed mother-son dyad of Mayang (Carlos Lucas's Chinese-Malay wife) and her son Luis Carlos, who makes his name as a composer and musician entertaining Manila's American and Americanized elite. After the rapid retreat of the U.S. in the face of Japanese imperial aggression, Luis Carlos will spend the war as a guerrilla soldier fighting the occupation; he survives, but his mother Mayang is killed after she follows him into the jungle. Finally, and despite his own experience as a guerrilla fighter, Luis Carlos is recruited by the murderous American colonel "Mad Uncle Ed" and works for the postwar U.S. counterinsurgency operation against the communist-led Hukbalahap peasant movement.[225]

Luis Carlos's status thus echoes the ambivalent agency of his grandmother, Maya. As the only product of his mother's illicit affair with the German chemist Hans Zangroniz (later rechristened Chris Hansen, and ancestor of Eliza Hansen), he is presented as Book Two's most sympathetic and sensitive character: earnest, rational, and preternaturally mature for his age. His artistic passion and disinterest in worldly gain is significant, I suggest, in that it borrows from the trope of the autonomous artist who stands outside, or in opposition to, official power structures. And yet Luis Carlos's allegiances are as hard to define as his bloodline—a mix of native, Spanish, Chinese, and German. His subsequent success—culminating in a grand performance for Manila's elite—is aided by his romantic connection to a beautiful "Eurasian chanteuse,"[226] mistress of the American military governor. A similarly ambivalent character appears in the figure of the Banyaga patriarch, whose name means "foreigner" or "stranger" in Tagalog. Another descendant of the friar who collaborates with the Spanish and the Americans in putting down the Philippine resistance, he eventually becomes a powerful business magnate and the patriarch of Adrian Banyaga's family line. Nevertheless, in a nostalgic gesture of anti-imperialist nationalism, the patriarch "goes up and down the archipelago buying all this relicary"[227] and memorabilia from the 1896 Philippine Revolution. We also have Anna's friend Eliza Hansen who, due to her relationship with a powerful general, sets up "office" in the coffee shop of the

Intercontinental Hotel and playfully undertakes an array of state functions, including the whimsical, if disastrous, mismatching of personnel to government posts.[228] In all these figures, Rosca complicates "the traditional figure of resistance as a subject who stands outside the state and refuses its demands."[229] The lines demarcating the state's inside and outside, (artistic) autonomy and complicity, are simply too difficult to map. If we are determined to find it, pure revolutionary subjectivity is attributed only to the peasants who fight instinctively against expropriating forces at every turn, but whose consciousness largely lies at the edges of the novel. Thus, rather than offer a lineage of the authentic Philippine national resistance that opposes the state (and which a number of other Marcos-era novels do, especially in vernacular languages),[230] the tripartite structure of *State of War* serves as the literary genre that *links* the contemporary Cold War state apparatus to various historically produced subject positions, whose interests are neither exclusively collaborative nor inherently resistant. As Nerferti Tadiar has pointed out, Marcos's "emergent crony capitalist state" depended on a social basis that was "comprised of practices of living and modes of subjectivity forged under conditions of post- and neocolonialism that are not easily categorized in terms of outright resistance or domination."[231]

A rethinking of the state in Rosca's novel helps us address the stubborn interpretive problem I have been grappling with throughout this chapter: the figuring of Third World authoritarianism beyond the monolithic, tyrannical police state and its human rights abuses. In this regard, and echoing Kim's satire of developmentalist logic, *State of War* reveals the less spectacular but more pervasive—perhaps even more "democratic"— violence effected for the reproduction of another Cold War transpacific capitalism. In a strikingly satirical scene during Book One's depiction of the festival, the town hall is temporarily converted into a conference center with a gathering of "businessmen, industrialists, intellectuals from all regions of the country" who come to debate national interests and development.[232] One of Eliza's mismatched government employees summarizes the state's economic logic in flawless bureaucratese: "The strategic intervention of authoritarian democratic bureaucratism . . . could hasten the trajectory of the critical path of implementation of development plans."[233] When a local resident points out the lack of available land, complaining that "there's barely enough space to bury a corpse,"[234] the bureaucrat promptly offers a solution: "The roots of our quandary lie in the tradition of encrypting remains horizontally. Astute re-education of our populace on the desirability of vertical burial can be a major step toward resolution of the problem."[235] What emerges as both authoritarian and ridiculous is the discourse of capitalist development as an unquestioned good.[236]

Indeed, as we've seen with other regional leaders, Marcos strenuously affirmed the link between development and authoritarian rule, even defining development as a "weapon" in meeting "internal subversion—the main threat.'"[237] Like Indonesia and South Korea and other "Asian Tigers," the Marcos economy was funded by huge flows of foreign investment and U.S. military loans. The country's historically weak bureaucracy, its reliance on agricultural exports, as well as Marcos's channeling of profits to his patronage network would, however, stymie its ability to grow on the model of the other export-oriented Tigers. Turning on its head the usual cause and result relation, Robert Stauffer has argued that the implementation of such a "transnational accumulation strategy" in the Philippines effectively *required* an authoritarian state.[238] Indeed, one "New Society" slogan would be "For the development of the Nation, discipline is necessary."[239] Explicitly enacted under the logic of national progress, Marcos's "New Society" poured money into those shiny signifiers of modernization—"dams" and "hydroelectric stations,"[240]—even as workers and peasants became poorer. Rosca's scenes of daring revolutionary resistance thus jockey with a canny satirical narrative mode to present a fuller picture of the state and the way it authorizes itself through both repression and the everyday discourse of development. She pokes fun at the Commander's men "who together and singly have decided to speak in four-syllable words . . . so that a new troop of servants had to be created to tote dictionaries."[241] In this way, the novel mocks bureaucratic developmentalism in order to portray the diffuse forms of violence that occur in its name. *State of War* goes beyond the depiction of the illiberal state apparatus overstepping its boundaries to figure the mutually enabling authorities of state and capital.

Such a figuring of the state as an ongoing and uneven process of accumulation strategies is precisely the "state of war" that the novel depicts. As we've seen, such entanglements are narrated via elements of the family saga, focusing on blood lines, racial mixing, inheritances, and progeny. In the final section of the novel, the revelry of the festival culminates in a bomb attack aimed at the Commander's entourage—"the Festival flung itself at the bus"[242]—inciting a brutal counterattack in which two of the three young protagonists are casualties: Eliza is killed, and Adrian seriously wounded.[243] Managing to escape, Anna Villaverde alone retreats to a peaceful and remote village, where she teaches the village children and listens to tape recordings of the rebel leader, the aptly named Guevarra. In the last pages of the novel, she prepares to give birth to her son, "the first of the Capuchin monks to be born innocent, without fate,"[244] presumably conceived during the festival with Adrian Banyaga. The narrative thus gestures to a future allegorized by Anna's unborn

baby, who will "be nurtured as much by her milk as by the archipelago's leg-
ends."[245] Despite the cycle of atrocities the novel has narrated, *State of War*
concludes by offering a profound figure of a biological reproduction that has
the potential to disrupt political reproduction.

In Rosca's telling, then, the authoritarian state is both genealogical—it
bears the imprint of colonial and kinship power structures—and generative,
that is, it is constantly reproduced anew in novel combinations of power. The
Marcos state is thus a "new configuration of both long-established rules and
recent innovations of practice."[246] And although certain characterizations con-
form to the binaries of ruthless state power (Mad Uncle Ed) and the committed hero of resistance (Anna Villaverde), in between these two extremes—and
taking up much more narrative space—are more typical and compromised
modes of agency. Echoing Pramoedya's narrative logic, Rosca's formal experimentation with temporality and historiography locates authoritarianism
firmly in the processes of reproduction of certain state and non-state authorities. The porous boundaries of the state precipitate uneven material, religious,
and genetic forms of authority. Via the historicizing and formalist reading it
demands, Rosca's bifurcated novel demonstrates how the expropriative logic
of the colonial state is reformed and recomposed in the Cold War–decolonizing conjuncture. Most profoundly, the novel reveals how the state cannot be
narrated *without* reproduction—of biological life, of bureaucracy, and of capitalism—at its center. In opening up the question of writing the state from one
of self-evident "resistance" against an already constituted tyranny, the critical
task has shifted from identifying scenes of imprisonment, torture, or state surveillance to the ways in which reproduction, inheritance, and genealogy
become active sites of struggle.

Conclusion

The Cold War literary imagination has often used the monolithic construct
of the repressive communist or Third World state against which to figure free
speech, individual rights, and tutelary democracy as its antidotes. "Solzhenitsyn" was the easiest shorthand for this model of reading. For all three exemplary Cold War dissident writers examined in this chapter, the postcolonial
capitalist-developmental state demands a different representational logic,
moving us beyond the "two-person drama" of transcendent artist versus
police state. In a nonfiction piece, Ninotchka Rosca has written of the twin
justifications "constantly used by [the Philippine] government": "economic
recovery and counterinsurgency. The two are both goal and process."[247]
Indeed, *State of War* prompts a new reckoning of postcolonial autocracy by

showing us the *longue durée* of these intertwined processes, and how they are
reproduced anew by different historical regimes. Through his scandalous satires, Kim's poetry breaks open the way colonial rule is resuscitated and revived
by forced Cold War alliances; that is, while Korean sovereignty is indefinitely
deferred, a U.S.- and Japanese-brokered transpacific capitalism is massively
expanded. Pramoedya, meanwhile, deploys a tale of police surveillance not to
lionize the dissident figure it targeted, but to retrieve as many possible political
alternatives to Suharto's regime as can be imagined. We are thus reminded
that authoritarianism is not the political antonym of the liberal capitalist
state (embodied, of course, in the U.S.), but is eminently capable of pulling
various kinds of authority—military, economic, religious, patriarchal—into its
service.[248]

My aim in such readings has been twofold. First is to better understand
how our reading practices around dissident literature and the state have been
forged, and subsequently congealed, by the long Cold War. Second, if we
"perceive the state less as art's habitual antagonist—the sovereign that censors
and bans, imprisons and exiles,"[249] my wager is that we can better make visible
the specific conditions and possibilities that obtain at the crossroads of decolonizing desires, Cold War securitization, and domestic dictatorship. Closer
comparative attention to such literary forms and genres may help us move
beyond the undifferentiated Cold War notion of a totalitarian state and its
"dissident literature," as well as a postcolonial longing for pure resistance.

I now leave the cultural works and debates of the Cold War period proper
and turn, in the following three chapters, to the ways the period's conflicts and
struggles remain embedded in our neoliberal, post–Cold War present. If "the
Cold War is the afterlife of colonialism,"[250] what are the afterlives of Cold War
decolonization?

PART II

Genres of Cold War Reckoning,
1997–2017

3
Separate Futures
Other Times of Southeast Asian Decolonization

Decolonization, Separation, Time

In the previous two chapters, we saw how tensions over Asia-Pacific decolonization were inexorably entangled with Cold War bipolarities, precipitating vexed debates during the 1960s and '70s around the role of literature in relation to freedom, revolution, authoritarianism, sovereignty, and solidarity. In moving to Part 2 of the book, we shift our attention to retrospective accounts of the decolonizing–Cold War conjuncture produced between the late 1990s and 2017. In each of the next three chapters, I explore the way writers and filmmakers cast their eye back to authoritarian regimes of an earlier era in order to critique sedimented—often triumphant—narratives of material progress, as well as to work through the relationship of such pasts to our ostensibly post–Cold War present.

There are various contexts and motivations for such a looking back. Authors of an older generation such as Mohamed Latiff Mohamed (born 1950, examined in this chapter) and Hwang Sŏk-yŏng (born 1943, addressed in Chapter 4) witnessed decolonization and the violence of Cold War fracturing firsthand. While their accounts are often informed by their personal experiences, they write with a backward interpretive glance that seeks to make sense of this complex era after the official end of the Cold War. By contrast, a younger generation of cultural producers, such as Singaporean novelist Jeremy Tiang, came of age after the years of decolonization and are "looking back at the past and questioning where we've come from, and maybe questioning the official narrative."[1] Even though topics such as Singapore's political repression and use of indefinite detention have had prior representation, those were "often couched in the language of victimhood," while there was little "investigation of the systemic oppression [and] . . . how this might be a continuation of colonial oppression."[2] The works I examine by Tiang and Sonny Liew (in this chapter), Tan Pin Pin, Joshua Oppenheimer, and Han Kang (in Chapters 4 and 5) constitute a retrospective accounting of "free world" authoritarianism by this younger generation of post–Cold War artists.

Whereas writers' conferences and dissident literature of a bipolarizing world were the focus of the first two chapters, this chapter considers novels loosely structured as *Bildungsromane*, or "novels of formation," to probe one of the major historical motifs of decolonization: separation. In postcolonial studies, the bloody 1947 Partition which produced India and Pakistan is probably the best-known (and most studied) of these fractures, exemplifying the contradictions inherent in the transition from multiethnic empires to postcolonial nation-states. Other divisions in Asia—especially North and South Korea; North and South Vietnam; the PRC on the Mainland and KMT-held Taiwan—would soon come to embody new kinds of contradictions, echoing both the partitioned subcontinent and divided Germany. While a large number of studies (especially in Area Studies) have examined these more visible geopolitical divisions, in this chapter I read three retrospective fictional narratives that look back at how the global Cold War intersected with decolonization in the case of the complex fracturing and suturing of Singapore and Malaya/Malaysia.[3] Beginning with Mohamed Latiff Mohamed's 1997 fictionalized memoir centered on the Singaporean Malay community, *Confrontation* (*Batas Langit*, or The sky's the limit, 1997), the chapter then examines Jeremy Tiang's *State of Emergency* (2017), which recounts the drama of decolonization through a multigenerational family story against the background of the Malayan Emergency. Finally, I turn to Sonny Liew's graphic novel *The Art of Charlie Chan Hock Chye* (2016), a metafictional critique of Singapore's transformation from colonial port city to gleaming "first world oasis."

The chapter is primarily interested in how Mohamed Latiff's, Tiang's, and Liew's novels reveal decolonization, as it unfolded under the emerging pressures of the Cold War, to be less a neutral historical marker of territorial separation and more a complex spatial and temporal opening. My thinking is influenced by Gary Wilder's exploration of the conjoined "problem of freedom and the politics of time" in his study of anti-colonial thought and the end of the French empire. In his book *Freedom Time*, Wilder argues against the typical "understanding of time as a neutral medium within which history takes place" and instead treats it as a "productive historical force of its own."[4] In her theorization of political transformation, which Wilder draws on, Hannah Arendt has stressed the "hiatus . . . between liberation from the old order

and the new freedom . . . between a no-more and a not-yet."[5] Bhakti Shringarpure has also forwarded a careful rethinking of time and Cold War decolonization in her book *Cold War Assemblages*. There she argues for the "triple
bind of time" that formerly colonized populations face: first, the "pre-historic,
anterior" time of colonial rule; then the "urgent, emergent" time of decolonization; and finally the Cold War's "temporal ruptures, meant to stymie the
birth of independent nations."[6]

I suggest that the three texts examined in this chapter open up this time of
the "no-more," the "not-yet," and the "triple bind" to critical scrutiny. Together,
they recover a range of anticipated, liberatory futures—Malay, communist,
and liberal—that would soon be overshadowed by Singapore's capitalist
authoritarian path under the People's Action Party (PAP). The texts are of
interest precisely because of their sustained backward glances from *after* the
apparent conclusion of the Cold War, aesthetic gazes that reappraise and
reinspect those multiple times of decolonization that have been disavowed in
the nation's march to progress. Rather than present decolonization as merely
the "exit narrative" of the colonizer,[7] these works address the time between the
"no-longer" of colonization and the "not-yet" of independence. Such time is
enlarged, stretched out, and held open to alternative significance. I read *Confrontation*, *State of Emergency*, and *Charlie Chan* as offering accounts of
decolonization as a multilayered struggle over the terms of separation and the
possible futures thereby made possible or impossible. Narratives of postcolonial separation and independence thus offer revised accounts of postcolonial
state-formation not simply by critiquing the afterlives of colonial epistemes,
but as processes in which once-imaginable futures were actively fought for
against bipolar realignment and reincorporation.

To be sure, these are very different novels. They emerge from a complex
milieu of multilingual and multigeneric cultural production, and are certainly not the first representations of the trials of Singapore's and Malaya's
decolonization.[8] Mohamed Latiff Mohamed, born in 1950 and educated in
Singapore, is one of the country's most established and respected Malay-
language poets, novelists, and educators. A three-time winner of the Singapore Literature Prize (for poetry and short fiction), he has actively promoted
Malay literature and culture during his long career. In addition to numerous
works of poetry, he is the author of other works centered on the Malay experience in Singapore, including *The Widower* (*Ziarah Cinta*, 1998), and the short
story collection *Lost Nostalgia* (*Nostalgia yang hilang*, 2004). Our two other
authors, also winners of the prestigious Singapore Literature Prize, are Anglophone authors and of a younger generation, as mentioned above. Prior to his
debut novel *State of Emergency* of 2017, Jeremy Tiang, born in 1977 and of

mixed Chinese and Sri Lankan background, published short fiction and worked extensively as a translator of Chinese literature, translating novels by Wong Yoon Wah, Zhang Yueran, Yeng Pway Ngon, and Su Wei-chen. Sonny Liew, born in 1974, grew up in Malaysia, studied in Singapore, the UK, and in the U.S., and (like Tiang) had Singapore government arts funding for *The Art of Charlie Chan Hock Chye* withdrawn due to its sensitive political content. The graphic novel went on to win the Singapore Literature Prize in 2016 as well as several Eisner Awards. Despite their differences, I argue that all three texts uproot sedimented historical narratives by exploring the dialectics of separation that attend liberation. At the literary level, they do this by foregrounding the conjuncture of youth, decolonization, and futurity. By offering greater complexity both to the *Bildungsroman* narrative form and to postcolonial renderings of the dependent/independent nation, these texts figure the temporal stakes of bipolar decolonization and show how the latter reactivates colonial "genres of rule."[9] In this chapter, therefore, I continue to think about how the Cold War was not just an ideological standoff between superpowers but a (Third) world-making project, and to consider literature's role in complicating existing representations of such worldings.

Nusantara, or Wholeness

In one of the most memorable scenes of Mohamed Latiff's *Confrontation*, members of a Malay political party meet to discuss strategies for the upcoming General Elections of 1959, which would allow Singapore its own elected parliament for the first time (ahead of formal independence with the merger with Malaysia in 1963). The party leader, Pak Ariff, expresses his vision of an expanded Malay state that would supersede the humiliating fragmentation of the colonial era and find its rightful place at the UN:

> We want a bigger state for the entire Malay archipelago, the Nusantara. We have been divided for too long, chopped to pieces. We have been slashed off like a tree branch. We want to join our biological siblings again. We oppose the separation imposed on us by the colonisers. We want the Nusantara flag to flutter all over the world. We want our language, the language that is spoken by hundreds of millions of people, to be recognised and respected, to be spoken at the UN. That is our manifesto.[10]

Using the traditional Malay word for the archipelago, *Nusantara*, Pak Ariff expresses his desires through the metaphor of a tree that has been unnaturally severed. The choice of figure confirms Pheng Cheah's observations on the

way postcolonial national imaginaries frequently assume an organicized concept of culture (the "tree branch") as that which can best overcome individual
finitude and project society into the future.[11] Separation and unification are
thus dialectical terms at decolonization. If independence is typically sought
through the detachment or separation from the colonizers—the very process
that transforms the colony into a sovereign nation—it is simultaneously conceived as a suturing force that will make the hitherto fragmented colonized
polity whole once more. On closer inspection, this suturing has two dimensions: that of territorial/ethnic restoration after the departure of the colonizers,
and that of the organic realignment *between* a people and a state.

In terms of the first, we can bear in mind that for most of the colonial
period Singapore and Malaya were administered by the British through a variety of legal and territorial entities—Singapore as part of the Straits Settle-
ments, along with Malacca, Penang, and Dindings—and the rest of Malaya
though the Federated and Unfederated Malay States. The 1824 Anglo-Dutch
treaty ensured the enduring formation of two separate colonial states: British
Malaya and the Dutch Indies. Large-scale immigration from China and the
Indian subcontinent, encouraged by the British, resulted in a multiethnic
colonial landscape. As in other former colonial territories, the resulting complexities and lack of ethnic-territorial isomorphism were legacies left for the
postcolonial state to resolve. Timothy Brennan has argued for a constitutive
asymmetry between modern European nationalisms and those of the postcolonial world: "If European nationalism was a project of unity on the basis of
conquest and economic expediency, insurgent or popular nationalism [of the
Third World] . . . is for the most part a project of consolidation *following an
act of separation* from Europe. It is a task of *reclaiming community* from within
boundaries defined by the very power whose presence denied community."[12]
In terms of the second dimension—the suturing of the gap between the state
and the people—Odd Arne Westad has noted that

> the colonial state was always the representative of the imperial center
> and of the colonists, never of any indigenous group, however collabo-
> rationist such a group may be. As such, the state therefore emerges as
> something extraneous to indigenous peoples, even at the elite level.
> The "foreignness" of the state led to a constant need for policing at
> all levels.[13]

These observations underscore the contradictory pushes and pulls of decolonization; at once an "act of separation" *from* Europe, it is also a process that
must reconcile and enfranchise divided multiethnic polities *within* the new
boundaries of the nation-state. Put otherwise, decolonization is tasked with

indigenizing the state and reconciling it to its hitherto alienated citizens. We must also recall how crucial separation was to the everyday governance of the colony, especially the division of racial and ethnic groups through labor. Under British colonial rule, Singapore and Malaya were governed as "racialized populations [who] were given cultural autonomy in religious and customary spheres, were assigned to different occupational roles and social spaces, and were encouraged to meet only in the market place."[14] In Singapore, "the lowest colonial jobs, such as postmen and rank and file policemen, went to some Malays."[15] On the peninsula, where the Chinese had long been merchants and traders, Chinese and Indian laborers worked as rubber tappers and miners in the lucrative imperial industries of rubber and tin mining, especially in the Kinta Valley; Malays, largely in *kampungs*, were entitled to some protected land on reservations and low-level government jobs.[16] The backward glance of *Confrontation*, I suggest, demonstrates how these dialectics of separation, reconciliation, and wholeness are profoundly complicated by the shift from a colonial to a bipolar power structure. Its portrayal of decolonization is one that crosshatches anti-imperial and bipolar struggles waged over territories, ethnic communities, ideologies, and—most importantly—futures.

But what would these futures look like? By the late 1950s and early '60s, and with a rising sense of the worldwide inevitability of decolonization, most believed that Singapore's and Malaya's independent futures would be closely tied. It is to this uncertain moment of separation and incorporation that Mohamed Latiff's *Confrontation* firmly returns us. A fictionalized memoir of childhood, the novel presents a social landscape undergoing radical transformation, elements of which are beyond the young protagonist's understanding but all too clear for the reader. Told through the naïve eyes of young Adi, *Confrontation* opens with an unflinching account of the hardships and personal tragedies that fill his working-class neighborhood of Kampung Pak Buyung in the 1950s at the end of British colonial rule. In assessing Mohamed Latiff's poignant rendering of this crucial moment in Singapore's history, Angelia Poon Mui Cheng has read the novel as offering contemporary readers "the fleeting glimpse of a different future in which Malays in Singapore would have been part of a majority in a larger country rather than a minority in a small nation-state."[17] *Confrontation* may be therefore read as a critical reflection on nationalist historiography and the contingent means by which majorities and minorities were decided.

Another way to read the novel's attention to localized violence and social decay is to understand it less as a childhood memoir of an authentic ethnic community—indeed Kampung Pak Buyung is ethnically mixed—than as an indictment of the colonial state, which is more or less absent for Adi and his neighbors. While Adi finds comfort climbing the old banyan tree at the village center, he and his community are continually beset by poverty and social dysfunction: alcoholism, opium addiction, gang violence, unwanted pregnancies, child abuse, incest, and madness. The state, indeed, is only present when police and ambulances arrive to arrest people or clean up the bodies after gang violence or murder. In other words, the novel quietly depicts the state's *absence* in any terms other than its disciplinary mode; local authorities provide little or no basic infrastructure, housing, health care, or personal security. In Gramscian terms, it may be understood as a version of the "night watchman" state, "whose functions are limited to the safeguarding of public order and respect for the laws."[18] The latter is usually thought of in opposition to Hegel's notion of the "ethical state," the "autonomous, educative and moral activity of the secular state."[19] Rather than a presentation of Malay culture as a discrete community undergoing the vicissitudes of decolonization, at stake in *Confrontation* is the portrayal of the minimalist colonial state and the alternative futures it incites. That is, the emphasis on poverty and social dysfunction instructs us on how to read the contrasting vectors of the novel: Adi's gradual political awakening and the contours of a possible decolonized Malay state imagined against both colonial rule and the escalating pressures of the Cold War.

In the social world of the novel, the project of reclaiming independence is largely articulated by Abang Dolah, Adi's politically active, educated neighbor and friend who refuses to work for the colonial state but teaches the Quran, plays music, and is a *bomoh* (witch doctor) on the side. Abang Dolah pins his hopes on a pro-Malay political party in the coming general elections, and it is through his hopes for decolonization that the growing tensions of the time are focalized. As we saw in the scene of the Malay political party, for Abang Dolah, Adi, and other Malays, the future postcolonial state is imagined as much more than the formal achievement of independence. The creation of an unalienated state based on territorial recovery is also the concrete means by which to redeem the specific social injustices experienced under negligent colonial rule. The political discussions incorporated into the novel disclose how anti-colonialism was expressed in collective desires for a state no longer "extraneous to" the people, as Westad puts it, but organically connected to them. For Malays especially, a recuperated Nusantara is what will restore the ethno-territorial wholeness destroyed by the colonizers. It is therefore not insignificant that a central pillar of Abang Dolah's resistance to the colonial state is his refusal to work for it despite his education level, as his autonomy over his labor marks him as relatively less alienated by colonial society. The obvious comparison is with Adi's own father, who embodies all the tragedies of colonial life: He works for a colonial shipyard painting boats but ensures the continued poverty of his family by gambling away most of his income. When he is rendered unable to work due to diabetes, his family is too poor to afford medical care and can only look on as he slowly dies. Abang Dolah, therefore, seems to be the one who is poised to lead Adi into a liberated, redeemed postcolonial future.

Adi's political interest, nurtured by Abang Dolah and Singapore's expected merger with Malaya (the latter which had gained independence in 1957), is awakened in part by the prospect of a new Malay-language secondary school in which he may move beyond the usual expectation of a seventh-grade education. Attending the school, his world opens as he reads Malay and Indonesian writers for the first time. As Siti Nuraishah Ahmad notes, "Adi's star rises with that of Malaysia—he is among the first batch of students to attend a Malay-medium secondary school, learning Malay language and literature, English, mathematics and science instead of the colonially-prescribed gardening and basket-weaving of the recent past."[20] Adi's expanded educational opportunities directly parallel the expanded horizons of greater postcolonial Malaysia. David Lloyd and Paul Thomas have noted the privileged role of the classroom for the reconciliation of culture and state, where "the teacher prefigures the role of the state as ultimate representative of ethical subjectivity."[21] Adi's new Malay-language high school exemplifies this function and constitutes the novel's clearest expression of a utopian, redemptive future as it will be actualized through a reconstituted Nusantara state. Where before he was, at best, indifferent to school, he now thrives in his new literature class and spends his spare time reading classics of Malay and Indonesian literature. Abang Dolah remarks, "How lucky for you Adi, to live in the Malaysian era."[22] Adi's expectations rise accordingly:

> Adi had heard that Singapore would become the "New York of Malaysia." It was planned that a national mosque would be erected at the Padang as a symbol of Islam and a united Malaysia. Adi was delighted. The grandest mosque ever built. It was all like a dream. He felt very fortunate, and as though he was in the midst of a great carnival. New campaigns and events such as "Malay Language Week" and "Malay Language Month" turned out to be fascinating. From trishaw pedallers to ministers, everyone raced to learn the language.[23]

Not only will Adi's future take place in a realignment of culture and state, but he imagines a remarkably syncretic future: A modern, cosmopolitan, Malay-speaking, Islamic Singapore will center a "united Malaysia." While less than the full recovery of Nusantara, the hitherto foreign colonial state is now the site of an ethical restoration of Malay wholeness, where linguistic and Islamic pride conjugates with capitalist modernity ("the New York of Malaysia"). Importantly, while a restored ethno-nationalism is here overlaid with a gleaming urban modernity, it is not the only political imaginary the novel alludes to. At the Malay political party meeting already mentioned, Pak Ariff, a representative of a leftist party, refuses the suggestions of an alliance with another party in part because "we want the working class to hold power; we want to distribute wealth equally. . . . They, on the other hand, worship capitalists."[24] He specifically blames the Malay feudal class for colluding with the British and selling out their brethren. What we see in these contestations is the range of competing, possible paths by which the postcolony will overcome the "foreignness" of the state via an imagined "ethical state." These various nations or states "of intent" include socialist desires for a restructuring of the colonial economy, territorial unification across the archipelago, participation in global governance and the UN, and expressions of Malay and Islamic nationalism.[25]

We may further scrutinize the question of a redemptive, decolonized state through the coming-of-age form, or *Bildungsroman*, of Mohamed Latiff's novel. In Franco Moretti's classic study of the European *Bildungsroman*, there are several salient aspects of the genre he calls the "'symbolic form' of modernity."[26] If, for Moretti, the European *Bildungsroman* arises because of the "hitherto unknown mobility" of subjects brought about by the "destabilizing forces of capitalism"[27] on traditional life forms, it would seem that the reorganization of societies at decolonization renders this genre more appropriate.[28] The genre's well-known "conflict between the ideal of *self-determination* and the equally imperious demands of socialization"[29] may take on an unavoidable geopolitical dimension of national allegory à la Jameson's famous essay: The trials of youthful protagonists stand in for nationalist struggles in tension with the demands of postwar global restructuring.[30] Or, more straightforwardly, the genre centers "postcolonial adolescents [who] occupy a new role not only as disillusioned rebels but also as embryonic citizens insisting on a [social] voice and a presence."[31] Most salient for my reading of *Confrontation* is the question of future reconciliation within the state. Interestingly, Moretti claims that the European version of the genre is particularly hostile or indifferent to questions of the state:[32] "The state," he explains, "embodies a 'mechanical' and 'abstract' form of social cohesion, intrinsically remote and foreign to the countless articulations of everyday life: this is why its exercise of power appears of necessity to be an outside coercion, a force inclined by its very nature to be arbitrary, violent."[33]

Moretti goes on to discuss the way (European) civil society possesses another kind of authority that "merges with everyday activities and relationships, exercising itself in ways that are natural and unnoticeable."[34] In other words, when the ethical state is doing its job correctly, the very boundary through which civil society articulates with it—and does some of its work—is unnoticeable. Conversely, we might argue that it is precisely the original lack of isomorphism between civil society and the colonial state that allows decolonizing imaginaries to question and experiment with the very boundary separating them.[35] Thus, the future Malay state imagined in *Confrontation* is a contested but potentially emancipatory force. Its founding involves the redrawing of state territory, as well as the state's own boundaries vis-à-vis society through the reorganization of the colonial economy, the re-centering of religion and Malay culture ("Malay Language Week"), and the overturning of colonial education policies. I argue that in the postcolonial *Bildungsroman*, contra Moretti, the protagonist's growth involves reimagining the state-society boundary itself as part of the movement from alienation to liberation.[36] As a consequence, in *Confrontation*, the state and its vicissitudes are the central organizers of plot and character development: The characters' fortunes literally rise and fall with the fate of the merger of the two former colonies. As we saw in Chapter 2, the postcolonial state is both "us" and "not us"; it is the foreign prosthesis *and* a potentially redeemable site of reconciliation. In emphasizing this ambiguity, the novel reveals the way the upheavals of bipolar decolonization prolong the "night watchman" function of the state as it responds to the Malayan Emergency and Indonesia's *Konfrontasi* (or low-level war) with anti-communist surveillance and repression.

Despite being a Malay nationalist and complaining of "wicked" communist instigators,[37] Abang Dolah is arrested during a purge of leftists, which we can assume to be Operation Cold Store of 1963, a crackdown Chua Beng Huat has called "the darkest episode in the history of Singapore's road to independence."[38] Abang Dolah is detained by the government's Special Forces, who repurposed the notorious colonial-era Internal Security Act (ISA) to allow for indefinite detention for suspected communists and radical nationalists. After being held without trial for months, he is forced to postpone his wedding with longtime partner Kak Habsah; when released, he is weakened, disillusioned, and newly religious. As Abang Dolah's health deteriorates due to cancer, the narrative follows a parallel trajectory in which the merger with Malaysia falls apart, Indonesia launches its *Konfrontasi* against the new state (perceived by Sukarno as a Western neocolonial construct), and race riots and instability result in the eventual separation of Singapore from the Union in 1965. Adi's world has already come tumbling down following the race riots of 1964, forcing him, his mother, and young adopted sister to move out of multiethnic Kampung Pak Buyung into an ethnically homogenous Malay neighborhood.

The shrinking of his world into a sterile block of concrete barrack houses echoes the population management tactics of New Villages (to be discussed shortly), as well as indexes the larger, geopolitical shrinkage that Singaporean Malays experienced. Fittingly, Abang Dolah dies along with the dream of a unified Malaysia.

The complex political turmoil of Singapore's and Malaya's decolonization—the Emergency, merger, anti-left purges, race riots, *Konfrontasi*, separation—are narrated partially and with great confusion by the young Adi. Even the usually politically savvy Abang Dolah finds it inexplicable that his anticolonial hero Sukarno and their Indonesian "siblings"[39] would attack Malaysia, and no reason for his own arrest and detention is ever determined, although we might surmise that his refusal to work renders him suspicious. But it is not, I contend, merely the limited communal tragedy or the misapplication of the ISA that is at stake. More important, the novel discloses the emergence of a political rationality based on the postcolonial state's pragmatic survival, rather than its radical transformation, in this new geopolitical matrix. For Singapore's PAP government, led for three decades by Lee Kuan Yew, the anticommunist purges would be equated to a "'life and death' struggle for the survival of the nascent island-nation."[40] In its view, the risk of a socialist future—or any future which did not see the nation-state as the articulation point with the global economic order—was no future at all. Abang Dolah's political desires and Adi's bright future in a recovered, unalienated lifeworld are all but foreclosed.

The result is that the continued "foreignness" of the colonial state is reproduced not only in terms of ethnic identity—the city-state will now be majority Chinese—but in terms of the state's very relationship to its citizens: Other social futures of Singapore are written out, whether communist or not, in the PAP's single-minded attempt to defend the nation's economic viability in a hostile region. Accordingly, by the end of the novel Adi's only option is to resume his place at the bottom of the racial division of labor. *Confrontation's* postcolonial *Bildungsroman* thus implies that there were not just communal winners and losers in the outcome of decolonization: the Chinese majority versus the Malay minority, or vice versa. It brings to light how the colonial state's disciplinary, or night watchman, functions are not overcome but deliberately reactivated by the postcolonial state to foreclose the possibility of alternative futures. As pragmatic state-led capitalist development emerges as the only way to inoculate Singapore against ethnic tensions and the regional communist threat, the state's priorities will be to control trade unions, mobilize bodies productively, and facilitate profitable transnational investments.[41]

At one level, we might read the novel's melancholy resolution as indicative of the durability of imperial governance. In Ann Laura Stoler's account, "degrees of imperial sovereignty"[42] are those in which "colonial infrastructure and arrangement, be they legal, pedagogic, military or territorial, have continued to exert their force"[43] beyond the moment of the colonizers' departure. But these infrastructures continue to "exert their force" not merely through the powerful half-life of European colonial modernity, but via their reworking in terms of a "particular power structure of domination invented and realized along the bipolarization of modernity."[44] This structure bears down with special intensity to control the temporal openings of decolonization. At the narrative level, such an arrangement confirms—albeit via a different political genealogy—a more fundamental paradox that Moretti notices of the *Bildungsroman* form: "the disturbing symbiosis of homeland and prison."[45] In the following analysis of Tiang's *State of Emergency*, we will see how separation and detention become the state's twin weapons of temporality. In the process, the formerly foreign, prosthetic state is reproduced anew.

Arrested Futures of the Ma Gong

Whereas *Confrontation* provided us with a window in which a restored, redeemed Malay world could briefly be imagined, Jeremy Tiang's *State of Emergency* weaves together a story of different anticipations that attended the same historical transformation. Its emphasis is not those once-possible Malay futures in Singapore, but foreclosed leftist ones, specifically those of the Malayan Communist Party (MCP), known colloquially as the *Ma Gong*. To be sure, the geopolitical shifts and contexts that led to the repression of the Ma Gong were complex and many. Briefly, the end of the Pacific War and the departure of the Japanese from Southeast Asia saw the prompt return of the British to Malaya, the French to Indochina, and the Dutch to Indonesia, all intent on a second colonial conquest. The MCP's armed wing, the Malayan National Liberation Army (MNLA), was a guerrilla force born as the Malayan People's Anti-Japanese Army (MPAJA) and supported during the war by the British; it now turned its efforts on the returning British to fight for independence. The British, who had limited negotiations on the postwar restructuring of Malaya to Malays only, "alienated the non-Malays and effectively drove them toward supporting the cause of the leftist anti-colonial movement."[46] Meanwhile, the revenues from Malayan tin and rubber had gained in importance as the British lost other colonial resources in India and Burma. Tensions over reviving the colonial economy while preventing the spread of communism further intensified when British planters tried to remove wartime squatters to reinstate rubber crops. Such acts increased hardships while adding fuel to the emerging tensions between Kuomintang-backed triads, or organized gangs, and Mao-inspired communists in the region, following Mao's 1949 victory and the KMT's retreat to Taiwan. These tensions would erupt in the armed communist insurgency that the British termed the Malayan Emergency (1948–60).[47] An attempted colonial reprisal turned anti-communist repression, the Emergency both sped up and slowed down decolonization. Even though the British were forced to abandon their fantasy of a long-term reconquest after their return in 1945, the Emergency delayed their own departure as "Britain would not leave Malaya until the insurrection was defeated."[48] One of the long-term effects of the Emergency was the production of a lingering anti-leftist episteme.[49] Anti-communism would become the entry price for postcolonial elites who wanted to remain within the sphere of Western security and markets, while the struggles of the Ma Gong, some of whom were still fighting in the jungle as late as 1989, have largely been forgotten.

It is perhaps not surprising that the Ma Gong's controversial role at decolonization has been repeatedly sidelined by official nationalist histories in Singapore and Malaysia. As Theophilus Kwek has noted of *State of Emergency*, "the author's task is to re-imagine and re-instate those whose lives have been erased from public memory."[50] Consisting of six chapters, each narrated by a different member of an extended family, Tiang's novel spans the years from 1948 and the beginning of the Malayan Emergency, through 1955 and Singapore's Hock Lee Bus Drivers' Strike, the merger of the two countries in 1963, separation in 1965, independence, Operation Spectrum in 1987, to around 2015. The different chapters function as something of a jigsaw puzzle at the levels of both character and politics. While connected in the larger tapestry of historical events, a number of family members are lost or separated from each other, and vast periods of time are omitted from the narrative. Likewise, the development of the postcolonial state—the focus is Singapore, not Malaysia—is narrated through selected historical moments rather than in a linear fashion.

A brief overview of the chapters is warranted. In the first, "Jason," narrated analeptically by the elderly Jason Low from around 2015, we learn of a life marked by the early loss of his sister Mollie to the random violence of *Konfrontasi*, and his wife Siew Li, to the Ma Gong. Siew Li, who had already been detained as a teenager by the British in the 1950s, is forced to flee Singapore and the PAP mop-up of leftists following 1963's Operation Cold Store; she reluctantly leaves behind the young couple's baby twins, Janet and Henry. In her own chapter which follows Jason's, we witness Siew Li's emerging socialist consciousness as a girl in a Chinese middle school; the chapter follows her life until the moment she is warned of her impending arrest and escapes to Malaysia. She will later end up in the jungle near the Thai border with the guerrilla Ma Gong forces. In the next chapter, "Nam Teck," a youth of the same generation as Jason and Siew Li, grows up in a New Village in Malaya, loses his father to counterinsurgency violence, and eventually also "goes inside" to join the underground communist movement in the 1960s. "Revathi" jumps ahead to 1970 and is told through the lens of a Malayan-born journalist who breaks the story of the 1948 Batang Kali massacre in the British press. Revathi's narrative retrospectively gives details to the harrowing story of Nam Teck's family and the hardships brought by the Emergency. "Stella," meanwhile, is focalized through Mollie's daughter (and Henry and Janet's cousin) and is set in Singapore in 1987 against the backdrop of the supposed "Marxist Conspiracy." This chapter tells of the months of detention and interrogations the young schoolteacher undergoes as part of the state's attempt to flush out leftist conspirators it believes are attempting to overthrow the state. Finally, "Henry" narrates the return of Jason's middle-aged son who has lived his adult life in the UK. Journeying back to Singapore to attend his father's funeral, he decides to retrace the life (and death) of his mother, Siew Li, among the Ma Gong. He eventually reaches the border area between southern Thailand and Malaysia and meets her aging partner Nam Teck, and a previously unknown half-sister.[51] With extraordinary precision and economy, Tiang uses this limited cast to sketch a fragmented, but powerful, portrait of leftist and anti-leftist energies during Singapore's and Malaysia's untidy decolonization. More so than Mohamed Latiff, Tiang also presents the years of Emergency, independence, merger, and separation as a necessarily transnational and multiply intercepted story. It includes intrusions, separations, and attachments that cut across the mixed ethnic populations of Singapore and Malay(si)a, as well as Indonesia, Thailand, the UK, and the Philippines. If *State of Emergency* is structured as a jigsaw puzzle, it is a sprawling and compelling one.

Although formally not a *Bildungsroman*, the three chapters I shall focus on here—"Siew Li," "Nam Teck," and "Stella"—arguably take the form of mini coming-of-age stories. Like *Confrontation*'s Adi, the characters in these narratives refract the historical problem of decolonization through the prism of youth, but their stories examine questions of geopolitical transformation through communist futures rather than Malay ones. Siew Li, to begin with, is a schoolgirl in Singapore when she first hears a speech by Lim Chin Siong, "so stirring and strong."[52] Lim is the charismatic young labor leader who will eventually lead the breakaway party Barisan Sosialis (Socialist Front) after the PAP's purge of leftists.

Now she was listening for it, she could hear there was also something in the air, the possibility that this was a crucible, and everything the nation could become was here in this moment. Lina was right. War had levelled everything, and here was a chance to blaze through the world and make it fair again.[53]

Siew Li's sense of anticipation and temporal acceleration is overpowering: The struggles of World War II have sped up the time of decolonization and opened up "everything the nation could become." Shortly after, while detained by the British ("the state of emergency justified anything"),[54] she ponders fellow detainee and student leader Lay Kuan: "So many ways to be a person, thought Siew Li. She felt unformed, as if she could be any shape at all."[55] By the time of the merger with Malaysia in 1963, Siew Li is a mother and married to Jason, a straitlaced, English-educated civil servant; she works first for a union and then for Lay Kuan, who is now a Barisan Sosialis candidate up for election to the Legislative Assembly.[56] But entering the union with Malaysia exacerbates the tensions between the PAP and the pro-British Malay leader, the Tunku Abdul Rahman, bringing accusations that the Barisan is a subversive, anti-national force.

> The election took place five days after merger, their first as part of another country. The night before, the main party warned that Malaysia would send in troops and renew the state of emergency if Barisan were to win. This was scarily plausible—Emergency had only ended three years previously, why wouldn't it start again? They also claimed, spuriously, that every vote for Barisan was a vote for Sukarno, that Barisan was conspiring with the Indonesians to bring Singapore down through Konfrontasi. Perhaps that's why people voted the way they did, out of fear. Lay Kuan thought so. She won her seat, as did a dozen others from Barisan. Not enough to claim power, but something.[57]

Siew Li tries to remain optimistic after Lay Kuan wins a place in the assembly: "Could the system be changed from within, after all? The leftists could no longer be ignored. This would be a new era, she was sure of it."[58] The just-opening future, however, is rudely cut short as three weeks later Siew Li and other leftists are forced to flee to avoid arrest and indefinite detention. The left and its visions of a remade world are effectively removed from Singapore's future, precipitating new separations; Siew Li never returns to see her family again. As her friend Lina puts it years later in an interview with journalist Revathi, "What kind of government would separate a mother from her children?"[59]

Nam Teck is the other character who envisions a new future via communism. In both "Siew Li" and "Nam Teck," Tiang provides us with rich and
sympathetic portrayals of everyday men and women who joined the Malayan
communists, a representation that echoes Han Suyin's classic *And the Rain
My Drink* (1956).[60] But reversing the chronology of communism and detention
in Siew Li's narrative, Nam Teck has already spent most of his youth in confinement. He grows up in Seminyih, one of the so-called New Villages that
were created as part of the British counterinsurgency strategy during the
Malayan Emergency. Nam Teck's father, as will be fully revealed in Revathi's
chapter, is one of approximately twenty-five plantation laborers who is shot
dead in a mass killing at the beginning of the Emergency in 1948. The blood-
bath at Batang Kali arises when the British suspect the villagers of sneaking
supplies to the Ma Gong; the men are killed, the village razed, and the women
and children dumped at the next village. Nam Teck's childlike narrative
echoes Adi's incomprehension of the larger geopolitical events that buffet his
family's life: "When they were alone, Auntie Poh told him Baba was dead, shot
by bad people, the government men who always made trouble."[61] A few years
later, the British come and tell them they must again move villages.

> In the meantime, the bad men put up a fence around the new village,
> then another one farther away. These were made of barbed wire, two
> and a half metres high, topped with three-cornered spikes. There was
> only one entrance, and anyone going in and out was searched. His
> mother was no longer allowed to bring any food with her when she
> went out to work, in case she gave it to the people in the jungle. She
> was often pale with hunger when she came back from the plantation.[62]

These resettlement camps—literal concentration camps—have previously been
rendered into powerful poetic form by Wong Yoon Wah in his bilingual 2012
collection *The New Village*. Wong, who grew up in a New Village, describes the
daily surveillance of the villages and the way village men were often forced to
work with police, as this stanza from "Inspection Post of the Concentration
Camp" reveals:

> since "Operation Starvation"
> my papa and the policemen
> jointly guard the New Village exits
> with rifles and carbines they stop
> each grain of rice from slipping out
> making sure that within a year
> all forest shadows shall starve to death[63]

As in Wong's poems, the Ma Gong of Nam Teck's childhood are spectral presences at the edge of plantations and forests, who brought fear to the peasants and plantation workers. Nam Teck's mother tells him later, after he has grown up and moved to Kuala Lumpur, "If you were tapping rubber, and a man came up to you and said, *Bring me rice tomorrow*—well, then, you found a way, or you were dead."[64] And yet in his aunt's narrative, it is the British who are the "bad men." While the ruthlessness of the Ma Gong has been sedimented into British, Singaporean, and Malaysian national histories of the Emergency—and the movement was certainly not without its excesses—Tiang uncovers the broader conditions of violence that resulted from both the insurgency and its suppression. Significant here is the way the British counterinsurgency mobilized a specific infrastructure of space and time—the segregation of the New Villages and the waiting game of "Operation Starvation"—to combat the communist threat.

In their account of the Malayan Emergency, historians Christopher Bayly and Tim Harper describe the New Village program, which largely took place during the years 1950–52 under direction of General Harold Briggs and High Commissioner Gerald Templar. A "key component" of British counterinsurgency strategy, it involved the removal and resettlement of approximately one million mostly Chinese workers and peasants—since most of the Ma Gong were ethnically Chinese, other racial groups were less targeted—and constituted a reign of counter-terror by the British security forces. These often poorly trained forces, drawing on manpower from across the crumbling Empire, retaliated against communist attacks by razing entire villages and often mistook "couriers, helpers and bystanders, villagers, students and . . . young women" for communist "bandits."[65] Complementing the New Villages was the extraordinarily high rate of detention of suspected communists. Fiona Lee has further shown how an Orientalist discourse was repurposed for "the Emergency's bipolar logic of war": "The containment of the 'red threat'"—now figured as a racial problem—is therefore "a means of integrating the Chinese into the emergent postcolonial nation."[66] What Heonik Kwon has called the "bipolarization of modernity," in this rendering, might best be understood as a hermeneutic which allows the state to "sort" the population in ways most advantageous to the reproduction of capitalist futures. Nevertheless, the unqualified "success" of the British in putting down the insurgency has rarely been questioned, and the New Village strategy would soon be taken up in another decolonizing-turned-Cold War conflict and renamed "strategic hamlets" by the U.S. in Vietnam.[67]

In retrospect, we can see how British counterinsurgency tactics construct a multilayered racial and spatiotemporal infrastructure that *bridges* colonial and bipolar modes of governance. That is, the New Village program had the effect of re-spatializing and re-racializing colonial settlement and labor patterns in order to preserve colonial-capitalist social relations over all others. That rural Chinese were made further economically vulnerable by separating them from their previous means of subsistence has been an overlooked component of this process. We can here recall the importance of the Marxist notion of the separation of workers from the means of production as the central logic of primitive accumulation. Famously, "the capitalist relation presupposes a *complete separation* between the workers and the ownership of the conditions of the realization of their labour,"[68] resulting in the double bind of "free workers" who are "free from, unencumbered by, any means of production of their own."[69] Such a separation is violently enforced on the Malayan rubber tappers and prefigures the effect of the 1965–66 anti-communist massacres in Indonesia, which have been described as "one specific, epochal moment in the history of capitalism."[70] As we'll see in more detail in Chapter 5, widespread violence there not only killed hundreds of thousands of suspected communists (and also targeted the ethnic Chinese minority), but "destroyed the economic livelihood of millions of families" and provided the "freedom for capital to implement work schemes that disadvantage workers."[71] The strict policing of New Villages can be viewed, similarly, as the weaponization of space and time with the goal of eliminating non-capitalist postcolonial futures. Moreover, "What Templar achieved was co-ordination of Emergency work with the everyday business of government,"[72] an alignment that would prove remarkably resilient. By imaginatively reaching back into the personal histories shaped by the Emergency, Tiang depicts the enduring effects of everyday anti-communist governance that emerged at Singapore's and Malaya's bipolar decolonization. "Emergency," then, is not a temporary measure; rather, anti-communist securitization becomes the foundation for the postcolonial state's most durable economic and political rationalities. The novel's epigraph from Walter Benjamin's well-known "Theses on Philosophy" thus refers equally to the Malayan Emergency that officially ended in 1960, and to the ensuing decades of PAP governmentality: "The tradition of the oppressed teaches us that the 'state of emergency' in which we live is not the exception but the rule."[73]

Nam Teck, significantly, is not initially inspired to join the communists, although the government's rough policies and massive incarceration rates during the Emergency did fuel MCP membership. The Emergency is officially over by the time he moves to Kuala Lumpur where, as a mechanically-minded seventeen-year-old, he finds work in a repair garage. Initially content to earn his living and explore the new temptations of the city, he experiences the looming geopolitical shifts—especially the coming merger with Singapore—with a mixture of curiosity, excitement, trepidation, and pragmatic concerns. Noting that 1962 was "turning out to be a very strange year" since the "British were supposed to have left, but lingered awkwardly like bad guests at a party,"[74] he wonders about the new country he will soon be living in:

> What did it mean, to carve a new thing out of chunks of land like this? Who would be in it? Would Brunei, Sarawak, Singapore? . . .
> Nam Teck wondered what language they would speak in this new world. He had Cantonese and Mandarin, but only passable Malay and no English at all.[75]

A new worker at the garage, Ah Lam, recently arrived from China, introduces Nam Teck to the heady, underground world of Malaya's leftists. Thinking he is attending a "cultural night," Nam Teck is both fascinated and troubled when the evening turns out to be one of revolutionary plays and party songs: "And it was thrilling, the ideas he'd heard, the thought of a new world full of youthful energy, the past swept away. Without even realising, he'd started singing too, his face as bright as if he believed."[76] His recruitment to the MCP—he will eventually go underground in the jungle and have a child there with Siew Li—is achieved less by a rational political decision than by an affective experience in which another future, "a new world full of youthful energy," is made tangible. In Tiang's rendering, the agency of the communists lies precisely in their ability to seize a new future from out of the old colonial system of divisions and inequities, the latter now bubbling to the surface in the form of race riots and political tensions. Nam Teck is critical of those simply struggling to get ahead within the existing system: "These people had no thoughts in their head except survival, which meant only chasing after the next bit of money, the next promotion."[77] His diagnosis of the scrabble for a "promotion" echoes the temporal logic I discussed in the introductory chapter, in which developmental states chase advancement within the existing, hierarchical world system. In contrast, Nam Teck's conversion to the Ma Gong is predicated on the possible creation of a different and unalienated futurity. As he reminds himself when he is in the jungle: "He tried not to think of his old life. *Look forward*, he chided himself, *think of the world to come*."[78] And it is in the jungle that he experiences the intimations of an ethical, division-less state to come. Recalling the experience of Adi's Malay literature class in *Confrontation*, Nam Teck wonders "if this is what university would have been like . . . the camaraderie, the joy and energy of youth."[79]

In *Futures Past*, historian Reinhart Koselleck traces the profound conceptual shifts in notions of past, present, and future from the ancient to modern

periods (in European thought). One of the defining characteristics of modernity—defined here largely by the Enlightenment and the French Revolution—is the acceleration of time, which for the first time becomes a "human
task" rather than a providential aspect of God's will.[80] Koselleck further notes
that a characteristic of absolutist states is the "struggle against all manner of
religious and political predictions," thus enforcing "a monopoly on the control
of the future."[81] Both observations, I suggest, can be transposed to the context
of Cold War decolonization. The sense of acceleration—the "urgent, emergent"[82] time of a new, ethical society—is perhaps the central temporal thrust
of Nam Teck and Siew Li's experiences. The state, in turn, may be understood
as what put the brakes on this temporal hastening or, more accurately, it seeks
a "monopoly on the control of the future." It restricts and forecloses the futures
that can be imagined not just by the Ma Gong, who go into hiding, but even
those imagined by moderates.

The narrative of "Stella," to which I now turn, set in 1987, brings into dramatic relief how the continued state repression of leftists effectively forecloses
a whole range of possible—even liberal—"worlds to come." The novel's focus
on Stella's detention is an obvious indictment of Singapore's authoritarian
rule; but more important, I suggest, is the way this chapter reveals the creative
reappropriation of colonial counterinsurgency techniques for the postcolonial
period. It is also the chapter in which we hear the state "state" at length: The
extended interrogation scenes allow for the full exposition of the government's
anti-communist, developmentalist logic. Like Abang Dolah's detention in
Confrontation, it is at first unclear why Stella, a quiet Catholic schoolteacher
who volunteers with her church group on weekends, would be a target of the
state. In a grueling interrogation, her interviewers throw ice water on her and
force her, shivering, under an air conditioning vent. They relentlessly ask her
about her volunteer church group, which offers support and resources for
abused and underpaid Filipina domestic workers. In a third person narration
of her motivations, Stella recalls that her actions were inspired by witnessing
how Singapore's "rush towards prosperity" ignored both local homeless people
and the thousands of impoverished workers from Indonesia and the Philippines who arrived to work "in people's homes for insultingly low wages."[83] Her
interrogators, dismissing her thinking in a caricature of socialism, espouse the
cold calculation of development logic:

> "Do you want us all to be the same? You think everyone in society
> should earn the same money? That's not possible. Some people work
> harder than others, some people are cleverer. If we did what you people
> want, then our society will never progress, and soon our women will

have to go and be maids in other people's countries. Stella, we know who you are, you don't have to pretend any more. . . . You want to destroy our society. You want to bring us all down to your level. Stella, we know that you are a Communist."[84]

"Progress" here, of course, means exactly the "getting ahead" or surviving within the system that Nam Teck had already critiqued. Instead of an ethics of solidarity, mutual care, or equality, the state offers only the promise of rising prosperity based on the uneven, but "fair," distribution of goods via the principle of meritocracy. Any act outside this logic, such as helping foreign workers, is necessarily read as an attack on the state's very sovereignty. This extends to sexuality, where Stella's same-sex relationship during college is taken as further evidence of her non-normative, anti-government stance.[85] What Stella has so grievously committed is a contradiction of the state's understanding of futurity, both political and reproductive. Later, the interrogators will point to Singapore's leap in material wealth as irrefutable evidence of the state's wisdom: "We used to be poor. . . . Look at our airport. Look at our housing. . . . Why are you attacking our progress? Why do you want to throw all this away?"[86] After months of detention, Stella realizes that she will not be released until she confesses. She eventually does so, partly because of her ailing father's health, and returns home to find she has been stripped of her job, her friends, her church community, her reputation. When some of her fellow former detainees attempt to sue the government for wrongful detention and mistreatment, they are promptly rounded up again and detained as proof they were communists all along.[87] Stella recognizes the risks and reluctantly signs a declaration that denounces the allegations of mistreatment: "There was so little left of herself, she couldn't afford to lose any more."[88] Tiang's poignant narrative shows not only the PAP government's cynical repurposing of the British ISA detention apparatus for its own purposes; it discloses how the practices of everyday emergency governance work to sustain a monological view of the nation's future as one of promotion, prosperity and heteronormativity.

In an interview I conducted with Tiang, the author spoke of what Singapore's triumphant leap into modernity has occluded:

When a lot of people, including critics of the PAP, talk about Singapore history, it's presented as a kind of inevitability: that of course it worked out this way, but actually, there were a couple of moments when it very much could have gone quite differently. . . . We can't be sure what a leftist Singapore would have looked like, but I think it's worth imagining, bearing in mind the PAP government for the first couple of decades called itself a socialist government. . . . They played both sides,

claiming to be Socialist while saying "but these Communists will desta-
bilize us."[89]

Tiang's comments align with his novel's attempts to restore a temporal complexity to decolonization, challenging the unfolding of official postcolonial
history as "a kind of inevitability." Not simply the "event" of the colonizers'
departure, the separating-suturing process of decolonization is a complex historical opening that—albeit briefly—holds within it multiple and contested
potential futures. If the vision of future wholeness we saw in Mohamed Latiff's
novel was one of a redeemed Malay polity and territory, *State of Emergency*
provides imaginative access to the tenacious communist struggles for a world
liberated from both colonial rule and capitalist pragmatism. Whether the Ma
Gong would have been able to achieve that truly ethical, proletarian state
which would, in Gramsci's words, "put an end to the internal divisions of the
ruled . . . and create a technically and morally unitary social organism,"[90] is a
point of historical speculation. What the novel does reveal is how the elimination of leftist futures during the Malayan Emergency was reworked into an
indispensable infrastructure of illiberal rule for the postcolonial state. We also
see the forging of a key conceptual circuit breaker of the global Cold War, in
which anti-colonial struggles for new, liberated futures are recast into an intolerable red threat.

Comics and Counter-histories

In turning to Liew's graphic novel, *The Art of Charlie Chan Hock Chye*, we
must begin by noting how difficult it is to describe its genre. Ostensibly a biography of "Singapore's greatest comic book artist"—the fictional Charlie Chan
Hock Chye, as "presented" by Sonny Liew—the novel switches between a
dizzying array of illustrative and narrative modes. Alternating between an
artist's retrospective, a biographical documentary, a private scrapbook, and a
counter-history of the nation, it is largely composed of Chan's own oeuvre of
comics, sketches, studies, and scrapbooks, as well as "documentary" strips that
present Chan's life story and personal interviews conducted by his "biogra-
pher" Liew. As a whole, to quote Philip Holden, the work makes "questions of
multiple layers of authorship, partiality and perspective"[91] its essential textual
logic. At the same time, it plays with the ability of the graphic novel to move
creatively between image and word, panel and page, especially in its incorporation of Chan's own artworks in a metafictional biographical mode.

     Despite the many generic differences from the previous two texts,
Liew's novel also returns to the question of youth during the decades of

Singapore's decolonization and early post-independence years; it thus shares the formal narrative concern for intertwined national and individual *Bildung*. Like *Confrontation*, it features a sidelined, peripheral protagonist. Charlie Chan, the antihero of Liew's fictional biography, grows up in unremarkable conditions in colonial Singapore, the son of Hokkien-speaking owners of a provisions store. Like Adi, Siew Li, and Nam Teck, Chan is a youth at the end of the colonial period, his maturation coinciding with that of Singapore's, such that the major political events of the era become the subject of his early comics. In "Ah Huat's Giant Robot" of 1956, for example, Chan uses the genre of a children's adventure comic to present us with a robot and schoolboy duo who support the anti-British riots and the Hock Lee Bus Drivers' Strike. Indeed, throughout the novel, Liew's multi-genred mode skillfully and playfully interweaves Chan's life story with that of Singapore. However, in direct contrast to the triumphant story of Singapore's post-independent rise to economic success—with which the novel frequently takes issue—Chan's own life story is defined by failure and disappointment: His cartoons never make it big; he doesn't marry, leave home, or ever make a decent income from his art. Echoing the central themes of family loss in both *Confrontation* and *State of Emergency*, Chan is unable to pay for expensive overseas medical treatment for his father, who dies after an unsuccessful heart operation.[92]

While not involved directly in the politics of the day, Chan produces artwork that is highly critical of the authoritarian path the PAP takes. A strip resembling a *Mad* comic pokes fun at the PAP's white-washed nationalist histories, while in other strips "founding father" Lee Kuan Yew himself appears variously as mouse-deer, a domineering company boss, an alien, and a destructive specter. One of the book's central narrative threads is the consideration of alternative versions of Singapore's history rendered through the contrast between the two main political figures at decolonization. First is Lee Kwan Yew, the Cambridge-educated anti-colonial lawyer who became the pragmatic and autocratic leader of the People's Action Party, leading the country for three decades and widely known as the "Father of Singapore." His antagonist is the Chinese-educated trade unionist Lim Chin Siong, the radical leader originally affiliated with the PAP (who had a cameo appearance in the "Siew Li" chapter of *State of Emergency*). Lim led the leftist party Barisan Socialis after many members were forced to leave the PAP; he was detained for six years under the PAP's anti-leftist purge, Operation Cold Store—alluded to in both previous texts—and was ultimately forced out of politics and into exile in England. As Holden points out, Liew juxtaposes the personal with the political in terms of two sets of relationships that the novel formally stages "as a contrast between idealism and pragmatism"[93]: Lim and Lee, on the one hand, and Chan and his early comics business partner, Bertrand Wong, on the other. Thus "Lee and Lim's story is frequently placed alongside that of Charlie and Bertrand, and readers are encouraged to make associations between the two."[94] The juxtaposition is used less to draw a one-to-one causal correspondence between national histories and personal lives, than to raise questions about how such historical and social transformations are made sense of as retrospective objects.

Two sections of Liew's novel can again help us parse the relationship between Cold War decolonization, separation, and the competing logics of futurity; both assume an understanding of the Lee/Lim dichotomy. In Chapter 6, "Sang Kucing and the Ants," Liew presents us with a series of unpublished comics that Charlie Chan created in his "Bukit Chapalang" series of 1963–65. As Liew's introductory notes to the chapter tell us,[95] "Bukit Chapalang" (Malay for "Hodgepodge-of-things Hill") is a retelling of a series of popular Malayan folktales known as the Sang Kancil stories about a clever mouse-deer or *kancil*. The strip's conventional appearance seems appropriate for a mass or juvenile audience where regular-sized panels frame animal characters and their adventures against a simple jungle landscape. In Chan's version, however, the strip becomes a witty, damning political allegory: Sang Kancil is the wily and quick-witted avatar of Lee Kuan Yew, while Sang Kucing—the cat—is Lim Chin Siong, whose left-leaning followers are represented by the ants. Chan's "Bukit Chapalang" strip narrates the story of Singapore's merger with Malaya, the imprisonment of Lim Chin Siong and other leftists in 1963, and the race riots of 1964, all with deceptive levity. The British colonial era is referred to as "the time of the Crocodiles"; Malaysia is coyly represented as the theme park "Hinterland," and the purpose of entry (read territorial merger) for Sang Kancil is "entertainments."

As with Mohamed Latiff's and Tiang's novels, Chan's account of the merger and separation raises difficult questions around multiethnic populations, the use of anti-communist violence to suppress political opposition, and beliefs about the economic viability of postcolonial nation-states. Liew is similarly critical of the egregious abuses of individual rights that occurred under Operation Cold Store of 1963. Yet where in *Confrontation* the repression of leftists was an inexplicable personal tragedy that befell Abang Dolah and in *State of Emergency* becomes the linchpin of the narrative action, *Charlie Chan* focuses on the elite political machinations behind the scenes, which ultimately result in the PAP's arrest of Lim or, as the strip puts it, "putting him in the locker."[96] In the scene in Figure 3, we see the orangutan (Malayan leader Tunku Abdul Rahman) complaining to Sang Kancil (Lee Kuan Yew) about Sang Kucing (Lim Chin Siong) and his ants (communists): "I certainly

The Tunku's fears were heightened after Lim Chin Siong and his supporters formed the Barisan Sosialis following their expulsion from the PAP in 1961. Believing the Barisan to be a communist party, he was concerned that Singapore might become a "Little China" under Lim, a base and stepping stone from which communism could be propagated to Malaya.

Figure 3. Strip from "Bukit Chapalang," in *The Art of Charlie Chan Hock Chye.*

don't want them at my doorstep." As the strip explains, the merger was motivated in part by Malaya's fear of having an independent communist outpost "at its doorstep," and required the simultaneous annexation of Sarawak and Sabah (the Squirrelteers and Hamsteers) to ensure Malay demographic dominance in the union. "Bukit Chapalang" thus presents a revisionist—and still PAP-proscribed—account of the blunt geopolitical realities of the merger and separation, whereby state-formation is a wager that balances population arithmetic, economic survival, and fear of the "catchy chorus" of communism. We derive pleasure from this narrative precisely because it distills a set of complex historical actions into a visual allegorical register, heightened all the more by the incongruous form of its genre.

Yet "Bukit Chapalang," I want to argue, is more than an irreverent counternarrative to a well-known piece of national history. The strip itself must be read at several levels, as both a private and a public enunciation. In its 2015 "presentation" by Sonny Liew, it enters public discourse as a historical counternarrative, and Liew's own clarifying captions ensure that the reader does not miss the message. But in terms of the novel's own internal narrative logic, it is a strip that was unpublishable during the actual merger of 1963–65, as the museum-like cataloguing of each of Chan's artworks indicates: the strip is labeled, "*Bukit Chapalang, c. 1963–1965. Chan Hock Chye. Unpublished.*"[97] As already noted, much of the biographical trajectory of Chan's life concerns his failure to find an audience for his work. In this sense, the future that is foreclosed for Charlie Chan is a politically and culturally *liberal* one, in which dissent, freedom of expression, and artistic criticism of the state would be welcomed in the marketplace of ideas. The biographical narrative, then, portrays Chan's ideological and aesthetic commitments as wasted energies. While his former partner Bertrand—the pragmatist whose life evokes the "Singapore Story" writ small—goes on to become a successful businessman and patriarch of a large family, Chan refuses to accept artistic compromise. He chooses a low-paid, low-prestige job as a night watchman (ironically enough) in order to have space and uninterrupted time to continue his art.[98] His aging parents, meanwhile, continue to nag him about marriage and taking over their store, neither of which he does. Over the course of the novel, we see Chan transformed from an optimistic, talented young comic artist to something of a recluse who refuses to take on commercial work because of its "stupid clients"[99] and lack of artistic autonomy. In the end, as Liew himself tells us in the small first-person strip placed along the bottom gutter of Chan's virulently anti-PAP comic "Sinkapor Inks," Chan decides to "sever all links with the public sphere and patronage" to ensure "true freedom of expression."[100] Lacking an audience or market, Chan's artistic and political liberalism thus remain impossible to articulate within the novel's own world.

If one dominant visual rhythm of the text is the interspersing of Chan's (largely unpublished) works with strips narrating his personal and artistic disappointments, each failed comic thus demands to be read in two ways: in its own right as revisionist political commentary on the events of the time and as evidence of those foreclosed liberal futures, in which Chan *could have* flourished. Chan's life story is one more melancholic response to the alienating developmental state: He detaches from the social and economic worlds it has created and commits ever more firmly to private artistic representations of the PAP's democratic failures.[101] Eschewing the pragmatism of his former partner Bertrand who comes to recognize "how important economic stability is to the bottom line,"[102] Chan labors his whole life, but never finds a home in the productive, efficient, and investment-friendly First World "oasis" that Singapore becomes. *Charlie Chan's* failed *Bildung*, therefore, results from the inability to reconcile individual artistic expression with the state but not, of course, in the ways validated by free speech organizations like PEN or Amnesty. The ethical state, once again, is elusive.

The second and final section I want to examine occurs toward the end of the novel. Whereas *Confrontation* and *State of Emergency* offered us "glimpses" of alternative futures that never were, the graphic novel genre allows Liew to go further in alternative history-making. In the strip "Days of August," we are presented with an explicit counter-history of modern Singapore in which Lim Chin Siong, the imprisoned and exiled leader of the Barisan Socialis, has become the prime minister instead of Lee Kuan Yew. Beginning in the mode of a banal TV interview with its small, TV-shaped panels (Figure 4), a reporter

THANKS, SIMON! WE'LL BE HEARING FROM P.M. LIM HIMSELF IN A LIVE BROADCAST OF HIS ANNUAL BIRTHDAY SPEECH IN JUST A LITTLE WHILE.

BUT FOR THOSE OF YOU WHO CAN'T WAIT, HERE ARE SOME HIGHLIGHTS FROM OUR *EXCLUSIVE* INTERVIEW WITH THE PRIME MINISTER LAST YEAR, AT THE ISTANA!

A CULT OF PERSONALITY?

YES, I'VE HEARD THAT BEFORE.

YOU KNOW, ALL MY LIFE, I'VE HAD THESE LABELS THROWN AT ME.

COMMUNIST, DEMAGOGUE, DICTATOR...

CHARLATAN.

RRMMBLL

BUT ANYONE WHO'S PAID ANY ATTENTION TO THE *FACTS* WILL KNOW THAT I ONLY DID WHAT WAS *NECESSARY* FOR SINGAPORE.

Figure 4. Television-shaped panels of "Days of August," from *The Art of Charlie Chan Hock Chye*.

nonchalantly reviews a national history in which the Barisan Socialis party won the 1963 elections, the Singapore-Malaya merger never happened, and Lim Chin Siong is the "father of Singapore."[103]

Complicating the established political contrasts between the two leaders—Lee Kuan Yew as the authoritarian pragmatist and Lim Chin Siong as the radical labor leader of the masses—the TV report reveals the latter to have been a moderate all along whose leadership barely differs from Lee Kuan Yew's. Although he avoids the failed merger with Malaya, Lim's achievements include taming the trade unions, leading with a "mild cult of personality," and achieving "progress and stability"[104] for the country. It is even hinted that he exiled his political opponent, Lew Kuan Yew. The result is a prosperous Singapore apparently identical to the actual one.[105]

Liew's graphic tale, I suggest, knowingly plays on the fact that it is almost impossible to imagine the future of Singapore otherwise, even had its political history turned out differently. The comic's value is not merely to offer a case of "what could have been," but to provide a more radical insight about Cold War decolonization: The very task of *imagining*, from the present, the post-colonial state as vehicle of emancipative, redemptive futurity is at once absolutely necessary and almost impossible. We are given pause by the familiar, gleaming image of Singapore's skyline placed within a fictional counter-history, itself framed within the biography of an artist who never existed. As Ann Cvetkovich has noted of the graphic novel's form, its interplay of words, texts, and panel sequences disrupts "standard modes of public discourse"[106] while it plays with our expectations of the visual and its privileged relationship to "evidentiary truth."[107] "Days of August" ups the ante on its own metafictiveness in the final section when the news broadcast is interrupted by reports of terrorist attacks and a mysterious vigilante figure in white; the format also changes from neat television-shaped panels to irregular-shaped frames that use the former comic as content, employing yellow bubbles in a separate meta-narrative. A convoluted story line takes over, revealing the mysterious man in white to be a monstrous, time-and-space-rending Lee Kuan Yew. But the alternative future of "Days of August" is also a world in which Chan himself has found success. He is a prominent artist whose "contributions to the nation have been remarkable," according to the prime minister.[108] We then learn that the "Days of August" Chan had actually been working on is a speculative fiction comic inspired by Philip K. Dick's *The Man in the High Castle*, in which it is Lee Kuan Yew and not Lim Chin Siong who won the 1963 election. Chan's attempt to "placate or stave off the forces threatening to destroy their present world" by depicting this "alternative" world fails, and a giant specter of Lee Kwan Yew declares himself "merely the force that returns the world to how it has to be."[109] The two possible worlds—the one in which Lee is prime minister, and the one in which Lim is—thus become impossibly entangled, pushing the time-bending narrative to its limit. In another authorial sleight of hand, "Days of August" ends by rewinding time altogether and dropping Chan and Lim Chin Siong back into the 1950s Singapore of the book's beginning—and the novel's earlier black and white graphic style—ready to start their (failed) lives and careers all over again.[110] Liew's melancholy point, we might surmise, is that even the unsuccessful artist's life is worth living for itself.

Ultimately, such intricate narrative and visual folding evidence the graphic novel's potential to reimagine those other futures of decolonization that were discarded in the nation's race to success and prosperity—at the same time that it gestures toward the very difficulty of doing so. Liew's heterogeneous, unclassifiable graphic novel dislodges the historical certainty of Singapore's authoritarian rise to success. It ruminates on success, failure, and historical destiny by playfully and subversively giving expression to those "what ifs" of other temporalities.

Conclusion

In reflecting on the long shadow of repressive state instruments wielded at decolonization, Bayly and Harper note the way "the continuing threat of communism and communalism" has profoundly affected the postcolonial era.

> In the aftermath of its revolutionary hour, and scale of the violence it unleashed, not only was communism all but obliterated, but in the process so too were a panoply of other alternatives. Liberalism never recovered from the shocking blows to civil society during these years of upheaval. The post-independence elites saw it as a dangerous thing: it was, in Lee Kuan Yew's striking phrase, "anti-national." In this new atmosphere many of the great figures of the popular movements faced long periods of imprisonment, exile or exclusion. But the vanquished also were struck out of national narratives, and almost vanished from historical memory itself.[111]

In this chapter, I have considered the way that fictional reappraisals of Singapore's and Malaya's decolonization restore those "other alternatives"—and other futures—to our historical understanding of the past. We have seen how decolonizing struggles become refracted through the tectonic fault lines of the global Cold War in ways that foreclosed alternative futures for postcolonial societies. Through its infrastructures of surveillance and detention—the everyday policing of futurity itself—the PAP forcibly rerouted anti-imperialist world-making into anti-communist nationalism, while excising those alternative imaginaries "from historical memory." Mohamed Latiff, Tiang, and Liew, through exploring the twinned problem of youth for both protagonists and nations, offer fine-grained critiques of the way Cold War and nationalist epistemes have worked to contain and re-signify certain problems of decolonization, showing how anti-liberal and anti-leftist epistemes remain congealed in the postcolonial state's political rationality. These works are provocative fictional returns to what could have been during the "no-more" and "not-yet" time of decolonization.

Together, the novels' depictions of postcolonial future-making remind us that "the world-historical transformation known as 'decolonization' was simultaneously an emancipatory awakening of peoples and a heteronomous process of imperial restructuring."[112] If different strains of anti-colonial nationalism imagined and anticipated the ethical suturing of people and state, the complications and intrusions of the global Cold War reined in such desires. Against teleological mappings of this region which celebrate their developmental achievements, these texts excavate the violent legacies of decolonization's separations and re-incorporations. The result for their protagonists is a kind of homelessness specific to the postcolonial genre of *Bildung*: The state remains, to all extents and purposes, a foreign one. In place of the imagined unity and restoration of community and state, of labor with self, of aesthetics and life, Cold War decolonization results in their melancholy separation. In the next chapter, we will further investigate the fate of those other futures by turning to stories of "imprisonment, exile and exclusion" that have lingered into the present.

4

The Wrong Side of History

Anachronism and Authoritarianism

The Meritorious Dictator

In her film from 2013, *To Singapore, with Love*, documentary filmmaker Tan Pin Pin tackles the question of Singaporean political exiles living outside the exceptionally well managed but famously still authoritarian city-state. Hwang Sŏk-yŏng's 2000 novel *The Old Garden* (*Oraedoen chŏngwŏn*) chronicles the aftermath of the South Korean military's crushing of the 1980 Gwangju Uprising. Both texts raise questions about these countries' periods of simultaneous political repression and remarkable economic growth, allowing us to dwell on the ambivalent social memory of regimes that are so often viewed with admiration for their economic achievements. They further complicate the story of "model minority" Asian postcolonial modernity that this book has been concerned to refute, instead underscoring the complex imbrication of decolonization, development, and the global Cold War. In the preceding chapter, I examined the multiple "futures past" that attended decolonization, and the ways they were arrested and foreclosed by national developmentalist priorities. Whereas there I reckoned with the entanglements of Cold War anticommunist authoritarianism via the question of youth and narratives of *Bildung*, this chapter does so through questions of age, specifically via aesthetic genres that worry over history, teleology, and anachronism. And whereas Chapter 3 explored texts that excavated those competing emergent futures that were cut short, this chapter chooses cultural texts for the way they present overlooked conflicts of the global Cold War as repressed elements of the present. Anticipating the following chapter's emphasis on transitional justice, it seeks to think through the legacies of authoritarian capitalism in ways that do not

adhere to usual teleologies of "miracle" development, the transition to democracy, or post–Cold War liberalization. It therefore troubles the usual historical
turning point of 1989 or 1991 that supposedly demarcates the Cold War period
from our "one world" of uninhibited globalization, in which the high-growth
development of Singapore and South Korea retrospectively confirms the folly
of alternative modes of development.

First, some brief introductions to the texts and the conceptual questions
guiding this chapter. Tan Pin Pin is an acclaimed documentary filmmaker
from Singapore. Her films—such as the award-winning *Singapore Gaga*
(2005), *Invisible City* (2007), and, more recently, *In Time to Come* (2017)—have
explored the city's soundscapes, stories and spaces that lie beyond official histories. In *To Singapore, with Love*, Tan returns to several foundational moments
in Singapore's postcolonial history. Her film's subjects—a variety of political
activists, trade-unionists, and former Malayan Communist Party members—
were forced to leave Singapore as a result of intense state repression during
Operation Cold Store, the 1963 elimination of leftist political forces (a period
fictionalized in all three of the novels discussed in the preceding chapter), as
well as subsequent government crackdowns directed at suspected communist
student leaders and activists. At these moments, the state employed the indefinite detention powers of its notorious Internal Security Act (ISA), in place
since the end of the colonial era. The film profiles the former student leader
and successful human rights lawyer Tan Wah Piow; the surgeon Ang Swee
Chai, who was exiled with her late husband, the democracy activist Francis
Khoo; Ho Juan Thai, a former Chinese-language proponent; the journalist
Said Zahari, who was imprisoned for seventeen years; and a number of former
Malayan Communist Party (MCP) members living in Thailand. Intercutting
scenes and interviews of the exiles in their various locations—London, Southern Thailand, and Malaysia—the film is less a documentary investigation into
the repressive mechanisms of the People's Action Party (or PAP, Singapore's
only ruling party since independence) and more a reflection on the personal
struggles, memories, and experiences of Singaporeans who have lived much
of their lives in exile as a result of state repression. The film opens, for example, with Ho Juan Thai at his home in London, cooking Singaporean-style
noodles and prawns and explaining, "You still try to cook your own Singapore
food" in order "not to feel defeated."

In a fictional narrative mode, Hwang Sŏk-yŏng's *The Old Garden* brings to
life the repression of the radical left under South Korea's long years of military
dictatorship (1961–87). A generation older than Tan, Hwang himself is perhaps
South Korea's best-known contemporary dissident writer. Born in colonial
Manchuria in 1943, he made his name writing workers' literature in the 1970s

as well as an extended allegory, *Chang Kil-san*, of the Park Chung Hee dictatorship. In 1985, he published a scathing account of South Korea's role in the Vietnam War,[1] and in 1989 took an unauthorized visit to North Korea for which he spent five years in prison upon his return to the South. Influenced by Hwang's own experiences of the Gwangju Uprising in 1980, *The Old Garden* is narrated by two voices: The first is that of political activist Oh Hyun Woo (O Hyŏn-wu), who has just been released after eighteen years' imprisonment for his involvement in a left-wing anti-government organization. The other, in the form of her posthumous diaries and letters, is that of his former lover Han Yoon Hee (Han Yun-hŭi), who dies two years prior to Hyun Woo's release. Hwang's novel is especially interested in reconstructing the complex political climate of 1979–80 when the South Korean military regime saw the transfer of power from Park—whose two-decade rule ended with his assassination in 1979—to General Chun Doo Hwan (Chŏn Tu-hwan). Told from the novel's diegetic present of 1997, Hyun Woo and Yoon Hee's story addresses the afterlives of political repression and Cold War authoritarian rule through a reflection on extended imprisonment as a kind of internal exile. Through the twin motifs of exile and anachronism, both Tan's and Hwang's texts explicitly grapple with the problem of thinking about the past violence of anticommunist capitalist states that has often been occluded by their ability to maintain remarkable growth rates. In that sense, the dissenting subjects of Tan's and Hwang's works are anachronistic remnants from the "wrong side of history": from the side that appears to have been mistaken about the alternatives to capitalist development in the former Third World, or the Global South. In "looking back" at authoritarianism through the tropes of exile, homelessness, and anachronism, Tan and Hwang offer powerful critiques not just of authoritarianism, but of the very space and time of model postcolonial development.

Let us recall that these two countries have long held anomalous status in comparative studies of the postcolonial or developing world. In the three decades following decolonization, Singapore and South Korea were two of the most lauded of Asian Tiger success stories, boasting unparalleled average GDP growth rates of 6–7 percent, with some years close to 15 percent (compared to 2–3 percent typical for OECD countries); they confounded the trend of Global South underdevelopment and became models of successful export-led industrialization. The World Bank's 1993 publication *The East Asian Miracle: Economic Growth and Public Policy* consolidated the narrative of their "miraculous" growth and exemplary status. In answering the basic question: "What caused East Asia's success?" the authors cite a series of sound "market-friendly" development policies alongside qualities such as "pragmatism and flexibility."[2] With a more critical lens, Andre Gunder Frank and other dependency theorists also early identified the Tigers as models for a (then) new kind of industrial development that replaced the emphasis on import-substitution with export-led growth and anti-communist "political stability."[3] The model of "free production zones" and "world market factories" would be widely imitated around the Global South.[4] In writing of the powerful "example" set by South Korea, Singapore, Hong Kong, and Taiwan, Caroline Hau notes that Marcos sought to legitimize his own martial law by citing "the example set by experiences of authoritarian neighbors" and "the developmental state's promise of 'efficiency.'"[5] In just a few decades, Singapore "model" development would allow it to become a global expert in urban-economic management recipes, selling know-how and advice to hundreds of cities in the Global South through the Singapore Cooperation Enterprise and the "World Bank–Singapore Urban Hub." Despite its high levels of labor precarity, South Korea has moved rapidly from the Asian Tiger manufacturing model to a high-tech, neoliberalized flexible market; it now boasts the world's eleventh largest economy, a huge cultural export industry, and is a major investor in China, Southeast Asia, and beyond.[6]

Such overdetermined narratives of "success" and "model" have made it difficult to think about the relationship between repressive authoritarian governments and economic development. The critic Paik Nak-chung clarifies the conceptual problem at hand in his essay "How to Think about the Park Chung Hee Era":

> It has by now become a platitude to say that, while Park must be condemned as a dictator and gross violator of human rights, he deserves praise for leading the country out of poverty and building a strong, industrialized nation. How do we go beyond this all too facile "striking of [a] balance" and particularize the manner in which the two contrasting appraisals are to be combined, specify the precise weight to be given to each, and *determine the actual relationship* between the two aspects?[7]

Paik goes on to describe General Park's regime as "meritorious service in unsustainable development"—unsustainable both in terms of its "unabashed environmental destruction" and because Park's militaristic rule "could not go for long."[8] He concludes by warning against the "Park Chung Hee nostalgia of our day."[9] Writing in 2011, his comments anticipate the reappearance of the Park dynasty in the form of Park's daughter, Park Geun-hye (Pak Kŭn-hye), president from 2013 until her ouster in 2017. Lee Kuan Yew, we must note, while wielding enormous personal and political power through the remarkably resilient People's Action Party, did not come to power in a military coup. And unlike South Korea's years of brutal military dictatorship, Singapore has had regular elections, despite the fact that opposition parties are often forced out of the playing field by other means. Nevertheless, the lack of democratic freedoms in Singapore—famously justified by Lee's invocation of "Asian Values"—has often been seen as a fair "trade-off" for the city-state's efficiency and prosperity. Indeed, throughout his career, Lee frequently pointed to other "messy, chaotic" postcolonial democracies as Singapore's "negative Other"[10] to shore up the PAP's authoritarian tendencies. That his son Lee Hsien Loong is the current prime minister confirms the successful recipes of his father.

In what follows, I attempt to move beyond "striking a balance" with regard to the specific problem of "meritorious dictatorship" in Singapore and South Korea. I do this by engaging with two texts that invite us to reckon with state violence and repression from "the wrong side of history," that is, from the perspectives of political dissidents, communists, and student leaders whom (neoliberal) history can only view as misguided, anachronistic, or superfluous to the triumphant narrative of capitalist modernity. I thus view both Singapore and South Korea as emphatically Cold War–postcolonial formations: I describe how a triumphalist neoliberal episteme has occluded those other stories of the region, while a postcolonial critical lens has paid too little attention to the new forms of bipolarized authority structuring the region. Tan's and Hwang's texts are valuable precisely because they necessitate a conceptual return to, and reassessment of, a particular configuration of decolonization, authoritarianism, and development at a moment when other futures were imaginable; this chapter thus builds on the preceding chapter's investigation into the multiple times of decolonization. How do these texts open up conceptual space for imagining other forms of postcolonial liberation beyond the advantageous insertion of the nation into circuits of global capitalism?[11] And how, I ask, do Tan's film and Hwang's novel map the unresolved continuities between an apparently "past" moment of contested decolonization and today's economically successful, post–Cold War states?

Exiles of Modernity: Tan Pin Pin's *To Singapore, with Love*

All of the documentary subjects in *To Singapore, with Love*, in differing ways, attest to the heartbreak of exile in terms of a fierce nationalist identity and tenacious love for Singapore—hence the film's title. In accordance with Edward Said's poignant 1984 essay on exile, the "essential sadness" of exile emerges as a set of paradoxes:[12] Most distinctly, it is dialectically entwined with nationalism, "like Hegel's dialectic of servant and master, opposites informing and constituting each other."[13] Such nationalist devotion seems at odds with both the peripatetic, cosmopolitan lives these exiles have been forced to live, and the deep criticisms they have leveled at the Singaporean state. Yet Ho Juan Thai, who fled the country in 1977 after he was accused of inciting violence as a "Chinese chauvinist," dreams of nothing more than giving his two young sons Singaporean citizenship so that (somewhat surprisingly) they can fight in the Singapore Armed Forces. The surgeon Ang Swee Chai, who fled around the same time, describes how her life in the UK has been one of incessant struggle due to the hardships she and her husband faced as refugees and her own homesickness. She recalls, in an interview with the offscreen filmmaker, desperately wishing to be working as a doctor back in Singapore: "Oh how I wish[ed] I was operating on Singapore patients!" The exiled democracy activist and lawyer Tan Wah Piow explains that now that his livelihood in England is secure, "the real problem is how to get back to Singapore." Even the former militant Malayan Communist Party members speak fondly of their ties to Singapore. The married couple Tan Hee Kim and Yap Wan Pin, who now run a small noodle factory in Thailand, refuse to give up their communist beliefs, a condition that the Singaporean state insists upon if they want to return. Nevertheless, as Tan Hee Kim says, "We long to go back to Singapore." This sentiment is confirmed by their pile of Chinese-language newspapers from Malaysia and Shanghai through which they keep abreast of all things Singaporean.[14]

At a superficial level, the film is staged around the binary of what Ang Swee Chai says in her interview, "see[ing] things in terms of Singapore/non-Singapore." Notably, there is only one scene in the entire film that is recognizably shot in Singapore, which is the moment Ho Juan Thai's wife and sons arrive at Changi Airport for a family celebration. Ho himself is stuck in a hotel in Johor Bahru on the other side of the causeway that connects peninsula Malaysia to the island-nation, where he participates in his mother's ninety-fourth birthday party via Skype. Shots of him looking wistfully over the narrow passage of water toward Singapore's shore are the film's purest visual expression of the aesthetics of exile and, not surprisingly, this scene is used as the film's publicity still: the lone figure defined by his longing for homeland and loved ones (Figure 5).

Said notes that exilic nationalism is, on the one hand, precisely the ideology that "affirms the home created by a community of language, culture and customs; and by so doing, *it fends off exile*, fights to prevent its ravages."[15] On the other, as Sophia McClennen points out, "the exile's nationalism is constructive of an *alternative*: it is active."[16] What deserves attention, then, is the fact that the film's exilic subjects continue to desire Singapore, but do so in

Figure 5. Ho Juan Thai looks toward Singapore from Malaysia in *To Singapore, with Love*. Image courtesy of Tan Pin Pin.

terms of radically *competing versions* of the postcolonial nation: of its national culture(s), its political and economic orientations, and its very borders. Ho Juan Thai, for example, was persecuted for his advocacy of the Chinese language—the linguistic heritage of many Singaporeans—at a time when affiliation with China was dangerously equated with communism and ethnic communalism. Among other activities, Francis Khoo (Ang's husband) protested against the Vietnam War and, by extension, Singapore's complicity with U.S. imperialism; Tan Wah Piow fought against worker exploitation at the massive Jurong Industrial Estate. At an earlier moment, the MCP members resisted the PAP suppression of the Barisan Sosialis, or Socialist Front, the party that emerged after the PAP expelled its left-wing members in 1961. Such contestations thus range from workers' rights, cultural and linguistic policy, foreign relations, and Cold War alignments.

Presented collectively in the film, these dissident figures form their own alternative territorial figuring *and* political imagining of Singapore, offering national, regional, and global imaginaries far more complex and multilayered than the binary of Singapore/non-Singapore. Indeed, Tan's curating of these disparate exilic lives constitutes something like an archipelago of other Singapores, a political and spatial alternative to the Singaporean state's monological and insular narratives of success. Such a logic is reinforced at the formal level. In the film, similar scenes or cities are occasionally juxtaposed with a slight delay in identifying titles, leaving the viewer momentarily disoriented as to whether or not we have left one location for another. For example, the film cuts suddenly from a scene of Tan Wah Piow walking down a London street to Yap Wan Pin negotiating with a taxi driver on a road in Hat Yai, Thailand. These simultaneous filmic and geospatial disjunctures produce a concatenation of spaces, a series of discontinuous but interpenetrating islands of exilic space.

The film not only challenges the unitary spatial imaginary of Singapore but also emphatically questions its temporal underpinnings. The progressivist, teleological account of Singapore's success has been well captured by long-time prime minister and founding father Lee Kuan Yew in his best-selling memoirs, *The Singapore Story* (1998) and *From Third World to First* (2000). His writings helped legitimize the national myth of the tiny colonial trading port that made the incredible leap to become Asia's model "world-class" city and oasis of First World modernity. In contrast, in *To Singapore, with Love*, London, Hat Yai and Betong in Thailand, and Johor Bahru and Shah Alam in Malaysia function as multiple external vantage points through which to contest Singapore's smooth temporal narrative of postcolonial development. The London office of the lawyer Tan Wah Piow holds a veritable library of Singapore's (authoritarian) political history, just as Yap Wan Pin and Tan Hee Kim's unassuming noodle shop in Yat Hai doubles as a reading room for contemporary Singaporean affairs. He Jin and Shu Shihua's house in Bangkok holds a photographic archive of the MCP's long and forgotten struggle in the Thai-Malaysian jungles. Such personal archives—comprising photos, memories, newspaper clippings, and musical recordings—function as anachronistic counter-archives to Singapore's official histories. One way to read the film's aesthetics of exile, then, is to see these anachronistic lives and memories as challenging the PAP's hegemonic spatial-temporal logic, which has claimed its own path of development as the only possible form of decolonization for the vulnerable city-state.[17] It is for these reasons, I would argue, that the film was banned in Singapore, earning a "Not Allowed for All Ratings" classification in 2014. As Tan noted, this has caused *To Singapore, with Love* to also "be in exile."

In part, the difficulty of examining other histories—and their futurities—beyond the overriding "Singapore Story" is due to the prevalence of what I alluded to in the Introduction as "Three-Worlds ideology."[18] Sharad Chari and Katherine Verdery critique this viewpoint by calling for a more "integrated analytical field [that] ought to explore intertwined histories of capital and empire . . . and the ongoing effects of the Cold War's Three-Worlds ideology."[19] They note two particular effects of the Cold War era: first, the "domination of modernization theory in western social sciences" epitomized by

W. W. Rostow's stagist theory of economic growth from 1960[20] and, second, "decades of censorship (including self-censorship) of a Marxist intellectual tradition," especially pronounced in the United States and those aligned with it.[21] The goal of Tan's film, I suggest, is not merely to recuperate the personal costs of political activism, nor to "strike a balance" in acknowledging the less savory side of the Singaporean miracle.[22] Rather, it opens a space for us to reflect on the way the now celebrated "Singapore Story" was *predicated on* a number of irreducibly Cold War political, economic, and temporal assumptions that often wrote out the struggles of Marxists and leftists.[23] Methodologically, we find that the decades following formal independence are structured less by the familiar postcolonial idioms of resistance to metropolitan colonial power and its cultural hierarchies. Rather, a bipolarized power structure and its abiding logic of anti-communist national development authorized certain forms and ideologies of modernization, and not others. In one memorable scene in Bangkok, for example, former members of the MCP, He Jin and Shu Shihua, reminisce over photos taken in the jungle in Betong, near the Malaysian border, where the movement maintained a guerrilla force until 1989. They hold up a photo of a smiling couple in outdated military fatigues against a jungle backdrop (Figure 6). The average viewer cannot but be slightly temporally unmoored when He Jin remarks that the photo was taken "just before" they left the jungle, probably in the late 1980s, a period when Singapore was already gaining worldwide attention as a "first world oasis" in Southeast Asia, while Malaysia was ascending the ranks as a second-tier

> Was this taken when we were about to leave the jungle?

Figure 6. He Jin and Shu Shihua reminisce about their time in the jungle in *To Singapore, with Love*. Image courtesy of Tan Pin Pin.

"Newly Industrializing Economy," in the language of the World Bank. Such a scene destabilizes Singapore as a paragon of uncontested capitalism as frequently read through the linear timeline of modernization theory. Rather, Singapore's (and Malaysia's) modernity must be understood both in terms of the foundational role of regional communist movements at decolonization and the prolonged socialist ideologies with which the state aggressively competed until 1989.

In another of the film's memorable scenes, Chan Sun Wing, a former MCP member, sits in a small, neat, but slightly dingy courtyard in Hat Yai, Thailand (Figure 7). Framed by overflowing potted plants and a washing line, the elderly man sits down on a plastic chair in the center of the frame, unhurriedly takes out a piece of paper, and reads the following poem in Mandarin Chinese:

Thoughts on Changing Citizenship: 17th May 2006
I changed my citizenship!
Born and bred a Singaporean
Who would've thought I'd leave home for half a century
And spend 12 years stateless in Thailand, despite being a nation builder
Today, I became an IC-carrying[24] Thai citizen
Reluctantly, yet gratefully
Reluctant, for it is not that I don't love Singapore
Grateful, for the generosity of the Thais
My smallpox vaccination from the colonial times is still on my left arm
Kretya Ayer, Cross Street, Ang Siang Hill, Tanjong Pagar, Pasir Panjang, Clifford Pier
Our youthful stomping grounds
How can we forget?
In Upper Cross St where the Japanese drop the first bomb
Of both sides of Temple Street lay bodies to be collected, along with their stench
The white flags raised, we surrendered
The Japanese dogs leave, the British monkeys return
The Union Jack rises once again
In the old Kallang airport, thousands cry "Merdeka!"
Amidst the wind and rain we surged
from self-governed to Independence
All these things I have seen
The History that I have witnessed
I still have so much to tell you

Figure 7. Chan Sun Wing reads a poem to Singapore in *To Singapore, with Love*. Image courtesy of Tan Pin Pin.

> Singapore, oh Singapore
> If only you knew
> How your present and your future still preoccupy me every day.
> WRITTEN ON 25TH MAY, 2006, SOUTH THAILAND, HAT YAI
> —CHAN SUN WING

It is, of course, another iteration of the poetics of exile, specifically framed by the anguish of taking another country's citizenship. When I asked the filmmaker about how this striking scene came about, Tan explained,

> He wrote the poem in 2006. When I read it, I had to find a way to have it in the film. It explained his life story and his decisions in a succinct and moving way, better than any interview could have done. I had conceived of *To Singapore, with Love* as love letters to Singapore by the exiles. I saw the poem as a letter by a lover to his ex-love on why he had to take on a new lover. So it made sense for Chan Sun Wing to read his apologia to camera, to us, he whom we are unlikely to ever meet.[25]

In Chan's poem, the anguish of exile is indeed figured as betraying a loved one: "It's not that I don't love Singapore." Notably, his poetic recitation is the only time in the film when a subject directly addresses the camera rather than the filmmaker offscreen; that we learn no more details of his life beyond the poem makes Chan's reading all the more affecting. The poem tacks vividly between quotidian personal memories and the larger sweep of twentieth-century history. Starting with "My smallpox vaccination from the colonial times," Chan reminisces about the spaces of his childhood in British Singapore: "Kretya Ayer, Cross Street, Ang Siang Hill, Tanjong Pagar . . . ." He then provides an abridged version of World War II and the struggle for decolonization: "The Japanese dogs leave, the British monkeys return."[26] The moment of liberation—signaled by the Malay word for independence, "Merdeka"—resonates across the archipelago, and is an event poetically attuned with the forces of the natural world: "Amidst the wind and rain we surged/from self-governed to Independence." The poem reaches a crescendo in the last few lines: "All these things I have seen/The History I have witnessed/I still have so much to tell." The poem's poignancy is produced in the gap between the speaker and an unwilling, absent, or lost interlocutor: "I still have so much to tell you [*jiang bu wan*, literally: the telling cannot be completed]." It is not simply that Singapore is spatially absent or removed, but that the Singapore that *could have heard* and assimilated Chan's version of nationalist attachment—his time in the jungle, the MCP experience, his twelve years of statelessness—no longer exists. It must be summoned via Chan's memory and the poetic figure of apostrophe, "Singapore, oh Singapore," while the memory of this future continues to exert psychic and physical pressure on the present: "How your present and your future still preoccupy me [*guadu qianchang*, literally: anxiety hangs in my belly] every day."[27]

Chan's memory of national independence remains squarely at odds with that of the "Singapore Story" narrative and prompts unanswered questions: What should independence have meant for this aging, exiled MCP fighter? Anachronistically, how can we remember the future of Singapore he imagined in 1963? Chan's alternative poetic rendering of Singapore's decolonization and its possible futures thus indexes the suppression of an entire political imaginary that nevertheless persists into the present. Syed Aljunied notes, "In Singapore, as in Malaya (later Malaysia), leftist activists were cast as 'fanatics,' 'extremists,' 'communists' and 'radicals' who sought to challenge the moral economy of the ruling regime. They were construed as wishing to stunt 'progress' and 'development' through their outright refusal to submit to the rule of capital that colonialism set in place."[28] Telling a very different story of these leftists, Chan's melancholy poetry recitation forces us to recast Singapore's independent development as a complex and contested product of Cold War decolonization rather than the unproblematic start date of the always anticipated "Singapore Story." The scene works, moreover, by foregrounding its unusual aesthetic mode: Chan's recitation departs from the usual documentary

genres of interviews, archives, and "slice of life" scenes, yet it conveys the specific sensibility of exile "better than any interview would have." Rubbing up
against teleological state narratives, Chan's scene works to return the island-
nation—so often extracted and abstracted by its exceptionality—to its regional
archipelagic location and its Cold War formation, opening up room for alternative, unrepentant historical perspectives.

Said suggests that the exile-nationalism dialectic requires a "working
through" of attachment and rejection, and on its other side lies a kind of ethical cosmopolitanism.[29] In the film, this is the journey taken by surgeon Ang
Swee Chai. In an interview toward the end of the film, she describes her outrage and sadness at learning about the plight of the Palestinians, and her
epiphany in realizing that, like herself, "the whole nation of Palestine is in
exile—none of them can go home." She recounts how, with her husband Francis, she established a medical humanitarian organization, Medical Aid for
Palestinians. Accompanying her narrative are photos of a slightly younger Ang
with survivors amid the rubble of Palestinian towns. In her clipped British-
inflected accent, she speaks movingly at a televised rally describing the suffering of Palestinians living under Israeli occupation. Palestinians outside their
homeland, as she puts it, not only have to face death but face death as refugees
with those profound uncertainties, "Where are you going to be buried? . . . .
How are you going to meet up with your family?" That she has worked through
her own nationalist attachments seems confirmed by her ethical care for those
whose collective plight is overdetermined by the very problem of homelessness. I want to consider this scene in relation to the one it precedes in the film,
in which Chan recites his poem. Tan's very deliberate juxtaposition of these
two emotional, and explicitly transnational, epiphanies—Ang's identification
with Palestinians as a nation in exile, and Chan's poetic declaration of love for
Singapore at the moment of taking Thai citizenship—at first seem to offer
another contrast of success versus failure. Ang's story, in this light, seems the
legible, successful model of Said's cosmopolitan "working through," which
"transcend[s] national and provincial limits."[30] Chan's poem, meanwhile,
expresses an unapologetic and almost jealous attachment to the country
he cannot forget; he is precisely the one who has failed to work through his
exilic predicament. Yet their very contrast—the eloquent, Anglophone
humanitarian doctor, and the unrepentant, unapologetic Chinese-speaking
communist—do more than invite us to ponder the diversity of Singapore's
exilic experiences. At the affective and aesthetic level, they prove to be equally
compelling responses to exile. Moreover, they complicate our assumptions
around the radical excesses that had to be removed from Singapore for its
pursuit of success: Ang is the model well-educated, hardworking Singaporean

doctor now acting in solidarity with Palestinians in the occupied territories; Chan, who fought a literal guerrilla war as a communist, becomes a poet of homesickness after being given a new home.

We might say that Tan's documentary subjects and her remarkable film archive the potentialities of other futures of Singapore beyond the pragmatist, hypermodern city-state we know today. Her exploration of the dialectics of inside/outside, exile/nationalism, Third World/Cold War, island/archipelago, and decolonizing history/globalizing present raises crucial questions around the politics of remembering postcolonial state repression, via untimely memories that emerge from the "wrong side of history." As Gary Wilder has written of anti-colonial thinkers Aimé Césaire and Léopold Senghor, to look back on unrealized projects for emancipation beyond the event of independence involves "remembering futures that might have been."[31] But such reflections do so not only in the name of a liberal effort to offer a "balanced" assessment of the meritorious dictator. Rather, they offer up such imaginaries in the name of alternative visions of collective life that persist in the multiple and competing desires for a homeland.

Dictatorship and Homelessness: Hwang Sŏk-yŏng's *The Old Garden*

In turning to Hwang Sŏk-yŏng's novel *The Old Garden* (*Oraedoen chŏngwŏn*), we must reckon with significant differences between its context and that of Tan's film. To start, the PAP's targeted anti-leftist purges of the 1960s and '70s must be contrasted with the generalized violence that followed the Chun Doo Hwan military coup of 1980, as well as the different landscapes of public memory in contemporary Singapore and South Korea.[32] Unlike the prompt 2014 banning of Tan's film in Singapore, representations of the 1980 Gwangju Uprising and the broader 1980s democracy movement that followed it have, by now, become mainstream in South Korea. By the 1990s, citizens' eyewitness accounts and official investigations into the massacre brought the southwestern capital of Chŏlla Province to national attention, and much subsequent political and historical analysis has attempted to fully determine the causes and events of the government's brutal repression of the Uprising. (The Uprising's significance for the country's 1990s "transition to democracy" is further discussed in the next chapter.) Multiple studies have revealed the event was a complex, ten-day affair that initially began as a student protest against General Chun and in particular his arrest of the Chŏlla opposition politician, and later president, Kim Dae-Jung. The violence escalated after elite paratroopers— apparently specially trained for anti-communist combat in North Korea—were sent in to restore order, waging indiscriminate violence on the demonstrators. The citizens retaliated: They staged mass street protests of 20,000–30,000 people, began arming themselves, and managed to hold the city for five days before the military entered the city with a heavy arsenal of tanks to crush the Uprising. The most conservative estimates put the death toll at around 500, with another 3,000 injured.[33] As Jang Jip Choi puts it, "Not since the Korean War had the civilian population been so brutally victimized by the military."[34] The Gwangju 5.18 People's Uprising (*o-il-p'a minjung hangjaeng*), or the Gwangju 5.18 Democratization Movement (*o-il-p'a minjuhwa undong*) as it is officially known, is now memorialized by public monuments, a museum, and a yearly memorial service in Korea. In the process, however, the multivalent struggles of workers, farmers, and students of which it was composed—like the larger 1980s anti-government movement—have tended to be conscripted by the liberal, linear narrative of the "democratization movement."[35]

Whereas Singapore's dominant narrative has been the "Singapore Story" of postcolonial pragmatism and miraculous development, South Korea's self-narrative is somewhat more complicated. On the one hand, it shares Singapore's bootstrapping exit from colonial subordination and wartime poverty, albeit with Japan as its former colonial master and the United States as direct neocolonial power. Yet unlike Singapore, on the other hand, it is one site in the larger so-called "transition to democracy" political map of Asia in the 1980s and '90s alongside the Philippines, Taiwan, Indonesia, and Malaysia, which all saw the end of martial law or dictatorship between 1986 and 1998. Largely figured in the West as a political zero-sum game between a receding authoritarianism and an awakening popular democracy movement (with the United States as paradoxical guide and hindrance), the democracy "transition" story tends to privilege the moment of free elections (1986 for the Philippines, 1987 for South Korea, 1991 for Taiwan, and so on), occluding a myriad of historical complexities and persisting injustices.[36] In South Korea's case, it especially misses the Cold War episteme whereby the peninsula's Cold War division and U.S. military presence in the South persist beyond the official end of the superpower contest; the two Koreas are, in fact, technically still at war following the 1953 armistice.[37] Some of these convoluted temporal effects come into focus as we "look back" at South Korea's authoritarianism of the 1970s and '80s.

Hwang's novel sets out in a different direction from much 5.18 scholarship and collective memorializing that, while filling in the historical record and honoring its victims, has attempted to recast peripheral Gwangju as a "Mecca" of democracy activism and central to the "transition to democracy" narrative.[38] His layered and polyvalent account of 5.18 prevents the Uprising's assimilation into an evolutionary narrative focused on the arrival of electoral democracy.[39] *The Old Garden* does this by pushing the direct experience and events of the 5.18 event to the background and presenting a wider account of the period focalized through his two main protagonists, Hyun Woo (Hyŏn-wu) and Yoon Hee (Yun-hŭi), both eccentric to the massacre itself. Indicating that 5.18 both is and isn't the focus of the novel, the center of narrative gravity becomes the tiny hamlet of Kalmae (Kalmoe) in the mountains of Chŏlla Province where Hyun Woo is forced to go underground during the anti-leftist crackdown that followed the Uprising. Yoon Hee—always ambivalent regarding radical politics—is a local schoolteacher who is drawn into helping him; they eventually fall in love and spend a secluded, blissful summer in their mountain retreat. Kalmae, I suggest, operates as a kind of space of internal exile, a space both inside and outside the nation, a retreat from politics, but also its place of reimagining. In this sense *The Old Garden* might be read as the spatial inverse of *To Singapore, with Love*. Where the latter takes place outside the formal territory of the nation, *Garden* unfolds both from the non-place of prison, the black hole at the center of the South Korean military regime where Hyun Woo will be detained for almost two decades, and from the politically insignificant village of Kalmae.[40]

The novel's supple rendering of 5.18 is partly achieved through the formally complex arrangement of different perspectives and voices. One plot strand involves Hyun Woo's anti-government radicalism, his organization's clandestine work around Seoul, his meeting Yoon Hee in Chŏlla Province, and his eventual arrest and eighteen years of imprisonment. Told through Hyun Woo's first person narrative, this arc consists of a series of flashbacks from the novel's diegetic present of 1997—the year, not insignificantly, of the Asian Financial Crisis and South Korea's humiliating IMF bailout.[41] Yoon Hee, who dies of cancer two years prior to Hyun Woo's release, tells her own intersecting, meandering story through the letters, diaries, and notebooks that Hyun Woo finds when he returns to their former residence in Kalmae. Despite sharing narrative space on the page, the two lives are adjacent and asynchronous, rather than connected. One effect of Hwang's temporally disjunctive narrative is that the novel refuses to present the 1980s in terms of a unified political character; in a sort of double vision, "we see the 1980s not only through the eyes of political activists but of ordinary citizens [*p'yŏngbŏmhan sosimin*] distanced from them."[42] Hwang's fragmented narrative form has the further advantage of incorporating multiple voices beyond the main protagonists[43] and disrupting the typically gendered hierarchy of "political actor" versus "love interest." During Hyun Woo's long years in prison, his world narrows to the slow-moving microdramas of prison life, while it is Yoon Hee who goes on to live a life inflected by all the contradictions of Cold War South Korea. Unmarried, she bears their daughter Eun Gyul (whom Hyun Woo is unaware of until his release), returns to graduate study, runs her own art school in Seoul, and is swept up in the 1980s anti-government student movement. She eventually moves to Berlin to study art, the latter episode suggesting another comparative Cold War lens through which to read the Korean peninsula.

Let's look more closely at Hwang's intricate staging of narrative voices and its temporal effects. In a much commented upon passage in the novel, Hyun Woo and Yoon Hee look down from Kalmae over the city of Gwangju, one year after the massacre, and hold an impromptu memorial service for its victims. In this scene, I argue, the present can be perceived only as a moment out of time. Yoon Hee records the episode in her diary, addressed in the second person to Hyun Woo.

> We opened a bottle of soju and poured some into the lid of the rice bowl, and we knelt down to each other. I was a little embarrassed— your somber silence made me feel uneasy. . . . You took out a piece of paper and began reading out loud. You started with a year and month and date, some long sentences that I can no longer remember. But I do remember the last sentence, about longing for a new, different world.[44]

In a melancholic tone, Yoon Hee goes on to observe that "the classic revolutionary age [kojŏnjŏgin hyŏngmyŏng ŭi segi] was already finished."[45] The scene is nevertheless imbued with a "longing for a new, different world," and an invocation of a united peninsula: In Hyun Woo's transcribed words, "From Baekdoo [in the North] to Halla [in the South], I can see the beautiful land of Korea as one. But you are all gone now. What kind of world did you picture in your mind? [dangsin dŭrŭn ŏtdŏn sesangŭl kŭrida kasyotnayo, literally: What kind of world had you been drawing when you left?]."[46] The "longing for a new, different world" is circumscribed both by geopolitical boundaries and a sense of postcolonial belatedness: The age of "classic" revolutions has been foreclosed by a bipolar world order. Note that at the formal level, the scene is marked by an unusually convoluted narrative temporality. Yoon Hee's diary entry is narrated in the second person ("You [dangsini] took out a piece of paper. . . . You started with . . .") while its addressee, Hyun Woo, is himself addressing the absent victims of Gwangju. Furthermore, he is privy to Yoon Hee's written account only some years after she has died. The point of such a layered narrative construction with its multiple addressees and temporalities, we might surmise, is that the significance of 5.18 cannot be wholly relegated to any one historical moment: It resides neither in Hyun Woo's flashbacks of the anti-government struggle nor in the novel's diegetic present of the late

1990s. Rather, the out-of-sync, second person address of Yoon Hee's belated diary entry is an attempt to collate the discrepant desires and temporalities that point both forward and backward to a "new, different world."

The past and present are conjugated slightly differently in one of Yoon Hee's earlier notebook passages, in which she meditates on her father's life. Yoon Hee knew him only as an alcoholic, broken man who was cared for begrudgingly by Yoon Hee's hardworking and thrifty mother. Only when he is close to death does she come to understand his past political passions and unrealized dreams, as well as the lifelong persecution he suffered in the South as a result of his leftist commitments. She relates his story of returning from his studies in Japan (the colonial metropole) and joining both the Preparation Committee for Founding the Nation (Chosŏn kŏn'guk chunbi wiwŏnhoe) and the Communist Party in the heady postliberation milieu where youth and political groups of all stripes flourished.[47] The next few years, however, saw the hardening of political ideologies in the lead-up to the Korean War, particularly through events like the Taegu uprising of 1946 and the mass violence on Cheju Island in 1948 (the latter is discussed in the following chapter).[48] Her father eventually fights for the North in the civil war, is taken prisoner, and very narrowly escapes death.

Yoon Hee's father's story attests to the nonlinear historicity of the peninsula's tumultuous decolonization, division, and subsequent authoritarianism. The year 1972—the year of Park Chung Hee's notorious Yusin ("Revitalizing") reforms—is usually known as the beginning of the state's more repressive and overtly military rule;[49] correspondingly, it is the year of radicalization for many of Hyun Woo's generation. But as Yoon Hee's narrative reveals, it is also the year that a new "Law of Society's Safety" (sahoe anjŏn pŏb) mandates that "anyone who once infringed on the Anti-Communist Law . . . be reinvestigated,"[50] imperiling Yoon Hee's father and the family anew. To secure a sponsor and avoid imprisonment he must beg for the support of his powerful but despised brother-in-law, a conservative lawyer. In another section of her posthumously read diary, Yoon Hee imagines what her father would have gone through:

> Ah, I can picture that day, my father meeting my mother at the market and together going to my uncle's law office to beg for clemency. I can imagine my father's return home. After sending my mom back to the market, he walks down the busy, unheeding street in the middle of the day, in the world where no one believes in his future. On the grand avenues full of government buildings, where the whole street would freeze during the daily ceremony of lowering the national flag, my father tries to breathe and wander around the dark corridors of foreign bookstores and used bookstores. And he buys the book on Goya for

me, feeling the same way he did when he first saw the Goyas in Tokyo
as a young man from a colony. Those black-and-white images are like
fearful groans issuing from war and oppression [*chŏnjaenggwa apje ŭi
kongp'oro kadŭk ch'an sinŭm kat'ŭn hŭkbaek hyŏngsangdŭrŭl*].[51]

Yoon Hee's father, a former colonial subject, nationalist, and communist, walks
the streets of Seoul as an outsider, "in the world where no one believes his future
[*i sahoe esŏnŭn amudo chasin ŭi changnaerŭl midŏjuji annŭn . . . kŏri*]." He is
spatially and temporally at odds with the symbols and aspirations of the rapidly
rising and militarized nation, with its "grand avenues full of government buildings" and flag ceremonies. Reprising his existence as a colonial subject in Tokyo,
he is the anachronistic remnant of a decolonizing desire that has been eliminated for the smooth functioning of the capitalist developmental state. In this
scene of intense alienation, vividly reimagined by his artist daughter, the only
legacy her father passes on is the intensity of aesthetic engagement.

The couple's impromptu memorial service in Kalmae and Yoon Hee's
imaginative reconstruction of her father's experience in downtown Seoul
share several features. Both point to the way that responses to authoritarian
political repression demand a critique of Cold War decolonization as much as
opposition to politically repressive state forms. In other words, the development rationality of postcolonial South Korea simultaneously represses and
reactivates anti-colonial liberationist desires. Like *To Singapore, with Love*, the
novel deploys a temporal layering through the use of anachronistic subjects
and their memories. But unlike Tan Pin Pin's literal examination of exile, *The
Old Garden* proceeds through a series of affiliated moments when the postcolonial nation itself becomes estranged territory, blurring the boundaries
between colonial, decolonizing, and postcolonial time.

There is one more important parallel with Tan's film. This is the pronounced role of the aesthetic, specifically, the rhetorical figure of ekphrasis,
usually understood as the verbal description of a work of visual art. It is no
coincidence that the character of Yoon Hee is an artist; as she writes in one
diary entry, "A painting is a way of seeing."[52] As already mentioned, Hwang
mobilizes a multiperspectival and analeptic narrative structure that incorpo-
rates Hyun Woo's and Yoon Hee's consciousnesses in overlapping but discrepant fashion. The novel's most striking expression of discrepant subjectivities is
surely the portrait Yoon Hee paints of Hyun Woo during their brief summer
together—at the very moment, he only later realizes, when she was newly
pregnant with their child.

Although she originally paints the portrait of Hyun Woo during their summer in Kalmae, in the last years of her life Yoon Hee inserts her own self-
portrait onto the canvas to create an impossible, asynchronous representation

of the couple. Having come across it after her death, Hyun Woo attempts to decipher its meaning through this extended ekphrastic description:

> Her high cheekbones, the little lines under her eyes and the gray in her hair, her cheeks painted with overlapping colors, together they betrayed her withering youth and her solitude. But her eyes were calm and collected, and there was that mysteriously tender smile. Here were a thirty-two-year-old man and a woman in her forties, depicted in different colors and distinctive tones, standing side by side and watching the world beyond the canvas. She was right behind me, not looking at what was right in front of her but staring at something far away, over my shoulder. Where was I looking, so nervous and pained? And where was she looking years later, with the hindsight of her age? Which way in the world were we going [*segye ŭi ŏnŭ panghyangŭro kanŭn kiriŏssŭlkka*]?
>
> In our garden, asters and cosmos began to bloom. Yoon Hee's school was about to start again. Our friends in Kwangju, those who had somehow survived and gone through humiliating trials, were released from prison on the thirty-sixth anniversary of the liberation [August 1981], some pardoned, others paroled. . . . Around that time, Yoon Hee was almost done with my portrait. It became all that was left of my youth.[53]

The painting, with its intimate connection to the political events of 1980, stands as a figure for what the novel seeks to perform in its looking back at 5.18. Yoon Hee's portrait poignantly refracts political time through biological time, as the "hindsight of her age" (*chagi sidae ŭi nunŭro*, literally, "[looking] through the eyes of her era) promises insight into the meaning of both Hyun Woo's long years in prison, as well as the meaning of the country's anniversary of liberation from Japan. It stands in not only for the tragedy of broken lives and sundered families, but also the discomfiting temporal legacy of those who fought for another kind of future, made unavailable by the time of the novel's present. The portrait indexes the disjunctural temporality of Cold War postcoloniality against the simple arithmetic of the "thirty-sixth anniversary of the liberation."

If the overthrowing of dictatorships in the postcolonial world is often told as a narrative of "political liberalization" and "transitions" disconnected from decolonizing formations, *The Old Garden* defiantly refuses such neat evolutionary trajectories. It shows, instead, how the energies and sacrifices that brought the military government to an end were simultaneous critiques of a Cold War logic that produced the "division system" and authoritarian structures on both sides of the 38th parallel.[54] Like Chan Sun Wing's poetry recitation in *To Singapore, with Love,* the moment of explicit aestheticization plays with the strictures of narrative time. Yoon Hee's portrait is irreconcilable with dominant redemptive histories of the liberalizing nation, although neither does it allow for an "unreflecting identification with these protagonists."[55] It redeems neither the couple's love nor the political radicalism of the era. Rather, it poignantly raises the problem of the hindsight of age—of looking back at dictatorships—as a profound object of intellectual and aesthetic inquiry, demanding new and revised ways to answer the enduring question, "Which way in the world were we going?"

Untimely Postcolonialism

Sandro Mezzadra and Federico Rahola have noted that postcolonial studies is not beholden to "an absolute persistence" of colonial power. On the one hand, the field is interested in the persistence of "vertical" threads of domination and exploitation and, on the other, "the ambivalent role played by the failure of a set of real, historically enacted projects of liberation from those very forms of domination and exploitation."[56] Put otherwise, the failures of liberation projects have produced their own regimes of repressive power. What does this equation look like, however, if the "historically enacted projects of liberation" have been beset not by failure but—in a certain measure—by developmentalist successes? By interrogating their governments' repression of radical nationalist and anti-imperialist energies, Tan's film and Hwang's novel once again reject the notion of authoritarianism as a preparatory stage to be passed through on the way to a fully developed capitalist democracy. Instead, their figures of anachronism and exile trouble the Cold War logics of time and space and reveal these states to be complex products of decolonizing desires, colonial reactivations, and bipolar geopolitics.

This chapter has thus worked toward unsettling the temporality of the "post" itself as a prefix that supposedly separates distinct epochs: postauthoritarian, postcolonial, post–Cold War. For Singapore—keeping in mind it has not had a transition to the "postauthoritarian" moment—the exemplary postcolonial narrative of national independence and development yields to an alternative, nonlinear temporality produced by unrepentant exiles beyond the illiberal city-state. In South Korea, despite the violent intersections of decolonization, division, and U.S. militarization, residues of other imagined futures remain as untimely and unresolved components of the present. In different ways, South Korea and Singapore invite a reckoning with our assumed post–Cold War epistemology: first on the question of successful but authoritarian development, and second on the ongoing proscription of leftist historiographies.

I conclude by returning to the opening of *The Old Garden*, in which we find Hyun Woo recently released from prison and struggling with unfamiliar modern technology. He is confounded by cell phones—the "small object that looked like a transistor"[57]—as well as elevators and new high-rise architecture. In so many ways, he functions in the narrative as a living anachronism, a fairy-tale character who has awoken with astonishment to find the world changed, and whose role is precisely to allow us to see this world anew. Through their respective techniques of disjunctive narratives and the aestheticization of memory, Tan's and Hwang's works stage and archive the incompatible temporalities of liberation that subtend postcolonial development and modernity. In their formal attentiveness to experiences of exile and dislocation, they present us with subjects of suffering and sacrifice from the wrong side of history, who emerge unredeemed, unvindicated, and unassimilated by a neoliberal historical reckoning. These anachronistic figures carry with them energies and demands not just for another world that was never realized, but for the ongoing right to help define our political futures. In the next and final chapter, I extend my examination of postcolonial untimeliness by probing the temporalities of postauthoritarian transitional justice and the still-open wounds of translocal anti-communist violence. Is it possible to render a notion of justice through the aesthetic inspection of pain, suffering, and culpability? How can we do so in a way that does not reproduce either the neoliberal triumphalism of the "end of history" or the civilizational binary of Western-bestowed human rights and an illiberal Asia?

5

Killing Communists, Transitional Justice, and the Making of the Post–Cold War

September 30, May 18, and Transitional Justice

Toward the end of Joshua Oppenheimer's 2012 documentary, *The Act of Killing* (*Jagal*), we are presented with a scene of young women in gorgeous costumes dancing against the lush background of a waterfall. In the center is Anwar Congo, a former death squad member who killed hundreds in the 1965–66 anti-communist, or September 30, massacres in Indonesia, and his sidekick Herman Koto. Against the stunning backdrop and the uplifting soundtrack of Matt Monro's 1966 hit "Born Free," two bedraggled communists who have miraculously returned from the dead remove their neck wires—the efficient killing method Anwar claims to have developed and which features in almost every scene of the film (Figure 8).

Oppenheimer's film follows the production of a film-within-a-film, whereby Anwar and several of his friends were asked to write and reenact the 1965–66 killings in any way they wanted. These perpetrators—who acted with the support of the Indonesian military and helped kill between 500,000 and 2 million communists and suspected leftists—choose to reenact the massacres by way of a generic mash-up of Hollywood westerns, detective thrillers, and musical numbers, an appropriate choice since for Anwar, an American movie buff, "killing is acting."[1] Oppenheimer has called *The Act of Killing* a film less interested in producing facticity than in documenting "the imagination of the killers,"[2] and much scholarship has rightly focused on the way the film brilliantly tacks between documentary and cinematic fantasy, the real and the imaginary.[3] As a result, "the film renders the distinction between

Figure 8. "Dead" communists remove the wires that killed them in the film-within-a-film of *The Act of Killing.*

authentic/fake, performance/re-enactment, reality/fantasy to be ultimately undecidable."[4]

Notably, the waterfall scene is a repetition of the one that began the film. But whereas the opening scene presented the number in rehearsal mode, the second time we are viewing its final, post-production version such that, dieget-ically, the "film-within-the-film" blends into Oppenheimer's film itself.[5] After removing his neck-wire, one communist forces a smile, pulls out a medal and places it around Anwar's neck, thanking him "for executing me and sending me to heaven." The scene pushes the killers' heroic self-image to the point of absurdity, and would be ludicrous if we did not know by now that Anwar and his accomplices are actually still treated as national heroes for wiping out the communist threat. A previous scene has shown Anwar and his friends from the paramilitary group Pemuda Pancasila appearing on TV to promote their film-in-progress. In the interview, they are enthusiastically praised by an attractive young talk-show host and the studio audience for their national ser-vice of exterminating the enemy. The aesthetic treatment seen in the waterfall scene is, therefore, less fantastical than we might suppose.

In what version of our post–Cold War world can this lingering imaginary of the communist enemy be possible? If the preceding chapter sought to inter-rogate the use of anachronism as a narrative structuring device that complicates nationalist teleologies of success, this chapter thinks more directly about the constitution of the post–Cold War era itself, a period typically signaled by the fall of the Berlin Wall in 1989, the collapse of the Soviet Union in 1991, and the People's Republic of China's transformation to a hybridized form of state capitalism. In what ways, I ask, does the mass killing of communists and suspected communists in certain Third World countries complicate the story of communism's ideological death in which, as Thatcher famously stated in her eulogy of Reagan, the Cold War was won "without firing a shot"?[26] This chapter suggests that the uncomfortable "living on" of communist specters in places such as Indonesia and South Korea demands a rethinking of the assumptions of the bloodless victory of liberal capitalism. It also posits, as Hwang Su-Kyoung has put it, "the rationale and legacy of anti-communist violence . . . as a distinct phenomenon . . . [that] deserves attention in its own right."[7] The texts that will help us with such a rethinking are Joshua Oppenheimer's diptych of documentaries on the 1965–66 mass killings in Indonesia, *The Act of Killing* (2012), already briefly introduced, and its sequel *The Look of Silence (Senyap)* (2014). Alongside these, I examine Han Kang's novel *Human Acts (Sonyŏni onda* [Here comes the boy]) (2014), a lyrical exploration of the Gwangju Uprising that tells of the 1980 military crackdown against anti-dictatorship protests in that South Korean city (also the subject of Hwang Sŏk-yŏng's *The Old Garden* discussed in the preceding chapter). Both Oppenheimer (born 1974) and Han (born 1970) are of a younger generation of artists who did not personally experience the violence of these atrocities, with Oppenheimer approaching his subject from a non-Indonesian perspective. Like others of their generation, they critically look back on the violence of the Cold War from a post-socialist moment. Han is an acclaimed South Korean author best known for her Booker Prize–winning 2007 novel, *The Vegetarian (Chaesik-ju'ŭija)*,[8] while Oppenheimer, an American, began research into these two films through work on his 2003 film, *The Globalisation Tapes*, a coproduction with the Independent Plantation Workers' Union of Sumatra. We should note that *The Act of Killing*—which won numerous documentary film awards around the world—and the *Look of Silence* were co-directed with an anonymous Indonesian director.

I choose these texts not as representative or authoritative cultural pronouncements on these events; there is by now a large corpus of works on both September 30 and May 18.[9] Rather, Oppenheimer's and Han's texts stand out for their complex engagement with the narrative and temporal conventions of transitional justice and its most common legal genre, the truth commission; I suspect this has contributed to the fact that both have circulated widely beyond their local context. I frame my analysis in terms of the borrowing across legal and aesthetic genres for several reasons. First, as powerful cultural texts that look back from our near-present to inspect atrocities of past decades, it is difficult not to read Oppenheimer's and Han's works in terms of truth commissions and the documentation of human rights abuses more generally, or as part of what Julie Stone Peters has called the late-twentieth-century "culture of testimony."[10] The films and novel include testimonial-like narratives and interviews, witness statements, reenactments, and the cataloguing of perpetrators' acts and victims' suffering, although both do so in highly mediated ways that are anything but a straightforward presentation of evidentiary truth.[11] Nevertheless, these works critically reflect on the violence of past "free world" authoritarianism by participating in a "normative human rights narrative of atrocity, suffering, testimony and redress."[12]

Beyond the obvious human rights aspects of these texts, I am also interested in the specific *temporality* that transitional justice and its imaginative renderings traffic in. If the very idea of a truth commission is to produce the "authoritative account of dictatorship,"[13] such tribunals have been necessary to the production of the broader historical notion of "transition" as well as to a post–Cold War, post-socialist common sense. In Priscilla B. Hayner's influential study of transitional justice, *Unspeakable Truths*, she writes on the nature and goals of those "official bodies set up to investigate and report on a pattern of past human rights abuses."[14] Arising in the 1980s and 1990s to address human rights abuses in newly post-conflict societies, truth commissions are distinct from the legal inquiries of criminal cases because of their broader intent "to address the past in order to change policies, practices, and even relationships to the future, and to do so in a manner that respects and honors those who were affected by the abuses."[15] By definition, "transitional justice" is directional. The technologies of inquiries and commissions are possible only after the "transition" from a civil war, major conflict, or authoritarian regime, thereby allowing a country to reckon with past violence in its journey toward liberal democracy. The goals and forms of transitional justice therefore say as much about a post-conflict or post-authoritarian periodization as they do about the nature of the atrocity. As Hayner points out, what is at stake in transitional justice is precisely the futurity of the collective. Notwithstanding the struggles of individual survivors, "society as a whole must find a way to move on, to recreate a liveable space of national peace, build some form of reconciliation between former enemies, and secure these events in the past."[16]

But how does a society "secure these events in the past"? In one sense, the notion of transitional justice relies on an evolutionary narrative whereby repression recedes as a more liberal and open democracy emerges, allowing silenced voices from the past to speak. Yet as a phenomenon deeply tied to the collapse of the Soviet Union and dictatorships in Latin America and Africa, the concept is also a reinscription of the way global Cold War conflicts were resolved or "managed" in terms that could "secure the globalized system of liberal economy."[17] Writing on the failed Grenada Revolution of 1979–83 and the trials that followed it, David Scott avers that transitional justice, above all, "aims to draw a line between an illiberal past and the *liberalizing* present."[18] Greg Grandin and Thomas Miller Klubock concur that, contra the linear evolution of nation-states toward "liberal and constitutional forms of government," truth commissions "indexed the shift from the global crisis of the 1970s—where escalating cycles of conflict and polarization often led to either repressive dictatorships or deadlocked civil wars—to the post–Cold War would-be *pax* neoliberal."[19] Building on work by these scholars, I explore the way that the narrative, moral and *temporal* forms of truth commissions, as they are taken up by film and literature, grapple with the task of producing the "now" as "the time not possible before."[20]

This chapter is especially interested in how we reckon with the mass killings of suspected communists in a liberal narrative logic that at once testifies to, *and reconfirms the necessity of*, the death of communism. In thinking carefully about how the figure of the communist is rendered in the work of both Oppenheimer and Han, I want to ask what forms of justice can and cannot be imagined by these texts. At the same time, I probe the genres of human rights in ways that exceed the "postideological international" ethos of transitional justice that legitimizes liberal universalism.[21] Crystal Parikh has fruitfully suggested that we can think of the intersection of human rights and literature (or film) in terms of how the imaginative text "shap[es] the notions of human personhood, good life, moral responsibility, and forms of freedom that rights claims seek to address."[22] By paying close attention to the aesthetic forms that represent abuses and atrocities, such as novels and life-writing, she suggests, we can also ask questions about "the social and political norms by which suffering and violence . . . and the distribution of social goods (e.g. security, pleasure, comfort) are imagined and justified."[23] Accordingly, I am interested in how, during the Cold War anti-communist regimes of Indonesia and South Korea, the distribution of suffering and social goods is organized around the figure of the communist. Furthermore, we will see how the communist is the transit point for mediating the gap, as Ariel Heryanto puts it, between "the somewhat 'abstract' global and structural context (the cold war) that created the conditions for the series of events in 1965 and . . . the 'concrete' lived experiences of individuals within their immediate social environment and relationships."[24] This figure is also, however, what sutures ongoing problems

of decolonization with our contemporary moment of uneven neoliberal capitalism in ways that frustrate the truth commission's role of drawing a clear line
between past and present. In other words, I'm interested in showing how the
specificity of anti-communist violence subtends narratives of transitional justice in ways that trouble the periodization of "post–Cold War" and "post-
authoritarian." What makes Oppenheimer's and Han's texts so intriguing is
precisely the way they each render a particular aesthetic of *killing communists*
in our post-socialist present.

Before moving to the analysis of the texts, let's again recall the historical
events that they reference. Oppenheimer's two films revolve around one of the
deadliest—but still little understood—conflicts of the Cold War, when up to
two million communists or PKI (Partai Komunis Indonesia) members, suspected communists, sympathizers, family members, and ethnic Chinese were
slaughtered across the archipelago following the still-debated events of September 30, 1965. On this date, six high-ranking military leaders were assassi-
nated in what was supposedly an attempted coup by the PKI. The military
quickly took over in the ensuing national crisis, effectively clearing the way for
Major General Suharto (who mysteriously avoided assassination) to step in
and replace an ailing and politically discredited President Sukarno. Sukarno,
of course, had been a key figure of the Bandung Conference in 1955 and one-
time leader of the Third Worldist, non-aligned movement. By the early 1960s,
however, Sukarno himself had shifted both to the left and to more autocratic
methods, as he precariously balanced his two largest power bases, the military
and the PKI. With the latter constituting the largest non-bloc Communist
Party in the world at the time,[25] U.S. strategists feared a communist Indonesia
would tip "the balance toward communism in Malaysia and then on through
mainland Southeast Asia."[26] Recent scholarship has shown the extent to which
these Cold War tensions precipitated interference from foreign governments,
especially the U.S.'s support for Indonesia's military as an anti-communist
bulwark.[27] The massive bloodletting of 1965–66 effectively destroyed the
country's left, and fervent anti-communism would underwrite the next three
decades of Suharto's New Order regime. Since the post-Suharto, *Reformasi*
era of the late 1990s, the National Commission on Human Rights (Komnas
HAM, established in 1993) has made ongoing efforts to push the government
into holding official investigations into 1965, without success.[28] As yet no
killers have ever been brought to justice. Moreover, as we saw in Anwar's TV
appearance, the PKI and leftists remain demonized as the nation's number
one enemies in official histories and mainstream public perception.

The subject of Han's novel *Human Acts*, the 1980 5.18 Gwangju Uprising (*5.18
Gwangju hangjaeng*), or Gwangju 5.18 Democritization Movement (*Gwangju*

5.18 *minjuhwa undong*), as it is now known, resembles the Indonesian killings in certain ways. As described in the previous chapter, the Uprising was also preceded by a military coup—a successful one—in early 1980, which followed the assassination of President Park Chung Hee in December 1979, the dictator who had ruled South Korea with increasing repression for almost two decades. In the chaotic months following Park's death, mass protests were staged around the country in expectation of a loosening of the military regime. Instead, one of Park's top generals, General Chun Doo Hwan (Chŏn Tu-hwan), staged his own coup; martial law and the dissolving of the national assembly quickly followed. On May 18, 1980, students and citizens in the southwestern provincial capital of Gwangju rose up in mass protest only to be viciously attacked by the military. Popular outrage manifested in even larger demonstrations across the city such that the military retreated and the citizens took over control of the city, arming themselves by raiding local armories and police stations. After citizens had held the city for almost a week, special troops reentered with tanks to brutally put down the Uprising, indiscriminately killing hundreds and injuring thousands. While the Gwangju Uprising was the subject of a high-profile inquiry and trial of military and political leaders during the 1990s (more on this later), the trial focused on the Seoul command and excluded prosecution of the soldiers involved. Anthropologist Linda S. Lewis notes that despite the mid-1990s investigations, "it has never been made clear who gave the order to open fire on civilian protestors, nor has anyone been held specifically responsible for that decision."[29] In Han Kang's poignant epilogue to *Human Acts*, she describes the months of research she did in the 5.18 archives and the frustrating lack of justice for such brutal acts: "When I first started poring over the documents, what had proved most incomprehensible was that this bloodshed had been committed again and again, and with no attempt to bring the perpetrators [*choe'in*] before the authorities. Acts of violence committed in broad daylight, without hesitation and without regret [*choeŭisikdo mangsŏrimdo ŏmnŭn hannaj ŭi p'ongnyŏk*]."[30]

The preceding accounts do not, of course, deny or condone the violence and excesses of various communist regimes in Asia, epitomized by the brutal policies of the PRC's Cultural Revolution from 1966 to 1976 and the Khmer Rouge's mass killings of 1975–79 in Cambodia.[31] Instead, my goal is to draw attention to the way that killing communists—with "killing" deployed as a transitive verb—has been subordinated in the dominant Cold War episteme to *killing* in its adjectival form—that is, murderous—communists.[32] Further, in both the September 30 events and the 5.18 Uprising, we must also note the murky role of the United States. In Indonesia, it is fairly certain the CIA played a role in encouraging the purge, which followed years of domestic interference by the U.S.,[33] while in South Korea the vast U.S. military forces based there were—as they still are—controlled through a power-sharing agreement between the U.S. and South Korea, unavoidably raising the question of American complicity or at least tolerance of the civilian massacre. And we cannot ignore the decades-long military and economic support provided by the U.S. for both the Indonesian and South Korean dictatorships, in a pattern all too familiar across the Third World.

Narrating Atrocity

In this brief section, I examine some of the ways that our cultural texts intersect with, borrow from, and trouble the narrative conventions of truth commissions and transitional justice. In his work on the relationship between literature and truth commissions in the context of South Africa's Truth and Reconciliation Commission, Paul Gready observes the efflorescence of literary and cultural production both during the commission's hearings and following the 1998 publication of its first five-volume report. Examining novels by J. M. Coetzee, Zoë Wicomb, and others, Gready shows how "culture has meditated upon the meanings of its keywords (truth, justice, reconciliation), retold its stories and reinvented its meta-narrative and metaphors . . . suggesting ongoing processes of reworking and the presence of the past in the present."[34] Literature and culture are able to address "the uncomfortable truths" and "unfinished business" of the commission.[35] In this sense, literature has more than a supplementary relationship to truth commissions. In his study of the same commission, Mark Sanders has elegantly theorized the "interdependence" of law and literature,[36] arguing that the "ambiguity in all languages that . . . designates the literary, abides at the very nub of forensic procedure."[37] Grandin, meanwhile, in an overview of decades of counterrevolutionary violence in Latin America, has described Gabriel García Márquez's *One Hundred Years of Solitude* (1968) as a kind of "gypsy's prophecy" or "anticipatory truth commission, a revelation of terror yet to come."[38] In different ways, Gready, Sanders, and Grandin point to the way that literature and culture might help constitute, and challenge, the forms and assumptions of transitional justice.

We can begin a comparison between Oppenheimer's and Han's works by looking at the ways they each draw from the temporal arc implicit to truth commissions, whereby we ideally move from suffering and truth-telling to reconciliation, justice and healing. *The Act of Killing* is partly driven by a narrative progression that moves toward the moral redemption of Anwar Congo, the movie-ticket scalper and former death squad member, who is initially completely remorseless. In the process of planning out and acting in the film-within-a-film on the killings, he gradually becomes aware of the enormity of his crimes. After shooting a particularly violent scene of the burning of a communist village, children and extras are visibly shaken and traumatized by the reenactment. Observing the way the reenactment has merged with the atrocity itself—evidenced by the crying children, exhausted extras, and smoldering wreckage of the village—Anwar begins to see his actions from a different perspective and confesses to the filmmaker, "Honestly what I regret is . . . I never thought it would look this awful."[39] The "awful" truth of the past seems, finally, to emerge after decades of political impunity. The heroic aesthetic of killing communists that Anwar and his colleagues have enjoyed creating for the big screen turns on itself and, by the end of the filming, their actions are revealed to be no more than murder, torture, and cruelty. It is precisely this self-doubt, this dawning remorse, that begins to redeem Anwar and the other killers toward a moral trajectory of reconciliation.[40]

In contrast, *The Look of Silence* may perhaps be described as taking the form of a frustrated truth commission. Rather than focus on the perpetrators, the sequel film revolves around the victims of 1965, in particular, Adi, an optician who performs eye exams as he surreptitiously interviews the men responsible for his own brother's death. In interview after painful interview, Adi tells his clients of his brother's gruesome death, which occurred as part of a three-month-long orgy of killing at Snake River, Medan. Leading with questions like "How do you see these events?" he is continually rebuffed by the perpetrators who dismiss him with comments like "the past is the past" and justifications that communists were known to be irreligious and sleep with each other's wives.[41] As the details of the horrific violence pile up in these interviews, it is the killers' remorse—rather than official punishment—that Adi yearns for, and which equally structures the viewer's response. As Adi tells his mother when she implores him to drop his inquiries, reconciliation is the goal: "If they felt regret, we could forgive them."[42] If anything, the failures of *The Look of Silence* only confirm the logic of transitional justice by underscoring the impossibility of individual justice when the larger political conditions for truth-telling and "moving on" are not there.

Similarly focused almost solely on victims rather than perpetrators, Han's *Human Acts* is structured by the moral arc of truth-telling and mourning. The novel is an exquisitely crafted, complex text made up of six intersecting chapters, each told from the perspective of a different character caught up in the events of 5.18 and lingering on the painful experiences and reverberations of the event. These include the central protagonist/victim Dong-ho, a middle-school student who joins the protests; the victim's friend; the victim's fellow protestors; the victim's mother; and so on. In one chapter, the narrative even goes beyond the many gruesome details of death and torture to provide an account of the victims' bodies *after* death. The following is narrated by Jeong-dae (Jŏng-dae), friend of Dong-ho, whose spirit witnesses his own body's decomposition after the soldiers remove the dead.

> Following the gestured instructions of one who looked to be in charge, they [the soldiers] stacked the bodies in the neat shape of a cross [*yŏl-sipja ro ch'agok ch'agok momdŭrŭl ssaha'ollyŏssŏ*]. Mine was second from the bottom, jammed in tight and crushed still flatter by every body that was piled on top. Even this pressure didn't squeeze any more blood from my wounds, which could only mean that it had all leaked out already. With my head tipped backwards, the shade of the wood turned my face into a pallid ghost of itself, eyes closed and mouth hanging half open.[43]

Part of an entire chapter narrated by Jeong-dae's spirit, this description mediates between the dead and the living; the spirit can sense the moment of others' deaths, but not ascertain the details. Yet formally, it is presented as simply another eyewitness account of the killings, another partial testimony among others, albeit one from beyond the grave.[44] Deborah Smith's translation, which takes some liberties with the Korean, tends to emphasize the novel's human rights framing even further; Han's poetic chapter titles in Korean—"The Young Bird" (*orin sae*), "Black Breath" (*kŏmŭn sum*), and "Metal and Blood" (*soe wa p'i*)—are replaced by something like dated witness statements: "The Boy. 1980"; "The Boy's Friend. 1980"; and "The Prisoner. 1990." Such titling certifies Han's novel as, above all else, a work of testimony and mourning in a form that could not take place for almost two decades after the Uprising.[45]

The novel's movement from truth-telling to mourning and healing is most explicitly narrated in the chapter-length author's epilogue. Titled "The Writer. 2013" in the English translation, but the more evocative "*nun dŏp'in lampŭ*" ("The Snow-covered Lamp") in Korean, the chapter recounts Han's motivations for writing the novel. Raised in Gwangju until the age of nine but living in Seoul by the time of the Uprising, Han first hears of the massacre by eavesdropping on the whispered conversation of adults and sneaking a look at a clandestine photo book of the victims, whose bloody images are seared in her memory. A personal connection drives the novel's shape: A boy, Dong-ho, on whom the central character of the novel is based, had lived in her family's former house in Gwangju, and his story becomes the connective tissue of the book. The epilogue narrates Han's return to Gwangju in winter 2013 in order to research the event at the 5.18 archives at Chonnam National University. Her "initial intention was to read each and every document I could get my hands on," but the nightmares soon become intolerable.[46] She also searches for Dong-ho's photos and records at the middle school he attended, visits the site of the old house (now torn down) and interviews anyone who knew the family. Most poignant is her interview with Dong-ho's brother who relates not only the tragedy of the boy's death, but the painful process of having the body exhumed in 1997 for reburial in the official May 18 National Cemetery. He describes the harrowing experience of exhumation and reburial, which involves cleaning his brother's bones with his elderly mother: *"I was worried that the skull would be too much for our mother, so I hurriedly picked it up myself and polished the teeth one by one. Even so, the whole experience clearly shook her to the core [kŭ irŭl igigiga himdŭsyŏtdŏnkabonda]."*[47] Following Dong-ho's personal story to its last possible moment, the epilogue concludes with the author visiting the snow-covered cemetery and lighting three candles next to Dong-ho's grave. The author's own journey from childhood rumors and half-knowledge to full knowledge and moral accounting thus constitutes its own transitional justice narrative in miniature, the aesthetic result of which the reader finds holding in her hands. Yet it also operates at the level of national allegory, whereby the suffering of the Gwangju people must be investigated, remembered, redeemed, and properly mourned by the citizenry at large.

Read thus, Oppenheimer's and Han's works function as filmic or literary truth commissions: They are instances of aestheticized truth-telling in the absence of full knowledge and official justice. The events of 1965–66 and 1980 are brought to ethical scrutiny by showing how the atrocities of the past continue to exert pressure on the present in the ongoing demands for truth, justice, reconciliation, and proper mourning. Beyond these striking narrative conventions, however, how might Oppenheimer's and Han's works grapple with reconciliation not just between victims and perpetrators, but between the nation's authoritarian past and its apparently democratic, post–Cold War present? How do these texts narrate the temporal "from" and "to" of transitional justice, and in what ways can cultural texts offer an "alternative grammar of transition" in which truth-telling follows an "unpredictable calendar"?[48]

Killing Communists

Let us return to the scene with which we began: the fantasy of the smiling dead communist. We have already noted the generalized impunity of the killers in contemporary Indonesia, which might explain the bizarre, grotesque scene of the communist who is grateful for his own death. There is, however, a more concrete historical referent. In a scene in *The Look of Silence*, Adi watches an

NBC news clip from 1967. As an American journalist speaks with locals in Bali about the recent killings, one man explains to him, "Now Bali has become more beautiful without communists" and, more puzzlingly, insists that "some of them want[ed] to be killed." The journalist looks confused, but the report proceeds without comment and cuts to a Goodyear rubber plantation in Sumatra, where the footage shows a number of surviving, bedraggled communists who are now forced to work the plantation at gunpoint. What is such an affront to the contemporary viewer of Oppenheimer's films is that the 1965–66 killers and their defenders seem *just* as convinced of the ideological righteousness of killing communists now as during the 1967 NBC news report. We might say that it is the time warp that transports the liberal, post–Cold War viewer back into the midst of the bipolar standoff that makes both *The Act of Killing* and *The Look of Silence* so disorienting. Over the course of the first film, Anwar repeatedly refers to a social geography that is indelibly stained by the presence of communists: This area, he remarks in one scene, was a "communist neighborhood"; in another we see Chinese merchants who are still treated as communists to extort; the background sound of a call to prayer prompts Anwar to inform us that the muezzin himself "used to be a communist"; while in *The Look of Silence*, an angry perpetrator accuses Adi of being a "secret communist" during a tense interview. The contemporary social world of Indonesia is peopled with undead communists.

In 2012, a whole issue of the leading Indonesian news magazine *Tempo* was devoted to *The Act of Killing*, constituting one of the most important public interventions to date into the ongoing silence around the killings. In an opinion article, the editors begin by restating the methods and logic of reconciliation:

> Reconciliation cannot begin with a denial, but with an admission.
> That is what we need to hear from the people responsible for the 1965
> mass killings, and those who supported them. As in the phrase "truth
> and reconciliation," the order of the words shows the first is a prerequi
> site for the second.[49]

They then point out Indonesia's illogical and anachronistic attachment to the perceived communist threat and call for an end to the official government ban on communism, which has amounted to a ban on investigating 1965:

> There is no reason for us to fear communism. The ideology is long
> bankrupt. The Soviet Union is no more and China is now as capitalist
> as the United States. The idea of a classless society is an obsolete and
> futile utopia.
>   Therefore there is no longer any need for a ban on spreading com
> munist teachings such as Marxism and Leninism. . . . There must be

no more bans on books about 1965—or anything else. What needs serious attention is the stigmatization of communism and its victims. The long-held belief that communism equals atheism is mistaken. In other words, there is no need to worry about communism, because as an ideology, it is really nothing special [*biasa saja*, or "so-so"].[50]

Their argument goes something like this: *We are post–Cold War; global communism has been confirmed dead by history and is no longer a threat, so let us now tell the truth about this atrocity!* We are reminded here of Jacques Derrida's comments on communism's lingering spectrality in the wake of the collapse of the Soviet bloc. In his 1993 book, *Specters of Marx*, Derrida ventriloquizes the triumphalism of Francis Fukuyama's well-known "end of history" argument: Communism "is only a spectre without a body, without a present reality, without actuality . . . it was *only* a spectre, an illusion, a phantasm, or a ghost: that is what one hears everywhere today."[51] I want to argue that Oppenheimer's films reveal a different post–Cold War haunting than Derrida's Marxist hauntology. To do so, Oppenheimer presents a distinct aesthetic of communist haunting, one that refracts the event of large-scale killing through the social and economic world that was created in its aftermath. There are three iterations of this aesthetic mode I wish to examine: first are the scenes of consumer stupor set in a big, glassy shopping center, where one of Anwar's fellow perpetrators, Adi Zulkadry,[52] wanders through the displays with his family; second, the barely contained violent display of militarized homosociality in the Pemuda Pancasila rallies; and, third, the brief interview and home tour with Haji Arif, a successful businessman and Pemuda Pancasila member.

Of the first iteration, we can immediately note the contrast between the shots of the sterile shopping center with the melodramatic acting, over-the-top costumes and energy of the reenactment scenes. In two scenes, the camera simply follows Zulkadry as he, his wife, and grown daughter languorously wander through a gleaming mall. In the first scene they sit at a café table, a look of supreme boredom on Zulkadry's face as his daughter and wife take selfies together. In the second, we see them stroll through a department store, running their hands over merchandise and staring at watches and perfume displays, while Zulkadry's voice-over recites the methods used for killing their victims: "We shoved wood in their anus until they died. . . . We hung them. We strangled them with wire. We cut off their heads." Interspersed with these scenes of distracted consumerism are lingering, static shots that portray sales clerks waiting for customers, their forced posture and sleek uniforms aligning the humans with the commodities that surround them (Figure 9).

These odd juxtapositions of sterile, zombie-like mall culture crowded with Western brand names remind us that Suharto's "New Order" Indonesia was

Figure 9. A sales clerk waits for customers in *The Act of Killing.*

not about terror and military repression alone. As we've seen in earlier chapters, the elimination of communists was also a moment of "primitive accumulation," which produced "a cheap and submissive labor force" attractive to foreign capital and left the country free to prioritize export-oriented economic growth.[53] Meanwhile, General Suharto explicitly supplanted Sukarno's Third Worldist, decolonizing ideology of "revolution" with one of technocratic, Western-oriented "development," or *pembangunan.*[54] The shopping mall functions as a metonym for the everyday world that resulted from the elimination of leftists, indexing Indonesia's rise in the ranks of newly industrializing Asian-Pacific economies. Heryanto summarizes the constitutive link between Suharto-era authoritarianism and economic expansion:

> Those coercive elements [of the regime] coexist alongside, and in juxtaposition with, convivial entertainment, festive activities, and the spectacle of fun, humor and laughter. In Indonesia and its neighboring countries, cold war authoritarian repression ran in tandem with sustained economic growth, industrialization, and an expanding desire for global consumerism. Such jarring cognitive dissonance and irony is illustrated abundantly in the film [*The Act of Killing*].[55]

Oppenheimer's film, therefore, is not only an investigation into individual guilt and responsibility for "acts of killing" from a moment that is constitutively different from the past; it gestures toward the very continuity between past atrocity and present prosperity. Recalling that the task of the U.S. and its allies was to ensure "Indonesia's full integration into a liberal international political and economic order over which they presided,"[56] we can better understand how demands for *economic* reconciliation during the Cold War years have stymied *political* reconciliation and transitional justice in the present.

The second iteration of this aesthetic, which can be traced more briefly, concerns the Pemuda Pancasila, which can be translated as "patriotic youth."[57] These scenes work with little need for formal juxtapositions. Here, young men in garish orange camouflage uniforms gather in fields or stadiums and are egged on by both their thuggish leaders and well-dressed government officials and parliamentary representatives. The latter, amazingly, have no shame associating with a paramilitary organization whose regular functions include political intimidation and the protection of illegal businesses. The legitimacy of paramilitary organizations as integral to the political system was made possible, as Taufik Abdullah points out, by the fact that Suharto's New Order state stressed the ultra-nationalist Pancasila as the "ideological foundation of all social and political organizations."[58] These scenes are visual evidence of the way state-sponsored violence against leftists has been normalized as the everyday functioning of a de-radicalized society. Additionally, the militarization of the Suharto government deployed a logic that twinned developmentalism with anti-communism in a recipe echoing other regional autocrats. Thus, "'long-term' military control of politics was justifiable since modernization was a decades-long national project," and the communist threat of instability to that project could be countered only by "military surveillance in all fields of national life."[59]

Finally, in the third iteration (Figure 10), the soft-spoken businessman Haji Arif patiently explains why the political elite cannot do without the organization. In a gentle voice mixing English with Indonesian, he states the obvious: "Everyone is terrified of the paramilitaries." He then explains that when a business wants to expropriate land, for example, the organization "helps" and makes the sale happen at whatever price the buyer wants. Furthermore, the youth group "doesn't allow for political protests" when politicians visit. Visually, Haji's calm exposition is paired with a tour around his mansion, its rolling grounds, and a special display room of his most prized possession—a collection of ostentatious jeweled and crystal figurines, each of which, we are assured, is "very, very limited." This scene, I insist, should be read as another version of the aesthetics of killing communists. Haji's enormous house and his room of priceless treasures are exactly the material index of the unchallenged ability to concentrate wealth, land, resources, and political power. In this aesthetic logic, grasping the truth of the communist purge requires no colorful reenactments, no contemplative acts of memory or mourning, and no digging

Figure 10. Haji Arif with his collection of crystal figurines in *The Act of Killing*.

up of bodies. It is to Oppenheimer's credit that he succeeds in capturing not only the aesthetic forms of the perpetrators' imaginations, but the everyday aesthetic results of the larger social "common sense" that was produced as the enduring aftermath of the massacres: shiny, soporific malls; hyper-masculinist displays of militarized power; and mansions full of treasures. As the press notes from the film's anonymous co-director put it, "the true legacy of the dictatorship" is "the erasure of our ability to imagine anything other."[60]

Anthropologist Heonik Kwon has written elegantly of the way that the bipolarization of political forces flashes up with special violence in the decolonizing world. Drawing on examples from Korea, Vietnam, and Indonesia, he notes that anti-communist violence was often justified by "essentialized idioms of differences and often targeted the collective social units to which these individuals belonged."[61] In common expressions like "red seed" or "red blood line," the ideology of communism is seen as something biological, genealogical, and inheritable, requiring nothing less than its elimination from the roots.[62] As Oppenheimer's films reveal, the communist body is that upon which unlimited, almost imponderable, transgenerational violence may be inflicted. In Indonesia, the national body must be constantly purified anew, a logic evinced in the "clean-self" (*bersih diri*) and "clean environment" (*bersih lingkungan*) movements that justified continued vigilance against communists. Former PKI members, their children, and even grandchildren were marked as such on their national ID cards enabling discrimination in certain jobs and educational opportunities. As we saw earlier with the Malayan Emergency, the Chinese community—with their status as perpetual foreigners and assumed links to the PRC—were especially targeted. The logic of colonial racial governance is reconstituted in the targeting of certain races as always already potential communists, enemies of the nation. The strategic adaptability of this logic is clear in the paradoxical fact that Chinese Indonesians bore the stigma as both anti-national communists and rapacious capitalists simultaneously.[63] The postcolony thus inaugurates what Kwon has called a "new bipolar color line," which "encompassed societies previously divided by the traditional color line, partly replacing the latter in significance and partly complicating it."[64]

Moreover, as Lisa Yoneyama has suggested, the arrangement of "Cold War justice has set the parameters of what can be known as violence and whose violence, on which bodies, can be addressed and redressed."[65] Indeed, in the world of Oppenheimer's films, the *only* violence that can be recognized is still that committed by the undead communist. These films, therefore, confound fundamental assumptions of truth-telling and reconciliation, which aim, as Grant Farred reminds us, for the past to be "narrativized into history [so that] the past can be sutured (in)to the present."[66] The figure of the undead communist, I argue, blocks such a reconciliatory suturing by laying bare the way our own post–Cold War *pax neoliberal* was partly achieved through such past violence. The careful aesthetic compositions of *The Act of Killing* and *The Look of Silence* unravel the logic of transitional justice whereby atrocities must be addressed in a present that is *differentiated* from the illiberal excesses of the past. Instead, we see how the "post–Cold War" period is haunted by an entrenched Cold War ontology, still populated with undead communists. Thus, in Indonesia the "specter of communism" is not the ghost of a discredited ideology put to rest by Fukuyama's "end of history." As in other parts of Asia, Latin America, and Africa, communism assumes a spectral quality not because of its historical insubstantiality—that "so-so" ideology as the editors of *Tempo* reassure us—but because of the hundreds of thousands of men and women who were slaughtered, tortured, imprisoned, and terrorized in the name of its supposed antonym, freedom.

As already mentioned, the national context of the Gwangju 5.18 Uprising and massacre is, in many ways, distinct from the killings in Indonesia, not least for there having been a special inquiry and trial. We must also acknowledge the differing infrastructure of killings: In Indonesia, death squads, gangsters, and paramilitaries did the state's dirty work, while the military, with help from the CIA, conveniently provided lists of suspected communists and transported political prisoners to killings sites, all while spreading propaganda about their murderous intent.[67] In South Korea, by contrast, the perpetrators were unambiguously the military acting on orders from the political leadership. In 1995 a special legislative act was decreed that enabled the prosecution of crimes related to 5.18 to proceed after the statute of limitations (15 years) had technically passed, and the decision from the special trial was handed down in 1997. Remarkably, the appellate court convicted the two most recent former Korean presidents, Chun Doo Hwan and Ro Tae Woo (No T'ae-woo), a number of high-ranking politicians, as well as *chaebol* (conglomerate) business leaders who supported them, with the somewhat tautological crime of "treason and homicide for the purpose of treason."[68] Legal scholar Han In Sup provides a useful overview of the way the inquiry shared characteristics of a truth commission (though it wasn't called as such). Beyond the criminal prosecution, it was guided by five principles, namely, "truth, justice, compensation, honor restoration and commemoration."[69] In Han In Sup's opinion, the "justice" portion of the process was relatively well served, given the high-ranking convictions. That all of the convicted were subsequently pardoned by the next incoming president, former dissident opposition leader, political prisoner, and Cholla-region native Kim Dae-jung is not insignificant and shall be discussed below. Despite the fact—alluded to in Han Kang's epilogue—that the individual perpetrators were never brought to trial, the Gwangju massacre was front and center of the country's transition to post-dictatorship in the 1990s during South Korea's first civilian government led by President Kim Young-Sam (1993–98). The 5.18 Uprising thus condenses a very different public memory than the events of 1965–66 in Indonesia.

Yet my focus in Han's novel is, again, the figure—or perhaps more accurately, the *absence*—of the communist and what it can reveal about the post-authoritarian transition. According to Han In Sup's account of the five principles of the special inquiry, literature, film, and architectural monuments would come under the fifth principle of "commemoration," which he defines as "a way to revive the memory of the original tragedy."[70] *Human Acts* is centrally organized around this task. Its penultimate chapter, narrated by Dong-ho's aging mother, is nothing short of heartbreaking in its depiction of the way lives are shattered and permanently haunted by loss. I suggest, however, that Han's novel may be better understood by the logic of the fourth category, "honor restoration." Han In Sup defines this as the "restoration of legal status and social position to those who were . . . stigmatized as rebels or rioters or were colored with red (communist)."[71] I suggest that at least part of the aesthetic remit of Han's novel is to re-humanize and redeem those who suffered not only the violence of the military, but also the biological, genealogical stigma of rebellion and radical leftism that attached (and still attaches) to the people of Gwangju. Recall that in the 1980s, official government reports of the Uprising blamed "wayward rioters" and "mobsters" for the turmoil and justified the military repression by claiming "that impure elements or armed

North Korean commandos might infiltrate Kwangju."[72] Although the Uprising was not fomented by North Koreans, the state's view that any civil unrest was *potentially* communist draws on a long history of interpretive authority that legitimates preemptive military violence. It is no wonder that, in a sort of reverse logic to Oppenheimer's films, there are no communists—dead or alive—in Han's novel.

Human Acts does such an exemplary job of restoring honor to—or perhaps "de-communizing"—the victims of 5.18 that the first revelation of the perpetrators' anti-communist logic arrives as something of a surprise. For the first half of the novel, Han provides allusive, partial accounts of middle-schooler Dong-ho's death, creating a foreboding that is finally discharged at the end of Chapter 4. This chapter is narrated by a former university student and protestor who was subsequently imprisoned and mercilessly tortured for several years; his punishment was especially harsh as he had been armed at the time of capture. Although the bulk of the chapter recounts his harrowing time in prison, its primary function in the larger narrative is to give testimony of Dong-ho's death. The latter occurs in the final, climactic standoff between the hard core of the citizen protestors—who had occupied the Provincial Office in the center of downtown and were armed—and the soldiers who return to retake the city. It is at this point in the narrative that Han characterizes an individual perpetrator for the first time in the novel. An officer who has just ordered the beating of a group of poorly armed students explains that "I was in Vietnam, you sons of bitches. I killed thirty of those Vietcong bastards with my own two hands. Filthy fucking reds [*ssip'al ppalgaengidŭl*]."[73] The narrator, who has been forced to the ground by other soldiers, witnesses Dong-ho's death in all its cruelty: "The bullets tore into those school kids without hesitation. My head inadvertently jerked up, and when he [the officer] whooped in the direction of his subordinates, 'As good as a fucking movie, right?' I saw how straight and white his teeth were."[74] Echoing the centrality of mediation and screen fantasies in *The Act of Killing*, the officer imagines himself the hero of a Hollywood action film, picking off the evil commies. But more relevant is the reader's realization that from the perspective of the state and military, the citizens of Gwangju simply *are* communists. Indeed, it is widely assumed that the particular brutality of the attacking soldiers was partly due to the fact of their being special forces intentionally trained for North Korean combat.[75] Whether the protestors were actual communists or simply vulnerable to communist collaboration was immaterial; as Hwang Su-Kyoung writes in her study of anti-communist violence before and during the Korean War, South Korean counterinsurgency campaigns could be "based on the suspicion that [leftist and workers' groups] *might* collaborate with the Soviet

Union if given half the chance."[76] By the time of the 1980 Uprising, of course, the communist threat was a much more tangible and regional threat, with China backing North Korea and South Korean troops only recently returned from Vietnam.

Grandin has written of the way "the slander 'Bolshevik' became continental currency" in prewar Latin America, while after World War II the "evolving Cold War offered a new repertoire of reference" with the backing of the new imperial hegemon, the U.S.[77] Anti-communism morphed into a global movement that mirrored the international left in scope and was able to translate local conflicts and social environments into a universal struggle. In Guatemala, the focus of Grandin's study, anti-communist students "affected an insurgent internationalism exuberant in tone and content, communicating with other anti-communist movements not only throughout Latin America but in Asia as well."[78] Han's novel reveals—most strikingly in this pivotal scene of Dong-ho's death—the powerful way international anti-communism produces a hermeneutic authority that legitimizes violence. The officer boasts, "I killed thirty of those Vietcong bastards," with the assumption that he is merely eliminating more of them. The scene forces us to recall the crucial pedagogical role of other Asian "Cold" War conflicts, and the fact that, in a lucrative deal between Presidents Johnson and Park Chung Hee, South Korea provided some 300,000 troops to support the U.S. in Vietnam.[79] As Daniel Y. Kim has noted, the novel demands to be read for the way its history "spans the distance between both that east Asian country [South Korea] and ones in southeast Asia, and also between that region and the US."[80] In Han's remarkably condensed aesthetic form, the perpetrator's logic points to the larger geopolitical conditions of anti-communist ideology in South Korea.

In temporal terms, the killer's boast also takes us further back to the moment of decolonization/division in 1945, that is, the simultaneous liberation from the Japanese, and the partition and occupation of the peninsula by the Soviets in the North and Americans in the South. As I've already argued, Cold War decolonization is less about an "exit narrative" in which the colonizers leave, and more an "entry, with considerable baggage, into a new world order."[81] In this view, Gwangju 1980 may better be understood as an aftershock of a more foundational violence that occurred during the political transitions of thirty years prior, that is, from colony of Japan to the South's military occupation by the United States and the establishment of the Republic of Korea in 1948. Following the period of the U.S. Army Military Government in Korea (USAMGIK), from 1945 to 1948, pro-U.S. Syngman Rhee was installed as first president of the Republic of Korea (he would be in power from 1948 until ousted by popular protests in 1960). At this transition moment during the Spring of 1948, people

of Cheju Island (Chejudo), off the southern tip of the peninsula, staged "protests against USAMGIK, the state of division, and the incumbent president
Syngman Rhee."[82] They were, in other words, explicitly voicing the problems
of decolonization and objecting to the solidifying of the Cold War boundary.
In response, and beginning as a campaign against a few hundred leftist rebels,
police repression morphed into an island-wide conflagration in which the
U.S.-directed South Korean military and police killed an estimated 8,000–
30,000 people, or roughly 10 percent of the island's population. People's various grievances were effectively "communized" by the government, which
assumed the rebellion either was instigated or *could* be instrumentalized by
the Soviet Union.[83] The paradigm-setting, orgy of anti-communist violence
on Chejudo is perhaps more directly comparable to events in Indonesia in
1965. Subsequently, South Korean society was "oversocialized with the politics
of anti-communism" for the next four decades,[84] and a robust discrimination
and shame attached to relatives of accused communists or survivors of anti-
communist violence. Thus, Hwang Su-Kyoung observes via Judith Butler's
work, until recently, "the actual victims of anti-communist violence . . . were
not treated as grievable lives."[85]

We see the enduring logic of the grievable and ungrievable in representations of Gwangju, 1980, as we did in Oppenheimer's films. To return to Han's
novel, the careful staging of the climactic scene at the Provincial Office with
its loathsome military officer shooting an unarmed schoolboy is meant, I
think, to distinguish Dong-ho and other innocents as far as possible from any
actual communists. The readerly pathos and moral outrage produced is precisely a function of the distance between Dong-ho, the frail teenager who
tends unclaimed victims' bodies, and the cinematically mediated image of
"filthy fucking reds." In other words, the monstrosity of the Chun Doo Hwan
regime is confirmed not only in the bloodletting of the massacre itself but also
in its blatantly erroneous epistemology, whereby middle-schoolers apparently
posed a political threat to the state. What is left intact in the logic of "restoring
honor" to Gwangju citizens in order to make them grievable, however, is that
the killing of *actual* communists remains acceptable, or even necessary. The
crime of the state lies primarily in the misdirection, rather than the illegality
or immorality, of anti-communist violence.

In Han In Sup's account of the 1995–97 trials, he explains that it was not
just the massacre's perpetrators, but Chun Doo Hwan's entire regime that was
on trial. One consequence of indicting the illiberal "evil regime"[86] of the past
was that Gwangju citizen-victims were "not only recognized as having suffered abuse, but were now honored as the defenders of the Constitution
because they had protested against the lawless military junta who pillaged,

massacred, and disgraced the constitutional order of the nation."[87] The notion of "honor restoration" thus erases the demands of radical anti-government politics via the logic of recuperation and reconciliation *within* the nation-state, casting the protestors as simply patriotic defenders of the nation. Lewis's study of the politics of memory around the Uprising confirms that by the late 1990s, the state largely "commemorated 5.18 for its pro-democracy legacy."[88] Interestingly, the Uprising is sometimes referred to as "Korea's Tiananmen Square," in a conflation of time (since it occurred well before Tiananmen) and ideology (blending anti-communist and communist). A parallel displacement and depoliticization seems to occur in Han's novel, in which there are no communists or leftists, but only patriotic citizens. The emphasis on personal, individualized suffering has tended to shade out links to the larger *minjung* (popular) movement of the 1970s and 1980s, with its militant labor movement and demands for "decolonization, represented by the achievement of reunification."[89] Instead, the class and anti-government nature of the Uprising was repackaged into an ideal symbol of civic value whereby Gwangju becomes the region's "Mecca of democracy"[90] and model human rights struggle, producing a transnational justice narrative of an illiberal past that appears "remade" by the liberal, post-ideological present.[91] Moreover, in a conjuncture where the dictates of neoliberalism awkwardly parade as post-authoritarian liberalism, President Kim Dae-Jung was forced to pardon those found guilty, since the verdict coincided with the chaos of the 1997–98 Asian Financial Crisis—the very crisis that also brought down Suharto's government. Dealing with mass layoffs, an IMF bailout loan, and the neoliberalization of the economy, 1998 was exactly the wrong year to reckon with the past collusion of state, business, and military violence in eliminating leftists from the country. Indeed, at the 1998 anniversary of the Uprising held in the new 5.18 cemetery, the acting prime minister went so far as to appeal to the memory of "May 18 democratic fighters" and their sacrifices as a model for accepting austerity measures in the context of the Asian Financial Crisis and IMF bailout package.[92] Han's novelistic aesthetic is structured by a similar conundrum: to represent 5.18 in a way that honors the victims' suffering and political agency but in a (neo)liberal present that obscures "the structural historical processes and political conflicts that gave rise to the human rights violations" in the first place.[93]

In another chapter of *Human Acts*, we see Han grapple more fully with the complex politicized landscape of South Korea in the 1970s and early '80s. Titled "The Eye (or pupil) of the Moon" (*Pam ŭi nundongja*), and translated as "Factory Girl. 2002," this chapter is narrated by Lim Seon-ju (Lim Sŏn-ju) some twenty-two years after the events of May 1980. Her story—or rather testimony—of imprisonment, torture, and lingering trauma focuses, as does

Han's larger project, on the lyrical investigation into human pain and suffering. Yet it nevertheless discloses the ways that the labor movement of the 1970s and '80s was deeply imbricated in the anti-dictatorship movement. Formally, Seon-ju's fragmented biographical segments are interspersed with her present-day dilemma of responding to a professor's request for her testimony; we thus learn that in the late 1970s Seon-ju was a teenage factory worker in a textile company and one of thousands of women who helped build the South Korean "miracle economy" by working 15-hour days for low pay. The second-person narrative bluntly recounts the conditions of this work: "The wages were half of what the men got paid for the same work. . . . You took pills to keep you awake, but exhaustion still battered you like a wave. . . . Hacking coughs. Nosebleeds. Headaches. Clumps of what looked like black threads in the phlegm you hacked up."[94] At eighteen, Seon-ju joins a women's labor protest against the company-dominated union. In a strike, she and other women are beaten by strikebreakers and police, and she ends up hospitalized for an intestinal rupture. In Seon-ju's understanding, the authoritarian government is inseparable from the abuses she experiences as a worker:

> You never forgot that the government actively trained and supported the strike-breakers, that at the peak of this pyramid of violence stood President Park Chung-hee himself, an army general who had seized power through a military coup. You understood the meaning of emergency measure no. 9, which severely penalized . . . practically any criticism of the government. . . .
>
> When President Park was assassinated that October, you asked yourself: Now the peak has been lopped off [*ije p'ongnyŏk ŭi chŏngjŏmi sarajyŏssŭni*], will the whole pyramid of violence collapse? Will it no longer be possible to arrest screaming, naked factory girls? Will it no longer be permissible to stamp on them and burst their intestines?[95]

Seon-ju's testimony allows us to understand that the resistance to the renewed dictatorship of Chun Doo Hwan is not an abstract defense of human rights or of the sanctity of the national constitution. It is grounded in the very concrete demands of working people and includes, simply, the right to decent working conditions and the right to not be beaten for those demands.

That spring, Seon-ju is drawn into the Gwangju Uprising after encountering a bus full of singing factory girls who dangle a banner proclaiming, "END MARTIAL LAW. GUARANTEE LABOUR RIGHTS [*kye'ŏm haeje, nodong samgwon pojang*]."[96] In giving the reader access to this wider political landscape, Han's preferred aesthetic mode of documenting lyrical suffering and personal trauma comes under some pressure. Seon-ju's first experience with the women's labor group, for example, involves sitting on a rooftop eating peaches, where she is told by an older member that the moon is called "the eye of the night [*pam ŭi nundongja rago haettda*]."[97] The union leader, Seong-hui, who teaches them labor law and to read hanja (Chinese characters), has a voice like a "primary school teacher" (162), while the girls in the bus on their way to the protest have "pale faces [that] put you in mind of mushrooms [*bŏsŏt katch'i ŏlguri ch'ang-baekhan yŏja*]."[98] Following the Uprising, Seon-ju's two years of imprisonment and torture—where she is assumed to be a North Korean spy—is narrated elliptically in terms of the horrendous physical abuse she undergoes and the lyrical account of her ongoing psychic trauma. On the one hand, then, the aesthetic again works to ban any potential communists from the narrative as it softens and feminizes—with "peaches," "moons," and faces like "mushrooms"—the labor movement that Seon-ju and her fellow workers participate in. We have already noted the way that official memorializations of 5.18 have worked to depoliticize and "domesticate" the event by downplaying the fact of armed resistance and focusing on nonviolence, victimhood, and military brutality.[99] According to this logic, if Gwangju victims are re-humanized—or de-communized—as the subjects of human rights, it would appear that they cannot also be subjects of political action other than defending an abstract "true" nation. Han's narrative thus walks the line between doing justice to the concrete demands of the labor movement, and avoiding the possible stain of leftist radicalism. The novel is symptomatic of the powerful, and enduring, construction of personhood during the Korean peninsula's Cold War, whereby leftists and communists were seen as an inhuman excess outside the nation, no matter the scale of actual violence heaped upon them.

On another level, however, we might read Han's characterization of Seon-ju as subverting the deeper ontological logic of communists and leftists as outside humanity. As in the discourse of totalitarianism examined in Chapter 2, a central trope of anti-communism was not the fear of loss of life per se, but "the loss of *self*, the subjugation of individual thought to an all-enveloping and unquestioned system of belief and behavior."[100] We might read Seon-ju's poetic testimony of her political awakening, especially her ability to connect the daily violence of factory work to patriarchal dictatorship, as an affirmation of her individuality within what otherwise could be dismissed as a de-individuating politics. Her story functions similarly to the way that "most of Latin America's testimonial literature . . . conveys how [leftist] politics helped *define* people's self-understanding"[101] rather than subtract from it. In this reading, Han refutes the dehumanizing logic attributed to leftist collective politics, although the specter of communism cannot quite come onto the page.

Finally, we can read Han's novel for what it reveals about the "unpredict-able calendar" of truth commissions and transitional justice. If the temporality of truth commissions "freezes the past into its distinct temporality," in certain cultural texts, by contrast, "the past survives as a political, affective, and mate-rial remainder in the present."[102] For Han, although this remainder is largely signified through individualized trauma and the body in pain, it also emerges in the political sense via the metaphor of radiation exposure (*p'ip'ok*). In her epilogue, she writes of the ongoing fact of state violence in contemporary, post-liberalized South Korea:

> In January 2009, when an illegal raid by riot police on activists and tenants protesting their forced eviction from central Seoul left six dead, I remember being glued to the television, watching the towers burning in the middle of the night and surprising myself with the words that sprang from my mouth: *But that's Gwangju.* In other words, "Gwangju" had become another name for whatever is forcibly isolated, beaten down and brutalised, for all that has been mutilated beyond repair. The radioactive spread is ongoing. [*P'ip'oki ajik kkŭtnaji anat-tda.*] Gwangju has been reborn only to be butchered again in an end-less cycle.[103]

In this violent reverberation of 1980, Han suggests that no clear line between the illiberal past and the liberal present can be easily drawn. Rather, "Gwangju" is a heuristic that allows for the recognition of ongoing repression and state terror in an era which has supposedly transcended such illiberalism; more directly, the raid reveals the inhumanity wrought by neoliberalism in its valu-ing of profits and markets over human life. Han's metaphor of radioactivity, however, need not be read as metaphorical at all. In Korean, *p'ip'ok* can also mean "being bombed"; thus another meaning of the sentence is, "the bomb-ing is still ongoing/unfinished." The extraordinary, mid-century violence which characterized the bipolar struggle over decolonization continues to structure the peninsula.

The Trials of the (post-) Cold War

A decade after the special 1995–97 trials, a broader South Korean truth com-mission addressed issues going back to the Japanese colonial era, including the period before and during the Korean War. Remarkably, in the commis-sion's final report in 2010, it found that 82 percent of the 9,609 petitions regard-ing wartime civilian massacres were attributable to South Korean state agents (the police, the military, and rightist groups associated with the state), and only

18 percent to the North Korean military and to leftist groups.[104] The main patterns of violence were: detention and execution of former communists and their supporters; retaliation against alleged communist collaborators; killings during the rooting-out of communists; and killings by U.S. bombings.[105] According to this evidence, anti-communist violence by the U.S.-backed South Korean state was a far more deadly force than the communist enemy themselves. Han In Sup has pondered the difficulty of approaching those turbulent founding years of the Republic:

> However, [in contrast to later periods under dictatorship] it was difficult to come to a consensus about how to deal with the military and police atrocities committed from 1948 through 1953. During these years, state terrorism had constituted a part of building the state itself.[106]

Officially formed in 1948, the South Korean state, it could be said, is anti-communist all the way down. The central role of "state terrorism" confirms Walter Benjamin's observation on the lawmaking function of violence, in which "violence crowned by fate, is the origin of law."[107] Similarly, we can posit 1965 as the foundational moment of both mass violence and state-building for the New Order government in Indonesia. Accordingly, *The Act of Killing* should not be read primarily as the indictment of certain individuals since "the crimes Anwar committed are constitutive of the state."[108]

The bipolar Cold War logic that seems to persist past its global use-by date reveals contradictions within the periodizations of both the Cold War and post–Cold War. If the legal technologies of transitional justice promise us entry into the time of the post-authoritarian now, or "the time not possible before,"[109] there is something strangely tautological about the time that liberalizes an *anti*-communist regime. That is, the transition to liberal democracy from the human rights abuses of the past must obscure the way that decades of anti-communist violence and terror *itself* played a major role in "liberalism's world-historical defeat of its principal Cold War political adversaries."[110] Such "sleights of hand" cover up a range of "illiberal" histories, but rhetorically guarantee entry into the post-ideological, universal time of the post–Cold War.[111] In a parallel argument from a different (post–) Cold War location, Chinese cultural critic Dai Jinhua has written of the multiple inversions and scramblings that Chinese historiography has had to undergo in order to legitimize that country's capitalist rise. For example, the 1972 Sino-U.S. Communiqué marked the start of Deng Xioaping's era of reform and opening, thus "beginning a post–Cold War era within the socialist camp even before the end of the Cold War. Time itself was foreshortened, displaced from the communist-utopian processes into global capitalist time."[112] If, for Marx, communism was a spectral presence from the future, in China today Marx-ism is "a phantom from the past that now and then emerges and takes place in the present."[113] The result is that in contemporary China "heterogeneous historical narratives that arose from the binary cultural logic of the Cold War [have] fought for ownership and narrative of history and time."[114] Oppen-heimer's films, the *Tempo* editorial, and Han's novel reveal another strange folding of (post–) Cold War time. In these particular struggles over narratives of history and time, the time of the Cold War leaks into, shapes, and subtends the post-transition, post-authoritarian liberal order. In these sites, the confir-mation of "global capitalist time" comes not from communism's historically verifiable exhaustion (the Soviet Union) or its inexorable evolution into the latest stage of capitalism (the PRC), but from the way anti-communism itself leveraged a certain path for Third World development.

I suggest, then, that the mass killings of *communists* in the past is the dis-avowed underside of the triumphalist end-of-history narrative that firmly pro-claims the "death" of *communism* in the present. We might understand Oppenheimer's and Han's texts less as poetic, imaginative efforts to stage alter-native truth-tellings of state violence, and more as revealing the enunciatory logic of a stalled exorcism, which, Derrida reminds us, "pretends to declare the death [of a person] only in order to put to death."[115] Put another way, the trials of transitional justice surreptitiously enact the larger trial and judgment of global communism. In Dai's words, such "victor's justice" demands nothing less than the "total negation of an alternative future other than capitalism,"[116] which also includes, importantly, writing out those paths which might have resulted in moderate social-democratic societies. Even as *The Act of Killing*, *The Look of Silence*, and *Human Acts* participate in the grammars of post-socialist common sense, they nevertheless point to its unacknowledged mate-rial conditions of possibility, whereby millions of suspected communists—as well as other futures and forms of justice—were killed off in sites where the Cold War was not "cold" at all. The figure of the communist, dead or alive, spectral or imaginary, not only occludes the actual richness and complexity of leftist movements and their desires. It condenses the contradictions and com-plicity of transitional justice with today's neoliberal order. He or she must remain outside humanity in order to shore up the humanity of the capitalist system that dictates our world today.

Epilogue
Authoritarian Lessons for Neoliberal Times

With the recent surge of right-wing populism and antidemocratic strongman leaders, many have read our current moment as a puzzling redux of twentieth-century authoritarianism and fascism. (Moreover, as this book goes to press, the unfolding novel coronavirus pandemic crisis is bringing authoritarianism, individual liberties, collective action, and capitalist futures into ever more strained configurations.)[1] If we take a more global perspective, however, it is difficult to see today's autocratic turn as a return after an interval of postwar democracy.[2] Instead, we might understand the current regimes of Trump, Johnson, Putin, Modi, Bolsonaro, Duterte, and others—whether of the global North or South—less as a surprising return after an absence and more as an expansion or intensification of a global phenomenon that never went away. My intention in these concluding remarks is not to assert that the "free world" authoritarian regimes studied in this book are direct precursors to today's crisis of democracy. Rather, I have been at pains to show that the coupling of capitalist development and Cold War authoritarianism was not a geographical anomaly nor a transitional phase, but an essential unfolding of the story of *both* decolonization *and* capital since World War II. Only through such a perspective can we appreciate the broader formation of what only appears to be the oxymoronic appearance of "freedom and authoritarianism."[3] Put otherwise, how can we think more capaciously about the dialectics of modern democracy, freedom, and authoritarianism if we include in our account the profound legacies of colonial dictatorships and the complications of Cold War decolonization? Although authoritarianism is clearly not a single substance, what light does a more global perspective on the phenomenon shed on today's illiberal turn?

In this brief coda I take up some of these questions. In what follows, I examine some recent political thought indicting neoliberalism for the rise of contemporary right-wing populism, and contrast this with accounts of neoliberalism that place decolonization at the center. I pair these theoretical and historical observations with a brief reading of a 2014 South Korean blockbuster film, *Ode to My Father* (*Kukje sijang*), directed by Yoon Je-kyoon (Yun Che-kyun). The latter, as a filmic plotting of the political-economic transformations of the developmental state, presents the struggles of decolonization as a nationalist tale compatible with neoliberalism's own self-narrative. Counterintuitively, I suggest that the U.S.-aligned region of the Asia-Pacific has preserved within it a form of antidemocratic capitalist development that provides a certain epistemological privilege for our neoliberal present. Its enduring logic, I stress, is not merely a lesson in realpolitik and forecasting disappointing outcomes. It demands that we interrogate more carefully the hinge of "freedom" around which we typically cast "liberal freedoms" in opposition to the authoritarian state.

In the introduction to their 2018 study, *Authoritarianism: Three Inquiries in Critical Theory*, Wendy Brown, Peter E. Gordon, and Max Pensky ponder the apparent return of illiberal regimes. They suggest that "the advent of the new era of antidemocratic politics, much of it with increasingly authoritarian features"[4] prompts a reexamination of Frankfurt School thinkers such as Adorno and Horkheimer who sought to understand "the slide into fascism in the 1930s."[5] Thus, "Notwithstanding the very real differences between the fascist movements of the mid-twentieth century and the antidemocratic movements of our time, critical theory remains of urgent relevance today, when many of the same phenomena . . . seem to have resurfaced in a new guise."[6] Acknowledging that their focus is on the "crisis of democracy in the Euro-Atlantic world,"[7] the authors imply that the period between World War II and the present has been, more or less, one of liberal democracy. Brown deepens this analysis—and extends it further in her 2019 book *In the Ruins of Neoliberalism*[8]—with an investigation into the way neoliberalism has prepared the ground for the current rollback of Western democracy. Focusing on the discourses of Trump in the U.S., Marine Le Pen in France, and those around Brexit in the U.K., Brown traces the way the concept of freedom undergoes a profound resignification. Central to her analysis are two strands characteristic of neoliberal thought. In the first, as freedom "is submitted to market means, it is stripped of the political valences that attach it to popular sovereignty and thus to democracy."[9] As David Harvey has noted, and Karl Polanyi before him, freedom here "degenerates into a mere advocacy of free enterprise."[10] Second, neoliberal freedom involves a moral dimension, "equated wholly with the pursuit of private ends,"[11] and results in the elevation of family values over social ones. Reviewing the thought of neoliberalism's major ideologues, Milton Friedman and Friedrich Hayek, Brown shows how the market becomes the quintessential realm of "freedom" and "choice" by way of its contrast to the necessary "coercion" of any political or collective system. By this logic, paraphrasing Hayek, "liberty prevails where there is no intentional coercion,"[12] where coercion is equated with any state or collective regulatory effort toward "equality, inclusion, access, and even civility."[13] Freedom thus paradoxically ends up legitimizing "social exclusion and social violence."[14] The result is bleak.

> When the nation itself is economized and familialized in this way, democratic principles of universality, equality, and openness are jettisoned, and the nation becomes legitimately illiberal toward those designated as aversive insiders or invading outsiders. Statism, policing, and authoritarian power also ramify since walling, policing, and securitization of every kind are authorized by the need to secure this vast expanse of personal, deregulated freedom.[15]

In both the second part of Brown's essay and in *In the Ruins of Neoliberalism* she explores the kind of subjectivity that is produced by a combination of white resentment and the neoliberal denial of the social. In this configuration, "freedom abandons all of the affinity with political self-determination found in Rousseau, Tocqueville, or Marx,"[16] and deteriorates into an impoverished, nihilistic freedom "which posits no value apart from that generated by price and speculative markets."[17]

A lucid theorization of the Euro-American world's autocratic turn, Brown's work does not simply "argue that the fascisms of the 1930s are 'returning.'"[18] She also acknowledges the neoliberal structural adjustment regimes in the Global South that began in the late 1970s, and briefly notes, following Quinn Slobodian, the way neoliberalism was "intellectually conceived and practically unveiled as a *global* project."[19] Yet Brown's North Atlantic focus does not allow us to see the constitutive role the decolonizing world played in contemporary neoliberal formations. First, we must complicate the zero-sum-game between "free" capitalist markets and the more substantive freedom of political self-determination raised above. As we have seen, U.S.-backed postcolonial regimes in the decolonizing Asia-Pacific could use the Cold War standoff to their advantage, wielding anti-communism as a means to discipline labor, gain entrance to lucrative military and trade alliances, and build export manufacturing economies just as Western economies were de-industrializing. Authoritarianism as "revolutionary promotion" was justified by reference to a deferred but imminent postcolonial sovereignty in the future—brought about by the various slogans we have seen of the "New Society," "New Order," or "Revitalizing Reforms." This book has provided a thick cultural-historical description of the conjoining of capitalism and illiberalism that occurred precisely in the name of political self-determination. Thinking through the global Cold War, we must also recall that the Western welfare state and its historic compromise between capital and labor was partially dependent on its opposition to the Soviet system, which "set itself up as a challenge to capitalism and so stimulated it."[20] Yet that "stimulation" manifested very differently in different parts of the world. In the North Atlantic, it forced capital to accede to some labor demands with increased rights and benefits, while in those Cold War frontiers of the decolonizing world—where U.S. Cold War administrators were making the world "safe for capitalism"—the "deification of the market" went hand in hand with the violent disciplining of decolonizing struggles.[21] As we saw in Chapters 1 and 2, in newly liberated Asia, the cultural and political meanings of "freedom," "revolution," and "liberty" became flash points where the demands of postcolonial sovereignty met the imperatives of bipolar economic and political restructuring. In Chapters 3, 4, and 5, I examined the ways those multiple "futures past" of decolonizing imaginaries were vehemently eradicated by developmentalist projects and security regimes, even while such imaginaries continue to haunt our present. Although Brown acknowledges the Cold War influence on neoliberal thinking—it was "born in the shadow of European fascism and Soviet totalitarianism"[22]—her story sidelines the way the contests and violence of the global Cold War *actively enabled* the hegemonic rise of neoliberal logic in Euro-America. Rather than see today's illiberalism as the disquieting "reappearance in a new guise" of mid-century fascisms, *Cold War Reckonings* has argued for another political genealogy where mass violence, social exclusion, and repression of "aversive insiders" occurred precisely under the banner of "freedom."

My larger claim is that we must situate the rise of neoliberal orthodoxy within the matrix of bipolarized, twentieth-century decolonization. Following neoliberalism's career from this particular vantage point of the postcolonial world allows a clearer understanding of the way the U.S. empire and local dictatorships worked in tandem to effect a rollback of Third Worldist demands, producing the triumphant victory of the "free" market. If we attend to the cultural texts and narratives born of this struggle, we gain a more nuanced sense of the way bipolar decolonization comprised a surprisingly dense web of historical forces, competing and desiring subjectivities, and multiple political imaginaries. It is also to suggest, as Chandan Reddy has done via queer critique in the U.S. context, that authoritarian state power and liberal democracy are not the antinomies we often assume.[23] Put simply, to understand our increasingly authoritarian present, a broader account of neoliberalism's original function as a brake on decolonization is needed.

We can look to several examples of recent scholarship that tell precisely this more global story of neoliberalism, which I hope my book complements. First is Quinn Slobodian's alternative account of neoliberal doctrine in his 2018 book *Globalists: The End of Empire and the Birth of Neoliberalism*. Slobodian's history of neoliberal thought—or "ordoliberalism," focusing on the Geneva School of economists—does not tell the typical story of market fundamentalism and the unleashing of markets from their social or governmental fetters. Instead, his study shows that neoliberalism worked by enthusiastically constructing new layers of international laws and regulations that would protect or "encase" the market from the dangers of nationalist and democratic forces. In sum, "What neoliberals seek is not a partial but a complete protection of private capital rights, and the ability of supranational judiciary bodies like the European Court of Justice and the WTO to override national legislation that might disrupt the global rights of capital."[24] Central to Slobodian's account is that figures such as Hayek were in large part responding to the perceived perils of "the end of empire" and Third World self-determination, a process that would endanger those "global rights of capital" through socialist and redistributionist claims.[25] In particular, the 1970s demands for a more just global economy via the New International Economic Order (NIEO)—which has been described as the "high noon of 'Third Worldism' and its vision of solidarity"[26]—prompted a fierce "countermove by neoliberals."[27] This pushback ultimately resulted in binding international legal mechanisms to contain such challenges and further enshrine the rights of transnational corporations.[28] Our twenty-first-century neoliberal consensus did not arise simply out of the "crisis of profitability and stagflation" of the 1970s[29]—the usual narrative—but by actively negating the Third World's brazen demands for social and economic decolonization. In Adom Getachew's recent examination of the career of the NIEO and the projects of Jamaica's Michael Manley and Tanzania's Julius Nyerere, she similarly shows how postcolonial nation-building required "anticolonial worldmaking," or the transformation of the global economy, to avoid the pitfalls of neocolonial underdevelopment. In her telling, a major factor in the NIEO's demise was the depoliticization of economic decision-making, which became merely "an arena of technical and legal expertise, better left to economists rather than politicians."[30] One of the central claims of *Cold War Reckonings* is that the non-communist postcolonies of Asia were key battlegrounds for the defusing of socialist redistributive demands, in part by recasting "freedom" as incorporation into the "free world."

Despite Slobodian's assertion that the Cold War is not particularly important to his narrative, he observes that during the 1970s "Hong Kong was a model for neoliberals."[31] The city was

> a model of a nonmajoritarian market economy that limited popular sovereignty while maximizing capital sovereignty with a much-touted free-trade policy, a robust bank secrecy law, and a low corporate tax rate. In many ways Hong Kong was the inverted version of the demands of the NIEO and the Global South in the 1970s.[32]

The singling out of Hong Kong deserves attention for its broader metonymic function. From a postcolonial perspective, the "nonmajoritarian"—read antidemocratic—character of the city was, of course, due to its still being a British crown colony at the time. Yet Hong Kong was also a "free world" trading and finance center on the edge of the vast communist territory of the PRC, and its famed entrepreneurialism, hardworking migrant population, and global economic outlook were very much shaped by the bipolar configuration. Due to its strong export-oriented industrialization, Hong Kong is regularly included in the quartet of first generation "Asian Tigers," along with South Korea, Taiwan, and Singapore. Such a grouping, I suggest, extends to the way the colonial, postcolonial, and bipolar overlapped in these sites in similarly complex ways, notwithstanding the fact that Hong Kong was ruled by foreigners for longer. Put simply, in the Cold War–decolonizing matrix, these locations functioned as authoritarian bulwarks against communism and as safe harbors for global capital.

Sites such as Hong Kong were therefore not simply fortuitous models of "non-majoritarian capitalism" that happened to fit neoliberal ideology and the tutelary "discipline of freedom"[33] appropriate to non-Western development. These "miracle" economies were, in fact, integral to the pushback against alternative political demands made by the NIEO since they constituted antidemocratic, heteronomous models of "miraculous" Third World development.[34] We might consider them paradigms of one definition of the neoliberal state, "a state apparatus whose fundamental mission [is] to facilitate conditions for profitable capital accumulation on the part of both domestic and foreign capital."[35] Their enduring influence (whether recognized or not) is evident in many sites around the Global South: in the dominance of export-oriented development, the craze for special economic zones, the deferral of democracy, and the optimization of domestic labor forces and industries for foreign direct investment. The regional repression, purges, and massacres of leftists—and the accompanying disciplining and exploitation of workers—is occluded by bootstrapping developmentalist stories. Nevertheless, because of their ability to industrialize, to a greater or lesser degree, these states and those that followed a similar formula constituted an influential example of the compatibility between capitalist development and antidemocratic rule, which lies at the heart of the neoliberal imagination. As C. J. W.-L. Wee writes of Singapore and Malaysia in the 1980s, "It is as if parts of the Non-Aligned Movement have reinvented themselves into the World Trade Organisation."[36] That such states are either viewed routinely as "sell-outs" (in a Third Worldist, non-aligned vision) or as unproblematic success stories of non-Western development that can be repeated (in the view of neoliberals and technocrats) indicates the need for a fuller accounting of their pivotal role in consolidating a neoliberal "common sense" of the world. It is such an account that this book has hoped to offer.[37]

In a different key, Joseph Slaughter has told a parallel story of neoliberalism's imbrication with decolonization, this time centered on human rights. Also from 2018, his essay "Hijacking Human Rights: Neoliberalism, the New Historiography, and the End of the Third World" recovers an earlier, more plural conceptualization of human rights that had been central to the discourses of Third Worldist national liberation and the watershed Bandung Conference of 1955. However, beginning in the late 1960s, these more open and collectivist notions of rights were "hijacked" and attenuated, resulting in the contemporary notion of human rights as limited to individual civil and political rights against a state. Paralleling Slobodian's account, the demise of the 1970s efforts for a NIEO, along with other struggles for international solidarity and self-determination, were central plot moves to the "rollback of human rights"[38] and the larger effort "to resubordinate the post-colonial world."[39] By the end of the 1970s, this had resulted in the more general discrediting of Third Worldist economic, social, and cultural rights that "human rights" had hitherto signified.[40] Crucially, Slaughter links post-1970s human rights to the neoliberalization of both "markets and sentiments."[41] The shift in human rights discourse to liberal concerns for individual prisoners of conscience thus aligned with "overt and covert operations to undermine communist and democratic socialist governments across the globe," as well as with "neo-liberal capital reforms around the world in the name of Structural Adjustment Programs."[42] To this compelling account, I would add that the developmental authoritarian states examined in this study have played a significant—but often overlooked—role in the larger repression of "communist and democratic socialist governments across the globe." That is, the complex internal contests between leftists, nationalists, anti-dictatorship movements, and pro-U.S. elites constituted a key terrain on which the struggle was fought both during the actual Cold War period and, more recently, around the historiography of the perceived "successes" and "failures" of the period. Paradoxically, what today is now recognized as the unfortunate "human rights violations" of those regimes can also be properly thought of as contributing to the erasure of those earlier, more capacious models of human rights.

One irony is that the strong-state models of Singapore, South Korea, and other would-be "tigers" were not themselves strictly free-market economies. As a number of critics have noted, a level of protectionism was tolerated in these countries by virtue of their Cold War security function.[43] As Joseph Jonghyun Jeon points out in his study of post-IMF South Korean cinema, that country "faced the end of favourable developmental conditions in the 1990s, as labor costs rose and competition increased from rapidly industrializing neighbors in the region."[44] After the devastating 1997 Asian Financial Crisis— which affected South Korea, Indonesia, and Thailand most severely—the IMF bailout package "radically reshaped the Korean economy" with the usual prescriptions of "trade liberalization, labor flexibilization and financialization oriented to global firms."[45] More succinctly, "Further neoliberalism was the answer."[46] The very sites that had helped to make capitalism safe from communism themselves had to be reined in by neoliberal restructuring. Ngũgĩ wa Thiong'o has pointed out a similar double bind pertaining to African postcolonial states, where Structural Adjustment Programs and economic liberalization are touted as the solution to their inefficient and anti-democratic regimes, even as the West continues to support those dictatorial leaders, underscoring the profoundly antidemocratic tendency of those "global rights of capital." Moreover, those austerity measures of neoliberalism— SAP reforms, debt regimes, the super-exploitation of labor, and minimalist social provisions—have long been familiar phenomena outside the West. "What is emerging is a very unholy alliance between the IMF, the World Bank and the West as a whole, and African civilian and military dictatorships."[47] Put simply, neoliberalism gets to have its cake and eat it too.[48]

I want to conclude with a brief reading of a cultural text that evidences the way a neoliberal plotting of history may be made compatible with certain Third World developmentalist narratives. Yoon Je-kyoon's 2014 Ode to My Father (Kukje sijang, or "International market" in Korean) is one of the highest-grossing films ever in Korean cinema, earning over $100 million at the box office.[49] Unlike the global consumption of K-pop or K-drama, however, it is not a film that drew a large international audience for reasons that will become clear. The film is a sweeping tale of the hardships of Yun Dŏk-su (played by Hwang Jung-min), who overcomes war, family tragedy, displacement, and poverty to become a successful market stallholder in the port city of Busan. At the same time, the film is the story of South Korea's stunning postwar industrialization of the 1960s, '70s, and '80s that produced its widely touted economic "miracle." Through the parallel "rags-to-riches"[50] tale of both the Yun family and the South Korean nation, we follow the newly decolonized, divided, and war-ravaged country's transformation into one of the world's largest economies and most successful high-tech societies. The film's global imaginary of upward mobility is metonymically figured in Busan's own trans-formation from colonial port city, destination for war refugees, regional center for the country's heavy industries, and finally to today's world-class metropo-lis.[51] Interestingly, there is only a single passing mention of Japan in the film, no Japanese language, and no explicitly Japanese cultural legacies—in fact, no reckoning with the typical postcolonial concerns of colonial violence, anti-colonial nationalisms, or hybrid identities. As we've seen already, for sites like the Korean peninsula, the decades following formal independence are less structured by the familiar postcolonial idioms of vertical resistance to colonial power and its cultural hierarchies,[52] and more by the way the "binary structure of the global order" (Kwon) subtended or, better, constituted decolonization. I am most interested in the historical vision the film stages, especially the structure of narrative repetition that frames both personal and national dra-mas. I then examine the transnational connections, or the film's global imag-inary of development, that such a historical vision implies. It is precisely the "fit" between the Cold War plotting of the film and our contemporary moment of neoliberal orthodoxy that I wish to elucidate.

The film is told largely in flashback mode from the perspective of the aging patriarch, Yun Dŏk-su, now a bad-tempered grandfather who resents his fam-ily's taken-for-granted prosperity. Its opening scene is one of material comfort and minor family conflict: Dŏk-su and his wife are left to care, reluctantly, for their numerous grandchildren as their own children depart for a carefree over-seas vacation. In dramatic contrast, the following flashback scene thrusts the viewer squarely into the midst of the violence and trauma of the Korean War. It is 1951 and we are in the port city of Hŭngnam, in today's North Korea, where thousands of civilian refugees are fleeing violence; the scene of mass terror and panic is captured in breathtaking, high-budget Hollywood style. Escaping with his family, the eight- or nine-year-old Dŏk-su is charged with taking care of his younger sister Mak-sun as they desperately compete with other refugees—many of whom are crushed or drowned in the process—in the attempt to board several U.S. warships which are evacuating the city. An impe-rious American general, at first unwilling to play the humanitarian, is eventu-ally persuaded to save the civilians and agrees to unload the ship's weapons to make room. In the chaos of boarding the ship, Dŏk-su loses hold of Mak-sun (Figure 11); his father decides to go back to look for her at the very moment the

Figure 11. The young Dŏk-su realizes he has lost hold of his sister, Mak-sun, as they struggle to board a U.S. warship evacuating Hŭngnam in *Ode to My Father*.

ship departs. The family unit is thus violently and tragically sundered, confirming the tight structural analogy between family and nation throughout the film. The film goes on to narrate Dŏk-su's life over the next decades as he struggles to provide for his mother and two remaining younger siblings in their new life as displaced people in Busan.

After arriving with nothing in Busan in 1951, Dŏk-su and his family are begrudgingly given a tiny storeroom to sleep in by his father's sister's family, and they begin their hard life in the Busan marketplace, the *Kukje sijang* of the film's title. Dŏk-su is ashamed by both his northern origins and his poverty; he is immediately accused of being a "commie" (*ppalgaengi*) by his new classmates, and after school he shines shoes on the street to make extra money. Confirming the disgraceful dependency of Koreans on the powerful Americans, Dŏk-su is one of the many ragged children who chase American jeeps in the hopes of receiving GI candy. When the North-South armistice is announced one day on a radio in the marketplace, Dŏk-su innocently asks the crowd if he can now go home; a member of the crowd tells him matter-of-factly, "Our country's weak so other countries came in, and now they fight and divide us up as they please." Dŏk-su understands the larger lesson: A weak nation caught in the bipolar confrontation of larger nations can rely only on its own sweat and blood in order to transcend such conditions.

Given the film's almost simplistic historical narrative, what might account for the film's staggering popularity among South Korean audiences? I suggest that it is not simply the nationalistic bootstrapping account of Korean history, but how its Cold War narrative figures a larger global history from mid-twentieth-century decolonization to early twenty-first-century globalization.

That is, Dŏk-su's life is not merely allegorical of the sufferings and tribulations of this small nation, but—despite its triumphalist plotting—convincingly indexes the global contradictions that shaped South Korea's major developmental achievements, resulting in the film's structuring affect of *ambivalence*. It does so by viscerally illustrating the nation's traumatic incorporation into the bipolar restructuring of the globe, emphasizing both the Cold War transnational economy and the transnational household.

Notably, the two extended flashback scenes that follow the initial war-time sequence are both set overseas. The first unfolds in the early 1960s when Dŏk-su takes a mining job in the Duisburg district of West Germany; the second is set in 1974 when he goes to Vietnam to work for a Korean company that supplies the U.S. military. The key to understanding South Korea's developmental story is thus *both* its tragic origins in division and war *and* its highly successful integration with Western bloc industries, war economies, and labor markets. Dŏk-su is precisely the figure who narratively traverses these personal, political, and economic levels. Take, for example, the flashback section of *Ode* set in West Germany. At the level of plot, Dŏk-su's labor allows him to send money home to his struggling mother and siblings, and it is in Germany that he also meets his future wife Yŏng-ja, who is there as a nurse in training. But structurally and historically, it is significant because the wave of guestworkers South Korea sent abroad in the 1960s and '70s—primarily construction workers to the Gulf States and West Germany—was critical to the country's economic rise. While the Duisburg section of the film includes the lighthearted story of Dŏk-su and Yŏng-ja's awkward courtship, it employs a super-realist aesthetic to depict the labor conditions they and their compatriots endure. Dŏk-su and his co-workers toil underground in unbearably dark, hot, dirty conditions, risking life and limb until a huge gas explosion seriously injures both Dŏk-su and his best friend Dal-gu, forcing them to return home. Nor does the camera gloss over Yŏng-ja's unglamorous work: We see her wipe excrement off elderly patients and wash and prepare corpses at the hospital morgue. In the film's diegetic present that immediately precedes this flashback, the elderly Dŏk-su witnesses some Korean students making fun of a South Asian couple at a local coffee shop in Busan. Dŏk-su becomes enraged in his attempt to defend the migrants' right to be there. The moral lessons for the modern Korean viewer are made clear. In a formal structure of repetition that the film employs several times, South Korea's promotion to the ranks of modern, developed nations catches on this moment of painful self-recognition: We got here because we too were once despised and exploited migrant workers. The critique, however, can go no further than this recognition. The film presents migrant labor as patriotic duty, simply a necessary step on the way to overcoming the country's shameful postcolonial predicament.

Dŏk-su has barely returned from Germany, married, and started a family when he is compelled to venture overseas again. Now 1974, this time it is to Saigon to earn U.S. dollars to help pay for his younger sister's wedding. The Vietnam War section of the film is again presented as a repetition, both in terms of Dŏk-su's own life narrative—he must leave his family again and risk his life for their material betterment—and in terms of geopolitics, where the Vietnam War is a veritable replay of the Korean War. But this is a repetition where Koreans have changed position. Working for a South Korean military supplier to the U.S., it is now Dŏk-su who rides in a jeep while ragged bands of Vietnamese children play in the street. Recognizing himself in the figure of small boy who is bullied over a candy bar, he goes out of his way to give the child an extra piece of chocolate. In a more traumatic replay of history, the next scene has Dŏk-su and his team loading up a boat of military goods for transport down a river. Just as they are about to pull out, a crowd of Vietnamese civilians arrives at the dock desperate to escape from the approaching Vietcong. Dŏk-su—echoing the cold-hearted American general in the Hŭngnam scene—initially refuses since the boat is already full. But after a beautiful young Vietnamese woman begs piteously for them to save them, he assents and—just like the Americans at Hŭngnam —unloads equipment to allow the civilians to board, with the added suspense of doing so under a Vietcong attack. An inter-title concludes the action-packed Vietnam sequence with "April 30, 1975: End of Vietnam War." We are suddenly back at the Busan *Kukje sijang*, and a trader is touting her market stall, "Look! We have new goods from Japan and the U.S." Cartons of Kool cigarettes, Cheerios, and Heinz products are suddenly prominent in Dŏk-su's and Yŏng-ja's storefront. A little later, a newspaper reveals the wedding picture of Dŏk-su's best friend Dal-gu and the young Vietnamese woman from the boat scene, proclaiming "First Korean-Vietnamese Marriage."

At least two aspects of the film's narrative align with the neoliberal view of history we have discussed. First, according to the film's aesthetic structure of repetition, Koreans may have been the colonized victims of twentieth-century history, but they are not destined to remain there. Where once their lives were at the mercy of American military power, through hard work and the benevolence of international markets they now command a similar authority over other decolonizing Asians. Where they once were a source of cheap labor to the West (or Middle East), they now are receivers of it. This essentially relational, or promotional, model of advancement clearly negates Third Worldist demands like the NIEO to overturn the entrenched hierarchy of the imperialist global economy, rather than merely ascend in its ranks.[53] More-over, the film makes clear that the motivation for Korean participation in the Vietnam War is not any lofty moral belief in anti-communism (although pre-dictably, the Vietcong are presented one-dimensionally as bloodthirsty killers and terrorists). Rather, the battlefield of bipolar confrontation in Vietnam is the pragmatic, depoliticized means by which South Korea is successfully brought into the "single, integrated market"[54] of the U.S. capitalist empire, with its attendant material benefits attested to by the new commodities in Dŏk-su's and Yŏng-ja's market stall. By naturalizing the trajectory of competi-tive, incorporated capitalist development, the film's Cold War episteme fosters an aspirational nationalist project that borrows legitimacy from anti-colonialist energies, even while it sidesteps the Third Worldist program of international solidarity and self-determination.

Second, the film's view of history imagines a transnationalism appropriate to a neoliberal world. The film's deliberate aesthetic of repetition notably offers no opportunity for South-South solidarity or collective action, confirm-ing that "the neoliberal state is necessarily hostile to all forms of social solidar-ity that put restraints on capital accumulation."[55] Genuine personal sympathies—for the Vietnamese street children and refugees, or South Asian migrant workers—can be addressed only at the level of individualized benev-olence and liberal incorporation: a kindness to strangers which allows access into the capitalist bloc via labor (for nations) or through marriage (for individ-uals).[56] In addition, the concluding section of the film reveals that Dŏk-su's long-lost sister Mak-sun had ended up in an orphanage in the North and was subsequently adopted and raised by Americans. In an emotional scene, they are reunited with the added pathos that Mak-sun can no longer speak Korean. The film suggests, then, only a diminished set of possible transnational rela-tions for South Koreans: those of the labor or military contract, or transna-tional marriage and adoption.

It is this naturalized, and enduring, Cold War view of Third World national integration that has served neoliberal thinking so well. Symptomatic of such an understanding is the controversy that arose after the film's release. For those on the right (including then-president Park Geun-hye, Park Chung Hee's daughter), the film appropriately honored the postwar generation of South Koreans whose sweat, blood, and patriotism resulted in the country's present gleaming modernity—explicitly visualized in the film by stunning vistas of Busan's hyper-modern port. Aligning with this view, the director has described his motivation for the film not in terms of any "political, social, or historical consciousness," but simply from the desire to honor his father who lived a difficult life and died young:[57] "Nowadays young people aren't aware of just how poor this country was and how much older people sacrificed for our development."[58] The left, however, objected to the fact that the film makes no mention of the human rights abuses of the Park regime or the fact that Korea was under military rule until 1987. Completely absent are the jailings, surveillance, anti-labor repression, and the Busan-Masan protests of 1979 which preceded the 1980 Gwangju Uprising. As a spokesperson for the leftist view put it, the film "effectively endorses the idea that the state can exploit its people."[59] More interesting is that the *only* historical debate available today is between heroic national development versus human rights abuses. Any alternative path to self-determination has been foreclosed by the neoliberal rendering of history, just as any notion of human rights as other than the supranational protection of individuals is erased.

Tellingly, in Yoon's film, the clearest marker of time between "then" and "now" is not dictatorship and post-dictatorship, or pre-1991 and post-1991, but simply the gap in material progress, most clearly marked by panoramic scenes of the present-day port of Busan (Figure 12). Politically and aesthetically, there is no demarcation between a world in which there are one or two (or three) competing social-political systems. At an obvious level this is because the peninsula remains divided but, at a deeper one, I suggest that it is because the Cold War was less experienced as an abstract ideology than through the material traumas and struggles of the developmental state itself. In a heartrending scene at the end of the film, the elderly Dŏk-su collapses in grief and tears at the still-fresh memory of losing his father in the Korean War. When his father appears to him in a kind of wish-image, he tearfully explains that he did his best to look after the rest of his family in his father's absence—but "it was so,

Figure 12. The elderly Dŏk-su and his wife sit overlooking a view of present-day Busan in *Ode to My Father*.

so hard." Meanwhile, his children and grandchildren are gathered for a lavish family celebration in the next room, singing, laughing, and oblivious to his suffering. The poignant emotional impasse here may be read as the affective surplus that cannot fit into the miraculous developmental story. Here, South Korea's painful reckonings with the Cold War can be viewed *only* as a success, symbolized by his family's celebration and the gleaming port.

At the beginning of this book, I discussed the way some postcolonial critics have lamented the post–Cold War horizon of liberal democracy for its inability to view postcolonial socialist attempts as anything but aberrant.[60] The controversy around Yoon's *Ode*, I argue, may be viewed as the other side of the same coin. The inexorable—albeit painful—logic of authoritarian, catch-up development is viewed as the *only* successful route of postcoloniality, writing out all other alternatives. I suggest that the film has attracted such large domestic audiences and spurred such fierce debates precisely because although its nationalist message is triumphant, its affective message remains one of deep ambivalence. The attempt to "strike a balance"[61] in terms of historical accounting—either triumphant development or human rights abuses—simply misses the point of this unbearable, devastating ambivalence of history.

Just five years after the release of *Ode to My Father*, Bong Joon-ho's 2019 hit *Parasite (Kisaengch'ung)* caused a sensation at the 2020 Academy Awards by being the first foreign-language movie to win best film (as well as best director, best screenplay, and best international film). His bitingly satiric film of egregious class inequality in contemporary Seoul follows the trials of the struggling basement-dwelling Kim family as they pose as high-class tutors and servants in the opulent home of the Park family. Bong's story of haves and have-nots—told through a quirky mix of horror, comedy, and haunted-house film genres—has resonated around the globe. Even the filmmaker was surprised at the film's wide appeal: "I tried to express sentiments specific to Korean culture, [but] all the responses from different audiences were pretty much the same. Essentially, we all live in the same country, called Capitalism."[62] That a South Korean film should deliver such a reverberating critique of twenty-first-century capitalism is perhaps not so surprising. Although departing from the narrative of nationalist triumphalism in *Ode to My Father*, the film similarly makes visible the contradictions of a transpacific developmental path that is coming to resemble capitalism everywhere. Yoon's and Bong's works, therefore, can be seen as belonging to the broader archive of literary and cultural genres that explore the Cold War–decolonizing matrix and its afterlives. They help us understand that today's rising authoritarianism is less a reappearance of a superannuated European political form—mid-century fascism—and more the revealing of neoliberalism's essential historical logic, a logic that has been global all along.

Finally, our own historical moment demands that we recognize the way in which the intensifying climate and ecological crisis (vividly allegorized in *Parasite*'s remarkable flood scene) is casting doubt on even the most triumphant stories of Asian development and prosperity. Amitav Ghosh has eloquently argued that we are only now coming to terms with empire's role in climate change and the way rapidly industrializing postcolonial Asia has played a "dual role as both protagonist and victim" in this crisis.[63] As Asia's remarkable capitalist expansion in the latter part of the twentieth century warrants closer scrutiny, it is my hope that we recognize the Cold War–decolonizing conjuncture as an entanglement of victorious development with profoundly antidemocratic, illiberal structures of domination. Such recognition, in turn, may allow us to produce better analyses and thus better political alternatives to our present.

Acknowledgments

As I write these acknowledgments during stay-at-home orders because of the COVID-19 pandemic, I have never been more aware of the communities and support networks that profoundly sustain the practice of scholarship. These brief pages are not adequate to acknowledge the myriad relationships that make this book a truly collaborative achievement. All deficiencies and oversights are my own.

First and foremost, this book literally could not have been written without the years-long friendship, camaraderie, and intellectual dialogue provided by my fabulous (and fun) writing group: Joseph Keith, Naomi Schiller, Krupa Shandilya, and Crystal Parikh. They read and commented on innumerable drafts with infinite care, generosity, insight, and patience; I am hugely indebted to them for all the ways they helped shape this book. As this book neared completion, I was fortunate to have a set of astute manuscript readers who engaged with my work and offered crucial feedback: My sincere gratitude to Philip Holden and Monica Popescu, who traveled in for the workshop, and to Rajeswari Sunder Rajan and Crystal Parikh (doing double duty). I thank the NYU English Department for supporting the workshop. Joseph Slaughter and one anonymous reader for Fordham University Press provided incisive comments and suggestions that helped make this a stronger book. And *Cold War Reckonings* could not have come into the world without the support, dedication, and no-fuss support of my editor Thomas Lay, as well as the fine work by Eric Newman, Teresa Jesionowski, and the superb staff at Fordham University Press.

Many colleagues at New York University (past and present) have been generous interlocutors and readers of this project, including Cristina Beltrán,

Lawrence Coderre, Guadalupe Escobar, Hala Halim, Wendy Lee, Sonya Posmentier, Ato Quayson, Anooradha Siddiqi, Shirley Wong, Robert Young, and Duncan Yoon. Maureen McLane has offered sage advice and regular doses of humor. I am in debt to the wonderful Mary Mezzano whose friendship and efficiency allowed me to write some of this manuscript during a time of heavy administrative duties. For years, NYU's Postcolonial, Race and Diaspora Studies Colloquium has been a constant source of community and conviviality, and I am grateful to faculty, graduate students, and guests who have made it the nourishing intellectual community it is. I am also deeply appreciative of NYU's Abraham and Rebecca Stein Fund, which generously supported this publication.

Beyond my own institution, Gary Wilder has been not only a friend, mentor, and collaborator, but working with him on *The Postcolonial Contemporary* (Fordham, 2018) opened up another intellectual community of extraordinary interlocutors. I am grateful to those contributors who helped shape what would become Chapter 4: Sadia Abbas, Anthony C. Allessandrini, Sharad Chari, Carlos A. Forment, Vinay Gidwani, Peter Hitchcock, Laurie Lambert, Stephen Muecke, Anupama Rao, and Adam Spanos. Neelam Srivastava gave encouragement and feedback (over delicious food) at exactly the right time; Cheryl Narumi Naruse has been a fellow traveler in all things Singaporean; Seonmin Kim offered generous last-minute research support and ongoing friendship from Seoul; and Martha Miller provided much-needed guidance and reassurance during the long slog of writing. Nihad Farooq, Amy Carroll, and Ranjana Khanna have offered their gracious support throughout the years.

I have been blessed with a number of outstanding research assistants who worked with me on this project. My deep thanks to Anindya Khairunnisa, Paris Liu, Shela Ramen, and Bomi Woo for their meticulous and multilingual work, and especially Paris who proofread and formatted the entire manuscript with an eagle eye. A number of artists and writers have shown exceptional generosity and patience: Tan Pin Pin and Jeremy Tiang graciously gave me interviews; Jee Leong Koh brought so many brilliant Southeast Asian authors and scholars into my orbit; Cyril Wong and Kim Chi-ha kindly gave permission to quote their poems; Heri Dono consented to using his wonderful painting as the cover image. I am also grateful for the hospitality shown to me by Magalí Armillas-Tiseyra, Pheng Cheah, Sujin Eom, Fiona Lee, and Elaine Ho, who gave me opportunities to present early parts of this project to different audiences. I owe thanks to Audrey Yue and colleagues at the University of Melbourne's School of Culture and Communication where the first inklings of the project were worked out.

Portions of this book have been previously published in other venues. Some sections of Chapter 1 and Chapter 2 were originally published as "Stories of the State: Literary Form and Authoritarianism in Ninotchka Rosca's *State of War*," in *Contemporary Literature* 58, no. 2 (2017): 262–89, by the Board of Regents of the University of Wisconsin System, and reprinted courtesy of the University of Wisconsin Press. An earlier version of Chapter 3 was published as "Separate Futures: Cold War Decolonization in Mohamed Latiff Mohamed's *Confrontation* and Sonny Liew's *The Art of Charlie Chan Hock Chye*," in *Discourse: Journal of Theoretical Studies in Media and Culture* 40, no. 2 (2018): 165–87, and reprinted courtesy of Wayne State University Press. Chapter 4, "The Wrong Side of History," was originally published in *The Postcolonial Contemporary: Political Imaginaries for the Global Present*, co-edited volume with Gary Wilder, published by Fordham University Press in 2018.

Many sustaining relationships predate and outlast the writing of a book. My mother, Taisoo Kim Watson, has been a rock of support and remains the inspiration for almost everything I do. My brother Tori, nephew Riley, and other family and friends in Toowoomba and Melbourne, are irreplaceable sources of sustenance. Finally, throughout the long gestation of this book, Bryce de Reynier has been there with unconditional love, support, and encouragement. He not only read chapters, debated title options, formatted images but— during the current pandemic—has been partner, caretaker, support network, and home-schooler all in one, and this book owes more to him than anyone else. And Mateo Watson de Reynier, with his sparkling mix of curiosity, impatience, and IT help, reminds me why it all matters.

Notes

Introduction. Ruling Like a Foreigner: Theorizing "Free World" Authoritarianism in the Asia-Pacific Cold War

1. Cyril Wong, *The Dictator's Eyebrow* (Singapore: Ethos Books, 2013), 17.

2. Ibid., 32.

3. Li Sui Gwee, "Cyril Wong in the Face of Power," introduction to *The Dictator's Eyebrow*, 6.

4. David Scott, *Refashioning Futures: Criticism after Postcoloniality* (Princeton, NJ: Princeton University Press, 1999), 199, 196.

5. Ibid., 151.

6. Ibid.

7. See Francis Fukuyama, *The End of History and the Last Man* (New York: Free Press, 1992).

8. I use the term "Asia-Pacific" aware of its problematic collapsing of coastal Asia and the Pacific Islands of Oceania, the latter of which are beyond the scope of this book. The other term available would be "East and Southeast Asia," which would imply that the book addresses the whole of this large region. "Asia-Pacific," by contrast, appropriately indexes a formation that partly stems from the U.S. hegemony in the region during the Cold War. See Christopher L. Connery, "Pacific Rim Discourse: The U.S. Global Imaginary in the Late Cold War Years," *boundary* 2 21, no. 1 (1994): 30–56, for the way the U.S. Cold War imaginary has shaped this geographical notion. See also Epeli Hau'ofa on the geographical imaginary of the Pacific, "Our Sea of Islands," in *We Are the Ocean: Selected Works*, by Epeli Hau'ofa (Honolulu: University of Hawai'i Press, 2008), 27–40.

9. The essay collection *Worlding Cities: Asian Experiments and the Art of Being Global* (Chichester; Malden, MA: Wiley-Blackwell, 2011) by Ananya Roy and Aihwa Ong, offers an interesting approach along these lines. The essays there argue that no

longer is the West the originator of urban forms of modernity; it is thus the "inter-references" and citationality of urban forms within Asia and across the Global South that deserve attention. The Asian Development Bank's 2011 forecast, "Asia 2050: Realizing the Asian Century," similarly decenters Euro-America from the core of capitalist modernity.

10. Chiang Kai-shek's Kuomintang regime in Taiwan is another important Cold War developmental state-formation, although Taiwanese texts largely remain beyond the scope of this book.

11. Language limitations mean that I read Anglophone and Korean texts in the original, and Indonesian/Malay texts in translation.

12. Sharad Chari and Katherine Verdery, "Thinking between the Posts: Postcolonialism, Postsocialism, and Ethnography after the Cold War," *Comparative Studies in Society and History* 51, no. 1 (2009): 12.

13. See Odd Arne Westad, *The Global Cold War: Third World Interventions and the Making of Our Times* (Cambridge: Cambridge University Press, 2007). Westad's expansive history argues for the overlooked impact of Cold War interventions and alignments in *creating* the Third World. The book has been profoundly important for opening up new scholarly perspectives of "the global cold war."

14. Ibid., 3.

15. Monica Popescu, *At Pen Point: African Literatures, Postcolonial Cultures, and the Cold War* (Durham, NC: Duke University Press, 2020), 2.

16. Kuan-Hsing Chen, *Asia as Method: Toward Deimperialization* (Durham, NC: Duke University Press, 2010), 119.

17. Bhakti Shringarpure, *Cold War Assemblages: Decolonization to Digital* (New York: Routledge, 2019), 191.

18. Heonik Kwon, "The Transpacific Cold War," in *Transpacific Studies: Framing an Emerging Field*, ed. Janet Hoskins and Viet Thanh Nguyen (Honolulu: University of Hawai'i Press, 2014), 76.

19. Ibid. Kwon is discussing Dipesh Chakrabarty's *Provincializing Europe* (Princeton, NJ: Princeton University Press, 2000) and Partha Chatterjee's *The Nation and Its Fragments* (Princeton, NJ: Princeton University Press, 1993).

20. Jodi Kim, *Ends of Empire: Asian American Critique and the Cold War* (Minneapolis: University of Minnesota Press, 2010), 4.

21. Ibid., 8.

22. Lisa Yoneyama, *Cold War Ruins: Transpacific Critique of American Justice and Japanese War Crimes* (Durham, NC: Duke University Press, 2016), 5. Sunny Xiang has also noted that the American Cold War in Asia turned war "from a historical event into a historiographical problem." See *Tonal Intelligence: The Aesthetics of Asian Inscrutability during the Long Cold War* (New York: Columbia University Press, 2020), 2. Beyond East and Southeast Asia, as Popescu and Shringarpure remind us, Southern Africa in particular witnessed violent, long-lasting Cold War conflicts.

23. Chari and Verdery, "Thinking between the Posts," 18.

24. Caroline Hau, *Elites and Ilustrados in Philippine Culture* (Manila: Ateneo de Manila University Press, 2017), 199. On the U.S.'s hegemonic web, see Bruce Cumings,

"Webs with No Spiders, Spiders with No Webs: The Genealogy of the Development State," in *The Developmental State*, ed. Meredith Woo-Cumings (Ithaca, NY: Cornell University Press, 1999), 92.

25. Westad, *The Global Cold War*, 36.

26. Greg Grandin, *Empire's Workshop: Latin America, the United States, and the Rise of the New Imperialism* (New York: Holt, 2006), 41.

27. Ibid., 75–76. We should note that Latin American right-wing autocrats—and we can extend the logic to Ferdinand Marcos or Chun Doo Hwan, who were warmly welcomed at the White House by President Reagan—were equally valuable in promoting economic stability and "protecting[ing] [U.S.] investments, as democracy led to a wave of strikes calling for . . . better wages, health care, social security and land and labor reforms." See Grandin, 41.

28. Crystal Parikh, *Writing Human Rights: The Political Imaginaries of Writers of Color* (Minneapolis: University of Minnesota Press, 2017), 12; italics added. See especially her chapter on "The U.S. Good Life, the UN World, and the Human Rights Record" for a cogent overview of the way the Cold War overdetermined the U.S.'s response to decolonization and notions of self-determination, both globally and within the U.S.

29. William Pietz, "The 'Post-Colonialism' of Cold War Discourse," *Social Text*, no. 19/20 (1988): 55.

30. Ibid., 56.

31. William Pietz notes that the discourse on totalitarianism, as found in George Kennan, Orwell, Koestler, and Arendt functions "as a substitute for the language of colonialism" (55), recycling Orientalist stereotypes of irrational and fetishist Asiatics (62) for the Soviet communist.

32. Ibid., 57.

33. Hannah Arendt, *The Origins of Totalitarianism* (San Diego: Harvest, 1966), 419.

34. Ibid., 413, 418.

35. Ibid., 475.

36. Ibid., 412.

37. Ibid., 221.

38. Ibid., 416. Importantly, this allows us to apply the logic of colonialism to the metropole and, like Aimé Césaire's famous 1955 *Discourse on Colonialism*, makes the ethical insistence that "that Fascism be viewed as a form of colonialism infesting Europe." See Sandro Mezzadra and Federico Rahola, "The Postcolonial Condition: A Few Notes on the Quality of Historical Time in the Global Present," *Postcolonial Text* 2, no. 1 (2006): 36–54.

39. Arendt, *The Origins of Totalitarianism*, 417.

40. Frantz Fanon reserves special vitriol for the national bourgeoisie, who are not even a real bourgeoisie but "an acquisitive, voracious, and ambitious petty caste, dominated by a small-time racketeer mentality, content with the dividends paid out by the former colonial power." *The Wretched of the Earth*, trans. Richard Philcox (New York: Grove, 2004), 119.

41. Ibid., 39.

42. Ibid., 36.

43. Shringarpure, *Cold War Assemblages*, 57.

44. Fanon, *Wretched of the Earth*, 41.

45. Ibid.

46. Ibid., 55.

47. Kwon, "The Transpacific Cold War," 68; italics added.

48. Mention must also be made of Mahmoud Mamdani's important book on the authoritarian postcolonial legacies of colonial rule in sub-Saharan Africa, *Citizen and Subject: Contemporary Africa and the Legacy of Late Colonialism* (Princeton, NJ: Princeton University Press, 1996). Mamdani pays particular attention to the way British indirect rule fostered authoritarian leadership. Other important works on states and state-formation in the Third World include Fernando Coronil, *The Magical State: Nature, Money, and Modernity in Venezuela* (Chicago: University of Chicago Press, 1997); Timothy Mitchell, *Rule of Experts: Egypt, Techno-Politics, Modernity* (Berkeley: University of California Press, 2002); Akhil Gupta, *Red Tape: Bureaucracy, Structural Violence, and Poverty in India* (Durham, NC: Duke University Press, 2012); and Naomi Schiller, *Channeling the State: Community Media and Popular Politics in Venezuela* (Durham, NC: Duke University Press, 2018).

49. Achille Mbembe, *On the Postcolony* (Berkeley: University of California Press, 2001), 118.

50. Chari and Verdery, "Thinking between the Posts," 21.

51. Gwee, "Cyril Wong," 6; Mbembe, *On the Postcolony*, 118.

52. Kwon uses the metaphor of "cross-hatching" to describe the two color lines of colonial history and bipolar history. See "The Transpacific Cold War."

53. Cécile Bishop usefully observes the ways that politicized literary criticism—exemplified by the field of postcolonial studies—grapples with the problem of "seem[ing] to privilege the political aspects of representation over aesthetic ones." Cécile Bishop, *Postcolonial Criticism and Representations of African Dictatorship: The Aesthetics of Tyranny* (London: Legenda, Modern Humanities Research Association and Maney Publishing, 2014), 7.

54. Ibid., 8.

55. See Magalí Armillas-Tiseyra's *The Dictator Novel: Writers and Politics in the Global South* (Evanston, IL: Northwestern University Press, 2019). Armillas-Tiseyra usefully juxtaposes works from Latin American and Africa to illuminate "the ways in which African dictator novels both evoke and amend their Latin American counterparts, transforming understanding of the dictator novel from a 'local' phenomenon that responds to national political questions into a transnational literary genre" (5).

56. The phrase is William Shawcross's. See his *Sideshow: Kissinger, Nixon, and the Destruction of Cambodia* (New York: Simon & Schuster, 1987).

57. Nixon, quoted in Grandin, *Empire's Workshop*, 85.

58. For background on the developmental state in postcolonial East Asia see, for example, Atul Kohli's "Where Do High-Growth Political Economies Come From?

NOTES TO PAGES 11–13

The Japanese Lineage of Korea's 'Developmental State,'" in *The Developmental State*, ed. Meredith Woo-Cumings (Ithaca, NY: Cornell University Press, 1999); Robert Wade's *Governing the Market: Economic Theory and the Role of Government in East Asian Industrialization* (Princeton, NJ: Princeton University Press, 1990); and Kim Hyung-A's *Korea's Development under Park Chung Hee: Rapid Industrialization, 1961–1979* (London: Routledge, 2004).

59. Meredith Woo-Cumings, "Introduction: Chalmers Johnson and the Politics of Nationalism and Development," in *The Developmental State*, ed. Meredith Woo-Cumings (Ithaca, NY: Cornell University Press, 1999), 23.

60. Walter LaFeber, "Rethinking the Cold War and After: From Containment to Engagement," in *Rethinking the Cold War*, ed. Allen Hunter (Philadelphia: Temple University Press, 1998), 36.

61. Cumings, "Webs with No Spiders, Spiders with No Webs," 92.

62. See Chapter 4 for a brief discussion of the World Bank's tone-setting 1993 publication *The East Asian Miracle*. Bruce Cumings notes the way Area Studies positioned nations differently as objects of study: "A part of Korea and a part of Vietnam had one epistemology, and the other parts, a totally different one. . . . In academe, communist studies for North Korea, North Vietnam, and China; modernization studies for Japan and the other halves of Korea and Vietnam." See "Boundary Displacement: The State, the Foundations and Area Studies during and after the Cold War," in *Learning Places: The Afterlives of Area Studies*, ed. Masao Miyoshi and H. D. Harootunian (Durham, NC: Duke University Press, 2002), 265.

63. Wong, *The Dictator's Eyebrow*, 26, 31.

64. See Aihwa Ong's *Neoliberalism as Exception: Mutations in Citizenship and Sovereignty* (Durham, NC: Duke University Press, 2006).

65. Philip Holden, "Histories of the Present: Reading Contemporary Singapore Novels between the Local and the Global," *Postcolonial Text* 2, no. 2 (2006): n.p.

66. Chua Beng Huat, *Liberalism Disavowed: Communitarianism and State Capitalism in Singapore* (Ithaca, NY: Cornell University Press, 2017), 47.

67. Ibid.

68. See references in footnote 58. For a fictional rendering, see Hwang Sok-yong's scathing 1985 novel on South Korea's participation in the Vietnam War: *The Shadow of Arms* [*Mugi ŭi kŭnŭl*], trans. Chun Kyung-ja (New York: Seven Stories Press, 2014).

69. Paul D. Hutchcroft, "Reflections on a Reversed Image: South Korea under Park Chung Hee and the Philippines under Marcos," in *The Park Chung Hee Era: The Transformation of South Korea*, ed. Byung-Kook Kim and Ezra F. Vogel (Cambridge, MA: Harvard University Press, 2011), 560.

70. Andrew Rosser, "Escaping the Resource Curse: The Case of Indonesia," *Journal of Contemporary Asia* 37, no. 1 (2007): 40, 43. Rosser notes that after Suharto came to power, the Dutch, British, and American firms that had commanded the Indonesia economy during colonialism were welcomed back, along with new Japanese investment. In addition, "the New Order began working co-operatively with the IMF and other Western donors to stabilise the Indonesian economy and promote its reintegration into the global capitalist system" (44, 49).

71. Robert Young, *Postcolonialism: An Historical Introduction* (Hoboken, NJ: Wiley-Blackwell, 2011), 181.

72. Chua further argues for the collectivist dimensions of Singaporean state capitalism with regard to its public housing and state savings scheme, a residue of the PAP's (People's Action Party's) socialist beginnings.

73. See, for example, the recent primer on the topic *Authoritarianism: What Everyone Needs to Know* (Oxford: Oxford University Press, 2018), by Erica Frantz.

74. Hannah Arendt, *Between Past and Present: Six Exercises in Political Thought* (New York: Viking Press, 1961), 93; italics added.

75. Ibid., 97.

76. Christopher J. Lee, "Between a Moment and an Era: The Origins and Afterlives of Bandung," in *Making a World after Empire: The Bandung Moment and Its Political Afterlives*, ed. Christopher J. Lee (Athens, OH: Center for International Studies, Ohio University, 2010), 19.

77. See the section "Between Revolution and Development" in Chapter 1 for more details. Recall, too, that Frantz Fanon presciently warned against the frantic attempt to catch up with Europe in 1961: "The notion of catching up must not be used as a pretext to brutalize man, to tear him from himself and his inner consciousness, to break him, to kill him." *The Wretched of the Earth*, 238.

78. Monica Popescu, *South African Literature beyond the Cold War* (New York: Palgrave Macmillan, 2010), 43.

79. Ibid., 44.

80. See Richard Wright, *The Color Curtain: A Report on the Bandung Conference* (London: Dennis Dobson, 1956).

81. Bhakti Shringarpure has written eloquently of the temporal dimensions of Cold War decolonization, although with a different regional focus. At decolonization, "The already subjugated populations are further subjugated by the promise of the revolutionary future in enabling the overcoming of the past. They are asked to wait, they are put on hold, or they are forced into the shock of over-acceleration." *Cold War Assemblages*, 81.

82. Theodore Hughes, *Literature and Film in Cold War South Korea: Freedom's Frontier* (New York: Columbia University Press, 2012), 137; italics added.

83. Robert B. Stauffer, in *The Philippines under Marcos: Failure of Transnational Developmentalism* (Sydney: Transnational Corporations Research Project, University of Sydney, 1986), 146.

84. Caroline Hau, *Elites and Ilustrados*, 203. The Marcos period may therefore be viewed "as an attempt, albeit a failed one, to create an authoritarian developmental state in the Philippines" (203).

85. Hilmar Farid, "Indonesia's Original Sin: Mass Killings and Capitalist Expansion 1965–66," in *The Inter-Asia Cultural Studies Reader*, ed. Kuan-hsing Chen and Chua Beng Huat (London: Routledge, 2007), 217.

86. Arendt, *Between Past and Present*, 109; italics added.

87. Wong, *The Dictator's Eyebrow*, 30.

88. As Neferti Tadiar stresses with regard to the Philippines, "It is a gross error, I believe, to view this kind of capitalism and its authoritarian state apparatus in culturally deterministic ways." *Things Fall Away: Philippine Historical Experience and the Makings of Globalization* (Durham, NC: Duke University Press, 2009), 208.

89. Writing on Singapore's development, C. J. W.-L. Wee has alluded to the curious gestalt-like quality of the passage from decolonizing nation to global capitalist hub that sheds self-determination for the pursuit of prosperity. See *The Asian Modern: Culture, Capitalist Development, Singapore* (Singapore: National University of Singapore Press, 2007), 23.

90. Ibid., 31.

91. Ann Laura Stoler, *Duress: Imperial Durabilities in Our Times* (Durham, NC: Duke University Press, 2016), 177.

92. Hughes, *Literature and Film*, 139. On further triumphalist notions of the Pacific, see Christopher L. Connery's "Pacific Rim Discourse: The U.S. Global Imaginary in the Late Cold War Years."

93. Wong, *The Dictator's Eyebrow*, 49.

94. Vijay Prashad, *The Darker Nations: A People's History of the Third World* (New York: New Press, 2007), 246.

95. Ibid., 248.

96. Among a vast literature on this topic, see, for example, Greg Grandin's chapter "The Third Conquest of Latin America: The Economics of the New Imperialism," in *Empire's Workshop*; Achille Mbembe's *On the Postcolony* (Berkeley: University of California Press, 2001); and Samir Amin's *Re-Reading the Postwar Period: An Intellectual Itinerary* (New York: Monthly Review, 1994).

97. Prashad, *The Darker Nations*, 255.

98. Ibid.

99. I have elsewhere examined the way that the Asian "miracle" economies exploited—rather than challenged—their subordinate role in the new international division of labor, especially in their turn to manufacturing export industries. See Jini Kim Watson, *The New Asian City: Three-dimensional Fictions of Space and Urban Form* (Minneapolis: University of Minnesota Press, 2011), especially Chapter 3, "Narratives of Human Growth versus Urban Renewal."

100. See also Annmaria M. Shimabuku's *Alegal: Biopolitics and the Unintelligibility of Okinawan Life* (New York: Fordham University Press, 2018) on the role of communists in postwar Okinawa.

101. Heonik Kwon, *The Other Cold War* (New York: Columbia University Press, 2010), 2.

102. Ibid., 79.

103. Paik Nak-chung, "How to Think about the Park Chung Hee Era," in *Reassessing the Park Chung Era, 1961–79: Development, Political Thought, Democracy,*

and Cultural Influence, ed. Kim Hyung-A and Clark W. Sorensen (Seattle: University of Washington Press, 2011), 87–88.

104. John D. Kelly and Martha Kaplan, *Represented Communities: Fiji and World Decolonization* (Chicago: University of Chicago Press, 2001), 5. See also Lee, "Between a Moment and an Era," 19.

105. Fredric Jameson, "Third World Literature in the Era of Multinational Capitalism," *Social Text* 15 (Autumn 1986): 81; italics added.

106. See Aijaz Ahmad's rejoinder to Jameson's essay in his "Jameson's Rhetoric of Otherness and the 'National Allegory,'" republished in *In Theory: Classes, Nations, Literatures* (London: Verso, 2008).

107. Ngũgĩ wa Thiong'o, *Writers in Politics: A Re-engagement with Issues of Literature and Society*, by Ngũgĩ wa Thiong'o (Oxford: James Currey, 1997), 129.

108. Ibid., 124.

109. Ibid., 131.

110. Jameson, "Third World Literature," 82. Ngũgĩ's magisterial 2006 novel *The Wizard of the Crow* (London: Harvill Secker, 2006), blends allegory, satire, and magical realism in its devastating portrayal of a fictionalized African regime.

111. Fanon, *Wretched of the Earth*, 173.

112. Jameson, "Third World Literature," 81.

113. Duncan Yoon, "'Our Forces Have Redoubled': World Literature, Postcolonialism, and the Afro-Asian Writer's Bureau," *Cambridge Journal of Postcolonial Literary Inquiry* 2, no. 2 (2015): 251.

114. Lee adapts this concept from Fredrick Cooper and Ann Laura Stoler's influential work, *Tensions of Empire* (Berkeley: University of California Press, 1997). Lee, "Between a Moment and an Era," 27.

115. It is for this reason, I suggest, that Prashad's study of the Third World's Non-Aligned Movement, *The Darker Nations*, must take the generic form of an elegy. Relatedly, I discuss what David Scott calls Fanon's exemplary "narrative of liberation" in Chapter 1.

116. See, for example, Peter Hitchcock's "The Failed State and the State of Failure," *Mediations: Journal of the Marxist Literary Group* 23, no. 2 (2008): 71–88, and Neil Ten Kortenaar, "Fictive States and the State of Fiction in Africa," *Comparative Literature* 52, no. 3 (2001): 228–45.

117. Stoler, *Duress*, 177.

118. Philip Holden, "Reading for Genre," *Interventions: International Journal of Postcolonial Studies* 12, no. 3 (2010): 445. Hitchcock notes more directly: "We know almost instinctively that there is at least one genre of postcoloniality: this genre is the novel." Peter Hitchcock, "The Genre of Postcoloniality," *New Literary History* 34, no. 2 (2003): 302.

119. Hitchcock, "The Genre of Postcoloniality," 312.

120. Ibid. Hitchcock is drawing from Tony Bennett's study of Mikhail Bakhtin.

121. Antonio Gramsci, *Selections from the Prison Notebooks*, ed. and trans. Quintin Hoare and Geoffrey Nowell Smith (New York: International, 1971), 119.

1. Writing Freedom from Bandung to PEN International

1. The conferences I concentrate on in this chapter are the five regional Asian Writers' meetings between 1962 and 1981; there were certainly many more PEN-sponsored meetings at individual national centers.

2. Vu Hoang-Chuong, "Contribution of Asian Writers," in *The Second Asian Writers Conference [1964]* (Bangkok: Sanan Bunyasirhibhandhu, 1965), 46.

3. The exceptions in Asia are Thailand, which was never colonized by Western powers, and of course Japan, itself an imperial power between 1895 and 1945.

4. For a fascinating study on the figure of the "free Asian" in Cold War U.S. discourse, see Sunny Xiang's *Tonal Intelligence: The Aesthetics of Asian Inscrutability during the Long Cold War* (New York: Columbia University Press, 2020).

5. Virgilio S. Almario. "Literary 'Consumerism': Notes on the Liberation of Philippine Critical Theory in Poetry," in *Literature and Social Justice: Papers Presented to the Second Asian Writers Conference [1981]* (Manila: Philippine Center of International P.E.N., 1982), 204.

6. Andrew Hammond, "On the Frontlines of Writing: Introducing the Literary Cold War," in *Global Cold War Literature: Western, Eastern and Postcolonial Perspectives,* ed. Andrew Hammond (New York: Routledge, 2012), 5.

7. This literary history is necessarily incomplete. Questions that remain to be investigated include, for example, who was *not* invited to the conferences; who refused to come or was not allowed to come; and what were the "behind the scenes" politics and networking at each conference.

8. Joseph Keith, *Unbecoming Americans: Writing Race and Nation from the Shadows of Citizenship* (New Brunswick, NJ: Rutgers University Press, 2013), 6.

9. See Gary Wilder, *Freedom Time: Negritude, Decolonization, and the Future of the World* (Durham, NC: Duke University Press, 2015), Chapter 4, "Freedom, Time, Territory."

10. "Our History," PEN International, accessed August 3, 2016, http://www.pen-international.org/our-history/.

11. "PEN Charter," PEN International, accessed August 3, 2016, http://www.pen-international.org/pen-charter/.

12. Rachel Potter, "Modernist Rights: International PEN 1921–1936," *Critical Quarterly* 55, no. 2 (2013): 72.

13. Ibid.

14. Ibid., 77.

15. Ibid., 74.

16. Frances Stoner Saunders, *The Cultural Cold War: The CIA and the World of Arts and Letters* (New York: New Press, 2001), 362. In 1960 PEN set up a Writers in Prison committee to facilitate appeals for the release of detained writers, such as Nigeria's Wole Soyinka. Saunders notes that PEN's "refusal to succumb to bias or *parti pris* coupled with a robust defense of freedom of expression . . . guaranteed the world-wide expansion of PEN during the Cold War years" (362).

17. Ibid., 1.

18. Peter D. McDonald, *The Literature Police: Apartheid Censorship and Its Cultural Consequences* (Oxford: Oxford University Press, 2009), 123. Also see Andrew Rubin's important work, *Archives of Authority: Empire, Culture, and the Cold War* (Princeton, NJ: Princeton University Press, 2012), especially for the way cultural works supported and circulated by the Congress for Cultural Freedom helped the transfer of "imperial authority" from Britain to the United States during the Cold War.

19. Saunders, *The Cultural Cold War*, 365. The 1966 International PEN Congress subsequently took place in New York City, under the apt theme of "The Writer as Independent Spirit." See Saunders, *The Cultural Cold War*, 367.

20. See also Writers and Free Expression website, https://writersandfree expression.com, headed by Rachel Potter.

21. "PEN Charter," n.p.

22. Domingo Castro de Guzman, "Notes on Art, Freedom, and Society," in *Literature and Social Justice: Papers Presented to the Second Asian Writers Conference [1981]* (Manila: Philippine Center of International P.E.N., 1982), 148.

23. See the next chapter's discussion on Ninotchka Rosca for more details on Marcos's crackdown on writers and journalists.

24. President Soekarno [Sukarno], "Speech," in *Selected Documents of the Bandung Conference: Texts of Selected Speeches and Final Communique of the Asian-African Conference, Bandung, Indonesia, April 18–24, 1955* (New York: Institute of Pacific Relations, 1955), 5.

25. Anne Garland Mahler, *From the Tricontinental to the Global South: Race, Radicalism, and Transnational Solidarity* (Durham, NC: Duke University Press, 2018), 13.

26. David Scott, *Refashioning Futures: Criticism after Postcoloniality* (Princeton, NJ: Princeton University Press, 1999), 198. As I discussed in the Introduction, for Scott, writing in 1999, such an era is emphatically over, superseded by a post-1991, neoliberal, unipolar world of U.S hegemony.

27. Christopher J. Lee, "Between a Moment and an Era: The Origins and Afterlives of Bandung," in *Making a World after Empire: The Bandung Moment and Its Political Afterlives*, ed. Christopher J. Lee (Athens, OH: Center for International Studies, Ohio University, 2010), 3.

28. Ibid., 4.

29. For more details on the AAWB, see Duncan Yoon's "'Our Forces Have Redoubled': World Literature, Postcolonialism, and the Afro-Asian Writer's Bureau," in *Cambridge Journal of Postcolonial Literary Inquiry* 2, no. 2 (2015): 233–52. Also see Hala Halim's "Lotus, the Afro-Asian Nexus, and Global South Comparatism," *Comparative Studies of South Asia, Africa and the Middle East* 32, no. 3 (2012): 563–83; and Rossen Djagalov's *From Internationalism to Postcolonialism: Literature and Cinema between the Second and Third Worlds* (Montreal: McGill-Queen's University Press, 2020).

30. Cirilo F. Bautista, "Philippine Literature: From National Liberation to Aesthetic Liberation," in *Literature and Social Justice: Papers Presented to the Second Asian Writers Conference [1981]* (Manila: Philippine Center of International P.E.N., 1982), 139–40.

31. Lee, "Between a Moment and an Era," 23.

32. Carlos P. Romulo, "Imagination and Asian Reality [The Fifth Annual José Rizal Lecture]," *Report of the Asian Writers' Conference,* published in *Comment: The Filipino Journal of Ideas, Discussion, and the Arts,* no. 17 (1963): 40.

33. Yoon, "Our Forces Have Redoubled," 245.

34. "The Role of the Writer in a Revolutionary Age [Conference Session]," *Report of the Asian Writers' Conference,* published in *Comment: The Filipino Journal of Ideas, Discussion, and the Arts,* no. 17 (1963): 88.

35. Ibid., 99.

36. Ibid., 90.

37. "Third Literary Session, Part B," in *Proceedings of the Third Asian Writers' Conference* (Taipei: Chinese Center, International P.E.N., 1970), 99.

38. Christina Klein, *Cold War Orientalism: Asia in the Middlebrow Imagination, 1945–1961* (Berkeley: University of California Press, 2003), 47–48. Such a perception of cultural isolation and "blockage" in the Soviet bloc is beginning to be challenged by scholars such as Rossen Djagalov, whose study of Second and Third World cultural exchange demonstrates the important transnational cultural networks that existed. See his *From Internationalism to Postcolonialism.*

39. *Lianhe bao* (*United Daily News*), June 6, 1970, 2. The unsigned editorial goes on to urge the development of, first, "a national literature [minzu wenxue], and second, the need to champion [baowei] the freedom of literature [wenxue ziyou]." Translations by Paris Liu.

40. We might pause to note the radical "makeover" that capitalism receives in this postwar, U.S.-promoted iteration. As we noted in the introductory chapter, one of the tasks of the United States in the decolonizing period of the Cold War was to cast itself as an anti-imperialist power and to challenge capitalism's long association with racial domination and exploitation, a link made explicit by thinkers such as V. I. Lenin, Rosa Luxemburg, M. N. Roy, Frantz Fanon, and many others.

41. "Third Literary Session [1970]," 105.

42. Ibid., 107.

43. The *United Daily News* also carried a report on the reception: "President Chiang Kai-shek and his wife stepped into the quaint and elegant hall to warm applause. Everybody stood up and moved forward in order to have a close look at the Asian anti-communist leader [yazhou fangong lingxiu] whom they have long admired, as well as the graceful and magnificent First Lady of the Republic of China." *Lianhe bao,* June 21, 1970, 1. Translation by Paris Liu.

44. The conference proceedings list that there were several "observers" from Vietnam.

45. One of the longest-standing Cold War boundaries still persists in the problem of two Chinas. Only a handful of countries currently have official diplomatic relations with the Republic of China, mostly small African or Pacific Island countries who are rewarded economically for doing so. Taiwan is forced to use "Chinese Taipei" as its official name for international forums such as the Olympics.

46. In fact, the ordinal numbering of the various conferences is confusing. The 1981 Manila conference is subtitled "Papers Presented to the *Second* Asian Writers Conference," even though the preamble to its Resolutions section states, "The *Fourth* Asian Writers' Conference . . . " The discrepancy may be reconciled by noting that the 1981 Conference was the second regional conference to be held in Manila, but fourth (or actually fifth) overall.

47. Y. C. Chen, "Opening Remarks," in *Thirty Years of Turmoil in Asian Literature: The Fourth Asian Writers' Conference, April 25th–May 2nd, 1976* (Taipei: Taipei Chinese Center, International P.E.N., 1976), 19.

48. Y. C. Chen, "Closing Remarks," in *Thirty Years of Turmoil in Asian Literature: The Fourth Asian Writers' Conference, April 25th–May 2nd, 1976* (Taipei: Taipei Chinese Center, International P.E.N., 1976), 61.

49. Heonik Kwon, *The Other Cold War* (New York: Columbia University Press, 2010), 6. Andrew Hammond has vigorously argued the fallacy of the "cold" war: "To designate the international conflict as 'cold' with its suggestion of inertia and equilibrium, is to do more than falsify the record. The act of understanding a historical period exclusively through the Western experience of that period partakes in the same hegemonic Euro-Americanism that defined the conflict itself, privileging a limited range of subjectivities and relegating all others to insignificance." See his essay, "From Rhetoric to Rollback: Introductory Thoughts on Cold War Writing," in *Cold War Literature: Writing the Global Conflict*, ed. Andrew Hammond (London: Routledge, 2006), 1.

50. Kwon, *The Other Cold War*, 6–7.

51. Chi-tsung Wang, "Literature in Agitated Time," in *Thirty Years of Turmoil in Asian Literature: The Fourth Asian Writers' Conference, April 25th–May 2nd, 1976* (Taipei: Taipei Chinese Center, International P.E.N., 1976), 169–70.

52. Although the 1976 Taipei conference was held several months before Mao's death that same year, the focus on Soviet dissident writers tends to obscure the looming threat of the Mainland.

53. See Sung-sheng Yvonne Chang's *Modernism and the Nativist Resistance: Contemporary Chinese Fiction from Taiwan* (Durham, NC: Duke University Press, 1993).

54. Hammond, "Global Cold War," 3. Such an aesthetic binary would itself come to characterize a major Taiwanese literary debate, dubbed the "Nativists versus Modernists" with Huang Chun-ming one of the leading figures of the former. Huang Chun-ming—also discussed at length in Yen Yuan-shu's paper—is recognized as one of the central figures of the *hsiang-t'u* (literally "homeland") or "nativist" literary movement that was opposed to the abstract aesthetics of Western-inspired

"modernist" writers and leaned toward social realist modes. The so-called "Nativists" sought to depict the fate of non-Mandarin speaking Taiwanese who were politically and economically marginalized by the KMT-affiliated population that retreated to Taiwan after 1949. For more on the literary debates in Taiwan, see June Yip's *Envisioning Taiwan: Fiction, Cinema, and the Nation in the Cultural Imaginary* (Durham, NC: Duke University Press, 2004); and Sung-sheng Yvonne Chang's *Modernism and the Nativist Resistance*.

55. "Fourth Literary Session," in *Thirty Years of Turmoil in Asian Literature: The Fourth Asian Writers' Conference, April 25th–May 2nd, 1976* (Taipei: Taipei Chinese Center, International P.E.N., 1976), 53.

56. Peter Elstob, "Message," in *Literature and Social Justice: Papers Presented to the Second Asian Writers Conference [1981]* (Manila: Philippine Center of International P.E.N., 1982), 1–2.

57. Carlos P. Romulo, "Opening Statement," in *Selected Documents of the Bandung Conference: Texts of Selected Speeches and Final Communique of the Asian-African Conference, Bandung, Indonesia, April 18–24, 1955* (New York: Institute of Pacific Relations, 1955), 17; italics in original. John Kotelawala, prime minister of Ceylon, similarly spells out the links between colonialism's legacy of poverty and the urgent need for the "common goal" of Third World development: "We, the nations of the new Asia and Africa, whatever our language, whatever our faiths, whatever our form of government, whatever the colour of our skin—black, brown or yellow—have one thing in common: we are all poor and underdeveloped." Kotelawala, "Opening Speech," in *Selected Documents of the Bandung Conference: Texts of Selected Speeches and Final Communique of the Asian-African Conference, Bandung, Indonesia, April 18–24, 1955* (New York: Institute of Pacific Relations, 1955), 10.

58. Jawaharlal Nehru, "India," in *Bandung: A Clarion Call for Afro-Asian Solidarity [18–24 April, 1955]* (Cairo: Afro-Asian Peoples' Solidarity Organisation, 1975), 19.

59. Dipesh Chakrabarty, "The Legacies of Bandung: Decolonization and the Politics of Culture," in *Making a World after Empire: The Bandung Moment and Its Political Afterlives*, ed. Christopher J. Lee (Athens, OH: Center for International Studies, Ohio University: 2010), 53. Chakrabarty cites a telling line from Richard Wright's observations of Indonesia recorded in *The Color Curtain* in 1956: "Where is the *engineer* who can build a project out of eighty million human lives, a project that can nourish them, sustain them, and yet have their voluntary loyalty." Wright, qtd., 53.

60. I thank Duncan Yoon for this observation.

61. Emmanuel Pelaez, "Opening Address," *Report of the Asian Writers' Conference*, published in *Comment: The Filipino Journal of Ideas, Discussion, and the Arts*, no. 17 (1963): 8.

62. "Second Literary Session, Part A," in *Proceedings of the Third Asian Writers' Conference* (Taipei: Chinese Center, International P.E.N., 1970), 54.

63. "Tradition and Modernity in Literature [Conference Session]," *Report of the Asian Writers' Conference*, published in *Comment: The Filipino Journal of Ideas, Discussion, and the Arts*, no. 17 (1963): 72.

64. Ibid., 74; italics added.

65. Alisjahbana is key figure in the debates around Indonesian literary culture in the post-independence period; see the next chapter for further discussion.

66. S. Takdir Alisjahbana, "Tradition and Modernity in Asian Literature," *Report of the Asian Writers' Conference*, published in *Comment: The Filipino Journal of Ideas, Discussion, and the Arts*, no. 17 (1963): 26.

67. Pelaez, "Opening Address," 8.

68. Reinhart Koselleck, *Futures Past: On the Semantics of Historical Time* (New York: Columbia University Press, 2004), 52; italics added.

69. Ibid.

70. Alisjahbana, "Tradition and Modernity in Asian Literature," 26.

71. "The Role of the Writer in a Revolutionary Age," 92.

72. Ibid.

73. Raul S. Manglapus, "Progress and the Writers of Asia," *Report of the Asian Writers' Conference*, published in *Comment: The Filipino Journal of Ideas, Discussion, and the Arts*, no. 17 (1963): 32.

74. F. Sionil José, *The Samsons, Two Novels in the Rosales Sage: The Pretenders and Mass* (New York: Modern Library, 2000), 432; italics added.

75. Leo Ching's comments were made as the discussant at the "Inter-Asian Literature between Colonial Modernism and Neoliberal Globalization" panel at the Association for Asian Studies, Toronto, March 2017.

We could also use the notion of "inter-imperiality" as defined by Laura Doyle. See her article "Inter-imperiality: Dialectics in a Postcolonial World History," *Interventions: International Journal of Postcolonial Studies* 16, no. 2 (2014): 159–96. In a related formulation, Lisa Yoneyama had importantly developed the notion of the "transwar" to describe the way U.S. postwar hegemony evolved from the defeat of Japanese imperialism in "a deeply conjoined, enduring interimperial complex of historical violence." See *Cold War Ruins: Transpacific Critique of American Justice and Japanese War Crimes* (Durham, NC: Duke University Press, 2016), ix.

76. See Kwame Nkrumah's *Neo-colonialism, the Last Stage of Imperialism* (London: Thomas Nelson & Sons, 1965).

77. Romulo, "Opening Statement," 14. Interestingly, at the 1970 conference, Indonesian delegate Taufiq Ismail partly blamed Sukarno's turn to autocracy (while neatly sidestepping General Suharto's altogether) as clearly "reminiscen[t] of some old British rule, authoritarian in character, yet with no efficient machinery of control." "First Literary Session, Part B [1970]," in *Proceedings of the Third Asian Writers' Conference* (Taipei: Chinese Center, International P.E.N., 1970), 35.

78. Gilbert Rist, *The History of Development: From Western Origins to Global Faith*, 4th ed. (London: Zed, 2014), 79. In Rist's authoritative account, he pinpoints

the postwar decades as crucial to the consolidation of "development" as a hegemonic concept. Crediting U.S. President Truman with inaugurating "the development age"—largely through the famous "Point Four" of his 1949 presidential address—Rist describes the way the newly paired notions of "underdevelopment" and "development" were largely accepted by the decolonizing Third World, replacing the discredited and antiquated civilizing mission of imperialism.

79. Recall from the introductory chapter Monica Popescu's observation that Soviet Asian republics were thought to be able to "speed up time" by implementing rational developmental strategies as directed by the state.

80. Rist, *History of Development*, 78.

81. Yip, *Envisioning Taiwan*, 22. A *United Daily News* article on the 1976 Asian Writers' Conference confirms Yip's observation: "Modernization can only be achieved through anti-communism, and only through modernization can anti-communist sympathies be made visible, and anti-communist campaigns more efficiently launched." April 26, 1976, 12. Translation by Paris Liu.

82. McDonald, *The Literature Police*, 171. McDonald is writing of the role of PEN South Africa.

83. José, *Mass*, 423.

84. Reynaldo Clemeña Ileto, *Filipinos and Their Revolution: Event, Discourse and Historiography* (Quezon City: Ateneo de Manila University Press, 1998), 188.

85. Although Filipino communists of the Partido Komunista ng Pilipinas (PKP) had been squarely routed in the U.S. counterinsurgency campaigns of the early 1950s, the party had resurrected itself in 1968 and would be increasingly significant in the 1970s as an underground movement—largely rural-based—in opposition to the Marcos regime. P. N. Abinales and Donna J. Amoroso, *State and Society in the Philippines* (Lanham, MD: Rowman & Littlefield, 2005), 200–201.

86. Caroline Hau notes that "the seeds for the toppling of the Marcos dictatorship were already sown back in 1979" with the second oil shock and the ensuing debt crisis following the U.S. Federal Reserve's decision to raise rates. *Elites and Ilustrados in Philippine Culture* (Manila: Ateneo de Manila University Press, 2017), 196.

87. Abinales and Amoroso, *State and Society in the Philippines*, 207.

88. The first presidential election in twelve years took place in the June preceding the conference; Marcos was reelected.

89. Mauro R. Avena, "The Filipino Writer and Social Justice," in *Literature and Social Justice: Papers Presented to the Second Asian Writers Conference [1981]* (Manila: Philippine Center of International P.E.N., 1982), 38.

90. Marcos's statement on declaring martial law on September 23, 1972, invoked the threat of a government overthrow by "lawless elements" whose "legal and moral precepts are based on the Marxist-Leninist-Maoist teaching and beliefs." Marcos, quoted in Abinales and Amoroso, *State and Society in the Philippines*, 206.

91. See Crystal Parikh's *Writing Human Rights* (Minneapolis: University of Minnesota Press, 2017) for the way literature responds to the postwar "human rights record."

92. A detailed 1978 article on Marcos's repression of journalism by E. San Juan Jr. indicts Lopez's liberalism and his dismissal of Marcos's draconian censorship laws "as a temporary expedient." "Marcos and the Media," *Index on Censorship* 7, no. 3 (1978): 45.

93. Salvador P. Lopez, "Some Reflections on Human Rights," in *Literature and Social Justice: Papers Presented to the Second Asian Writers Conference [1981]* (Manila: Philippine Center of International P.E.N., 1982), 195.

94. Ibid. Interestingly, Lopez confirms the apparent zero-sum game between individual political/civil rights and social economic development by reminding us of the way Cold War contests were actually constitutive of—and remain embedded in—the major human rights documents: "During the drafting of the Universal Declaration of Human Rights, the debate between East and West turned on the question of whether civil and political rights were more or less important than economic, social and cultural rights. . . . This divergence of opinion resulted in the splitting of the International Covenant on Human Rights, one covering civil and political rights, and another covering economic, social and cultural rights." Lopez, "Some Reflections," 191. It is perhaps an irony that while the very documents of human rights archive the history of Cold War binarism, the universal principles drawn from them are made to apply to political landscapes created by that very same bipolarism.

95. Ibid., 193.

96. Duk-yong Kang, "Literature and Social Justice," in *Literature and Social Justice: Papers Presented to the Second Asian Writers Conference [1981]* (Manila: Philippine Center of International P.E.N., 1982), 35–36.

97. Cecil Rajendra, "The Higher Duty of a Writer in a Developing Society," in *Literature and Social Justice: Papers Presented to the Second Asian Writers Conference [1981]* (Manila: Philippine Center of International P.E.N., 1982), 18.

98. Selina Hossain, "Literature and Social Justice," in *Literature and Social Justice: Papers Presented to the Second Asian Writers Conference [1981]* (Manila: Philippine Center of International P.E.N., 1982), 22.

99. Ibid., 23.

100. Ibid.

101. Castro de Guzman, "Notes on Art, Freedom, and Society," 147.

102. Hossain, "Literature and Social Justice," 23.

103. Michio Ochi, "Modernization in Japan," in *Literature and Social Justice: Papers Presented to the Second Asian Writers Conference [1981]* (Manila: Philippine Center of International P.E.N., 1982), 157.

104. Gloria F. Rodriguez, "A Look at Publishing in the Philippines," in *Literature and Social Justice: Papers Presented to the Second Asian Writers Conference [1981]* (Manila: Philippine Center of International P.E.N., 1982), 168.

105. Ibid.

106. Almario was a prominent proponent of the Filipino language literary movement. I thank Philip Holden for this insight.

107. Almario, "Literary Consumerism," 118.

108. Ibid., 119.

109. Fredric Jameson, "On Literary and Cultural Import-Substitution in the Third World," in *The Real Thing: Testimonial Discourse and Latin America*, ed. Georg M. Gugelberger (Durham, NC: Duke University Press, 1996), 176.

110. Ibid., 176–77.

111. Ibid., 186.

112. Sarah Brouillette, "UNESCO and the Book in the Developing World," *Representations* 127, no. 1 (2014): 49.

113. In his study of censorship in apartheid South Africa, Peter McDonald usefully contrasts (white) liberal forms of protest such as the petition, which stay "within the law," versus more radical protests that call into question structures of inequality and dependency. See *The Literature Police*, 173–74.

114. Norman Cousins, introduction to *Asian PEN Anthology*, ed. F. Sionil José (New York: Taplinger, 1966), xv.

115. "Report on the Proceedings," in *The Second Asian Writers Conference [1964]* (Bangkok: Sanan Bunyasirhibhandhu, 1965), 28.

116. Ibid.

117. Hala Halim, "Lotus," 572.

118. Ibid., 571.

119. "Role of Western Literature in the Asian Modernization Process [Conference Session]," in *Thirty Years of Turmoil in Asian Literature: The Fourth Asian Writers' Conference, April 25th–May 2nd, 1976* (Taipei: Taipei Chinese Center, International P.E.N., 1976), 58.

120. Ibid., 59.

121. Leo T. S. Ching, *Anti-Japan: The Politics of Sentiment in Postcolonial East Asia* (Durham, NC: Duke University Press, 2019), 7.

122. One of the most concrete manifestations of this repurposing was Japan's role in the Colombo Plan, the regional development plan inaugurated in 1950 by Commonwealth Asian and Pacific countries, backed by Britain, Australia, and eventually the United States. Gilbert Rist notes the allusion to Colombo in point 1 of the Bandung Conference's Final Communiqué. See Rist's *The History of Development*, 86n13.

123. Kuan-Hsing Chen, *Asia as Method: Toward Deimperialization* (Durham, NC: Duke University Press, 2010), 121.

124. Also interesting at the 1981 Manila Conference is a paper on the proposal for a "Know Our Region" translation program, funded by the Toyota Foundation. The program would focus specifically on translations of Southeast Asian literary works into Japanese, and vice versa. See 175–79.

125. The other three resolutions pertain to internal organizational matters: a vote of thanks (to the organizers F. Sionil José and Tessie José); a decision for PEN International to "find ways and means" to fund a PEN International Award in Literature; and a call for the Japanese government and the ASEAN standing

committee to disburse funding for cultural activities in Southeast Asian countries. See "Resolutions," *Literature and Social Justice: Papers Presented to the Second Asian Writers Conference [1981]* (Manila: Philippine Center of International P.E.N., 1982), 201–3. The latter carries an interesting, but never explicit, tone of imperial reparations.

126. "Resolutions [1981]," 201.

127. Ibid., 202.

128. Ibid.

129. Potter, "Modernist Rights," 74.

130. McDonald, *The Literature Police*, 167.

131. Kwon, *The Other Cold War*, 4.

132. Scott, *Refashioning Futures*, 201.

133. For other versions of the defeat of progressive Third World national projects, see also Aijaz Ahmad's *In Theory: Classes, Nations, Literatures* (London: Verso, 1992); Neil Lazarus's *The Postcolonial Unconscious* (Cambridge: Cambridge University Press, 2011); and Partha Chatterjee's "Empire and Nation Revisited," *Inter-Asia Cultural Studies* 6, no. 4 (2005): 487–96.

2. In the Shadow of Solzhenitsyn: Pramoedya Ananta Toer, Kim Chi-ha, Ninotchka Rosca, and Cold War Critique

1. Solzhenitsyn was accused by the Stalinist state of anti-Soviet propaganda and was imprisoned from 1945 to 1953. He won the Nobel Prize for literature in 1970, and his writings have been widely translated.

2. Amnesty's "Prisoner of Conscience Week" began in 1968, the UN Year of Human Rights.

3. Richard Bourne, "Amnesty Names Its Twelve Prisoners of Conscience," *Guardian*, November 13, 1972.

4. Kathleen Teltsch, "Worldwide Amnesty Group Asks Waldheim's Help in Freeing 12," *New York Times*, November 20, 1972.

5. Donald Kirk, "The Bold Words of Ki: In Korea, Officials Curse, Intellectuals Cheer," *New York Times*, January 7, 1973.

6. Robert Whymant, "'The Korean Solzhenitsyn' Strikes Back," *Guardian*, June 6, 1974.

7. Lourdes Gordolan, "Butch Dalisay, Ricky Lee, and Other Writers Remember Prison Life in Martial Law Era," *Rogue*, April 2012, http://rogue.ph/butch-dalisay-ricky-lee-writers-remember-prison-life-martial-law-era/.

8. See Brian K. Goodman's article on the emergence of the "dissident writer" in Cold War Czechoslovakia, "Philip Roth's Other Europe: Counter-Realism and the Late Cold War," in which he describes the "new image of the persecuted Czech intellectual, couched in an emerging language of dissent." Brian K. Goodman, "Philip Roth's Other Europe," *American Literary History* 27, no. 4 (2015): 719.

9. Neil Lazarus, *The Postcolonial Unconscious* (Cambridge: Cambridge University Press, 2011), 69. He likens such scholars to the character of Teacher in Ayi Kwei

Armah's 1968 novel, *The Beautyful Ones Are Not Yet Born*, who "retreats into political agnosticism and abandons his erstwhile activism" in the face of the generalized disappointments of the postcolonial era.

10. Ibid., 70.

11. Barbara Harlow, *Resistance Literature* (New York: Methuen, 1987), xvii.

12. Joseph R. Slaughter, "Foreword: Rights on Paper," in *Theoretical Perspectives on Human Rights and Literature*, ed. Elizabeth Swanson Goldberg and Alexandra Schultheis Moore (New York: Routledge, 2012), xii.

13. Ibid.

14. Matthew Hart and Jim Hansen, "Introduction: Contemporary Literature and the State," *Contemporary Literature* 49, no. 4 (2008): 493. In Chinua Achebe's *Anthills of the Savannah* (London: Heinemann, 1987), journalist character Ikem confirms exactly this view of the oppositional artist: "A genuine artist, no matter what he says he believes, must feel in his blood the ultimate enmity between art and orthodoxy," 100. A 1984 essay on underground protest literature in Marcos-era Philippines by Rosario Torres-Yu also expresses this opposition: "Literature possesses a subversive force inherent in its language and imagery which enables it to be free, to a certain extent, from the language of the establishment." Rosario Torres-Yu, "The State of Philippine Literature," in *The Politics of Culture: The Philippine Experience*, ed. Nicanor G. Tiongson (Manila: Philippine Educational Theater Association, 1984), 16.

15. William Pietz, "The 'Post-Colonialism' of Cold War Discourse," *Social Text*, no. 19/20 (1988): 56.

16. Peter Benenson, quoted in Slaughter, "Foreword: Rights on Paper," xi.

17. Slaughter, ibid., xii.

18. Ibid., xi.

19. Richard Bourne, "Amnesty Names Its Twelve Prisoners of Conscience," *Guardian*, November 13, 1972. Emphasis added.

20. Jonathan Power, "Last Words for a Hero of the Pen," *Los Angeles Times*, July 30, 1988.

21. Ibid.

22. Robert Whymant, "'The Korean Solzhenitsyn' Strikes Back," *Guardian*, June 6, 1974.

23. Peter D. McDonald, *The Literature Police: Apartheid Censorship and Its Cultural Consequences* (Oxford: Oxford University Press, 2009), 10.

24. Slaughter, "Foreword: Rights on Paper," xiii.

25. I draw this phrase from Josephat Kubayanda's essay, "Unfinished Business: Dictatorial Literature of Post-Independence Latin America and Africa," *Research in African Literatures* 28, no. 4 (1997): 38–53

26. Unfortunately, due to language limitations, I am reliant on Max Lane's translation in reading Pramoedya's works. Nevertheless, these translations themselves have circulated widely and have formed part of the corpus of postcolonial transpacific literature.

27. House of Glass was composed orally on Buru island during Pramoedya's detention during the late 1970s.

28. Swami Anand Haridas, "Profile: Pramoedya Ananta Toer," *Index on Censorship* 7, no. 5 (1978): 50.

29. Ibid., 51.

30. I discuss the 1965–66 massacre in more detail in Chapter 5.

31. Like the French in Indochina and the British in Malaya, the Dutch colonial power had returned after the defeat of Japan to retake their Southeast Asian possession. The bloody struggle, from 1945 to 1949, is known as Indonesia's national revolution.

32. Tony Day, "Still Stuck in the Mud: Imagining World Literature during the Cold War in Indonesia and Vietnam," in *Cultures at War: The Cold War and Cultural Expression in Southeast Asia*, ed. Tony Day and Maya H. T. Liem (Ithaca, NY: Cornell University Press, 2010), 137.

33. Keith Foulcher, *Social Commitment in Literature and the Arts: The Indonesian "Institute of People's Culture," 1950–1965* (Clayton, VIC: Centre of Southeast Asian Studies/Monash University, 1986), 17.

34. Ibid., 17–18.

35. Ibid., 20–26.

36. Ibid., 46.

37. Haridas, "Profile: Pramoedya Ananta Toer," 50.

38. Foulcher, *Social Commitment*, 38.

39. Day, "Still Stuck in the Mud," 146–53. Foulcher notes that although socialist realist classics were encouraged, LEKRA itself never strictly held to the stylistic opposition of "good" socialist realism and "bad" bourgeois modernist literature. The concept of *kerakyatan* aesthetics (from *rakyat*, the people) was advocated without strict stylistic prescription, 36–39. Pramoedya encountered Steinbeck while in a Dutch jail. "Access to this library helped me to study English by reading John Steinbeck's *Of Mice and Men*—which also impressed me very much by its narrative technique." "Perburuan 1950 and Keluarga Gerilya 1950," trans. Benedict Anderson. *Indonesia*, no. 36 (1983): 37.

40. Foulcher, *Social Commitment*, 42–43.

41. Foulcher notes that in 1950 "the Indonesian market was flooded with American films" with 85 percent of films being American imports, 43.

42. Chapter 5 discusses the controversial coup of September 30, 1965, in more detail.

43. Haridas, "Profile: Pramoedya Ananta Toer," 52.

44. Foulcher, *Social Commitment*, 5.

45. Ibid., 6.

46. Pramoedya remained a threat to the military leaders of the New Order government despite his incarceration. In 1980, when the government planned to gradually release PKI prisoners, the Nation Defense Institute, Lemhannas, named the authors Pramoedya and Rivai Apin as prime examples of "diehards" "unwilling to renounce communist ideology." Lemhannas insisted that PKI supporters were a

latent threat to society and could maintain communist activities "through networks of cell members which were not formally organized," prompting years of "vigilance indoctrination" or *kewaspadaan*. Jun Honna, "Military Ideology in Response to Democratic Pressure during the Late Suharto Era: Political and Institutional Contexts," in *Violence and the State in Suharto's Indonesia*, ed. Benedict R. O'G. Anderson (Ithaca, NY: Cornell University Press, 2001), 57.

47. Chris GoGwilt, "Pramoedya's Fiction and History: An Interview with Indonesian Novelist Pramoedya Ananta Toer," *Yale Journal of Criticism* 9, no. 1 (1996): 151. Pramoedya wrote a biography, *Sang Pemula* (The Pioneer, 1985, also promptly banned), on Tirto, the Javanese journalist, doctor, entrepreneur and thorn in the side of the Dutch administration.

48. The close relationship between Pramoedya's novels and theories of postcolonial nationalism have been well noted. As GoGwilt puts it, "The formal structure of the first three novels, narrated by Minke, fits the genre of what Partha Chatterjee calls 'nationalism's autobiography,'" 154. See in particular Benedict Anderson, *Imagined Communities* (London: Verso, 1983), for the influence that Pramoedya's writings have on his well-known theory of nationalism.

49. Ananta Toer Pramoedya, *House of Glass: A Novel*, trans. Max Lane (New York: Penguin, 1992), 39.

50. Peter Hitchcock, *The Long Space: Transnationalism and Postcolonial Form* (Stanford, CA: Stanford University Press, 2010), 191.

51. Ibid., 194.

52. Ibid., 192.

53. Mary Durran, "Asking Forbidden Questions," *New Internationalist*, December 1989. https://newint.org/features/1989/12/05/endpiece.

54. GoGwilt, "Pramoedya's Fiction and History," 154.

55. Pramoedya, *House of Glass*, 52.

56. Ibid., 54.

57. Ibid., 117.

58. Hitchcock, *Long Space*, 196.

59. Pramoedya, *House of Glass*, 55.

60. Hitchcock, *Long Space*, 202.

61. Pramoedya, *House of Glass*, 55.

62. Ibid., 72.

63. Ibid., 341–42.

64. Ibid., 130.

65. Pramoedya's father was a teacher in a Boedi Oetomo school, and a supporter of its reform programs.

66. Pramoedya, *House of Glass*, 16.

67. Ibid., 166.

68. Ibid., 131.

69. The frequent insertion of other narratives and textual forms (letters, articles, interviews, oral stories) is well established in the previous three novels of the Buru quartet.

70. Ibid., 186.

71. Ibid.

72. For background on the workings of the Suharto state, see Joshua Barker's "State of Fear: Controlling the Criminal Contagion in Suharto's New Order," in *Violence and the State in Suharto's Indonesia*, ed. Benedict R. O'G. Anderson (Ithaca, NY: Cornell University Press, 2001): "Economically, 1973–1981 witnessed a tremendous oil boom which gave the state unprecedented revenues and leeway in pursuing policies of economic nationalism. By 1982, however, the first signs of the oil bust began to appear, leaving the state in a weakened position with respect to foreign capital," 23.

73. Andrew Rosser, "Escaping the Resource Curse: The Case of Indonesia," *Journal of Contemporary Asia* 37, no. 1 (2007): 50.

74. Honna, "Military Ideology," 55n3.

75. Naomi Schiller, *Channeling the State: Community Media and Popular Politics in Venezuela* (Durham, NC: Duke University Press: 2018), 14.

76. Ibid.

77. Pramoedya, *House of Glass*, 289.

78. Ibid.

79. Ibid., 289–90.

80. Ibid., 290.

81. Ibid.

82. Ibid.

83. Ibid., 234.

84. This attention is most visible in the character of Nyai Ontosoroh, or Sanikem, but evident in many other narrative diversions such as the powerful story of Surati, who rebels against her forced prostitution to a local Dutch sugar boss. See *Child of All Nations* (New York: Penguin, 1990).

85. Pramoedya, *House of Glass*, 235.

86. Alex Woloch, *The One vs. the Many: Minor Characters and the Space of the Protagonist in the Novel* (Princeton, NJ: Princeton University Press, 2009), 125.

87. Ibid., 130.

88. Pramoedya, *House of Glass*, 263.

89. Ibid., 177-178.

90. Ibid., 262. Also see *Child of All Nations* for Pramoedya's extended metaphor of Java's awakening. Early in that novel, Minke notes that "there was no movement at all. All Java was fast asleep, dreaming." *Child of All Nations*, 93.

91. Ibid., 265.

92. Ibid., 331.

93. See Carl Niekerk for his in-depth analysis of gender and sexuality in *This Earth of Mankind*. As he puts it, "All of these texts articulate an interest in gender as a means to come to a critical assessment of colonial politics." Carl Niekerk, "Modernity, Sexuality, and Gender in Pramoedya Ananta Toer's *This Earth of Mankind*," *Symposium: A Quarterly Journal in Modern Literatures* 65, no. 2 (2011): 90.

94. Dominic Boyer, "Censorship as Vocation: The Institutions, Practices, and Cultural Logic of Media Control in the German Democratic Republic," *Comparative Studies in Society and History* 45, no. 3 (2003): 539.

95. Pramoedya, *House of Glass*, 326.

96. Ibid., 335; italics added.

97. Hannah Arendt, "What Is Freedom?" in *Between Past and Future*, by Hannah Arendt (New York: Viking Press, 1961), 149; italics in original.

98. Ibid., 148. Arendt's anti-Marxism is part of this argument. For Arendt, true liberation is not to do with attaining the material necessities of life, which are the mere preconditions to real freedom: "In order to be free, man must have liberated himself from the necessities of life."

99. Ibid., 151.

100. Ibid., 169.

101. Pramoedya, quoted in GoGwilt, "Pramoedya's Fiction and History," 160.

102. Yong-hee Hong, *Kim Chi-ha Munhak Yon'gu* [Literary research on Kim Chi-ha] (Seoul: Si wa Sihaksa, 2000), 303–4.

103. Kim Chi-ha's real name is Kim Yŏn-gil.

104. The longer legacy of Kim Chi-ha's radicalism is difficult to evaluate. In 2012, to great surprise, Kim announced his avid support for the now-disgraced and deposed President Park Geun-hye (Pak Kŭn-hye, president from 2013 to 2017), daughter of General Park Chung Hee. As Youngju Ryu has noted in a recent essay, this produced the puzzling image of "an old icon of resistance chumming it up to the daughter of the man he had once had the guts to call fascist" (289). For a rich accounting of Kim's "apostasy," see Ryu, "From Martyrdom to Apostasy: Kim Chiha and the Politics of Death in South Korea's Democratizations," in *Beyond Death: The Politics of Suicide and Martyrdom in Korea*, ed. Charles R. Kim et al. (Seattle: University of Washington Press, 2019).

105. The essay's enduring power is evident in the fact that a new translation was published in 2019, from which I quote. In 2011, inspired by Camus's work, the acclaimed Haitian American writer Edwidge Danticat published her own reflections as a writer under the same title.

106. Shelly Killen, "Profile: Kim Chi-ha," *Index on Censorship* 7, no. 3 (May 1978): 50.

107. Albert Camus, quoted in Killen, "Profile: Kim Chi-ha," 50.

108. Albert Camus, *Create Dangerously: The Power and Responsibility of the Artist*, trans. Sandra Smith (New York: Vintage, 2019), 27.

109. Ibid., 41.

110. Ibid.

111. Killen, "Profile: Kim Chi-ha," 50.

112. Youngju Ryu, *Writers of the Winter Republic: Literature and Resistance in Park Chung Hee's Korea* (Honolulu: University of Hawai'i Press, 2015), 10. Chasil writers included Ko Un, Yŏm Mun-gu, Pak T'ae-sun, Hwang Sŏk-yŏng, and Yi Mun-gu. Ryu, *Winter Republic*, 14. See my discussion of Hwang Sŏk-yŏng in Chapter 4.

113. Ibid., 5.

114. Ibid., 11–12.

115. Fox Butterfield, "U.S. Aides Voice Concern to Seoul on Political Trials," *New York Times*, July 23, 1974.

116. Ryu, *Winter Republic*, 18.

117. Ibid., 28.

118. Ibid., 26.

119. Killen, "Profile: Kim Chi-ha," 50.

120. Kim Chi-ha, "Five Bandits," trans. Brother Anthony of Taizé, *Manoa* 27, no. 2 (2015): 94; *Ojŏk/Five Thieves*, trans. James Han and Kim Won-chung (Seoul: Tapke, 2001), 184. In general, I use Brother Anthony of Taizé's 2015 translation of the poem, "Five Bandits." Quotes from the Korean original refer to James Han and Kim Won-chung's bilingual edition *Ojŏk/Five Thieves*.

121. Ibid.

122. Won Ko, "Kim Chi-ha: Poet of Blood and Fire," *Bulletin of Concerned Asian Scholars* 9, no. 2 (1977): 23.

123. Chan J. Wu, "Introduction: Cosmic Buds Burgeoning in Words: Chiha Kim's Poetics of Full-Emptiness," in *Heart's Agony*, trans. James Han and Kim Won-chung (Fredonia, NY: White Pine Press, 1998), 24.

124. Ryu, *Winter Republic*, 49.

125. Ibid.

126. David R. McCann, "Kim Chi Ha's Messed-Up Poems," *Azalea: Journal of Korean Literature and Culture* 6 (2013): 358.

127. Kim actually used his own versions of the Sino-Korean characters for the bandits "by replacing the existing radical with the dog radical." Ryu, *Winter Republic*, 49. Brother Anthony of Taizé's translation approximates this well with his punning names. Earlier translations vary greatly: The 2001 translation by Han and Kim curiously uses the Greek terms—"plutocrat, aristocrat, bureaucrat"—erasing their specificity to Korea's modern history.

128. Kim Chi-ha, "Five Bandits," 95.

129. Ibid., 95-96; *Ojŏk/Five Thieves*, 192.

130. See Robert Wade for one of the clearest arguments linking the success of postwar South Korean and Taiwanese industrialization to earlier Japanese colonial development. *Governing the Market: Economic Theory and the Role of Government in East Asian Industrialization* (Princeton, NJ: Princeton University Press, 1990), 73–75.

131. Hyung-A Kim, *Korea's Development under Park Chung Hee: Rapid Industrialization, 1961–79* (London: Routledge Curzon, 2004), 82.

132. The high-ranking bureaucrat indicates the source of investment and loan money as he "oscillates between 'No, thank you' / and 'Yes yes, thank you'": revealingly, the words "thank you" are in transliterated English in the Korean text. "Five Bandits," 97; *Ojŏk/Five Thieves*, 200.

133. Kim Chi-ha, "Five Bandits," 96; *Ojŏk/Five Thieves*, 196.

134. Kim Chi-ha, "Five Bandits," 97.

135. Kim Chi-ha, "Five Bandits," 98; *Ojŏk/Five Thieves*, 204–6.

136. David Harvey notes that in South Korea's much celebrated graduation from internal development to outward investment, it (along with Taiwan) "export[ed] not only financial capital but some of the most vicious labor management practices imaginable as subcontractors to multinational capital." David Harvey, *The New Imperialism* (Oxford: Oxford University Press, 2003), 120.

137. Kim Chi-ha, "Five Bandits," 102; *Ojŏk/Five Thieves*, 232.

138. Heonik Kwon, *The Other Cold War* (New York: Columbia University Press, 2010), 43.

139. The broad outlines of this model—detached from the specificity of Japanese colonial development, the devastation of the Korean War and subsequent U.S. occupation—would become disproportionately influential around the developing world. Robert B. Stauffer, in *The Philippines under Marcos: Failure of Transnational Developmentalism* (Sydney: Transnational Corporations Research Project, University of Sydney, 1986), notes the problem with the EOI model being inherently ahistorical, where development experts are "blind to vastly different productive conditions left by defeated or retreating colonial powers" (151), as well as the all-important timing of the moment of entry into the export market.

140. Although Kim's aesthetic bears some similarity to Achille Mbembe's account of the "grotesque art of representation" (115) in *The Postcolony* (Berkeley: University of California Press, 2001), I am arguing that it results from a different historical and material genealogy. See my discussion in the Introduction.

141. Kim Chi-ha, "Five Bandits," 100.

142. Kim Chi-ha, *Ojŏk/Five Thieves*, 240.

143. Ryu, *Winter Republic*, 37.

144. Ibid., 37–38.

145. Tadashi Kimiya, "The Cold War and the Political Economy of the Park Chung Hee Regime," in *Reassessing the Park Chung Hee Era, 1961–1979: Development, Political Thought, Democracy, and Political Influence*, ed. Hyung-A Kim and Clark W. Sorensen (Seattle: University of Washington Press, 2011), 74.

146. Kimiya also writes of the many advantages the ROK gained by being the U.S.'s number one Asian ally in the Vietnam War, and that "one could argue that South Korea secured its economy by paying the cost of dispatching its military troops and fighting in the Vietnam War," 78.

147. Lisa Yoneyama, *Cold War Ruins: Transpacific Critique of American Justice and Japanese War Crimes* (Durham, NC: Duke University Press, 2016), 33.

148. Kwon, *The Other Cold War*, 42.

149. Thomas Borstelmann, quoted in Kwon, *The Other Cold War*, 38.

150. Kwon, *The Other Cold War*, 43.

151. Kim Chi-ha, "Five Bandits," 98; translation altered.

152. Fox Butterfield, "U.S. Aides Voice Concern to Seoul on Political Trials," *New York Times*, July 23, 1974.

153. See Chapter 1 for more background on Lotus and the AAWB.

154. See Rossen Djagalov's *From Internationalism to Postcolonialism* (Montreal: McGill-Queen's University Press, 2020) on the relationship of Second World internationalism and the postcolonial world. He is attentive to the way the Afro-Asian Writers' Association and its publications and prizes—like the Lotus Prize—constitute an alternate genealogy of postcolonialism.

155. "The Poet Kim Chi-ha" (Author profile), in *Lotus: Afro-Asian Writings* 30 (1976): 125.

156. Ibid.

157. Maher Shafik, Review of *Cry of the People and Other Poems*, in *Lotus: Afro-Asian Writings* 30 (1976): 138.

158. Ibid.

159. Ibid.

160. Ibid., 139.

161. Ngũgĩ would be the subject of his own article in the same 1978 issue of *Index on Censorship* which profiles Kim Chi-ha.

162. "K'enya chakga ŭnggugi 'Kim Chi-ha Ojŏk' ŭro put'ŏ k'ŭn yŏnggam" [Kenyan writer Ngũgĩ wa Thiong'o greatly inspired by Kim Chi-ha's "Five Thieves"], n.p. *MK Maeil Kyŏ ngje*, October 25, 2016. https://www.mk.co.kr/news/society/view/ 2016/10/ 744442/.

163. Ngũgĩ wa Thiong'o, "Africa and Asia: The History That Refuses to Be Silenced," in *Writers in Politics: A Re-engagement with Issues of Literature and Society*, by Ngũgĩ wa Thiong'o (Oxford: James Currey, 1997), 121.

164. Ibid., 122.

165. Ibid., 124. In her *Resistance Literature*, Barbara Harlow mentions that Kim Chi-ha's poetry is among the material confiscated by the Kenyan state when Ngũgĩ was detained, so his work is actually banned in two countries.

166. Kim explains the concept of *lumpenproletariat* by referring to Frantz Fanon's *The Wretched of the Earth*. Ryu, *Winter Republic*, 57.

167. Hala Halim has noted a "vestigial ethnocentric tendency" in *Lotus*, which at times "attributes a fixed essence to Afro-Asianness." "Lotus, the Afro-Asian Nexus, and Global South Comparatism," *Comparative Studies of South Asia, Africa and the Middle East* 32, no. 3 (2012): 579.

168. Ngũgĩ, "Africa and Asia," 124.

169. Paik Nak-chung, *The Division System in Crisis: Essays on Contemporary Korea*, trans. Kim Myung-hwan, Sol June-Kyu, Song Seung-cheol, and Ryu Young-joo (Berkeley: University of California Press, 2011), 7.

170. Ibid.

171. McCann, introduction to *The Middle Hour: Selected Poems of Kim Chi Ha* (Stanfordville, NY: Human Rights Publishing Group, 1980), 6.

172. Kim Chi-ha, *Cry of the People and Other Poems* (Hayama: Autumn Press, 1975), 67.

173. Ibid., 71.

174. Ibid., 67; "Pi'ŏ," in *Kyŏlchŏngbon Kim Chi-ha si chŏnjip* (Seoul: Sol, 1993), 55.

175. Kim Chi-ha, *Cry of the People*, 68; "Pi'ŏ," 55.

176. Kim Chi-ha, *Cry of the People*, 68.

177. Ibid., 90.

178. Ibid., 96.

179. Ibid., 94.

180. See Joseph R. Slaughter, "Hijacking Human Rights," for the way human rights were reconceived from including the projects of Third World nationalist self-determination, to a narrower version of supranational protection for individuals. By the 1970s, the discourse of human rights constructed "a new moral order in which the proper response to state oppression was not collective struggles for national liberation but individual dissidence." "Hijacking Human Rights: Neoliberalism, the New Historiography, and the End of the Third World," in *Human Rights Quarterly* 40, no. 4 (2018): 765. I return to this essay in the Epilogue.

181. Kim Chi-ha, *Cry of the People*, 82. Both "Five Bandits" and "The Cry of the People" also mention the tragic collapse of the Wawoo apartment block in Seoul 1970, blamed on rushed and shoddy construction.

182. See my *New Asian City* on the novel use of export-oriented development, which took over from import substitution as the model of Third World development. *The New Asian City: Three-dimensional Fictions of Space and Urban Form* (Minneapolis: University of Minnesota Press, 2011), 87–96.

183. Ryu, *Winter Republic*, 53.

184. Kwon, *The Other Cold War*, 24.

185. Ibid., 40.

186. John A. Lent, "The Philippine Press under Martial Law," *Index on Censorship* 3, no. 1 (1974): 47.

187. E. San Juan Jr., "Marcos and the Media," *Index on Censorship* 7, no. 3 (1978): 41.

188. Ibid., 42. San Juan Jr. notes that the registration of all duplicating machines with the Philippine Constabulary was required. Yet by January 1973, there were seventy-five clandestine newspapers, 44, 47.

189. Myra Mendible, "Literature as Activism: Ninotchka Rosca's Political Aesthetic," *Journal of Postcolonial Writing* 50, no. 3 (2014): 363.

190. Dinitia Smith, "Invite the Rich? PEN is Pondering," *New York Times*, January 24, 1996.

191. John Domini, "Exile and Detention," *New York Times*, January 1, 1984, BR14.

192. Caroline Hau, *Elites and Ilustrados in Philippine Culture* (Manila: Ateneo de Manila University Press, 2017), 60.

193. Oscar V. Campomanes, "Filipinos in the United States and Their Literature of Exile," in *Reading the Literatures of Asian America*, ed. Shirley Geok-lin Lim and Amy Ling (Philadelphia: Temple University Press, 1992), 51. See also Denise Cruz for an in-depth study of transpacific Filipinas from the colonial to early Cold War periods: *Transpacific Femininities: The Making of the Modern Filipina* (Durham, NC: Duke University Press, 2012).

194. Ibid.

195. Viet Thanh Nguyen, *Race and Resistance: Literature and Politics in Asian America.* (Oxford: Oxford University Press, 2002), 141.

196. Mendible, "Literature as Activism," 358.

197. Rocio G. Davis, "Postcolonial Visions and Immigrant Longings: Ninotchka Rosca's Versions of the Philippines," *World Literature Today* 73, no. 1 (1999): 64.

198. Oscar V. Campomanes and other critics have noted Rosca's intertextual references to Linda Ty-Casper's triangulated book *Awaiting Trespass* (New York: Readers International, 1985).

199. Pheng Cheah, "Of Other Worlds to Come," in *Delimiting Modernities: Conceptual Challenges and Regional Responses,* ed. Sven Trakulhun and Ralph Weber (Lanham, MD: Lexington, 2015), 15.

200. Harlow, *Resistance Literature,* 20.

201. Ibid., 22.

202. Ibid., 98.

203. Lazarus, *The Postcolonial Unconscious,* 66.

204. Barbara Harlow, *Barred: Women, Writing, and Political Detention* (Hanover, NH: University Press of New England, 1992), 252.

205. Ibid., 254.

206. Ibid.

207. Ibid., 247.

208. Works like McDonald's study of apartheid-era censorship in *The Literature Police* have also shown just how complex the notions of authorship, resistance, and state power actually are. He notes, for example, that even though PEN South Africa was open to writers of all colors who subscribed to its charter, "In practice, its membership was always overwhelmingly white," 167.

209. Akhil Gupta, David Nugent, and Shreyas Sreenath, "State, Corruption, Postcoloniality: A Conversation with Akhil Gupta on the 20th Anniversary of 'Blurred Boundaries,'" *American Ethnologist* 42, no. 4 (2015): 587.

210. Akhil Gupta, "Blurred Boundaries: The Discourse of Corruption, the Culture of Politics, and the Imagined State," *American Ethnologist* 22, no. 2 (1995): 393.

211. Ibid., 378, 389–91.

212. See Benedict Anderson, *Imagined Communities.*

213. Lazarus, *The Postcolonial Unconscious,* 76.

214. Crystal Parikh, *Writing Human Rights: The Political Imaginaries of Writers of Color* (Minneapolis: University of Minnesota Press, 2017), 23.

215. Dolores de Manuel, "Decolonizing Bodies, Reinscribing Souls in the Fiction of Ninotchka Rosca and Linda Ty-Casper," *MELUS* 29, no. 1 (2004): 108.

216. Mark Twain, quoted in E. San Juan Jr., *Philippine Temptation* (Philadelphia: Temple University Press, 1996), 3.

217. P. N. Abinales and Donna J. Amoroso, *State and Society in the Philippines* (Lanham, MD: Rowman & Littlefield, 2005), 174.

218. Parikh, *Writing Human Rights,* 112.

219. Peter Hitchcock, "Postcolonial Failure and the Politics of Nation," *South Atlantic Quarterly* 106, no. 4 (2007): 741.

220. Ninotchka Rosca, *State of War* (New York: Norton, 1988), 154.

221. Ibid., 156.

222. Ibid.

223. Ibid.

224. Ibid., 197.

225. Abinales and Amoroso note that during the war, the "PKP-led Hukbalahap distinguished itself as an effective guerilla army [against the Japanese], much like its Communist counterparts in Vietnam and Cuba." *State and Society in the Philippines*, 174.

226. Rosca, *State of War*, 267.

227. Ibid., 86.

228. Ibid., 97–98.

229. Timothy Mitchell, "The Limits of the State: Beyond Statist Approaches and Their Critics," *American Political Science Review* 85, no. 1 (1991): 93.

230. Rosario Torres-Yu gives a good account of the kind of resistance literature being produced in Filipino and other native languages, such as the novels *Gapo* by Lualhati Bautista and *The Brown Earth Is Gold* by Dominador Mirasol.

231. Neferti Xina M. Tadiar, *Things Fall Away: Philippine Historical Experience and the Makings of Globalization* (Durham, NC: Duke University Press, 2009), 186. Tadiar is here writing on Jose Lacaba, another writer imprisoned by the Marcos regime for subversive journalism.

232. Rosca, *State of War*, 139.

233. Ibid., 140.

234. Ibid.

235. Ibid., 141. This scene resonates strongly with the bureaucratic battle staged in Singaporean dissident playwright Kuo Pau Kun's *The Coffin Is Too Big for the Hole* (1984).

236. On the neutrality of development discourse, see James Ferguson's *The Anti-Politics Machine: Development, Depoliticization and Bureaucratic Power in Lesotho* (Cambridge: Cambridge University Press, 1990). Gupta in "Blurred," 383, also observes that "the implementation of development programs . . . forms a key arena where representations of the state are constituted and where its legitimacy is contested."

237. Marcos, quoted in Stauffer, *The Philippines*, 141.

238. In his extensive work on the Philippine political economy, Stauffer describes the Marcos regime's economic policy as a "transnational accumulation strategy" with a growth model based on huge flows of foreign private investment (from the United States and Japan), massive IMF and USAID loans, and the attempt at export-oriented industrialization in explicit imitation of South Korea and Taiwan, all which necessitated "political stability" enforced by militarized civic action. The result of such development policy was not just the "grotesque maldistribution

of income and wealth, [and . . .] malnutrition" but "the externalization of all costs of the development projects onto the poor and powerless, whether they be tribal peoples living in a region where dams are to be built or farmers standing in the way of agribusiness expansion" (*The Philippines*,146).

239. Tadiar, *Things Fall Away*, 194–95.

240. Rosca, *State of War*, 107–8. Although beyond the scope and intent of this book to discuss fully, there are several important reasons why development projects under Marcos resulted less in Asian Tiger levels of industrial or economic improvement and more in the "centralization of Marcos' patronage networks," as Paul D. Hutchcroft explains in "Reflections on a Reversed Image: South Korea under Park Chung Hee and the Philippines under Marcos," in *The Park Chung Hee Era: The Transformation of South Korea*, ed. Byung-Kook Kim and Ezra F. Vogel (Cambridge, MA: Harvard University Press, 2011), 555. These include the (as mentioned) historically weak and decentralized bureaucracy; the lack of a clear external enemy that South Korea and Taiwan both had, allowing a greater emphasis on development as national security; the Philippines' later arrival into the highly competitive field of export-oriented industrialization; and, crucially, the fact that its "postwar rehabilitation assistance" was provided by the United States—both former colonizer *and* rising superpower, as Hutchcroft further explains, 547, who at every turn sought to maintain the flow of profitable American-owned business interests.

241. Rosca, *State of War*, 339.

242. Ibid., 366. The festival bombing echoes the 1971 Plaza Miranda bomb that struck a Liberal Party campaign event in Quiapo, Manila. Hau, *Elites and Ilustrados*, 64.

243. Rosca, *State of War*, 366–68.

244. Ibid., 382.

245. Ibid.

246. Tadiar, *Things Fall Away*, 209.

247. Ninotchka Rosca, "'Total War' in the Philippines," *Nation*, June 19, 1989, 839. Recall Walter Benjamin's well-known passage: "The tradition of the oppressed teaches us that the 'state of emergency' in which we live is not the exception but the rule. We must attain to a conception of history that is in keeping with this insight. . . . One reason that Fascism has a chance is that in the name of progress its opponents treat it as historical norm." Walter Benjamin, *Illuminations*, trans. Harry Zohn (New York: Schocken Books, 1968), 257. Jeremy Tiang uses this quote as his epigraph to his novel, *State of Emergency* (Singapore: Epigram, 2017), discussed in the next chapter.

248. Chua Beng Huat, in "Disrupting Hegemonic Liberalism in East Asia," *boundary* 2 37, no. 2 (2010): 208, also reminds us of the need to disentangle forms of liberal democracy from capitalist accumulation. The Singaporean state has amply evidenced its ability to forge a "productive capitalist economy that combines private and state enterprises with a single-party state." He argues that this enables space for

"the privileging of the social" in a neoliberal context that otherwise has eliminated most claims to social welfare (211).

249. John Marx, *Geopolitics and the Anglophone Novel, 1890–2011* (Cambridge: Cambridge University Press, 2012), 49.

250. Bhakti Shringarpure, *Cold War Assemblages: Decolonization to Digital* (New York: Routledge, 2019), 85.

3. Separate Futures: Other Times of Southeast Asian Decolonization

1. Jeremy Tiang, "Going Inside," interview by Jini Kim Watson, *Singapore Unbound*, July 22, 2019, singaporeunbound.org/blog.

2. Ibid.

3. In terms of the book's regional focus, the most obvious decolonizing division is surely that of the Korean peninsula, where the North and South are still technically at war in one of the earliest and last remaining Cold War confrontations. See Paik Nak-chung's *The Division System in Crisis* (Berkeley: University of California Press, 2011); and Bruce Cumings's *The Origins of the Korean War* (Ithaca, NY: Cornell University Press, 2004). I have written elsewhere of Hwang Sŏk-yŏng's powerful literary rendering of division, war, and reconciliation in his novel *The Guest* (*Sonnim*). See "A Not-yet-postcolonial Peninsula: Rewriting Spaces of Violence, Division, and Diaspora," *Cambridge Journal of Postcolonial Literary Inquiry* 1, no. 1 (2014): 69–87.

4. Gary Wilder, *Freedom Time: Negritude, Decolonization, and the Future of the World* (Durham, NC: Duke University Press, 2015), 41.

5. Hannah Arendt, quoted in Wilder, *Freedom Time*, 76.

6. Bhakti Shringarpure, *Cold War Assemblages: Decolonization to Digital* (New York: Routledge, 2019), 63–64.

7. Christopher J. Lee, "Between a Moment and an Era: The Origins and Afterlives of Bandung," in *Making a World after Empire: The Bandung Moment and Its Political Afterlives*, ed. Christopher J. Lee (Athens, OH: Center for International Studies, Ohio University, 2010), 19.

8. In Singaporean Anglophone literature, a few important predecessors include Goh Poh Seng's class tale of disillusionment during the early PAP years, *If We Dream Too Long*; Floyd Fernando's *Scorpion Orchid* on racial tensions after independence; and Robert Yeo's explicitly political triptych of plays, the *Singapore Trilogy*. For more details of the Anglophone literary tradition in Singapore see *Writing Singapore: An Historical Anthology of Singapore Literature* (Singapore: NUS Press, 2009), edited by Shirley Geok-lin Lim, Philip Holden, and Angelia Poon. Mention must also be made of the pioneering Kuo Pau Kun whose early Chinese-language plays on class and social issues aroused government suspicions; he was detained in 1976 under the Internal Security Act.

9. Ann Laura Stoler, *Duress: Imperial Durabilities in Our Times* (Durham, NC: Duke University Press, 2016), 177.

10. Mohamed Latiff Mohamed, *Confrontation: A Novel*, trans. Shafiq Selamat (Singapore: Epigram, 2013), 102.

11. Pheng Cheah, *Spectral Nationality: Passages of Freedom from Kant to Postcolonial Literatures of Liberation* (New York: Columbia University Press, 2003), 216–17.

12. Timothy Brennan, "The National Longing for Form," in *Nation and Narration*, ed. Homi K. Bhabha (London: Routledge, 1990), 58; italics added.

13. Odd Arne Westad, *The Global Cold War: Third World Interventions and the Making of Our Times* (Cambridge: Cambridge University Press, 2007), 75.

14. Philip Holden, "Refusing the Cultural Turn: Amir Muhammad's Politics of Surfaces," in *Locating Life Stories*, ed. Maureen Perkins (Honolulu: University of Hawai'i Press, 2012), 19.

15. Chua Beng Huat, "Disrupting Hegemonic Liberalism in East Asia," *boundary 2* 37, no. 2 (2010): 101–2.

16. Christopher Bayly and Tim Harper, *Forgotten Wars: Freedom and Revolution in Southeast Asia* (Cambridge, MA: Belknap Press of Harvard University Press, 2010), 420–22.

17. Angelia Poon Mui Cheng, "Being in the World: Literary Practice and Pedagogy in Global Times," *Ariel: A Review of International English Literature* 46, no. 1–2 (2015): 267.

18. Antonio Gramsci, *Selections from the Prison Notebooks*, ed. and trans. Quintin Hoare and Geoffrey Nowell Smith (New York: International, 1971), 261.

19. Ibid., 262. Gramsci goes on to point out, however, that these two expressions need not be opposed "and in fact could be brought into conjunction."

20. Siti Nuraishah Ahmad, Review of *Confrontation*, by Mohamed Latiff Mohamed, trans. Shafiq Selamat, *Asiatic* 8, no. 1 (2014): 269.

21. Ibid., 20.

22. Mohamed, *Confrontation*, 127.

23. Ibid., 137.

24. Ibid., 102. Bayly and Harper also discuss the importance of a number of Malay communists including Musa Ahmad, who were influenced by Partai Kommunis Indonesia (PKI) leaders Alimin and Tan Malaka. In 1948, Musa Ahmad denounced the return of the British capitalists in terms of democracy, human rights, and anti-capitalism: "We are living in a democratic era in a world of revolution. . . . We are fighting to retain our human rights. . . . Our greatest enemies are the capitalists." Quoted in *Forgotten Wars*, 419.

25. Bayly and Harper describe the multiple "nations of intent" during the Malayan Emergency, 498. However, Adi's sole focus on Malay political parties that appeal to ethno-nationalism suggests the limits of these visions for multi-ethnic Singapore. Note that the novel refers to parties by their logos but withholds their names. The "flame" party refers to the PAP, while the "Buffalo's head" party is the pro-Sukarno Parti Rakyat (people's party). The other logos are less identifiable. My thanks to Philip Holden for this observation.

26. Franco Moretti, *The Way of the World: The Bildungsroman in European Culture*, trans. Albert Spragia (London: Verso, 1987), 15.

27. Ibid., 4.

28. See Joseph Slaughter's important work on the postcolonial *Bildungsroman* in his *Human Rights, Inc.: The World Novel, Narrative Form, and International Law* (New York: Fordham University Press, 2007).

29. Moretti, *Way of the World*, 15.

30. See Fredric Jameson, "Third-World Literature in the Era of Multinational Capitalism," *Social Text*, no. 15 (Autumn 1986).

31. Catherine Diamond, "Maturation and Political Upheaval in Lloyd Fernando's 'Scorpion Orchid' and Robert Yeo's 'The Singapore Trilogy,'" *Comparative Drama* 36, no. 1/2 (2002): 126.

32. Moretti, *Way of the World*, 52.

33. Ibid., 53.

34. Ibid.

35. For further discussion on the boundaries between state and non-state, see Chapter 2's discussion of Ninotchka Rosca's *State of War* (New York: Norton, 1988).

36. We can recall that for Gramsci, civil society must be *reconciled* to the economic structure of the (bourgeois) state. Gramsci, *Selections*, 208.

37. Mohamed, *Confrontation*, 121.

38. Chua Beng Huat, *Liberalism Disavowed: Communitarianism and State Capitalism in Singapore* (Ithaca, NY: Cornell University Press, 2017), 31.

39. Mohamed, *Confrontation*, 127.

40. Chua, *Liberalism Disavowed*, 47.

41. Chua Beng Huat's book *Liberalism Disavowed* offers a fascinating qualifier to one-dimensional readings of Singapore's capitalist development. Chua argues that while the PAP has successfully inserted itself into circuits of global capitalism, it maintains an underlying commitment to its earliest socialist principles in the rejection of private property rights and development of state—rather than "free"—market capitalism.

42. Stoler, *Duress*, 177.

43. Ibid., 176.

44. Heonik Kwon, *The Other Cold War* (New York: Columbia University Press, 2010), 4.

45. Moretti, *Way of the World*, 55.

46. Fiona Lee, "Epistemological Checkpoint," *Postcolonial Text* 9, no. 1 (2014): 4.

47. For more details on the postwar economic transformations, see Bayly and Harper, *Forgotten Wars*, 412–27.

48. Ibid., 498.

49. Such an episteme is satirically explored in Amir Muhammad's musical-documentary film *The Last Communist* (Lelaki komunis terakhir) (Red Films), 2006. See also Philip Holden's essay on Amir Muhammad's film, "Refusing the Cultural Turn: Amir Muhammad's Politics of Surfaces."

50. Theophilus Kwek, "'State of Emergency' by Jeremy Tiang," *Asian Review of Books*, August 22, 2017, n.p.

51. As part of a peace settlement in the late 1980s, the Thai government gave land to the MCP members, who had been living in the jungle until this point.

52. Jeremy Tiang, *State of Emergency* (Singapore: Epigram, 2017), 55.

53. Ibid.

54. Ibid., 65.

55. Ibid., 67.

56. Kwek notes in his review article that Lay Kuan's character is based on MP Loh Miaw Gong, who was elected to Singapore's Legislative Assembly in 1963, but promptly detained.

57. Tiang, *State of Emergency*, 85.

58. Ibid., 85-86.

59. Ibid., 173.

60. A more recent, complex, representation of the revolutionary fervor of the era and its disillusionments is provided in the Chinese-language *Unrest* (2002) by Yeng Pway Ngon. See *Unrest*, trans. Jeremy Tiang (Singapore: Math Paper Press, 2012).

61 Tiang, *State of Emergency*, 95.

62. Ibid., 96.

63. Yoon Wah Wong, *The New Village*, trans. Ho Lian Geok and Ng Yi-Sheng (Singapore: Ethos, 2012), 105.

64. Tiang, *State of Emergency*, 115.

65. Bayly and Harper, *Forgotten Wars*, 456. Mention must also be made of the thousands of resettled Orang Asli, or indigenous forest dwellers, who were assumed to have tight links to the communists. Of some 25,000 who were forcibly resettled into unfamiliar, barbed-wire towns, some 5,000–7,000 perished. See *Forgotten Wars*, 494.

66. Lee, "Epistemological Checkpoint," 6.

67. In terms of military innovations, the Malayan Emergency would be important for the development of "low intensity" warfare. The term was made famous by General Frank Kitson's 1970 publication *Low Intensity Operations: Subversion, Insurgency, and Peacekeeping* (London: Faber and Faber, 1971), which drew on his experience in a number of counterinsurgency efforts by the late British Empire in Malaya, Kenya, Aden, Cyprus, and Northern Ireland. My thanks to Patrick Deer for introducing his work to me.

68. Karl Marx, *Capital: A Critique of Political Economy*, trans. Ben Fowkes, vol. 1 (London: Penguin, 1990), 874, italics added.

69. Ibid.

70. Hilmar Farid, "Indonesia's Original Sin: Mass Killings and Capitalist Expansion 1965–66," in *The Inter-Asia Cultural Studies Reader*, ed. Kuan-hsing Chen and Chua Beng Huat (London: Routledge, 2007), 215.

71. Ibid.

72. Bayly and Harper, *Forgotten Wars*, 525.

73. Walter Benjamin, quoted in epigraph to *State of Emergency*.

74. Tiang, *State of Emergency*, 111.

75. Ibid.

76. Ibid., 120.

77. Ibid., 126.

78. Ibid., 135.

79. Ibid., 131.

80. Reinhart Koselleck, *Futures Past: On the Semantics of Historical Time* (New York: Columbia University Press, 2004), 12.

81. Ibid., 16; italics added.

82. Shringarpure, *Cold War Assemblages*, 63.

83. Tiang, *State of Emergency*, 190.

84. Ibid., 206.

85. Colonial-era laws outlawing homosexuality are still upheld in Singapore today, reminding us of the way anti-communist "containment" has often meant restrictions on sexuality and gender roles.

86. Ibid., 222.

87. Ibid., 241.

88. Ibid., 242.

89. Tiang, "Going Inside," n.p.

90. Gramsci, *Selections*, 259.

91. Philip Holden, "'Is It Manipulative? Sure. But That's How You Tell Stories': The Graphic Novel, Metahistory, and the Artist in *The Art of Charlie Chan Hock Chye*," *Journal of Postcolonial Writing* 52, no. 4 (2016): 517.

92. Sonny Liew, *The Art of Charlie Chan Hock Chye* (New York: Pantheon, 2016), 264.

93. Holden, "Is It Manipulative?," 517.

94. Ibid.

95. Liew, *Charlie Chan*, 125.

96. Ibid., 190.

97. Ibid., 185.

98. See the Introduction's discussion on Lee Kuan Yew and the "Singapore Story."

99. Liew, *Charlie Chan*, 227.

100. Ibid., 247.

101. The fate of Sonny Liew's own novel echoes the tensions of censorship and the state that still plague Singapore: An $8,000 government arts grant was revoked a few days before the book's publication when the content of his novel was discovered.

102. Liew, *Charlie Chan*, 216.

103. "Days of August" is set in 1996, the year that Lim died in exile. My thanks to Philip Holden for pointing out this observation.

104. Liew, *Charlie Chan*, 280.

105. Ibid., 275.

106. Ann Cvetkovich, "Drawing the Archive in Alison Bechdel's Fun Home," *Women's Studies Quarterly* 36, nos. 1–2 (2008): 112.

107. Ibid., 114.

108. Liew, *Charlie Chan*, 282.

109. Ibid., 284.

110. Ibid., 286.

111. Bayly and Harper, *Forgotten Wars*, 551.

112. Wilder, *Freedom Time*, 241.

4. The Wrong Side of History: Anachronism and Authoritarianism

1. See Hwang Sŏk-yŏng, *The Shadow of Arms* [*Mugi ŭi kŭnŭl*], trans. Chun Kyung-ja (New York: Seven Stories Press, 2014).

2. See "Overview: The Making of a Miracle," World Bank, *The East Asian Miracle: Economic Growth and Public Policy* (New York: Oxford University Press, 1993), 1–26. Note that the report uses "East Asia" to include Indonesia, Malaysia, Singapore, and Thailand.

3. Andre Gunder Frank, *Crisis: In the Third World* (New York: Homes and Meier, 1981), 100.

4. Ibid.

5. Caroline Hau, *Elites and Ilustrados in Philippine Culture* (Manila: Ateneo de Manila University Press, 2017), 204.

6. I have written elsewhere of the way that such developmental states were the result of a particular Cold War configuration, and decolonizing desires were recruited toward the "urgent national task [of] accelerated economic development." Jini Kim Watson, "Aspirational City: Desiring Singapore and the Films of Tan Pin Pin," *Interventions: International Journal of Postcolonial Studies* 18, no. 4 (2016): 174.

7. Paik Nak-chung, "How to Think about the Park Chung Hee Era," in *Reassessing the Park Chung Era, 1961–79: Development, Political Thought, Democracy, and Cultural Influence*, ed. Kim Hyung-A and Clark W. Sorensen (Seattle: University of Washington Press, 2011), 87–88; emphasis added.

8. Ibid., 89.

9. Ibid., 91. The logic of nostalgia for South Korea's authoritarianism can be clearly seen, for example, in the bootstrap narrative of the wildly popular film *Ode to My Father* [*Kukje sijang*] (dir. Yoon Je-kyoon, 2014), which I discuss in the book's Epilogue.

10. Hau, *Elites and Ilustrados*, 171.

11. I am, of course, paraphrasing Partha Chatterjee's argument: "Conservatory of the passive revolution, the national state now proceeds to find for 'the nation' a place in the global order of capital, while striving to keep the contradictions between capital and the people in perpetual suspension." Partha Chatterjee, *Nationalist Thought in the Colonial World: A Derivative Discourse?* (London: Zed Books, 1986), 168.

12. Edward Said, *Reflections on Exile and Other Essays* (Cambridge, MA: Harvard University Press, 2000), 173.

13. Ibid., 176.

14. Such dialectical tensions resonate with Sophia McClennen's observations that "exile is personal/individual and political/collective; . . . exiles write about the past and also about the future." Sophia McClennen, *The Dialectics of Exile: Nation, Time, and Language in Hispanic Literatures* (West Lafayette, IN.: Purdue University Press, 2004), 39.

15. Said, *Reflections on Exile*, 176; emphasis added.

16. McClennen, *Dialectics of Exile*, 26; emphasis added.

17. The oft-cited vulnerability of Singapore is neatly evoked in the political language of the "little red dot"—the tiny spot on the world map that must ever be wary of being swallowed up by larger neighbors. See Chua Beng Huat's discussion of state survivalism in *Liberalism Disavowed* (Ithaca, NY: Cornell University Press, 2017), 32–35.

18. Sharad Chari and Katherine Verdery, "Thinking between the Posts: Postcolonialism, Postsocialism, and Ethnography after the Cold War," *Comparative Studies in Society and History* 51, no. 1 (2009): 12.

19. Ibid., 19; italics added.

20. Ibid.

21. Ibid., 23.

22. Paik, "Park Chung Hee Era," 88.

23. As we see in other chapters, fierce anti-communism in both Singapore and South Korea was integral to the repression of labor utilized in their emerging manufacturing industries, in forming alliances with the U.S. military and capital interests, as well as linking the pursuit of national development and security. Chari and Verdery also note the role of actually existing socialisms as a competing model for social production and consumption. Hence, South Korea's comprehensive land distribution occurred not despite, but in competition with, the North's socialist planned economy, and Singapore's far-reaching social housing provision was also a response to the socialist development from which the state rhetorically distanced itself. See also Chua Beng Huat's *Liberalism Disavowed*, 74–97.

24. "IC" refers to "Identification Card."

25. Tan Pin Pin, personal correspondence, July 8, 2015.

26. Chan's poem draws on lyrics from a popular anti-colonial song "I Love My Malaya"—included in Sonny Liew's *The Art of Charlie Chan Hock Chye* —in which the Japanese are depicted as dogs and the British as monkeys.

27. My sincere thanks to Laurence Coderre for this translation.

28. Syed Muhd Khairudin Aljunied, "Political Memoirs as Contrapuntal Narratives," *Interventions: International Journal of Postcolonial Studies* 18, no. 4 (2016): 516.

29. Said, *Reflections on Exile*, 185.

30. Ibid..

31. Gary Wilder, *Freedom Time: Negritude, Decolonization, and the Future of the World* (Durham, NC: Duke University Press, 2015), 12.

32. As I point out above, both countries have been led by the children of former longtime authoritarian leaders, that is, Lee Kuan Yew's son Lee Hsien Loong and Park Chung Hee's daughter Park Geun-hye, deposed in March 2017, raising questions of both political and biological genealogies.

33. Gi-wook Shin, introduction to *Contentious Kwangju: The May 18 Uprising in Korea's Past and Present*, ed. Gi-wook Shin and Kyun Moon Hwang (Lanham, MD: Rowman and Littlefield, 2003), xvii.

34. Jang Jip Choi, "Political Cleavages in South Korea," in *State and Society in Contemporary Korea*, ed. Hagen Koo (Ithaca, NY: Cornell University Press, 1993), 35.

35. Notable fictional representations of 5.18 that precede Hwang's novel include Lee Chang-dong's powerful 1999 film *Peppermint Candy* (*Pakha sat'ang*), Han Kang's 2014 novel *Human Acts* (*Sŏnŏyni onda* [Here comes the boy]), discussed in the following chapter, and Jang Hoon's 2017 film *A Taxi Driver* (*T'aeksi unjŏnsa*). See also the collections of fiction and poetry published by the May Culture Series, under editorial direction by the prominent poet-activist Ko ŭn: *Sosŏl* (Kwangju: 5.18 Kinyŏm chedan, 2012) and *Si* (Kwangju: 5.18 Kinyŏm chedan, 2012).

36. For example, Paul Y. Chang represents the "dark ages" of Korean democracy as a single period stretching from Syngman Rhee's rule (1948–1960) until 1987. Paul Chang, *Protest Dialectics: State Repression and South Korea's Democracy Movement, 1970–1979* (Stanford, CA: Stanford University Press, 2015), 2.

37. The "drawn out caesura of the [1953] Armistice" only paused the Korean War, not ended it. Susie Jie Young Kim argues that this has effected "a landscape of temporal disorder that makes the pastness of the present more intrinsic." "Korea beyond and within the Armistice: Division and the Multiplicities of Time in Postwar Literature and Cinema," *Journal of Korean Studies* 18, no. 2 (2013): 290.

38. In 2011, the "May 18th Democratic Uprising against Military Regime in Gwangju" was included in UNESCO's Memory of the World Register, under the category "Human Rights Documentary Heritage." See Chapter 5 for more discussion on the post-dictatorship transition in South Korea (and Indonesia).

39. Another complexity missed by the broader Asian liberalization narrative is the *increasing* anti-Americanism that occurred after 5.18, which focused on the complicit role of the U.S. armed forces in the civilian massacre, as the occupying military force on the peninsula. In that sense, the United States, as Gi-wook Shin has argued, was not the model of democracy but rightly perceived as restraining it. See Shin, introduction to *Contentious Kwangju*, xxiv.

40. Critics have debated the role of Kalmae as either a place of utopian promise or merely an apolitical place of refuge and exile. See Kyŏngmi Kwŏn, "Chisikin chuch'e ŭi sangjon hyŏnsil insik kwa chŏhang ŭi sŏsa" [The recognition of survival reality of the intellectual subject and the narrative of resistance]. *Han'guk munye ch'angjak* [Korean literary creative writing] 1, no. 27 (2013): 208–11.

NOTES TO PAGES 148–154

41. That neoliberalization coincided exactly with the post-dictatorship transition will be discussed in the next chapter. On the 1997 bailout and its repercussions in South Korean society, see Jesook Song, *South Koreans in the Debt Crisis: The Creation of a Neoliberal Welfare Society* (Durham, NC: Duke University Press, 2009).

42. Jinho Kang, "Sosŏl kyoyukgwa t'aja ŭi jip'yŏng" [Novel education and the horizon of the other], *Munhak kyoyukhak* [Literary education] 13 (2004): 39.

43. Sŏk-yŏng Hwang, *The Old Garden*, trans. Jay Oh (New York: Seven Stories Press, 2009), 429–41. Two examples come to mind: first, the eyewitness accounts of the 5.18 violence that enter the novel via a political pamphlet Yoon Hee finds herself typing up, and, second, a blow-by-blow account of a valiant factory workers' strike that is incorporated in the form of long letters from her activist friend Mi Kyung.

44. Ibid., 184.

45. Ibid., 184; *Oraedoen Chŏngwŏn* (P'aju: Changbi, 2000), 1:215. I use the first page numbers to refer to Jay Oh's English translation of the text; the second refers to the Korean original, which was published in two volumes. The volume number precedes the colon, and the page number follows the colon.

46. Ibid. Recall, of course, that any engagement with the communist North was (and still is) ferociously proscribed by the South Korean state. The literal severing of geographical homeland—a spatial by-product of decolonization that effectively turned South Korea from peninsula to island—was a central object of critiques in the important Minjung [People's or Popular] Movement of the 1970s and 1980s. On the Minjung movement, see Namhee Lee, *The Making of Minjung: Democracy and the Politics of Representation in South Korea* (Ithaca, NY: Cornell University Press, 2007).

47. Hwang, *Old Garden*, 129.

48. For an overview of the period, see Choi, "Political Cleavages."

49. Chang, *Protest Dialectics*, 41.

50. Hwang, *Old Garden*, 79.

51. Ibid., 79; *Oraedoen Chŏngwŏn*, 1:92.

52. Hwang, *Old Garden*, 99.

53. Ibid., 218; *Oraedoen Chŏngwŏn*, 1:254–55.

54. Paik Nak-chung, "Coloniality in Korea and a South Korean Project for Overcoming Modernity," *Interventions: International Journal of Postcolonial Studies* 2, no. 1 (2000): 76–78.

55. Philip Holden, "Postcolonial Desire: Placing Singapore," *Postcolonial Studies* 11, no. 3 (2008): 353. Holden is writing of the temptation to identify with protagonists in leftist counter-histories in Singapore and Malaysia.

56. Sandro Mezzadra and Federico Rahola, "The Postcolonial Condition: A Few Notes on the Quality of Historical Time in the Global Present," *Postcolonial Text* 2, no. 1 (2006): n.p.; emphasis added.

57. Hwang, *Old Garden*, 15.

5. Killing Communists, Transitional Justice, and the Making of the Post–Cold War

1. Joshua Oppenheimer, "Membunuh, Bagi Anwar, Adalah Sebuah Akting" ["Killing, for Anwar, is an act"], trans. Anindya Khairunnisa, *Tempo*, October 1–7, 2012, http://majah.tempo.co/read/140715/joshua-oppenheimermembunuh-bagi -anwar-adalah-sebuah-akting.

2. Ibid.

3. See in particular Zahid R. Chaudhary, "This Time with Feeling: Impunity and the Play of Fantasy in *The Act of Killing*," *boundary 2* 45, no. 4 (2018): 65–101, and Alexandra Schultheis Moore, *Vulnerability and Security in Human Rights Literature and Visual Culture* (New York: Routledge, 2016).

4. Chaudhary, "This Time with Feeling," 95.

5. Ibid., 97.

6. Thatcher delivered the speech at the National Cathedral on June 11, 2004. The full text is available on the Margaret Thatcher Foundation website at www .margaretthatcher.org/document/110360.

7. Hwang Su-Kyoung, *Korea's Grievous War* (Philadelphia: University of Pennsylvania Press, 2016), 2.

8. See Daniel Y. Kim on the textual and thematic links between *The Vegetarian* and *Human Acts*. "Translations and Ghostings of History: The Novels of Han Kang," *New Literary History* 51, no. 2 (2020): 375–99.

9. See the preceding chapter's discussion on the 5.18 Uprising for a range of cultural representations. For filmic representations of September 30, see Barbara Hatley's essay, "Recalling and Representing Cold War Conflict and Its Aftermath in Contemporary Indonesia Film and Theater," in Tony Day and Maya H. T. Liem's *Cultures at War* (Ithaca, NY: Cornell University Press, 2010). Hatley's essay attends to documentary and fictional films with a focus on the "young, less-experienced filmmakers" for whom the "events of 1965 represent a remote, myth-shrouded subject" (267).

10. Julie Stone Peters describes "culture of testimony" as characterized by the "idealization of victimhood, of 'narrative' or 'story' and its healing powers and— above all—of the sufferer's individuated voice." "'Literature,' the 'Rights of Man,' and Narratives of Atrocity: Historical Backgrounds to the Culture of Testimony," in *Theoretical Perspectives on Human Rights and Literature*, ed. Elizabeth Swanson Goldberg and Alexandra Schultheis Moore (Hoboken, NJ: Taylor and Francis, 2011), 34.

11. Sophia McClennen and Alexandra Moore have written of a typical dual impulse when it comes to approaching human rights questions through literature. The debate, they write, is often "over human rights literature as truth-telling, as a representation of truth-telling, or as something imaginary that bears only a distant relation to juridical evidence." In short, "Is the text meant to be true? Or is it meant to be meaningful?" Introduction to *Routledge Companion to Human Rights and Literature*, ed. Sophie A. McClennen and Alexandra Schultheis Moore (Abingdon: Routledge, 2016), 14.

12. Moore, *Vulnerability and Security*, 202.

13. Han In Sup, "Kwangju and Beyond: Coping with Past State Atrocities in South Korea," *Human Rights Quarterly* 27, no. 3 (2005): 1026.

14. Priscilla B. Hayner, *Unspeakable Truths: Transitional Justice and the Challenge of Truth Commissions*, 2nd ed. (New York: Routledge, 2011), 4.

15. Ibid., 11.

16. Ibid., 3–4.

17. Lisa Yoneyama, *Cold War Ruins: Transpacific Critique of American Justice and Japanese War Crimes* (Durham, NC: Duke University Press, 2016), 13.

18. David Scott, *Omens of Adversity: Tragedy, Time, Memory, Justice* (Durham, NC: Duke University Press, 2014), 27.

19. Greg Grandin and Thomas Miller Klubock, "Editor's Introduction," *Radical History Review* 97 (2007): 1.

20. Grant Farred, "Many Are Guilty, Few Are Indicted," review of *In My Country*, directed by John Boorman, Sony Pictures Classics, 2004, *Radical History Review* 97 (2007): 155. If Hayner presupposes a more or less linear movement toward a future that seals repression and violence in the past, Farred—in his writing on the South African Truth and Reconciliation Commission of 1996–2001—has noted the way that such commissions are always governed by a more convoluted "logic of political temporality": "These commissions want to determine the historical 'truth' of the time before: the now represents its own epistemology, the time not possible before, the time that now makes possible a supposedly truthful rendering of the past, a rehabilitation of the past into a new political use."

21. Scott, *Omens of Adversity*, 131.

22. Crystal Parikh, introduction to *The Cambridge Companion to Human Rights and Literature*, ed. Crystal Parikh (Cambridge: Cambridge University Press, 2019), 1.

23. Ibid., 6.

24. Ariel Heryanto, "Great and Misplaced Expectations," *Critical Asian Studies* 46, no. 1 (2014): 162.

25. Moore, *Vulnerability and Security*, 196.

26. Geoffrey B. Robinson, *The Killing Season: The History of the Indonesian Massacres, 1965–66* (Princeton, NJ: Princeton University Press, 2018), 87.

27. Robinson writes that during the last years of Sukarno's rule, the United States chose to "build ties with the Indonesia army" to counter the communist threat. "Portraying the army as the only reliable anticommunist force in the country, US policy makers sought to encourage it to play a more direct role in politics, to see itself as a viable alternative to the country's civilian leadership, and more specifically, to act forcefully together with civilian allies to remove or replace Sukarno and the PKI" (Robinson, *The Killing Season*, 96; see also 95–101).

28. This is not to say that all information pertaining to 1965 has been repressed; Komnas HAM has made its own investigations and the government of Palu has made an apology to victims. A victims' advocacy and support group, Yayasan Penelitian Korban Pembunuham 1965–66, is also active. See *YPKP 65*, http://ypkp1965.org/.

29. Linda S. Lewis, *Laying Claim to the Memory of May* (Honolulu: University of Hawai'i Press, 2002), 87.

30. Han Kang, *Human Acts*, trans. Deborah Smith (London: Portobello, 2016), 214; *Sonyŏni onda* (Seoul: Changbi, 2014), 206. In a *New York Times* op-ed, "While the U.S. Talks of War, South Korea Shudders" (a moment when President Trump's sabre-rattling with North Korea was at its worst), Han wrote that *Human Acts* sought to address "the universal humanity that is revealed in the history of this world. I wanted to ask what it is that makes human beings harm others so brutally, and how we ought to understand those who never lose hold of their humanity in the face of violence." *New York Times*, October 8, 2017.

31. It may be surprising that the estimated death toll from Indonesia's anti-Communist purge rivals the toll from the 1975–79 Khmer Rouge regime, usually estimated at between 1.4 million and 2.2 million, and which remains one of the most notorious killing campaigns in the communist world.

32. I borrow the ambiguous use of the word "killing" from Rajeswari Sunder Rajan in her section on "Killing Women" in *The Scandal of the State: Woman, Law, and Citizenship in Postcolonial India* (Durham, NC: Duke University Press, 2003).

33. In Geoffrey B. Robinson's exhaustive history of the massacre, he writes, "The documentary and circumstantial evidence that has so far been unearthed makes it clear that the United States and its allies share both direct and indirect responsibility for the events of October 1, 1965 and for the violence that followed." *Killing Season*, 76.

34. Paul Gready, "Novel Truths: Literature and Truth Commissions," *Comparative Literature Studies* 46, no. 1 (2009): 164.

35. Ibid., 162.

36. Mark Sanders, *Ambiguities of Witnessing: Law and Literature in the Time of a Truth Commission* (Stanford, CA: Stanford University Press, 2007), 9.

37. Ibid., 4–5. More specifically, he shows how the "unfolding of the commission determined and continues to determine time, but is open as well to other temporalities: past and to come" (188).

38. Greg Grandin, *The Last Colonial Massacre: Latin America in the Cold War* (Chicago: University of Chicago Press, 2004), 171.

39. Joshua Oppenheimer, dir., *The Act of Killing* (2012), streaming video file.

40. Chaudhary notes that, "We might well long for a narrative arc for the film as a whole that leads from corruption, to killing, to remorse—the classic narrative arc—and the final scene [in which Congo vomits repeatedly at the scene of the killings] has been repeatedly criticized for somehow 'redeeming' Anwar Congo." "This Time with Feeling," 79.

41. Joshua Oppenheimer, dir., *The Look of Silence* (2014), streaming video file.

42. Ibid.

43. Han Kang, *Human Acts*, 51–52; *Sonyŏni onda*, 47.

44. The image of the bodies stacked in a cross allude to one of the best-known and earliest poems to be written about Gwangju, "Gwangju! Cross of Our Nation"

(A, a, Gwangjuyŏ, Urinara ŭi sipjagayŏ), from 1980, by Kim Jun Tae. The imagery of the title—and themes of sacrifice—are obviously inspired by the author's Christianity.

45. Sanders notes of apartheid rule in South Africa that the truth commission there revealed a regime based not only on racial oppression and exploitation, but a "systematic prohibition on mourning and a withholding of condolence." See Sanders, Ambiguities of Witnessing, 49.

46. Han Kang, Human Acts, 211.

47. Ibid., 223; Sonyŏni onda, 214.

48. Gready, "Novel Truths," 174.

49. "Requiem for a Massacre," Tempo (English edition), October 1–7, 2012, 11, https://magz.tempo.co/read/25496/requiem-for-a-massacre.

50. Ibid. Although these quotes come from the English edition of Tempo, I am grateful to Anindya Khairunnisa for her added translation from the original Indonesian version.

51. Jacques Derrida, Specters of Marx: The State of the Debt, the Work of Mourning, and the New International, trans. Peggy Kamuf (New York: Routledge, 1994), 47; emphasis added.

52. To avoid confusion with Adi, the brother of a 1965 victim, who is the focus of The Look of Silence, I will refer to Adi Zulkadry by his second name.

53. Hilmar Farid, "Indonesia's Original Sin: Mass Killings and Capitalist Expansion, 1965–66," in The Inter-Asia Cultural Studies Reader, ed. Kuan-hsing Chen and Beng Huat Chua (London: Routledge, 2007), 217.

54. Taufik Abdullah, "Introduction: The New Order: A Historical Reflection," in Indonesia in the Soeharto Years: Issues, Incidents, and Images, ed. John H. McGlynn et al. (Singapore: Lontar, 2007), xxi.

55. Heryanto, "Great and Misplaced Expectations," 166.

56. Robinson, Killing Season, 89.

57. "Pancasila"—which literally means "five principles"—is a nationalist ideology first promulgated by Sukarno and then further codified by the Suharto regime.

58. Abdullah, "Introduction: The New Order: A Historical Reflection," in Indonesia in the Soeharto Years: Issues, Incidents and Images, ed. McGlynn et al., xxiii.

59. Jun Honna, "Military Ideology in Response to Democratic Pressure during the Late Suharto Era: Political and Institutional Contexts," in Violence and the State in Suharto's Indonesia, ed. Benedict R. O'G. Anderson (Ithaca, NY: Cornell University Press, 2001), 55.

60. Quoted in Janet Hoskin and Viola Lasmana, review of The Act of Killing, Visual Anthropology 28, no. 3 (2015): 264.

61. Heonik Kwon, "The Transpacific Cold War," in Transpacific Studies: Framing an Emerging Field, ed. Janet Hoskins and Viet Thanh Nguyen (Honolulu: University of Hawai'i Press, 2014), 69.

62. Ibid., 71.

63. The association between the Chinese minority and communists during the killings is a complicated one. Robinson mentions the "long-standing, if fluctuating,

hostility toward ethnic Chinese" that "had roots dating back several hundred years" and was often mixed with economic resentment, as "Chinese Indonesians were widely perceived to be wealthy." Yet because "the PKI and other parties of the Left had a record of defending their interests, many Chinese Indonesians joined or supported them." See Robinson, *Killing Season*, 143.

64. Kwon, "Transpacific Cold War," 72.

65. Yoneyama, *Cold War Ruins*, 8.

66. Farred, "Many Are Guilty," 159.

67. For more details, see Robinson, *Killing Season*.

68. Han In Sup, "Kwangju and Beyond," 1009. Ironically, while communism was long synonymous with treason, the court's judgment flipped this logic in declaring treason the crime of the *anti-communist* military government.

69. Ibid., 1040.

70. Ibid., 1041.

71. Ibid., 1034. Even prior to the Uprising, the southwestern provinces of North and South Cholla have long had a reputation for radical and anti-government politics. Due to Korea's historical patterns of regionalism—and especially the series of presidents from the southeastern Gyeongsang provinces, the Cholla region was largely excluded from the country's heavy industrial manufacturing boom of the 1970s. U.S. observers of the Uprising originally put it down to regionalist sentiment.

72. Donald Clark, qtd. in Lewis, *Laying Claim*, 77–78.

73. Han Kang, *Human Acts*, 139; *Sonyŏni onda*, 133.

74. Ibid., 140.

75. Lewis quotes an account by a Korean journalist in 1980 who had asked a paratrooper why they had been so brutal: "He told me that they hadn't been fed for three days, that immediately before being sent into Kwangju they had been fed *soju* (rice wine) and also that they had been told they were being sent in to put down a communist insurrection" (qtd. in Lewis, *Laying Claim*, 83).

76. Hwang, *Korea's Grievous War*, 10. Similarly, the wartime massacre of 7,000 political prisoners in Taejon in 1950 by South Korean troops used "the pretext of 'preventing' collaboration with the North." 24.

77. Grandin, *Last Colonial Massacre* 185, 188.

78. Ibid., 186.

79. Kim Hyung-A, *Korea's Development under Park Chung Hee: Rapid Industrialization, 1961–79* (London: Routledge Curzon, 2004), 102.

80. Kim, "Translations and Ghostings of History," 384.

81. John D. Kelly and Martha Kaplan, *Represented Communities: Fiji and World Decolonization* (Chicago: University of Chicago Press, 2001), 9.

82. Hwang, *Korea's Grievous War*, 30.

83. Ibid., 50.

84. Ibid., 11.

85. Ibid., 189.

86. Scott, *Omens of Adversity*, 128. Scott is speaking about the assumed illiberal politics of "evil regimes" over merely bad individuals.

87. Han In Sup, "Kwangju and Beyond," 1,035.

88. Lewis, *Laying Claim*, 103.

89. Ibid., 156. I have previously written of the *minjung* movement and its multipronged critique of the division system, U.S. presence on the peninsula, and class and labor-based exploitation. See "The Redemptive Realism of Korean *Minjung* Literature," in *The New Asian City: Three-dimensional Fictions of Space and Urban Form* (Minneapolis: University of Minnesota Press, 2011), 227–50. See also Kenneth Wells, *South Korea's Minjung Movement* (Honolulu: University of Hawai'i Press, 1995), and Namhee Lee, *The Making of Minjung* (Ithaca, NY: Cornell University Press, 2007).

90. Lewis, *Laying Claim*, 109.

91. Scott, *Omens of Adversity*, 138.

92. Lewis, *Laying Claim*, 104.

93. Grandin and Klubock, "Editor's Introduction," 6.

94. Han Kang, *Human Acts*, 161.

95. Ibid., 165; *Sonyŏni onda*, 157–58. See Chapter 2 for poet Kim Chi-ha's run in with Emergency Decree number 9.

96. Han Kang, *Human Acts*, 166; *Sonyŏni onda*, 158.

97. Ibid., 143; 136.

98. Ibid., 166; 158.

99. Han In Sup, "Kwangju and Beyond," 1039.

100. Grandin, *Last Colonial Massacre*, 181; emphasis added.

101. Ibid., 183; emphasis added.

102. Farred, "Many Are Guilty," 156. Farred's analysis is of the 2004 film *In My Country*, based on Antjie Krog's *Country of My Skull*, an account of the South African TRC.

103. Han Kang, *Human Acts*, 216; *Sonyŏni onda*, 207.

104. Hun Joon Kim, "Transitional Justice in South Korea," in *Transitional Justice in the Asia-Pacific*, ed. Reneé Jeffrey and Hun Joon Kim (New York: Cambridge University Press, 2013), 245.

105. Ibid.

106. Han In Sup, "Kwangju and Beyond," 1042.

107. Walter Benjamin, *Reflections: Essays, Aphorisms, Autobiographical Writings*, ed. Peter Demetz and trans. Edmund Jephcott (New York: Schocken Books, 2007), 286.

108. Gerry Van Klinken, "No, The Act of Killing Is Not Unethical," *Critical Asian Studies* 46, no. 1 (2014): 177.

109. Farred, "Many Are Guilty," 155.

110. Scott, *Omens of Adversity*, 138.

111. Ibid.

112. Jinhua Dai, *After the Post–Cold War: The Future of Chinese History*, ed. Lisa Rofel (Durham, NC: Duke University Press, 2018), 4.

113. Ibid., 3.

114. Ibid., 8. Indeed, the enduring, nonlinear temporality of Cold War decolonization is again evidenced by the fact that both Indonesia and South Korea would not restore diplomatic relations with the region's communist power, the PRC, until the 1990s (South Korea would be the last Asian country to establish relations with its larger neighbor), almost two decades after U.S. President Nixon's visit to the Mainland in 1972.

115. Derrida, *Specters of Marx*, 59.

116. Dai, *After the Post–Cold War*, 20.

Epilogue: Authoritarian Lessons for Neoliberal Times

1. See, for example, Selam Gebrekidan's article "For Autocrats, and Others, Coronavirus Is a Chance to Grab Even More Power," *New York Times*, March 30, 2020.

2. Neil Lazarus, drawing on Samir Amin, writes how the long postwar boom of capitalist production in the North Atlantic was accompanied by a "settlement" between capital and labor, resulting in strong unions, social and economic benefits, and various forms of social democracy. Neil Lazarus, "The Global Dispensation since 1945," in *The Cambridge Companion to Postcolonial Literary Studies*, ed. Neil Lazarus (Cambridge: Cambridge University Press, 2004), 22–23. In contrast, "Throughout the Third World in the quarter-century following the Second World War, developmentalism (or modernization) produced relatively impressive economic results, even if these cannot be correlated with any necessary democratization" (35).

3. Wendy Brown, "Neoliberalism's Frankenstein: Authoritarian Freedom in Twenty-first Century 'Democracies,'" in *Authoritarianism: Three Inquiries in Critical Theory*, by Wendy Brown, Peter E. Gordon, and Max Pensky (Chicago: University of Chicago Press, 2018), 11.

4. Wendy Brown et al., "Introduction: Critical Theory in an Authoritarian Age," in *Authoritarianism: Three Inquiries in Critical Theory*, by Wendy Brown, Peter E. Gordon, and Max Pensky (Chicago: University of Chicago Press, 2018), 1.

5. Ibid., 3.

6. Ibid., 4.

7. Ibid., 2.

8. See Wendy Brown, *In the Ruins of Neoliberalism: The Rise of Antidemocratic Politics in the West* (New York: Columbia University Press, 2019).

9. Brown, "Neoliberalism's Frankenstein," 12–13.

10. Karl Polanyi, quoted in David Harvey, *A Brief History of Neoliberalism* (Oxford: Oxford University Press, 2005), 37.

11. Brown, "Neoliberalism's Frankenstein," 13.

12. Ibid., 15.

13. Ibid., 17.

14. Ibid., 11.

15. Ibid., 23.

16. Ibid., 29.

17. Ibid. On the subjectivities produced by neoliberalism, see also Chapter 5, "No Future for White Men," in Brown's *In the Ruins of Neoliberalism*, 161–88.

18. Brown, *In the Ruins of Neoliberalism*, 10.

19. Ibid., 18.

20. Samir Amin, quoted in Lazarus, "The Global Dispensation," 29.

21. Odd Arne Westad, *The Global Cold War: Third World Interventions and the Making of Our Times* (Cambridge: Cambridge University Press, 2007), 31.

22. Brown, "Neoliberalism's Frankenstein," 13.

23. See Chandan Reddy, *Freedom with Violence: Race, Sexuality, and the U.S. State* (Durham, NC: Duke University Press, 2011).

24. Quinn Slobodian, *Globalists: The End of Empire and the Birth of Neoliberalism* (Cambridge, MA: Harvard University Press, 2018), 12–13.

25. Ibid., 9.

26. Nils Gilman, "The New International Economic Order: A Reintroduction," *Humanity* 6, no. 1 (2015): 2. For more details on the NIEO, see this special issue of *Humanity* on the topic, edited by Nils Gilman.

27. Slobodian, *Globalists*, 259.

28. Ibid., 260.

29. Brown, *In the Ruins of Neoliberalism*, 18.

30. Adom Getachew, *Worldmaking After Empire: The Rise and Fall of Self-Determination* (Princeton, NJ: Princeton University Press, 2019), 173.

31. Ibid., 236.

32. Ibid.

33. Friedrich Hayek, quoted in Slobodian, 236.

34. Slobodian notes that Hong Kong (and I would argue the other Asian Tigers) actually became the model for mainland China's top-down industrialization program: "Deng Xiaoping's reforms started a process toward China's own form of nonmajoritarian capitalism, slowly introducing market freedoms without expanding political representation." Slobodian, *Globalists*, 236.

35. Harvey, *A Brief History of Neoliberalism*, 7.

36. C. J. W.-L. Wee, *The Asian Modern: Culture, Capitalist Development, Singapore* (Singapore: National University of Singapore Press, 2007), 23.

37. Although beyond the scope of this epilogue to address, the massive, ongoing protests in Hong Kong against the PRC's erosion of its autonomy—and the U.S.'s attempts to support Hong Kong in the name of human rights and democracy while continuing its economic relationship with the Mainland—brings into relief the lingering Cold War contradictions of the U.S. as defender of the "free world."

38. Joseph R. Slaughter, "Hijacking Human Rights: Neoliberalism, the New Historiography, and the End of the Third World," *Human Rights Quarterly* 40, no. 4 (2018): 755.

39. Ibid., 757.

40. Ibid., 755.

41. Ibid., 768.

42. Ibid., 757.

43. "Contrary to initial claims by neoliberals . . . , the success of the NICs [New Industrializing Countries] of East Asia was state-induced rather than market driven." R. N. Gwynne and C. Kay, quoted in Lazarus, "The Global Dispensation," 35. Also see Robert Wade, *Governing the Market: Economic Theory and the Role of Government in East Asian Industrialization* (Princeton, NJ: Princeton University Press, 2004); and Ha-Joon Chang, *The East Asian Developmental Experience: The Miracle, the Crisis, and the Future* (New York: Zed, 2006).

44. Joseph Jonghyun Jeon, *Vicious Circuits: Korea's IMF Cinema and the End of the American Century* (Stanford, CA: Stanford University Press, 2019), 10.

45. Ibid., 11.

46. Harvey, *A Brief History of Neoliberalism*, 97.

47. Ngũgĩ wa Thiong'o, *Writers in Politics: A Re-engagement with Issues of Literature and Society*, by Ngũgĩ wa Thiong'o (Oxford: James Currey, 1997), 130.

48. See also Kenneth Surin's rich study of the "low-intensity democracy" of the U.S.-dominated neoliberal regime, which ensures the continued impoverishment of the global south. Kenneth Surin, *Freedom Not Yet: Liberation and the Next World Order* (Durham, NC: Duke University Press, 2009).

49. Susie Jie Young Kim has noted that the "[Korean] war and the issue of division have . . . become a hallmark of the so-called Korean Blockbuster," inaugurated by the large production, hit films *Shiri* (*Swiri*, 1999) and *JSA: Joint Security Area* (*Kongdong kyŏngbi kuyŏk JSA*, 2000). See "Korea beyond and within the Armistice: Division and the Multiplicities of Time in Postwar Literature and Cinema," *Journal of Korean Studies* 18, no. 2 (2013): 287–313.

50. Steven Borowiec, "'Ode to My Father' Stirs the Box Office and Debate in South Korea," *Los Angeles Times*, January 31, 2015.

51. The country's heavy industrial push of the 1970s was centered along a belt of industrial cities including Pohang, Ulsan (the base of the massive Hyundai enterprises), Busan, and Masan. Young-Jin Choi and Jim Glassman have examined the way Hyundai's "networks were globally formed, integrated into the geographically expansive US military industrial complex (MIC) that emerged through Cold War alliances." Choi and Glassman, "Heavy Industries and Second Tier City Growth in South Korea: A Geopolitical Economic Analysis of the 'Four Core Plants Plan,'" in *Developmentalist Cities? Interrogating Urban Developmentalism in East Asia*, ed. Jamie Doucette and Bae-Gyoon Park (Leiden: Brill, 2019), 30.

52. This is not to say that anti-Japanese sentiment is not important to Korean nationalist thinking. See Leo T. S. Ching, *Anti-Japan: The Politics of Sentiment in Postcolonial East Asia* (Durham, NC: Duke University Press, 2019), especially Chapter 3 on the Korean "comfort women" issue.

53. See my discussion in the Introduction of Theodore Hughes and his notion of "promotion through the world system." Theodore Hughes, *Literature and Film in*

Cold War South Korea: Freedom's Frontier (New York: Columbia University Press, 2012), 137.

54. Aijaz Ahmad, *In Theory: Classes, Nations, Literatures* (London: Verso, 2008), 21.

55. Harvey, *A Brief History of Neoliberalism*, 75.

56. On the logic of Cold War familial incorporation, see Christian Klein's *Cold War Orientalism: Asia in the Middlebrow Imagination, 1945–1961* (Berkeley: University of California Press, 2003).

57. Je-kyoon Yoon, "Kukje sijang, sot'ong kwa hwahap ŭi yŏnghwa . . . inyŏm nollan tanghwang [*International Market*, a film of communication and harmony . . . and ideological controversy]," Interview on *JTBC*, January 6, 2015. Translation mine. http://news.jtbc.joins.com/article/article.aspx?news_id=NB10712210

58. Je-kyoon Yoon, quoted in Borowiec, "Ode to My Father."

59. Lee Taek-kwang, quoted in Borowiec, "Ode to My Father."

60. See my discussion in the Introduction and Scott, *Refashioning Futures: Criticism after Postcoloniality* (Princeton, NJ: Princeton University Press, 1999).

61. See Chapter 4's discussion of Paik Nak-chung in regard to assessing the legacy of Park Chung Hee's "meritorious dictatorship."

62. Eileen Jones, "*Parasite* Is Our Film," *Jacobin*, February 12, 2020, https://jacobinmag.com/2020/02/parasite-bong-joon-ho-academy-awards.

63. Amitav Ghosh, *The Great Derangement: Climate Change and the Unthinkable* (Chicago: University of Chicago Press, 2016), 92.

Bibliography

Abdullah, Taufik. "Introduction: The New Order: A Historical Reflection." In *Indonesia in the Soeharto Years: Issues, Incidents and Images*, edited by McGlynn et al., xx–xxiii. Singapore: Lontar, 2007.

Abinales, P. N., and Donna J. Amoroso. *State and Society in the Philippines.* Lanham, MD: Rowman & Littlefield, 2005.

Achebe, Chinua. *Anthills of the Savannah.* London: Heinemann, 1987.

Ahmad, Aijaz. *In Theory: Classes, Nations, Literatures.* 1992. London: Verso, 2008.

Ahmad, Siti Nuraishah. Review of *Confrontation*, by Mohamed Latiff Mohamed. Translated by Shafiq Selamat. *Asiatic* 8, no. 1 (2014): 268–70.

Alisjahbana, S. Takdir. "Tradition and Modernity in Asian Literature." *Report of the Asian Writers' Conference.* Published in *Comment: The Filipino Journal of Ideas, Discussion, and the Arts* 17 (1963): 17–26.

Aljunied, Syed Muhd Khairudin. "Political Memoirs as Contrapuntal Narratives." *Interventions: International Journal of Postcolonial Studies* 18, no. 4 (2016): 512–25.

Almario, Virgilio S. "Literary 'Consumerism': Notes on the Liberation of Philippine Critical Theory in Poetry." In *Literature and Social Justice: Papers Presented to the Second Asian Writers Conference [1981]*, 113–24. Manila: Philippine Center of International P.E.N., 1982.

Amin, Samir. *Re-Reading the Postwar Period: An Intellectual Itinerary.* Translated by Michael Wolfers. New York: Monthly Review Press, 1994.

Anderson, Benedict. *Imagined Communities: Reflections on the Origin and Spread of Nationalism.* London: Verso, 1983.

Arendt, Hannah. *Between Past and Present: Six Exercises in Political Thought.* New York: Viking Press, 1961.

———. *The Origins of Totalitarianism.* New ed. San Diego: Harvest, 1966. First published 1951 by Schocken Books (New York).

Armah, Ayi Kwei. *The Beautyful Ones Are Not Yet Born*. Boston: Houghton Mifflin, 1968.

Armillas-Tiseyra, Magalí. *The Dictator Novel: Writers and Politics in the Global South*. Evanston, IL: Northwestern University Press, 2019.

Avena, Mauro R. "The Filipino Writer and Social Justice." In *Literature and Social Justice: Papers Presented to the Second Asian Writers Conference [1981]*, 37–40. Manila: Philippine Center of International P.E.N., 1982.

Barker, Joshua. "State of Fear: Controlling the Criminal Contagion in Suharto's New Order." In *Violence and the State in Suharto's Indonesia*, edited by Benedict R. O'G. Anderson, 20–53. Ithaca, NY: Cornell University Press, 2001.

Bautista, Cirilo F. "Philippine Literature: From National Liberation to Aesthetic Liberation." In *Literature and Social Justice: Papers Presented to the Second Asian Writers Conference [1981]*, 135–41. Manila: Philippine Center of International P.E.N., 1982.

Bayly, Christopher, and Tim Harper. *Forgotten Wars: Freedom and Revolution in Southeast Asia*. Cambridge, MA: Belknap Press of Harvard University Press, 2010.

Benjamin, Walter. *Illuminations*. Translated by Harry Zohn. New York: Schocken Books, 1968.

———. *Reflections: Essays, Aphorisms, Autobiographic Writings*. Translated by Edmund Jephcott. New York: Schocken Books, 2007.

Birdsall, Nancy, et al. *The East Asian Miracle: Economic Growth and Public Policy*. The World Bank, 1993. http://documents.worldbank.org/curated/en/975081468244550798/Main-report.

Bishop, Cécile. *Postcolonial Criticism and Representations of African Dictatorship: The Aesthetics of Tyranny*. London: Legenda, Modern Humanities Research Association and Maney Publishing, 2014.

Boyer, Dominic. "Censorship as Vocation: The Institutions, Practices, and Cultural Logic of Media Control in the German Democratic Republic." *Comparative Studies in Society and History* 45, no. 3 (2003): 511–41.

Brennan, Timothy. "The National Longing for Form." In *Nation and Narration*, edited by Homi K. Bhabha, 44–70. London: Routledge, 1990.

Brouillette, Sarah. "UNESCO and the Book in the Developing World." *Representations* 127, no. 1 (2014): 33–54.

Brown, Wendy. *In the Ruins of Neoliberalism: The Rise of Antidemocratic Politics in the West*. New York: Columbia University Press, 2019.

———. "Neoliberalism's Frankenstein: Authoritarian Freedom in Twenty-first Century 'Democracies.'" In *Authoritarianism: Three Inquiries in Critical Theory*, by Wendy Brown, Peter E. Gordon, and Max Pensky, 7–44. Chicago: University of Chicago Press, 2018.

Brown, Wendy, et al. "Introduction: Critical Theory in an Authoritarian Age." In *Authoritarianism: Three Inquiries in Critical Theory*, by Wendy Brown, Peter E. Gordon, and Max Pensky, 1–6. Chicago: University of Chicago Press, 2018.

Campomanes, Oscar V. "Filipinos in the United States and Their Literature of Exile." In *Reading the Literatures of Asian America*, edited by Shirley Geok-lin Lim and Amy Ling, 49–78. Philadelphia: Temple University Press, 1992.

Camus, Albert. *Create Dangerously: The Power and Responsibility of the Artist.* Translated by Sandra Smith. New York: Vintage, 2019.

Castro de Guzman, Domingo. "Notes on Art, Freedom, and Society." In *Literature and Social Justice: Papers Presented to the Second Asian Writers Conference [1981]*, 142–55. Manila: Philippine Center of International P.E.N., 1982.

Chakrabarty, Dipesh. "Legacies of Bandung: Decolonization the Politics of Culture." In *Making a World after Empire: The Bandung Moment and Its Political Afterlives*, edited by Christopher J. Lee, 45–68. Athens, OH: Center for International Studies, Ohio University: 2010.

———. *Provincializing Europe.* Princeton, NJ: Princeton University Press, 2000.

Chang, Ha-Joon. *The East Asian Developmental Experience: The Miracle, the Crisis and the Future.* New York: Zed, 2006.

Chang, Paul. *Protest Dialectics: State Repression and South Korea's Democracy Movement, 1970–1979.* Stanford, CA: Stanford University Press, 2015.

Chari, Sharad, and Katherine Verdery. "Thinking between the Posts: Postcolonialism, Postsocialism, and Ethnography after the Cold War." *Comparative Studies in Society and History* 51, no. 1 (2009): 6–34.

Chatterjee, Partha. "Empire and Nation Revisited: 50 Years after Bandung." *Inter-Asia Cultural Studies* 6, no. 4 (2005): 487–96.

———. *The Nation and Its Fragments.* Princeton, NJ: Princeton University Press, 1993.

———. *Nationalist Thought in the Colonial World: A Derivative Discourse?* London: Zed Books, 1986.

Chaudhary, Zahid R. "This Time with Feeling: Impunity and the Play of Fantasy in *The Act of Killing.*" *boundary 2* 45, no. 4 (2018): 65–101.

Cheah, Pheng. "Of Other Worlds to Come." In *Delimiting Modernities: Conceptual Challenges and Regional Responses*, edited by Sven Trakulhun and Ralph Weber, 3–24. Lanham, MD: Lexington, 2015.

———. *Spectral Nationality: Passages of Freedom from Kant to Postcolonial Literatures of Liberation.* New York: Columbia University Press, 2003.

———. *What Is a World? On Postcolonial Literature as World Literature.* Durham, NC: Duke University Press, 2016.

Chen, Kuan-Hsing. *Asia as Method: Toward Deimperialization.* Durham, NC: Duke University Press, 2010.

Chen, Y. C. "Closing Remarks." In *Thirty Years of Turmoil in Asian Literature: The Fourth Asian Writers' Conference, April 25th–May 2nd, 1976*, 60–64. Taipei: Taipei Chinese Center, International P.E.N., 1976.

———. "Opening Remarks." In *Thirty Years of Turmoil in Asian Literature: The Fourth Asian Writers' Conference, April 25th–May 2nd, 1976*, 18–20. Taipei: Taipei Chinese Center, International P.E.N., 1976.

Ching, Leo T. S. *Anti-Japan: The Politics of Sentiment in Postcolonial East Asia.* Durham, NC: Duke University Press, 2019.

Choi, Jang Jip. "Political Cleavages in South Korea." In *State and Society in Contemporary Korea*, edited by Hagen Koo, 13–50. Ithaca, NY: Cornell University Press, 1993.

Choi, Young-Jin, and Jim Glassman. "Heavy Industries and Second Tier City Growth in South Korea: A Geopolitical Economic Analysis of the 'Four Core Plants Plan.'" In *Developmentalist Cities? Interrogating Urban Developmentalism in East Asia*, edited by Jamie Doucette and Bae-Gyoon Park, 17–43. Leiden: Brill, 2019.

Chua, Beng Huat. "Disrupting Hegemonic Liberalism in East Asia." *boundary 2* 37, no. 2 (2010): 199–216.

———. *Liberalism Disavowed: Communitarianism and State Capitalism in Singapore.* Ithaca, NY: Cornell University Press, 2017.

Connery, Christopher L. "Pacific Rim Discourse: The U.S. Global Imaginary in the Late Cold War Years." *boundary 2* 21, no. 1 (1994): 30–56.

Cousins, Norman. Introduction to *Asian PEN Anthology*, edited by F. Sionil José, xv–xvi. New York: Taplinger, 1966.

Cumings, Bruce. "Boundary Displacement: The State, the Foundations and Area Studies during and after the Cold War." In *Learning Places: The Afterlives of Area Studies*, edited by Masao Miyoshi and H. D. Harootunian, 262–302. Durham, NC: Duke University Press, 2002.

———. "Webs with No Spiders, Spiders with No Webs: The Genealogy of the Developmental State." In *The Developmental State*, edited by Meredith Woo-Cumings, 61–92. Ithaca, NY: Cornell University Press, 1999.

Cvetkovich, Ann. "Drawing the Archive in Alison Bechdel's Fun Home." *Women's Studies Quarterly* 36, no. 1–2 (2008): 111–27.

Dai, Jinhua. *After the Post–Cold War: The Future of Chinese History*, edited by Lisa Rofel. Durham, NC: Duke University Press, 2018.

Davis, Rocio G. "Postcolonial Visions and Immigrant Longings: Ninotchka Rosca's Versions of the Philippines." *World Literature Today* 73, no. 1 (1999): 63–70.

Day, Tony. "Still Stuck in the Mud: Imagining World Literature during the Cold War in Indonesia and Vietnam." In *Cultures at War: The Cold War and Cultural Expression in Southeast Asia*, edited by Tony Day and Maya H. T. Liem, 131–70. Ithaca, NY: Cornell University Press, 2010.

de Manuel, Dolores. "Decolonizing Bodies, Reinscribing Souls in the Fiction of Ninotchka Rosca and Linda Ty-Casper." *MELUS* 29, no. 1 (2004): 99–118.

Derrida, Jacques. *Specters of Marx: The State of the Debt, the Work of Mourning, and the New International.* Translated by Peggy Kamuf. New York: Routledge, 1994.

Diamond, Catherine. "Maturation and Political Upheaval in Lloyd Fernando's 'Scorpion Orchid' and Robert Yeo's 'The Singapore Trilogy.'" *Comparative Drama* 36, no. 1/2 (2002), 125–44.

Djagalov, Rossen. *From Internationalism to Postcolonialism: Literature and Cinema between the Second and Third Worlds*. Montreal: McGill-Queen's University Press, 2020.

Doyle, Laura. "Inter-imperiality: Dialectics in a Postcolonial World History." *Interventions: International Journal of Postcolonial Studies* 16, no. 2 (2014): 159–96.

Durran, Mary. "Asking Forbidden Questions." *New Internationalist*, December 1989. https://newint.org/features/1989/12/05/endpiece.

Elstob, Peter. "Message." In *Literature and Social Justice: Papers Presented to the Second Asian Writers Conference [1981]*, 1–2. Manila: Philippine Center of International P.E.N., 1982.

Fanon, Frantz. *The Wretched of the Earth*. Translated by Richard Philcox. New York: Grove, 2004. First published by F. Maspero (Paris) in 1961 as *Les Damnés de la Terre*.

Farid, Hilmar. "Indonesia's Original Sin: Mass Killings and Capitalist Expansion, 1965–66." In *The Inter-Asia Cultural Studies Reader*, edited by Kuan-hsing Chen and Beng Huat Chua, 207–22. London: Routledge, 2007.

Farred, Grant. "Many Are Guilty, Few Are Indicted." Review of *In My Country*, directed by John Boorman, Sony Pictures Classics, 2004. *Radical History Review* 97 (2007): 155–62.

Ferguson, James. *The Anti-Politics Machine: Development, Depoliticization, and Bureaucratic Power in Lesotho*. Cambridge: Cambridge University Press, 1990.

"First Literary Session, Part B." In *Proceedings of the Third Asian Writers' Conference*, 34–44. Taipei: Chinese Center, International P.E.N., 1970.

Foulcher, Keith. *Social Commitment in Literature and the Arts: The Indonesian "Institute of People's Culture," 1950–1965*. Centre of Southeast Asian Studies/ Monash University, 1986.

"Fourth Literary Session." In *Thirty Years of Turmoil in Asian Literature: The Fourth Asian Writers' Conference, April 25th–May 2nd, 1976*, 50–59. Taipei: Taipei Chinese Center, International P.E.N., 1976.

Frank, Andre Gunder. *Crisis: In the Third World*. New York: Homes and Meier, 1981.

Frantz, Erica. *Authoritarianism: What Everyone Needs to Know*. New York: Oxford University Press, 2018.

Fukuyama, Francis. *The End of History and the Last Man*. New York: Free Press, 1992.

Getachew, Adom. *Worldmaking After Empire: The Rise and Fall of Self-Determination*. Princeton, NJ: Princeton University Press, 2019.

Ghosh, Amitav. *The Great Derangement: Climate Change and the Unthinkable*. Chicago: University of Chicago Press, 2016.

Gilman, Nils. "The New International Economic Order: A Reintroduction." *Humanity* 6, no. 1 (2015): 1–16.

GoGwilt, Chris. "Pramoedya's Fiction and History: An Interview with Indonesian Novelist Pramoedya Ananta Toer." *Yale Journal of Criticism* 9, no. 1 (1996): 147–64.

Goodman, Brian. "Philip Roth's Other Europe: Counter-Realism and the Late Cold War." *American Literary History* 27, no. 4 (2015): 717–40.

Gordolan, Lourdes. "Butch Dalisay, Ricky Lee, and Other Writers Remember
    Prison Life in Martial Law Era." *Rogue*, April 2012. http://rogue.ph/
    butch-dalisay-ricky-lee-writers-remember-prison-life-martial-law-era/.
Gramsci, Antonio. *Selections from the Prison Notebooks*. Edited and translated by
    Quintin Hoare and Geoffrey Nowell Smith. New York: International, 1971.
Grandin, Greg. *Empire's Workshop: Latin America, the United States, and the Rise of
    the New Imperialism*. New York: Holt, 2006.
———. *The Last Colonial Massacre: Latin America in the Cold War*. Chicago:
    University of Chicago Press, 2004.
Grandin, Greg, and Thomas Miller Klubock. "Editor's Introduction." *Radical
    History Review* 97 (2007): 1–10.
Gready, Paul. "Novel Truths: Literature and Truth Commissions." *Comparative
    Literature Studies* 46, no. 1 (2009): 156–76.
Gupta, Akhil. "Blurred Boundaries: The Discourse of Corruption, the Culture
    of Politics, and the Imagined State." *American Ethnologist* 22, no. 2 (1995):
    375–402.
Gupta, Akhil, David Nugent, and Shreyas Sreenath. "State, Corruption,
    Postcoloniality: A Conversation with Akhil Gupta on the 20th Anniversary of
    'Blurred Boundaries.'" *American Ethnologist* 42, no. 4 (2015): 581–91.
Gwee, Li Sui. "Cyril Wong in the Face of Power." Introduction to *The Dictator's
    Eyebrow*, by Cyril Wong, 4–10. Singapore: Ethos Books, 2013.
Halim, Hala. "Lotus, the Afro-Asian Nexus, and Global South Comparatism."
    Comparative Studies of South Asia, Africa, and the Middle East 32, no. 3 (2012):
    563–83.
Hammond, Andrew. "From Rhetoric to Rollback: Introductory Thoughts on Cold
    War Writing." In *Cold War Literature: Writing the Global Conflict*, edited by
    Andrew Hammond, 1–14. London: Routledge, 2006.
———. "On the Frontlines of Writing: Introducing the Literary Cold War." In
    Global Cold War Literature: Western, Eastern, and Postcolonial Perspectives,
    edited by Andrew Hammond, 1–16. New York: Routledge, 2012.
Han, In Sup. "Kwangju and Beyond: Coping with Past State Atrocities in South
    Korea." *Human Rights Quarterly* 27, no. 3 (2005): 998–1045.
Han, Kang. *Human Acts: A Novel*. Translated by Deborah Smith. London:
    Portobello, 2016.
———. *Sonyoni onda* [Here comes the boy]. Seoul: Changbi, 2014.
Haridas, Swami Anand. "Pramoedya Ananta Toer." *Index on Censorship* 5 (1978):
    49–52.
Harlow, Barbara. *Barred: Women, Writing, and Political Detention*. Hanover, NH:
    University Press of New England, 1992.
———. *Resistance Literature*. New York: Methuen, 1987.
Hart, Matthew, and Jim Hansen. "Introduction: Contemporary Literature and the
    State." *Contemporary Literature* 49, no. 4 (2008): 491–513.
Harvey, David. *A Brief History of Neoliberalism*. Oxford: Oxford University Press,
    2005.

———. *The New Imperialism*. Oxford: Oxford University Press, 2003.

Hatley, Barbara. "Recalling and Representing Cold War Conflict and Its Aftermath in Contemporary Indonesia Film and Theater." In *Cultures at War: The Cold War and Cultural Expression in Southeast Asia*, edited by Tony Day and Maya H. T. Liem, 265–84. Ithaca, NY: Cornell University Press, 2010.

Hau, Caroline. *Elites and Ilustrados in Philippine Culture*. Manila: Ateneo de Manila University Press, 2017.

Hau'ofa, Epeli. "Our Sea of Islands." In *We Are the Ocean: Selected Works*, by Epeli Hau'ofa, 27–40. Honolulu: University of Hawai'i Press, 2008.

Hayner, Priscilla B. *Unspeakable Truths: Transitional Justice and the Challenge of Truth Commissions*. 2nd ed. New York: Routledge, 2011.

Heryanto, Ariel. "Great and Misplaced Expectations." *Critical Asian Studies* 46, no. 1 (2014): 162–66.

Hitchcock, Peter. "The Genre of Postcoloniality." *New Literary History* 34, no. 2 (2003): 299–330.

———. *The Long Space: Transnationalism and Postcolonial Form*. Stanford, CA: Stanford University Press, 2010.

———. "Postcolonial Failure and the Politics of Nation." *South Atlantic Quarterly* 106, no. 4 (2007): 727–52.

Holden, Philip. "Histories of the Present: Reading Contemporary Singapore Novels between the Local and the Global." *Postcolonial Text* 2, no. 2 (2006): n.p.

———. "'Is It Manipulative? Sure. But That's How You Tell Stories': The Graphic Novel, Metahistory and the Artist in *The Art of Charlie Chan Hock Chye*." *Journal of Postcolonial Writing* 52, no. 4 (2016): 510–23.

———. "Postcolonial Desire: Placing Singapore." *Postcolonial Studies* 11, no. 3 (2008): 345–61.

———. "Reading for Genre." *Interventions: International Journal of Postcolonial Studies* 12, no. 3 (2010): 442–58.

———. "Refusing the Cultural Turn: Amir Muhammad's Politics of Surfaces." In *Locating Life Stories*, edited by Maureen Perkins, 15–34. Honolulu: University of Hawai'i Press, 2012.

Hong, Yong-hee. *Kim Chi-ha Munhak Yon'gu* [Literary research on Kim Chi-ha]. Seoul: Si wa Sihaksa, 2000.

Honna, Jun. "Military Ideology in Response to Democratic Pressure during the Late Suharto Era: Political and Institutional Contexts." In *Violence and the State in Suharto's Indonesia*, edited by Benedict R. O'G. Anderson, 54–89. Ithaca, NY: Cornell University Press, 2001.

Hoskin, Janet, and Viola Lasmana. Review of *The Act of Killing*. *Visual Anthropology* 28, no. 3 (2015): 262–65.

Hossain, Selina. "Literature and Social Justice." In *Literature and Social Justice: Papers Presented to the Second Asian Writers Conference [1981]*, 22–30. Manila: Philippine Center of International P.E.N., 1982.

Hughes, Theodore. *Literature and Film in Cold War South Korea: Freedom's Frontier*. New York: Columbia University Press, 2012.

Hutchcroft, Paul D. "Reflections on a Reversed Image: South Korea under Park Chung Hee and the Philippines under Marcos." In *The Park Chung Hee Era: The Transformation of South Korea*, edited by Byung-Kook Kim and Ezra F. Vogel, 542–72. Cambridge, MA: Harvard University Press, 2011.

Hwang, Sŏk-yŏng. *Oraedoen chŏngwŏn*. P'aju: Changbi, 2000.

———. *The Old Garden*. Translated by Jay Oh. New York: Seven Stories Press, 2009.

Hwang, Su-Kyoung. *Korea's Grievous War*. Philadelphia: University of Pennsylvania Press, 2016.

Ileto, Reynaldo Clemeña. *Filipinos and Their Revolution: Event, Discourse, and Historiography*. Quezon City: Ateneo de Manila University Press, 1998.

Jameson, Fredric. "On Literary and Cultural Import-Substitution in the Third World." In *The Real Thing: Testimonial Discourse and Latin America*, edited by Georg M. Gugelberger, 172–91. Durham, NC: Duke University Press, 1996.

———. "Third World Literature in the Era of Multinational Capitalism." *Social Text, no.* 15 (Autumn 1986): 65–88.

Jeon, Joseph Jonghyun. *Vicious Circuits: Korea's IMF Cinema and the End of the American Century*. Stanford, CA: Stanford University Press, 2019.

Jones, Eileen. "*Parasite* Is Our Film," *Jacobin*, February 12, 2020. https://jacobinmag.com/2020/02/parasite-bong-joon-ho-academy-awards

José, F. Sionil, ed. *Asian PEN Anthology*. New York: Taplinger, 1966.

———. *The Samsons, Two Novels in the Rosales Sage: The Pretenders and Mass*. New York: Modern Library, 2000.

Kang, Duk-yong. "Literature and Social Justice." In *Literature and Social Justice: Papers Presented to the Second Asian Writers Conference [1981]*, 31–6. Manila: Philippine Center of International P.E.N., 1982.

Kang, Jinho. "Sosŏl kyoyukgwa t'aja ŭi jip'yŏng" [Novel education and the horizon of the other]. *Munhak kyoyukhak* [Literary education] 13 (2004): 33–62.

Keith, Joseph. *Unbecoming Americans: Writing Race and Nation from the Shadows of Citizenship*. New Brunswick, NJ: Rutgers University Press, 2013.

Kelly, John D., and Martha Kaplan. *Represented Communities: Fiji and World Decolonization*. Chicago: University of Chicago Press, 2001.

"K'enya chakga ŭnggugi 'Kim Chi-ha Ojŏk' ŭro put'ŏ k'ŭn yŏnggam" [Kenyan Writer Ngũgĩ wa Thiong'o greatly inspired by Kim Chi-ha's "Five Thieves," *MK Maeil Kyŏngje*, October 25, 2016. https://www.mk.co.kr/news/society/view/2016/10/744442/.

Killen, Shelly. "Profile: Kim Chi-ha." *Index on Censorship* 7, no. 3 (1978): 50–53.

Kim, Chi-ha. *Cry of the People and Other Poems*. [No translator noted.] Hayama: Autumn Press, 1975.

———. "Five Bandits." Translated by Brother Anthony of Taizé. *Manoa* 27, no. 2 (2015): 94–104.

———. *Ojok/Five Thieves*. Translated by James Han and Kim Won-chung. Seoul: Tapke, 2001.

———. "Pi'ŏ." In *Kyŏlchŏngbon Kim Chi-ha si chŏnjip* [Kim Chi-ha collected poems.] Seoul: Sol, 1993.

Kim, Daniel Y. "Translations and Ghostings of History: The Novels of Han Kang."
    New Literary History 51, no. 2 (2020): 375–399.
Kim, Hun Joon. "Transitional Justice in South Korea." In *Transitional Justice in the
    Asia-Pacific*, edited by Reneé Jeffrey and Hun Joon Kim, 229–58. New York:
    Cambridge University Press, 2013.
Kim, Hyung-A. *Korea's Development under Park Chung Hee: Rapid
    Industrialization, 1961–79*. London: Routledge Curzon, 2004.
Kim, Jodi. *Ends of Empire: Asian American Critique and the Cold War*. Minneapolis:
    University of Minnesota Press, 2010.
Kim, Jun Tae. *Gwangju, Cross of Our Nation/A, a, Gwangjuyŏ, urinara ŭi sipjagayŏ.*
    Translated by David McCann, Chae-Pyong Song, Melanie Steyn, Kyung Ja Chun,
    and Kevin Ilsub Lim. Seoul: Hans Media, 2014.
Kim, Susie Jie Young. "Korea beyond and within the Armistice: Division and the
    Multiplicities of Time in Postwar Literature and Cinema." *Journal of Korean
    Studies* 18, no. 2 (2013): 287–313.
Kimiya, Tadashi. "The Cold War and the Political Economy of the Park Chung Hee
    Regime." In *Reassessing the Park Chung Hee Era, 1961–1979: Development,
    Political Thought, Democracy, and Political Influence*, edited by Hyung-A Kim
    and Clark W. Sorensen, 66–82. Seattle: University of Washington Press, 2011.
Klein, Christina. *Cold War Orientalism: Asia in the Middlebrow Imagination,
    1945–1961*. Berkeley: University of California Press, 2003.
Ko, Won. "Kim Chi-ha: Poet of Blood and Fire." *Bulletin of Concerned Asian
    Scholars* 9, no. 2 (1977): 20–25.
Koselleck, Reinhart. *Futures Past: On the Semantics of Historical Time*. New York:
    Columbia University Press, 2004.
Kotelawala, Sir John. "Opening Speech." In *Selected Documents of the Bandung
    Conference: Texts of Selected Speeches and Final Communique of the Asian-
    African Conference, Bandung, Indonesia, April 18–24, 1955*, 12–20. New York:
    Institute of Pacific Relations, 1955.
Kuo, Pao Kun. *The Coffin Is Too Big for the Hole and Other Plays*. Singapore: Time
    Books International, 1990.
Kwek, Theophilus. "'State of Emergency' by Jeremy Tiang." *Asian Review of Books*.
    August 22, 2017.
Kwon, Heonik. *The Other Cold War*. New York: Columbia University Press, 2010.
———. "The Transpacific Cold War." In *Transpacific Studies: Framing an Emerging
    Field*, edited by Janet Hoskins and Viet Thanh Nguyen, 64–84. Honolulu:
    University of Hawai'i Press, 2014.
Kwŏn, Kyŏngmi. "Chisikin chuch'e ŭi sangjon hyŏnsil insik kwa chŏhang ŭi sŏsa."
    [The recognition of survival reality of the intellectual subject and the narrative
    of resistance.] *Han'guk munye ch'angjak* [Korean literary creative writing] 1, no.
    27 (2013): 207–35.
Kubayanda, Josephat. "Unfinished Business: Dictatorial Literature of Post-
    Independence Latin America and Africa." *Research in African Literatures* 28,
    no. 4 (1997): 38–53.

LaFeber, Walter. "Rethinking the Cold War and After: From Containment to Engagement." In *Rethinking the Cold War,* edited by Allen Hunter, 35–45. Philadelphia: Temple University Press, 1998.

Lazarus, Neil. "The Global Dispensation since 1945." In *The Cambridge Companion to Postcolonial Literary Studies,* edited by Neil Lazarus, 19–40. Cambridge: Cambridge University Press, 2004.

———. *The Postcolonial Unconscious.* Cambridge: Cambridge University Press, 2011.

Lee, Christopher J. "Between a Moment and an Era: The Origins and Afterlives of Bandung." In *Making a World after Empire: The Bandung Moment and Its Political Afterlives,* edited by Christopher J. Lee, 1–42. Athens, OH: Center for International Studies, Ohio University, 2010.

Lee, Fiona. "Epistemological Checkpoint." *Postcolonial Text* 9, no. 1 (2014): 1–21.

Lee, Namhee. *The Making of Minjung: Democracy and the Politics of Representation in South Korea.* Ithaca, NY: Cornell University Press, 2007.

Lent, John A. "The Philippine Press under Martial Law." *Index on Censorship* 3, no. 1 (1974): 47–58.

Lewis, Linda S. *Laying Claim to the Memory of May.* Honolulu: University of Hawaiʻi Press, 2002.

Liew, Sonny. *The Art of Charlie Chan Hock Chye.* New York: Pantheon, 2016.

Lloyd, David, and Paul Thomas. *Culture and the State.* New York: Routledge, 1998.

Lopez, Salvador P. "Some Reflections on Human Rights." In *Literature and Social Justice: Papers Presented to the Second Asian Writers Conference [1981],* 189–200. Manila: Philippine Center of International P.E.N., 1982.

Mahler, Anne Garland. *From the Tricontinental to the Global South: Race, Radicalism, and Transnational Solidarity.* Durham, NC: Duke University Press, 2018.

Mamdani, Mahmood. *Citizen and Subject: Contemporary Africa and the Legacy of Late Colonialism.* Princeton, N.J.: Princeton University Press, 1996.

Manglapus, Raul S. "Progress and the Writers of Asia." *Report of the Asian Writers' Conference.* Published in *Comment: The Filipino Journal of Ideas, Discussion, and the Arts,* no. 17 (1963): 27–32.

Marx, John. "Failed State Fiction." *Contemporary Literature* 49, no. 4 (2008): 597–633.

———. *Geopolitics and the Anglophone Novel, 1890–2011.* Cambridge: Cambridge University Press, 2012.

Marx, Karl. *Capital: A Critique of Political Economy.* Vol. 1. Translated by Ben Fowkes. London: Penguin, 1990.

Mbembe, Achille. *On the Postcolony.* Berkeley: University of California Press, 2001.

McCann, David R. Introduction to *The Middle Hour: Selected Poems of Kim Chi Ha.* Translated by David R. McCann, 1–8. Stanfordville, NY: Human Rights Publishing Group, 1980.

———. "Kim Chi Ha's Messed-Up Poems." *Azalea: Journal of Korean Literature and Culture* 6 (2013): 357–68.

McClennen, Sophia A. *The Dialectics of Exile: Nation, Time, and Language in Hispanic Literatures.* West Lafayette, IN: Purdue University Press, 2004.

McClennen, Sophie A., and Alexandra Schultheis Moore. "Introduction: Aporia and Affirmative Critique: Mapping the Landscape of Literary Approaches to Human Rights Research." In *Routledge Companion to Human Rights and Literature*, edited by Sophie A. McClennen and Alexandra Schultheis Moore, 1–20. Abingdon: Routledge, 2016.

McDonald, Peter D. *The Literature Police: Apartheid Censorship and Its Cultural Consequences*. Oxford: Oxford University Press, 2009.

Mendible, Myra. "Literature as Activism: Ninotchka Rosca's Political Aesthetic." *Journal of Postcolonial Writing* 50, no. 3 (2014): 354–67.

Mezzadra, Sandro. "How Many Histories of Labour? Towards a Theory of Postcolonial Capitalism." *Postcolonial Studies* 14, no. 2 (2011): 151–70.

Mezzadra, Sandro, and Federico Rahola. "The Postcolonial Condition: A Few Notes on the Quality of Historical Time in the Global Present." *Postcolonial Text* 2, no. 1 (2006): 36–54.

Mitchell, Timothy. "The Limits of the State: Beyond Statist Approaches and Their Critics." *American Political Science Review* 85, no. 1 (1991): 77–96.

Mohamed, Mohamed Latiff. *Confrontation: A Novel*. Translated by Shafiq Selamat. Singapore: Epigram, 2013.

Moore, Alexandra Schultheis. *Vulnerability and Security in Human Rights Literature and Visual Culture*. New York: Routledge, 2016.

Moretti, Franco. *The Way of the World: The Bildungsroman in European Culture*. Translated by Albert Spragia. London: Verso, 1987.

Nehru, Jawaharlal. "India." In *Bandung: A Clarion Call for Afro-Asian Solidarity [18–24 April, 1955]*, 17–24. Cairo: Afro-Asian Peoples' Solidarity Organisation, 1975.

Ngũgĩ wa Thiong'o. *Writers in Politics: A Re-engagement with Issues of Literature and Society*. Oxford: James Currey; Nairobi: EAEP; and Portsmouth: Heinemann, 1997.

Nguyen, Viet Thanh. *Race and Resistance: Literature and Politics in Asian America*. Oxford: Oxford University Press, 2002.

Niekerk, Carl. "Modernity, Sexuality and Gender in Pramoedya Ananta Toer's *This Earth of Mankind*." *Symposium: A Quarterly Journal in Modern Literatures* 65, no. 2 (2011): 77–98.

Nkrumah, Kwame. *Neo-colonialism, the Last Stage of Imperialism*. London: Thomas Nelson & Sons, 1965.

Ochi, Michio. "Modernization in Japan." In *Literature and Social Justice: Papers Presented to the Second Asian Writers Conference [1981]*, 156–63. Manila: Philippine Center of International P.E.N., 1982.

Oppenheimer, Joshua. "Membunuh, Bagi Anwar, Adalah Sebuah Akting." ["Killing, for Anwar, is an act."] *Tempo*. October 1–7, 2012. https://majalah.tempo.co/read/140715/joshua-oppenheimermembunuh-bagi-anwar-adalah-sebuah-akting

Oppenheimer, Joshua, dir. *The Act of Killing (Jagal)*. Final Cut for Real. 2012. Streaming video file.

———, dir. *The Look of Silence (Senyap)*. Final Cut for Real. 2014. Streaming video file.

"Our History." PEN International. http://www.pen-international.org/our-history/ Accessed August 3, 2016.

Paik, Nak-chung. "Coloniality in Korea and a South Korean Project for Overcoming Modernity." *Interventions: International Journal of Postcolonial Studies* 2, no. 1 (2000): 73–86.

———. *The Division System in Crisis: Essays on Contemporary Korea.* Translated by Kim Myung-hwan, Sol June-Kyu, Song Seung-cheol, and Ryu Young-joo. Berkeley: University of California Press, 2011.

———. "How to Think about the Park Chung Hee Era." In *Reassessing the Park Chung Era, 1961–79: Development, Political Thought, Democracy, and Cultural Influence,* edited by Kim Hyung-A and Clark W. Sorensen, 85–91. Seattle: University of Washington Press, 2011.

Parikh, Crystal. Introduction to *The Cambridge Companion to Human Rights and Literature,* edited by Crystal Parikh, 1–9. Cambridge: Cambridge University Press, 2019.

———. *Writing Human Rights: The Political Imaginaries of Writers of Color.* Minneapolis: University of Minnesota Press, 2017.

Pelaez, Emmanuel. "Opening Address." *Report of the Asian Writers' Conference.* Published in *Comment: The Filipino Journal of Ideas, Discussion, and the Arts,* no. 17 (1963): 5–10.

"PEN Charter." PEN International. http://www.pen-international.org/pen-charter/ Accessed August 3, 2016.

Peters, Julie Stone. "'Literature,' the 'Rights of Man,' and Narratives of Atrocity: Historical Backgrounds to the Culture of Testimony." In *Theoretical Perspectives on Human Rights and Literature,* edited by Elizabeth Swanson Goldberg and Alexandra Schultheis Moore, 19–40. Hoboken, N.J.: Taylor and Francis, 2011.

Pietz, William. "The 'Post-Colonialism' of Cold War Discourse." *Social Text,* no. 19/20 (1988): 55–75.

"The Poet Kim Chi-ha" (author profile). *Lotus: Afro-Asian Writings* 30 (1976): 123–25.

Poon, Angelia Mui Cheng. "Being in the World: Literary Practice and Pedagogy in Global Times." *Ariel: A Review of International English Literature* 46, no. 1–2 (2015): 257–73.

Poon, Angelia, Philip Holden, and Shirley Lim. *Writing Singapore: An Historical Anthology of Singapore Literature.* Singapore: NUS Press/National Arts Council, 2009.

Popescu, Monica. *At Penpoint: African Literatures, Postcolonial Studies, and the Cold War.* Durham, NC: Duke University Press, 2020.

———. *South African Literature beyond the Cold War.* New York: Palgrave Macmillan, 2010.

Potter, Rachel. "Modernist Rights: International PEN 1921–1936." *Critical Quarterly* 55, no. 2 (2013): 66–80.

Pramoedya, Ananta Toer. *Child of All Nations.* Translated by Max Lane. New York: Penguin, 1990.

———. *House of Glass: A Novel*. Translated by Max Lane. 1988. New York: Penguin, 1992.

———. "Perburuan 1950 and Keluarga Gerilya 1950." Translated by Benedict Anderson. *Indonesia* 36 (1983): 24–48.

Prashad, Vijay. *The Darker Nations: A People's History of the Third World*. New York: New Press, 2007.

Rajendra, Cecil. "The Higher Duty of a Writer in a Developing Society." In *Literature and Social Justice: Papers Presented to the Second Asian Writers Conference [1981]*, 18–21. Manila: Philippine Center of International P.E.N., 1982.

Reddy, Chandan. *Freedom with Violence: Race, Sexuality, and the U.S. State*. Durham, NC: Duke University Press, 2011.

"Report on the Proceedings." In *The Second Asian Writers Conference [1964]*, 27–33. Bangkok: Sanan Bunyasirhibhandhu, 1965.

"Requiem for a Massacre." *Tempo* (English edition). October 1–7, 2012. https://magz .tempo.co/read/25496/requiem-for-a-massacre.

"Resolutions." In *Literature and Social Justice: Papers Presented to the Second Asian Writers Conference [1981]*, 201–3. Manila: Philippine Center of International P.E.N., 1982.

Rist, Gilbert. *The History of Development: From Western Origins to Global Faith*. 4th ed. London: Zed, 2014.

Robinson, Geoffrey B. *The Killing Season: The History of the Indonesian Massacres, 1965–66*. Princeton, NJ: Princeton University Press, 2018.

Rodriguez, Gloria F. "A Look at Publishing in the Philippines." In *Literature and Social Justice: Papers Presented to the Second Asian Writers Conference [1981]*, 164–74. Manila: Philippine Center of International P.E.N., 1982.

"Role of Western Literature in the Asian Modernization Process [Conference Session]." In *Thirty Years of Turmoil in Asian Literature: The Fourth Asian Writers' Conference, April 25th–May 2nd, 1976*, 50–59. Taipei: Taipei Chinese Center, International P.E.N., 1976.

"The Role of the Writer in a Revolutionary Age [Conference Session]." *Report of the Asian Writers' Conference*. Published in *Comment: The Filipino Journal of Ideas, Discussion, and the Arts*, no. 17 (1963): 84–109.

Romulo, Carlos P. "Imagination and Asian Reality [The Fifth Annual José Rizal Lecture]." *Report of the Asian Writers' Conference*. Published in *Comment: The Filipino Journal of Ideas, Discussion, and the Arts*, no. 17 (1963): 37–43.

———. "Opening Statement." In *Selected Documents of the Bandung Conference: Texts of Selected Speeches and Final Communique of the Asian-African Conference, Bandung, Indonesia, April 18–24, 1955*, 12–20. New York: Institute of Pacific Relations, 1955.

Rosca, Ninotchka. *The Monsoon Collection*. St Lucia: University of Queensland Press, 1983.

———. *State of War*. New York: Norton, 1988.

———. "'Total War' in the Philippines." *The Nation*, June 19, 1989, 839–42.

Rosser, Andrew. "Escaping the Resource Curse: The Case of Indonesia." *Journal of Contemporary Asia* 37, no. 1 (2007): 38–58.

Roy, Ananya, and Aihwa Ong, eds. *Worlding Cities: Asian Experiments and the Art of Being Global.* Chichester; Malden, MA: Wiley-Blackwell, 2011.

Ryu, Youngju. "From Martyrdom to Apostasy: Kim Chiha and the Politics of Death in South Korea's Democratizations." In *Beyond Death: The Politics of Suicide and Martyrdom in Korea,* ed. Charles R. Kim et al., 287–314. Seattle: University of Washington Press, 2019.

———. *Writers of the Winter Republic: Literature and Resistance in Park Chung Hee's Korea.* Honolulu: University of Hawai'i Press, 2015.

Said, Edward. *Reflections on Exile and Other Essays.* Cambridge, MA: Harvard University Press, 2000.

San Juan, E., Jr., "Marcos and the Media." *Index on Censorship* 7, no. 3 (1978): 40–47.

———. *The Philippine Temptation: Dialectics of Philippines–U.S. Literary Relations.* Philadelphia: Temple University Press, 1996.

Sanders, Mark. *Ambiguities of Witnessing: Law and Literature in the Time of a Truth Commission.* Stanford, CA: Stanford University Press, 2007.

Saunders, Frances Stoner. *The Cultural Cold War: The CIA and the World of Arts and Letters.* New York: New Press, 2001.

Schiller, Naomi. *Channeling the State: Community Media and Popular Politics in Venezuela.* Durham, NC: Duke University Press, 2018.

Scott, David. *Omens of Adversity: Tragedy, Time, Memory, Justice.* Durham, NC: Duke University Press, 2014.

———. *Refashioning Futures: Criticism after Postcoloniality.* Princeton, NJ: Princeton University Press, 1999.

"Second Literary Session, Part A." In *Proceedings of the Third Asian Writers' Conference,* 49–66. Taipei: Chinese Center, International P.E.N., 1970.

Shafik, Maher. Review of *Cry of the People and Other Poems.* In *Lotus: Afro-Asian Writings* 30 (1976): 136–39.

Shimabuku, Annmaria M. *Alegal: Biopolitics and the Unintelligibility of Okinawan Life.* New York: Fordham University Press, 2018.

Shin, Gi-wook. Introduction to *Contentious Kwangju: The May 18 Uprising in Korea's Past and Present,* edited by Gi-wook Shin and Kyun Moon Hwang, xi–xxxi. Lanham, Md.: Rowman and Littlefield, 2003.

Shringarpure, Bhakti. *Cold War Assemblages: Decolonization to Digital.* New York: Routledge, 2019.

Slaughter, Joseph R. "Foreword: Rights on Paper." In *Theoretical Perspectives on Human Rights and Literature,* edited by Elizabeth Swanson Goldberg and Alexandra Schultheis Moore, xi–xiv. New York: Routledge, 2012.

———. "Hijacking Human Rights: Neoliberalism, the New Historiography, and the End of the Third World." *Human Rights Quarterly* 40, no. 4 (2018): 735–75.

———. *Human Rights, Inc.: The World Novel, Narrative Form and International Law*. New York: Fordham University Press, 2007.

Slobodian, Quinn. *Globalists: The End of Empire and the Birth of Neoliberalism*. Cambridge, MA: Harvard University Press, 2018.

Soekarno [Sukarno], President. "Speech." In *Selected Documents of the Bandung Conference: Texts of Selected Speeches and Final Communique of the Asian-African Conference, Bandung, Indonesia, April 18–24, 1955*, 1–5. New York: Institute of Pacific Relations, 1955.

Solzhenitsyn, Aleksandr. *One Day in the Life of Ivan Denisovich*. Translated by Ralph Parker. New York: New American Library, 2009. First published in Russian in *Novy Mir*, 1962.

Song, Jesook. *South Koreans in the Debt Crisis: The Creation of a Neoliberal Welfare Society*. Durham, NC: Duke University Press, 2009.

Stauffer, Robert B. *The Philippines under Marcos: Failure of Transnational Developmentalism*. Sydney: Transnational Corporations Research Project, University of Sydney, 1986.

Stoler, Ann Laura. *Duress: Imperial Durabilities in Our Times*. Durham, NC: Duke University Press, 2016.

Surin, Kenneth. *Freedom Not Yet: Liberation and the Next World Order*. Durham, NC: Duke University Press, 2009.

Tadiar, Neferti Xina M. *Things Fall Away: Philippine Historical Experience and the Makings of Globalization*. Durham, NC: Duke University Press, 2009.

Tan, Pin Pin, dir. *To Singapore, with Love*. 2013. DVD.

Thatcher, Margaret. "Eulogy for President Reagan." Video-linked speech, June 11, 2004, National Cathedral, Washington, DC. www.margaretthatcher.org/document/110360.

"Third Literary Session, Part B." In *Proceedings of the Third Asian Writers' Conference*, 97–126. Taipei: Chinese Center, International P.E.N., 1970.

Tiang, Jeremy. "Going Inside." Interview with Jini Kim Watson. *Singapore Unbound*. July 22, 2019. singaporeunbound.org/blog.

———. *State of Emergency*. Singapore: Epigram, 2017.

Torres-Yu, Rosario. "The State of Philippine Literature." In *The Politics of Culture: The Philippine Experience*, edited by Nicanor G. Tiongson. Manila: Philippine Educational Theater Association, 1984.

"Tradition and Modernity in Literature [Conference Session]." *Report of the Asian Writers' Conference*. Published in *Comment: The Filipino Journal of Ideas, Discussion, and the Arts*, no. 17 (1963): 44–83.

Van Klinken, Gerry. "No, The Act of Killing Is Not Unethical." *Critical Asian Studies* 46, no. 1 (2014): 176–78.

Vu Hoang-Chuong. "The Contribution of Asian Writers to World Understanding." In *The Second Asian Writers Conference [1964]*, 46–48. Bangkok: Sanan Bunyasirhibhandhu, 1965.

Wade, Robert. *Governing the Market: Economic Theory and the Role of Government in East Asian Industrialization*. 1990. Princeton, NJ: Princeton University Press, 2004.

Wang, Chi-tsung. "Literature in Agitated Time." In *Thirty Years of Turmoil in Asian Literature: The Fourth Asian Writers' Conference, April 25th–May 2nd, 1976*, 169–70. Taipei: The Taipei Chinese Center, International P.E.N., 1976.

Watson, Jini Kim. "Aspirational City: Desiring Singapore and the Films of Tan Pin Pin." *Interventions: International Journal of Postcolonial Studies* 18, no. 4 (2016): 543–58.

———. *The New Asian City: Three-dimensional Fictions of Space and Urban Form*. Minneapolis: University of Minnesota Press, 2011.

Wee, C. J. W.-L. *The Asian Modern: Culture, Capitalist Development, Singapore*. Singapore: National University of Singapore Press, 2007.

Wells, Kenneth, ed. *South Korea's Minjung Movement: The Culture and Politics of Dissidence*. Honolulu: University of Hawai'i Press, 1995.

Westad, Odd Arne. *The Global Cold War: Third World Interventions and the Making of Our Times*. Cambridge: Cambridge University Press, 2007.

Wilder, Gary. *Freedom Time: Negritude, Decolonization, and the Future of the World*. Durham, NC: Duke University Press, 2015.

Woloch, Alex. *The One vs. the Many: Minor Characters and the Space of the Protagonist in the Novel*. Princeton, NJ: Princeton University Press, 2009.

Wong, Cyril. *The Dictator's Eyebrow*. Singapore: Ethos Books, 2013.

Wong, Yoon Wah. *The New Village*. Translated by Ho Lian Geok and Ng Yi-Sheng. Singapore: Ethos, 2012.

Woo-Cumings, Meredith. "Introduction: Chalmers Johnson and the Politics of Nationalism and Development." In *The Developmental State*, edited by Meredith Woo-Cumings, 1–31. Ithaca, NY: Cornell University Press, 1999.

Wu, Chan J. "Introduction: Cosmic Buds Burgeoning in Words: Chiha Kim's Poetics of Full-Emptiness." In *Heart's Agony*. Translated by James Han and Kim Won-chung, 15–33. Fredonia, NY: White Pine Press, 1998.

Xiang, Sunny. *Tonal Intelligence: The Aesthetics of Asian Inscrutability during the Long Cold War*. New York: Columbia University Press, 2020.

Yen, Yuan-shu. "Social Realism in Recent Chinese Fiction in Taiwan." In *Thirty Years of Turmoil in Asian Literature*, 197–231. Taipei: The Taipei Chinese Center, International P.E.N., 1976.

Yeng Pway Ngon. *Unrest*. Translated by Jeremy Tiang. Singapore: Math Paper Press, 2012.

Yeo, Kim Wah, and Albert Lau. "From Colonialism to Independence, 1945–1965." In *A History of Singapore*, edited by Ernest C. T. Chew and Edwin Lee. 117-153. Oxford: Oxford University Press, 1991.

Yip, June. *Envisioning Taiwan: Fiction, Cinema, and the Nation in the Cultural Imaginary*. Durham, NC: Duke University Press, 2004.

Yoneyama, Lisa. *Cold War Ruins: Transpacific Critique of American Justice and Japanese War Crimes*. Durham, NC: Duke University Press, 2016.

Yoon, Duncan. "'Our Forces Have Redoubled': World Literature, Postcolonialism, and the Afro-Asian Writers' Bureau." *Cambridge Journal of Postcolonial Literary Inquiry* 2, no. 2 (2015): 233–52.

Yoon, Je-kyoon, dir. *Ode to My Father [Kukje sijang]*. CJ Entertainment. 2014. Streaming video file.

Young, Robert J. C. *Postcolonialism: A Historical Introduction*. Hoboken, NJ: Wiley-Blackwell, 2001.

Index

282

INDEX

writerly freedom, 4, 38, 46, 68
writers: AAWB, 35, 53, 78, 83; Afro-Asian
  Writers' Association, 228n154; Association
  of Writers for Freedom and Praxis, 77;
  crackdown on, 212n23; dissident, 59–60,
  220n8; nativist, 40; PEN Asian, 43; PEN
  Writers in Prison committee, 211n16; in
  prisons, 55, 60, 64, 66, 76, 77, 90, 220n1,
  222n46, 231n231; role of, 43
Wu Cheng, 78

Yap Wan Pin, 138, 140
Yeng Pway Ngon, 236n60
Yen Yuan-shu, 41, 214n54

Yeo, Robert, 233n8
Yip, June, 214n54, 217n81
Yoneyama, Lisa, 83, 171, 204n22, 216n75
Yoon, Duncan, 21, 35
Yoon Je-kyoon, 4, 25, 184, 190
Yoshimi Shun-ya, 54
Young, Robert J.C., 13
youth, 124–25, 156, 169. See also
  Bildungsroman
Yusin reforms, South Korea, 17, 84, 150

Zahari, Said, 134
Zhdanov, Andrei, 41
Zulkadry, Adi, 167, 245n52

Jini Kim Watson is Associate Professor of English and Comparative Literature at New York University. She is the author of *The New Asian City: Three-dimensional Fictions of Space and Urban Form* and editor, with Gary Wilder, of *The Postcolonial Contemporary: Political Imaginaries for the Global Present.*

www.ingramcontent.com/pod-product-compliance
Lightning Source LLC
Chambersburg PA
CBHW032119020426
42334CB00016B/1001